GETTING THE MOST FROM YOUR MICRO

ERNEST E. MAU

HAYDEN BOOK COMPANY, INC.
Rochelle Park, New Jersey

Acquisitions Editor: M.C. VARLEY
Production Editor: RONNIE GROFF
Art Director: JIM BERNARD
Original artwork: JOHN MC AUSLAND
Composition: MC FARLAND GRAPHICS AND DESIGN, INC.
Printed and bound by: HAMILTON PRINTING COMPANY

Neither the publisher nor the author makes any warranties, either expressed or implied, concerning this book or the procedures described herein, its quality, performance, merchantability, or fitness for any particular purpose, application, system, or component. Neither the publisher nor the author shall have any liability or responsibility to the purchaser or to any other person regarding liability, loss or damage, or criminal or civil action caused or alleged to be caused by the contents hereof. This includes but is not limited to any interruption of service, loss of business or anticipatory profits, governmental actions, or actual or consequential damages resulting from, arising out of, or in connection with the use or application of information and procedures described in this book.

While every effort has been made to ensure the accuracy of the information herein, the responsibility for determining whether any given action or combination of actions is suitable to any particular computer, system, peripheral, component, or installation rests solely and exclusively with the reader. In no event shall the publisher or the author be liable for damages of any kind as a result of omission, printing or other error, misstatement, misinformation, or misinterpretation. The reader is cautioned to apply the contents of this book with due care.

Library of Congress Cataloging in Publication Data

Mau, Ernest E.
Getting the most from your micro.

Includes index.
1. Microcomputers—Maintenance and repair. I. Title.
TK7888.3.M364 1983 621.3819'54 83-12815
ISBN 0-8104-6264-8

1 2 3 4 5 6 7 8 9 PRINTING

83 84 85 86 87 88 89 90 91 YEAR

ACKNOWLEDGMENTS

The author wishes to thank the management and personnel of companies that have participated in this project. Without their help in providing information, technical manuals, photographs, hardware, and software, this book would not have been possible. Throughout this book, their products often are mentioned and credited, but the author regrets that space limitations occasionally limit the coverage or force the omission of products, materials, and information graciously provided. Specifically, the author thanks the helpful individuals at: *Advanced Logic Systems; Advanced Micro Techniques; ALF Products, Inc.; Andromeda, Inc.; Applied Engineering; ATV Research; Basis, Inc.; Billings McEachern, Inc.; Blat Research & Development Corp.; Central Point Software, Inc.; Colonial Data Services Corp.; Communications Research Corp.; Compdent; Compulink Corp.; Computer:applications, Inc.; Computer Case Co.; Computer Station, Inc.; Control Technology, Inc.; Corvus Systems, Inc.; Creative Computing Software; Creative Software Development; Custom Computer Systems, Inc.; Davong Systems, Inc.; Digital Marketing; Diversified Software Research, Inc.; Electronic Specialists, Inc.; Epic Software/Epic Computer; Epson-America, Inc.; Fiberbilt/Ikelheimer-Ernst, Inc.; Franklin Computer Corp.; Gould, Inc.; Happ Electronics, Inc.; Hayden Software Co.; Hutton Industries, Inc.; International Business Machines Corp.; IMS International; Inmac; Innovative Computer Products; Intertec Data Systems; Ithaca InterSystems; Kay Computers, Div. Non-Linear Systems; Kensington Microware, Ltd.; Ladco Development Company; Langley-St. Clair Instrumentation Systems, Inc.; Last Electronics; Legend Industries, Ltd.; Lifeboat Associates, Inc.; Lobo Drives International; Macrotech Computer Products, Ltd.; Mark Four Imports; Masterworks Software, Inc.; Micro-Sci, Inc.; Microstand; Micro-Ware Distributors, Inc.; Mountain Computer, Inc.; National Field Sales; NEC Home Electronics; Nikrom Technical Products; Northwest Instrument Systems,*

Inc.; Novation, Inc.; Ohm/Electronics; Okidata Corp.; Omega Microware, Inc.; Omni Communication; Osborne Computer Corp.; Otrona Corp.; Panamax; Personal Computer Products, Inc.; Practical Peripherals, Inc.; Quadram Corp.; Quality Software; R.H. Electronics; RKS Industries; RockRoy, Inc.; SAFT America, Portable Battery Div.; Sanyo Business Systems, Computer Div.; Sensible Software; Shugart Associates; Soft CTRL Systems; SoftKey Publishing; SOLA Electric, Unit of General Signal; Sorrento Valley Associates; SSM Microcomputer Products; Street Electronics Corp.; Strobe, Inc.; Sun Research, Inc.; SuperSoft, Inc.; Sympathetic Software; The 3M Corporation; The Software Store; Topaz Electronics Div.; Toshiba America, Inc.; Tovatech; Videx, Inc.; XPS, Inc.; Xcomp, Inc.

The author recognizes that other companies provide useful products probably appropriate to and worthy of mention in a book of this scope. He has attempted to contact as many such companies as possible. Some declined to participate in this project, and their absence is regrettable, but at least they responded, and that response is appreciated.

Other companies, however, chose not to respond to inquiries concerning their products. In such cases, at least three attempts were made by mail and usually one additional attempt by telephone. In a few rare cases, companies ignored as many as six successive requests for information. Such companies must, of necessity, remain nameless and are not represented in this book.

TRADEMARKS

Trademarks and registered trademarks cited in this book include but are not necessarily limited to: *ACE-1000—Franklin Computer Corp.; ADDS and Regent—Applied Digital Data Systems, Inc.; AIO-II—SSM Microcomputer Products, Inc.; Alspa—Alspa Computer, Inc.; Altair and MITS—Pertec Computer Corp.; Apple, Apple II, Apple II Plus, Apple III, Applesoft, and Disk II—Apple Computer Inc.; Apple-Cat II—Novation, Inc.; Apple-Cillin—XPS, Inc.; Apple-Verter—ATV Research; Appli-Card—Personal Computer Products, Inc.; Atari—Atari, Inc.; Attache—Otrona Corp.; Back It Up II, Super Disk Copy, and Disk Recovery—Sensible Software, Inc.; BADLIM—Blat Research & Development Corp.; BASIS-108—Basis, Inc.; Clean Cycle—Inmac Corp.; CompuServe—CompuServe, Inc.; Cool-Mark II—Mark Four Imports; DataLife and Verbatim—Verbatim Corp.; Decision 1—Morrow Designs; Diagnostics II, Disk Edit, Disk Doctor—SuperSoft, Inc.; Disk Doctor—Creative Computing Software; Disk Edit II—Softkey Publishing; Disk Fix—The Software Store; Disk Prep—Sympathetic Software; DiscSavers—RockRoy, Inc.; Diversi-DOS—Diversified Software Research, Inc.; DPatch—Advanced Micro Techniques; File Fix—Alan Miller; Hazeltine—Hazeltine Corp.; I-Protect—Langley-St. Clair Instrumentation Systems, Inc.; IBM—International Business Machines Corp.; KayPro—Kay Computers Div., Non-Linear Systems; Kleen Line—Electronic Specialists, Inc.; Line 2—Topaz Electronics Div.; Locksmith, The Inspector, Watson, and The Manager—Omega Microware, Inc.; Macrodisk—Macrotech Computer Products, Ltd.; Master Diagnostics + plus—Nikrom Technical Products, Inc.; Masterdisk and Masterdos—Masterworks Software, Inc.; Mayday—Sun Research, Inc.; Microline—Okidata Corp.; Micromodem II and Hayes—Hayes Microcomputer Products, Inc.; MicroStand—Standard Computer Products; MX-80 and HX-20—Epson America, Inc.; Nibbles Away II—Computer:applications, Inc.; Osborne—Osborne Computer*

Corp.; PenultiCopy—ALF Products, Inc.; PerfectData—Innovative Computer Products; PKASO—Interactive Structures, Inc.; Plexa-Lok—Last Electronics; Qume and Sprint—Qume Corporation; QWK—Hutton Industries, Inc.; RAMCard and SoftCard—Microsoft, Inc.; Ramlok—Ladco Development Co., Inc.; Ramplus and ROMPlus—Mountain Computer, Inc.; ROMBoard—Andromeda, Inc.; Sinclair—Sinclair Research, Inc.; Soft Disk—Legend Industries, Ltd.; Solatron/Acuvolt—SOLA Electric; SooperSpooler—Compulink Corp.; Sprint 5—Qume Corp.; Super Fan II, Super RAM II, and Guardian Angel—R.H. Electronics; Surge Sentry—RKS Industries; Synergizer—Advanced Logic Systems; System Saver—Kensington Microware, Ltd.; Tellus and Darina-AX—Shell Oil, Inc.; Texwipe, Clearview Terminal Wipes, and Micro Duster—The Texwipe Co.; The Filer and Copy II Plus—Central Point Software, Inc.; VENTOP—Tovatech; VIC—Commodore Computer Systems, Inc.; Videoterm and Enhancer II—Videx, Inc.; Xerox and Diablo—Xerox Corp.; Z-80—Zilog, Inc.; Z-Card—Advanced Logic Systems, Inc.

The author has attempted to reference all known trademarks cited in this book. In general, all product names are trademarks or registered trademarks; they have been "flagged" accordingly at the first appearance in text and are usually owned by the company cited in context. Apologies are extended to any trademark owners whose product is mentioned in the book but is not listed here and to any trademark owners not listed correctly. If the author is advised in writing of an omitted or mis-cited trademark, the oversight will be corrected in the next edition.

PREFACE

We've all heard about the so-called "computer revolution" sweeping the world and changing the way we live. Over the past few years, most aspects of our daily lives have gradually shifted into the domain of the mighty electronic machine. Our bank accounts are held in computers. Our insurance policies are written and priced by computers. The bills we receive are prepared by computers. The products we buy are often designed, manufactured, and sold—to varying degrees—by computers. Our tax returns are examined and recorded by computers. Even our homes are falling prey to computer-controlled appliances, computerized video games, and ingenious personal computers that do everything from balancing our checkbooks, through planning our menus, to helping us write our personal correspondence.

Even greater impact soon will be evident as projects already in planning are implemented: computerized information and buying services through cable television; large-scale implementations of electronic mail services; a "cashless" society based on computer-controlled electronic fund transfers ("EFT" systems); national and international news networks coming into our homes; video-display newspapers. All these and many more are coming, and it won't be too long before they are here.

No one knows for sure whether these changes are good or bad. Both sides usually can be argued with about equal success. What we do know is that computers are useful tools. By one definition, a machine is a device for performing a task, and computers perform many tasks that relieve people of tedious, tiresome chores. Not only that, but they usually perform tasks faster and more accurately than the human mind ever could. In particular, computers are nicely suited to handling large amounts of information and performing routine or repetitive calculations.

Yet there's a gremlin in the works ready to disrupt the best of plans. The little beastie goes by many names—"machine malfunction," "computer failure," "downtime," and even the misidentified "computer error." We all know the critter exists; we've all seen it at one time or another. Think about the times you've gone into a bank to transact some business and been told, "The computer is down." More than likely you've heard the same statement when getting an insurance estimate, trying to convince a company to correct a computerized billing error, or even trying to buy something over the counter of a department store. And that's just on a personal basis. The problem is just as severe within companies and corporations when employees don't get paychecks, executives don't get letters and reports typed and printed, a whole assembly line comes to a standstill, and so on. All because "the computer is down."

It doesn't make any difference what level we examine. From the multimillion-dollar mainframes installed in large corporations to the $99 home video computer, malfunctions occur. Sometimes they happen frequently, other times infrequently, but they do happen sooner or later. After all, a computer system is a device. Whether a device is a mechanical one, an electronic one, or a combination of these, it will fail eventually.

Since we have to accept the occurrence of computer malfunctions as unavoidable facts of life, we then have to look at four considerations to minimize their impact. One is preventing unnecessary equipment failures so those that do occur are due to things beyond our direct control. Another is eliminating practices and procedures that lead to failures as a result of improper operation, negligence, or outright carelessness. A third is reducing the seriousness of a failure when it does occur by implementing methods to minimize lost work and information. The fourth involves finding ways to return the computer to operational status with speed and with as little out-of-pocket expense as possible.

Those are the things to which this book is dedicated. I have a specific objective in mind—to save you money, to reduce your lost time, and to alleviate the annoyance you'll experience when your machine goes down. To accomplish that, I'm going to discuss a variety of subjects that include general care and operation of your equipment, specific preventive steps you can implement, methods and procedures for backing up your system's operation, and some things you can do to fix minor problems on your own.

I will be limiting my discussions to microcomputer systems. These generally are the systems priced below $20,000 and commonly found in small businesses, professional offices, and homes. The problems faced by businesses using "micros" for accounting, word processing, inventory control, billing, direct mailing, and the like aren't much different from those faced by individuals using their "home" or "personal" computers for letter writing, education, game playing, budget management, and similar pursuits. In fact, the differences are only a matter of scale.

The home user is likely to be inconvenienced by a machine failure but usually isn't threatened with loss of income or serious financial burdens as a result. On the other hand, the business user may suffer anything from the loss of one employee's or one department's production to a complete shutdown of the entire facility.

Oddly, the importance of computer care and maintenance in small businesses is not always in direct proportion to the sizes of the businesses. It's normal to assume that a larger business would suffer more damage from a system breakdown than a small business, but that often is not the case. In a multi-employee company, a computer probably supports specific tasks such as accounting, word processing, or some other function used by one department or one individual. When the computer is out of operation, only the one employee of that department ceases to function while the rest go about business as usual. But a single-individual enterprise such as that of a professional writer, accountant, or consultant may have the entire business built around one machine. When that machine fails, the entire business comes to a screeching halt. Often it's the one-person business that has the greater interest in minimizing failures and reducing downtime in the interest of basic survival.

Regardless of the size of your system, the number of hours you use it, whether it's for business or personal applications, or the size of your budget, you will find useful and important information in this book. I must point out, however, that there's no practical way of covering every equipment brand, every system type, or every application. There are too many systems, devices, gadgets, and packages even to attempt a detailed explanation of each. Instead, much of what you'll be reading is intended as "generic," concentrating on things that can be applied to systems in general. Because the equipment was available to me, I'll use an older Altair® S-100 bus computer, a new Morrow Designs' Decision 1™ S-100 bus computer, and an Apple II® or Apple II Plus® computer for examples.

Those of you with other systems must interpret my advice and remarks in the context of your own machines and applications. There shouldn't be any real difficulty in doing so, although some of my discussions may not be applicable to your system, may need alteration to work with your equipment, or may require you to consult a service technician or other professional for something another user would be able to do on his or her own. Those situations are unavoidable, and I apologize to those who might be inconvenienced. Covering every possible variation on every statement I make would have taken volume after volume and never would have been complete.

Bear in mind that I'm trying to provide the broadest information base to the greatest number of users, whether their applications are business-oriented or personal. At the same time, I have to accommodate novice users as well as intermediate and experienced users. To that end, I've included information that falls under the heading of "common sense" but often is overlooked, forgotten, or ignored. In other cases, I've covered complicated but risky procedures that could be beyond a particular individual's capabilities or that might involve voiding warranties, violating service contracts, and so on. In those cases, I provide specific cautions and warnings, and items described with such notations are intended only for technically competent users who feel comfortable performing them and are willing to assume the associated risks.

I wish you the best of luck with your system and may you have long, uninterrupted intervals of error-free computing.

Ernest E. Mau

CONTENTS

ONE

SO YOU HAVE A SMALL COMPUTER . . .

"Say, have you heard about . . ." So begins a classic tale of woe about small-computer ownership. It seems there was someone who bought a $5000 microcomputer for use in a home-operated business. It doesn't matter whether the person was an accountant, writer, lawyer, consultant, or something else. The story ends the same no matter what the application.

Anyway, this person picked up the machine from the dealer, took it home, plugged it in, and nothing happened. Taking it back to the dealer, the user was told they didn't service that equipment. It had to be shipped to the manufacturer. But there was a catch! It seemed the factory was backlogged with repair orders and had a four- to six-month waiting list. Here was someone who bought a computer in good faith, paid the money, and ended up with a depleted bank account and no working machine. Even worse, the user had no idea when or even if a working unit would be available—some versions of story have the equipment shuttling back and forth for months or even years but never becoming operational.

I'll admit it does sound a bit farfetched, and I've not actually met anyone who's suffered exactly that situation, but I have seen things that make it seem all too possible—even probable. I do know people who have trouble getting repair work done on their computers, most often because some retail outlets do not employ trained service technicians. Others ordered equipment from mail-order houses to cut a few dollars off local prices, later discovering that local dealers service only items they sold. Still others committed to expensive monthly service contracts, a year or two later seeing "guaranteed" 24-hour service grow to more like 24 days or having contracts canceled outright.

I direct your attention to these things because they should make you stop and think. They are things retailers, distributors, and manufacturers don't like to bring up for fear of losing a sale.

THE FACTS OF LIFE

When you are working with computer systems and their components, it's an irrefutable fact of life that something is going to fail. It might happen today, tomorrow, next week, next month, or next year, but it is going to happen. The philosophy is summed up by two corollaries to Murphy's Law. First, "Everything put together falls apart sooner or later." Second, "If there is a possibility of several things going wrong, the one that will cause the most damage will be the one to go wrong."[1] When you accept those two statements, you're ready to cope with computer ownership and can plan to do something about the problems.

I'm probably beginning to make you nervous. Good! You should be nervous! Nervousness breeds caution, and caution makes for better, more frequent, and more thorough examination of your equipment and your maintenance needs. Now I'm going to shake you up a little more by telling a story I know is true. I can vouch for it because it happened to me and created a situation that remains unresolved as I write this book. The story is a bit long, but stay with me because I'm making a point.

A Tale of Many Troubles

This tale begins in 1978. I've changed the names, not to protect the innocent but to avoid being sued by the guilty. Anyway, I decided I needed a business microcomputer. I won't go into why I needed one or the details of what I intended to accomplish with it. It's sufficient that I needed a machine for word processing, general data handling, and repetitive and tedious information manipulations. After spending six months sizing up systems, I finally decided on one. It had the right equipment or "hardware," came with word-processing "software," and was programmable with exactly the right language to let me design some complex programs of my own.

The system, let's call it the "Spiffy 8080," had been marketed for a couple of years, starting as a hobbyist's machine and then being converted into a full-scale business system. The dealer, "Starstruck Data Devices," seemed adequately versed on the machine and had both a full-time service technician and a full-time programmer. After long deliberation I purchased a $15,000 system, complete with large monthly bank payments. Besides the normal 90-day warranty, I signed a service contract bearing additional payments of 1 percent of the original system purchase price per month. The contract clauses provided service at my location (on-site) within 24 hours of a phone call, "loaner" equipment when repairs would take more than 24 hours, and so on. I thought I had all bases covered.

---

1 Arthur Bloch, *Murphy's Law 1982 Calendar,* (Price/Stern/Sloan Publishers, Inc., Los Angeles), 1977, 1980.

Maintenance problems began less than 12 hours after delivery and installation by the dealer. For the first two months, major failures hit one after another, requiring more than 30 service calls in eight weeks. There were times I had to make two, three, or even four calls the same day, often placing a new call before the technician could drive the 20 miles from my place back to his office. The malfunctions struck every component and every peripheral. They included bad solder joints, missing wires, partially cut interconnect cables, burned-out circuit chips, faulty power supplies, defective diskettes, programming errors in the software, and just about anything else you care to name.

By the third month, the technician had quit Starstruck Data Devices and was never replaced. Instead, Joe Fixit, a partner in the company, supposedly took over all service responsibility. With that, even minor failures became major events—and major hassles. Joe didn't like working on computers. Joe didn't like driving to customers' sites. Joe did like to blame the user for anything and everything that went wrong, with nasty comments like "Now what did you do to it?" One day, Joe absolutely refused to fix a disk-drive failure, which prompted an irate call to the manufacturing company's president to have him apply the necessary leverage. Properly reprimanded, Joe finally showed up and fixed the equipment, but that day marked the start of a continuous decline in the dealer's support of the system.

By the second year, equipment failures had decreased to about one incident every two months, and I had the system up and running about five weeks out of every six. But the service interval—the time between my call to the dealer and getting the unit operational—began to increase. Joe was out of town for a week. Joe had other customers ahead of me. Joe wouldn't be available for ten days. One excuse after another. And then there was the day when I had been waiting, with inoperable equipment, over two weeks and knew this was the day Joe Fixit was supposed to be in town. At 4:30 in the afternoon, he called and said, "I don't have the time for you." I never saw him again.

From that day on, I was required to diagnose my own failures, inform the dealer of what I thought was wrong, receive replacement parts by mail or courier, and then install the replacements myself. Once, they sent a salesman over to install a new disk drive, but he hadn't the vaguest idea how to do it. I wound up installing it myself. Eventually, it got to the point where a single hardware failure could shut down the computer and my entire business for weeks, and the dealer never would honor the "loaner" clause of the contract because they never had a unit "available" to lend.

The best I could hope for was that the dealer would send some third party out for special items such as my terminal or letter-quality printer. Occasionally they did; other times they found moonlighting service technicians who might show up at 9:00 at night. But the dealer, unable to provide their own service while continuing to accept contract payments, would not contract for third-party service and often held up their payments until all available third parties finally refused to work on the machine.

The final incident came during the summer of 1982. I had a disk drive malfunction, so I called for service or parts. Remember I had been paying more than $100 a month for the contract. I was informed abruptly that the dealership no longer found it convenient to service or provide parts for my machine and that my contract was canceled retroactively to the preceding month. The contract was "open-ended," having no expiration date and subject to cancellation only upon my nonpayment, my negligence of the machine, or my abuse of the machine—none of which had occurred.

The result: I was stuck with a machine I couldn't trust in my business because parts and service weren't readily available. I had no luck reselling the unit because it had long since been declared obsolete. I still owed the bank $5000 on a useless computer, yet I had to purchase a new master system at additional expense. I had to re-license all accumulated operating software because the original licenses were valid only for the one unit. In short, the outright cancellation of parts and service by the dealership, violating the terms of their own contract, cost me more than $15,000. I couldn't even file suit because laws of the state in which I reside don't allow recovery of legal expenses unless specified in the contract (it was not specified), so it would have cost me more in out-of-pocket legal expenses than the other losses justified.

The only redeeming factor was that I "jury rigged" the old system long enough to transfer most of my disk files to the new machine. If I had not been able to save four years' of accumulated custom software and data, my losses would have been even greater and probably would have shut down my business permanently.

The Care and Maintenance Choices

The principal point and the one I want to stress is that you have two choices for taking care of your equipment. One is to rely on outsiders for all care and maintenance, whether they be dealership personnel, factory representatives, or "third-party" service companies. But as I've shown, you can't trust anyone you can't control directly. Even a written contract isn't worth the paper on which it's typed if one party or the other refuses to honor it and the injured party doesn't have the financial resources to enforce it through the courts.

Your other alternative is to learn to fend for yourself. That means knowing something about your equipment, how it works, how to take care of it, and how to fix it. It doesn't mean becoming a technician; after all, you can't be expected to do everything. Instead, you learn to do routine things that lengthen the life of the unit, learn to diagnose system "errors" and failures to discover what kinds of problems or potential problems you face, and learn to fix numerous little failures that don't require extreme technical expertise. Then you can rely on outsiders to repair major malfunctions.

Those are the things I'm presenting in this book. Whether you're a professional user or a hobbyist, I emphasize things you can do without being a technical expert. I stress the routine, usually common-sense procedures often overlooked or ignored in haste or because of lack of guidance, and I suggest "fixes" to many of the common but often minor failures you can expect to see. This book is not a comprehensive in-depth repair manual, nor do I expect you to use it as such. While I can get you past many problems, I can't eliminate the need for trained service personnel to perform complex tasks.

THE THINGS YOU CAN DO

You'll probably be amazed at the number of things you can and should do to care for your system. Some are obvious; others are not. Some should be viewed as mandatory; others can be treated as optional. All can be beneficial in reducing downtime and repair costs for virtually any business or recreational system regardless of who's using it, what tasks it performs, or where it's installed

Preventive vs. Remedial Procedures

Throughout this book, the tasks, methods, and procedures generally fit into either of two broad categories, namely preventive and remedial operations. The preventive items keep the equipment operating at peak performance levels while minimizing outright failures that could result from carelessness or negligence. Typically, preventive steps are characterized as "care" of a computer system. Remedial items apply to fixing something after it fails or malfunctions. The remedial steps are considered "maintenance" items.

Most information deals with proper care of equipment. Just a few considerations under this heading are conditioning power lines, cleaning keyboards and disk drives, and connecting peripheral equipment. There are, of course, many other areas I'll be describing as well. These are the things any computer user can accomplish without having to call on a technician. Most important, they are the things that do the most to keep a system operational as long as possible and extend the useful life to its maximum.

Because of the many differences between brands and models of computers and peripherals, I present less information on "fix-it" maintenance. It's impossible in any one book to provide all the maintenance procedures for the thousands of individual items available for personal and small-business systems. Instead, I provide guidelines and specific examples of what I've been able to do with my own systems. That should get you started, and you can modify my presentations to coincide with your specific needs.

Whether dealing with preventive or remedial procedures, you must account for the peculiarities of your own equipment, and I strongly recommend that you obtain service and maintenance manuals for every item you have installed. Sometimes it's difficult to obtain those manuals, but they are available for most computers and peripheral devices. If you have to pay for the manuals, do it! They'll easily pay for themselves. If you have to throw a temper tantrum to coerce a supplier into providing the information, do it! It might be good practice for the tantrums you'll want to throw later when you run into major problems.

You may have to obtain service and maintenance information from some manufacturer other than the one who made and marketed the computer. For example, you might purchase a computer "package" complete with disk drives, a video display, and a printer—all bearing the brand name of the computer. But the drives, display, and printer may all be O.E.M. (original equipment manufacturer) devices made by other companies and relabeled by the computer supplier. The service and maintenance information may be available only from the original component manufacturers, so they are the ones you have to identify and contact.

Software vs. Hardware

Preventive care and remedial maintenance considerations extend to both hardware and software. The hardware applications usually are obvious, but the software deserves special consideration. It may seem a little strange to think of maintaining something as intangible as data or programs, but it can be a crucial concern. It's common for the investment in software to far exceed the cost of the hardware, especially when the purchase price of "off-the-shelf" programs is combined with the value of time spent developing specialized programs and data. If something destroys one or more programs or some large collection of data, it can be extremely costly.

As I'll show later, software does require maintenance. By way of clarification, I consider magnetic media such as floppy disks and cassette tapes as much parts of the software category as the programs and information they store. Since media actually constitute a gray area, being neither true hardware nor true software, some people might argue with me about including them in the software category. However, the media serve no function other than to store and transport the software, so I feel they are closer to being software than hardware. As a result, there are care and maintenance procedures such as protecting the media and contents, retrieving erased information, restoring damaged information, and so on.

I put a heavy emphasis on software and media care. First, this is the easiest care for the user to perform. Second, it is the most neglected area of care. Third, failure to preserve and protect the media and contents usually results in serious and costly problems a few weeks, months, or years down the road. Fourth, software failures often cannot be distinguished from hardware failures, causing unnecessary but costly service calls when nothing the technician can fix is wrong.

Negligence vs. Abuse

There are two species of users who run headlong into serious care and maintenance problems that could be avoidable. The worst is the abusive user—the individual who knows better but goes ahead and does things wrong anyway or deliberately avoids taking care of the equipment. In short, this type of user mistreats the system by driving it beyond its capabilities or limits, failing to take prompt action to remedy minor failures before they become major ones, ignoring the advisories printed on equipment and supply packages, and simply abusing the components. People who have developed bad habits to the extreme of deliberately abusing their installations aren't likely to be helped much by my presentations. All I can do is offer condolences and pity them for the expenses they must be incurring just to keep their equipment operational.

The other type is the negligent user who simply doesn't know enough or doesn't care enough to do anything about the problems. As a result, the equipment is neglected or abused, but not with intent. Most often, this user thinks of the computer as a modern wonder machine that will solve all problems and run indefinitely. With a little time, study, and thought, there shouldn't be any problem adjusting day-to-day operating methods to accommodate effective care and maintenance procedures. The result: lowered operating costs, decreased downtime, and a greater satisfaction with the computer and its capabilities.

In some ways, maintaining a computer system is like maintaining the family car—another machine that takes some attention to keep in operation. Periodically, a car needs clean air and oil filters, while a computer needs clean air intakes for proper ventilation. A car needs occasional tuneups with timing adjustments, clean spark plugs, and a check of the wiring. A computer system needs disk-drive adjustments and cleaning, as well as a thorough check of cable and plug-in connections to make certain nothing has worked loose. A car needs the right kinds of batteries and fuel, while the computer requires proper electrical power and power conditioning. The analogies go on and on, including the final one: if the car is neglected, it breaks down; if the computer system is neglected, it breaks down too!

THE THINGS TO EXPECT

Before plunging into the "meat" of this book, it's advisable that you know something more about the basics of computer care and maintenance. The information is presented here by way of introduction, and remaining chapters of this book will elaborate on many of the subjects.

The Mythical Computer Error

A logical place to start is by talking about so-called "computer errors." After all, things that look like errors are the things that should prompt you to look for a problem in your system, particularly if errors occur repetitively.

We've all heard about computer errors. The big ones even make the newspapers. It's reached a point where we willingly excuse the bugaboos in our daily lives when we hear that familiar statement, "It's a computer error!" Just think about how many times you've heard or read it. Delivered merchandise is wrong, so it's a "computer error." You pay your bills every month, but the utility company threatens to cut off service, so it's a "computer error." You receive a paycheck for a tenth of your normal salary, and it's another "computer error." Well, I say, "bunk" or an equivalent in long strings of nasty four-letter words whenever someone tries that excuse in my presence.

A simple fact: *people make mistakes, computers do not!* A computer does exactly what it's told to do within the constraints of its design and its operating environment. The machine doesn't think for itself, it doesn't write its own programs, and it can't deviate from the instructions given to it by its human programmers and operators.

Most errors blamed on computers are errors by the people using them. A keyboard operator misplaces a decimal point or omits a line of data. A printout gets misplaced in a stack of papers. Eventually, these and others might be called computer errors to keep the blame away from where it belongs—on users themselves.

Human error also is found in computer programming. A programmer can overlook conditions that occur only a few times in thousands of processing operations. Later, the computer encounters the unanticipated conditions and handles them improperly. Sometimes, the program is just "bad." It might have been written by someone who didn't know enough about the language or the problem. It might contain outright "blunders." It may not have been tested thoroughly. The user may be trying to do things for which the program wasn't designed. Regardless, the error isn't in the computer, it's in the program written by a human.

Other causes of the supposed computer errors include design or manufacturing faults as well as unpredictable external influences on the machines' operation. There are such things as equipment failures. A circuit chip fails. A disk drive jams. A diskette wears out. Wire connectors work loose. Contacts get dirty. The equipment overheats. The power is interrupted or is faulty. Someone walks across a carpet and discharges a static burst to the equipment. The list goes on and on, but all these "interferences" may appear either as complete system failures or as the so-called computer errors. Yet the computer doesn't control its own environment and can't be held accountable for adverse external influences.

The subject of care and maintenance affects the last category directly. Good preventive care and thorough maintenance contribute to a reduction in problems due to external or internal causes. Just remember that these are not true computer errors but malfunctions, failures, or whatever else you want to call them. In all my work with computers, I've not seen anything that would be a true computer error. I've never found a computer that was in good working order, was properly programmed, and was receiving accurate data but provided erroneous outputs.

Typical Problem Areas

The problem areas typical users can and should anticipate usually fall into one of several possible categories, namely electronic failure, mechanical malfunction, magnetic-media deficiency, power disturbance, and miscellaneous interruption. Each will be dealt with at greater length in other chapters. However, the following sections present some general background.

Electronic Failures. Of the problem categories, the one likely to cause the fewest problems is electronic failure. Those are the problems generated by an integrated circuit going bad, a solder joint breaking, a wire becoming detached, a circuit board cracking, and so on.

All modern microcomputers have benefited from the expansion of the technology into home and personal uses. To penetrate that market, manufacturers had to produce highly reliable machines that could be kept operational with a minimum of technical expertise. The result is that today's micros perform better, last longer, and have fewer electronic problems than those of just a few years ago. Occasionally, there may be some problems with a chip "burning out" or some similar fault, but these things are infrequent.

All but the simplest electronic failures usually require the assistance of a trained service technician. Few users are capable of performing or are inclined to go through elaborate testing and diagnostic procedures to isolate and repair a single failed circuit—even technicians rarely do that. Instead, the failure is systematically isolated to a component or group of components, say a circuit board, and that section of electronics then is replaced in its entirety. Most computer dealers and service organizations return the defective board to the manufacturer for factory repair.

Known as *card-level maintenance,* this often is the fastest, cheapest, and most successful remedial treatment for an electronic failure. On a parts basis, a whole circuit board may cost more than a single circuit chip, but the job is far less labor intensive than *circuit-level maintenance.* With labor costs ranging anywhere from $50 to over $100 an hour, the difference could amount to hundreds or even thousands of dollars.

There is a catch, however. There's a peculiar pattern known in the electronics industry as *infant mortality* or *instant mortality.* It means that if a component is going to fail, it's most likely to fail soon after being used the first time. Dealers and technicians can testify that the majority of electronic failures occur within the first 24 to 100 hours of operation. As the equipment is subjected to electrical currents, heat buildups, and other traits of normal use, the weakest components often "let go" almost immediately. Once operational for a few days, most early mortality should be eliminated, and the electronics should be good for months or years of uninterrupted service.

This draws attention to the need for a dealership "burn-in" of all computers and associated equipment. If you're dealing with anything more elaborate than an inexpensive video-game computer, it's unwise ever to ask for or accept your equipment in a sealed factory carton. All equipment should be thoroughly burned in by the dealer before you accept delivery. That means plugging it in, switching it on, and running it for a minimum of 24 hours. Longer burn-in intervals are highly recommended, and you should strive to make the supplier run the units for 48, 72, 96, or more hours to ensure the elimination of infant-mortality failures.

After that, your primary problem will be protecting the electronics from certain hazards. Things like high-voltage power-line surges, rapid power fluctuations, overheating, static discharges, and strong magnetic fields all can have detrimental effects on the electronics and destroy components. At the least, failure to provide adequate protection causes things that look like computer errors and shortens the useful life of the system.

Mechanical Malfunctions. Do you think it strange to mention mechanical malfunctions while talking about electronic devices? Think about it! A computer is based on electronic circuits, but many peripherals and connected controls either are mechanical or contain mechanical components. Printing mechanisms, disk drives, keyboards, and switches all have moving parts. If you recall high-school general science, you'll remember that moving objects are subject to friction. Friction causes wear. Wear eventually leads to a failure in the component.

To be blunt, expect more trouble from mechanical failures than from any other problem category. Parts become contaminated, wear out, or just break under stresses of everyday use. Printers jam. Keys stick. Switches fail to make or break contact. Motors change speed. Disk drives slip out of alignment. Parts supposed to slide against each other won't. Parts that aren't supposed to slide will. All these thrills and more await the unwary computer user.

While manufacturers have made significant progress in improving the reliability of electronics, they've not done as well with the mechanics. The situation is better than it used to be, but it's still not good. Some ingenious types have tried to eliminate mechanical parts completely by using touch-sensitive keyboards (like elevator buttons), touch-screen overlays for video displays, light pens, and magnetic induction printer drives, but none has been able to replace mechanical parts completely.

As a user, you have to pay special attention to the mechanical functions of your system. That means inspecting, cleaning, lubricating, adjusting, and replacing parts when and where necessary. Many things you can do yourself. It's not a major undertaking to lubricate a printhead or clean the heads of a disk drive. Other things such as totally realigning disk drives are beyond most users' capabilities and require a technician's assistance. Just be alert, and keep a careful eye on the moving parts.

Media Deficiencies. Another major problem area involves care and maintenance of magnetic media. All *interchangeable* magnetic media such as reel-to-reel tapes, cassette tapes, cartridge tapes, floppy disks, and hard disks require meticulous attention. A possible exception would be the popular Winchester hard disks that operate in a closed environment and therefore aren't subjected to the same hazards as the interchangeable media.

Taken as a group, magnetic media are the most sensitive parts of a computerized operation—they might be considered the weak links in computer technology because they are vulnerable to many damaging influences. The entire system relies on magnetic media to store programs and data—the software—essential to all operations. In most systems used for professional or business purposes, the software often costs several times more than the hardware. Even in personal or recreational computers, the software costs can easily meet or exceed the original hardware costs. As a result, damage to or deficiencies in the media and the data transfers to and from the media can have effects ranging from merely annoying to catastrophic.

I said that media are vulnerable. They or the software they contain can be damaged or destroyed by heat, magnetic fields, airborne contamination, dirty drive heads, improper storage, mishandling, bending, and so on. Even new media never before run through the machine can be troubled by surface contamination, scratches, abrasions, poor oxide coatings, inclusions, and a host of other problems. If that isn't enough, magnetic media wear out eventually. The base material holding the oxide can become brittle with age. Adhesive holding the oxide to the base material can deteriorate. Destruction of the physical media can occur during a drive failure or head crash, and even as the result of a power interruption to the drive mechanism.

With all the things that can and often do go wrong, magnetic media have to be viewed as the most likely area to be damaged by actual user neglect or negligence. Although you could do considerable harm in other areas as well, you're far more likely to damage media than the hardware components as a direct result of your actions or inaction.

The things you'll have to do include cleaning recording heads of disk and tape drives, testing and retesting media integrity, adopting protective operating and handling procedures, maintaining a high level of cleanliness in the area, using only high-quality media, and getting into the habit of backing up everything and anything you buy or create.

Power Disturbances. Power-line disturbances and disruptions are yet another area demanding your attention. It doesn't matter whether you run on residential or commercial power lines; sooner or later you'll see power problems. If you're lucky, your utility company provides "clean" power, and you won't have to go through major expenses to protect your equipment. If you're unlucky, you'll be hit with things like low- and high-frequency noise on the lines, high voltages ("overvoltages"), low voltages ("undervoltages"), voltage spikes ("surges"), voltage drops ("brownouts"), and outright power failures ("blackouts"). If you use your computer purely as a hobbyist, you'll probably be able to squeeze by with little or no special power-line conditioning. On the other hand, if you're a serious user or apply the machine to business and professional pursuits, you may have to cough up the cash for some costly protective equipment.

The effects of power disturbances can vary widely. One that causes you to lose your place in a complex game rates as mildly annoying. One that costs a few hours of word processing effort is extremely irritating. One that wipes out whole disks and "fries" your electronics is a calamity. All are possible depending on how you use your computer, what preventive steps you've taken, how well and how often you've backed up your magnetic media, and similar factors.

In a later chapter, I'll be discussing power-line conditioning at greater length. While you won't be able to control the occurrence of power disturbances, you'll see ways to protect equipment from their effects. Of course, protection comes only at a price—usually a substantial price. You'll have to judge for yourself how much you're willing to spend to protect your investment in hardware and software, but I recommend that you examine the chapter carefully. I feel every computer should be protected to the limit of the user's budget, even if buying such protective devices delays the purchase of other components.

Miscellaneous Interruptions. Finally, there is a myriad of other problems that don't fit neatly into a specific category. Static electricity is one. Walk across a carpet and discharge a spark to the computer, and you could do anything from "glitching" data to frying a circuit chip. Carry a chip or a circuit board across that same carpet and you run a high risk of ruining it.

If you sit at your console with a magnetized key chain or screwdriver in your pocket, don't be surprised if you see some unpredictable computer behavior. The same holds true for putting a telephone near the system—the system could go haywire when hit by a magnetic field as the phone rings. Expose the system to excess heat and it might shut down, malfunction, or suffer permanent damage. If you get too close with a radio-frequency transmitter such as a walkie-talkie, CB radio, or radio telephone, you might see some strange results in your computations when some portion of the electronics acts as a receiver for the transmitted signal.

I could go on and on just listing the potential problems you could encounter. Instead, I'll stop here and leave further explanations and possible remedies for other chapters, where they'll be more appropriate.

Some Routine Advice

Not everything that can go wrong is preventable. No matter how hard you try to prevent them, you'll still have some problems. What you can do is minimize those problems so they occur less often, their effects are less severe, and the recovery is faster than if you ignored the situation.

As a general recommendation before we get down to specifics in the next chapter, examine your actual or proposed installation. Can you keep it clean? Have you cleared away all nonessential metallic objects? Can you control the temperature in the area? Do you have grounded electrical outlets? Have you removed all devices containing magnets or electromagnets (phones, speakers, transformers, flashlights, stereo amplifiers, etc.)? Is the area secured against intrusion by children, pets, or other unauthorized people and creatures? Have you allowed working and ventilation space around all components of the system? Have you either removed any carpeting or installed a special "anti-static mat?"

If you answered "no" to any of these questions, plan to do some work around the installation. I strongly advise that you tend to these items immediately and that you don't progress to the other chapters until you've done so. If you answer "yes" to all the questions, you've already eliminated three-quarters of the potential causes of computer malfunctions and failures.

While you're at it, make certain you've installed smoke and rising-water detectors at and around the installation. The first gives you early warning of a fire, the second warns of a flood. You should also install at least one fire extinguisher near the equipment, using one specifically approved for electronic equipment. Dry-chemical and carbon-dioxide extinguishers are not good choices. Chemicals ruin the electronics, and cold carbon dioxide hitting a hot machine can shock, crack, and destroy sensitive components. The best extinguishers use substances that evaporate quickly, leave no residues, and require no cleanup, such as the Halon™ 1211 extinguishers available from Inmac.

Throughout, be aware of the seven deadly hazards—the seven gremlins of computer usage. Individually and collectively, they should be viewed as mortal enemies of your system to be slain at every opportunity. Specifically, the seven are:

1. Dirt or contamination. Cleanliness is a must for all computer usage on any scale. Dust, dirt, airborne chemicals, and the like can cause problems, especially in combination with other computer enemies. Practice good housekeeping at all times, and perform inspections and cleanings at regular intervals.

2. Excessive heat buildup can be devastating to any component. Most computer components eliminate heat through normal convection or forced-air cooling, but blockage of vents, plugging of filters by dust, operation near heaters or in direct sunlight, and other factors can cause

too much internal heat for the system. Take care where and how you install the system and be sure to perform periodic cleanings.

3. Stray magnetic fields are hard to detect and eliminate. They are, after all, invisible. You can start by getting all unneeded metallic objects away from the computer, including screwdrivers, paper clips, staplers, and other tools. Remove anything with a bell, buzzer, speaker, horn, or transformer (the coils have magnetic fields). Even at that, one component of the system still can cause problems for another. The "flyback" transformer of a video terminal can interfere with the disk drives. The motors in a printer can erase disks.

4. Static electricity is deadly to electronics and magnetic media alike. Virtually anything moving generates static, including you moving through the air or walking across the floor. Even moving parts of computer peripherals, such as spinning disk drives, can cause their own static. You'll have the most problems if you live in a dry climate, and you'll probably not be able to eliminate the problems entirely. Nevertheless, do what you can. Be sure the computer is grounded. Avoid carpeted areas. Since I work at home, I even go so far as not to wear shoes when working on or near the computers.

5. Power disturbances are things you can't prevent, but you can minimize them if you're willing to spend the money. There are numerous products available to cut down on voltage surges, eliminate noise, and even provide backup or standby power. The prices range from as low as $30 to many thousands of dollars. Refuse to pay the money, and you'll just have to take your chances, but don't be surprised if you have problems.

6. Mechanical wear on moving parts is another unavoidable difficulty. Nothing that moves does so without friction, and friction causes wear. Be sure you check your manuals for lubrication requirements on things such as fans, motor shafts, printer mechanisms, and so on. Follow the advice to the letter, and be sure you get the right lubricant on the right part at the right time.

7. Mishandling is a major source of malfunctions. Drop a device like a disk drive just an inch down onto a table and you could jar the entire mechanism out of alignment. Misplace a connector coupling by one pin, and you could blow out some circuitry—perhaps even "smoke" an entire unit. Pull or insert a chip improperly, and you could bend the pins, later damaging the electronics because the pin doesn't engage properly. In general, treat the unit with care, checking, rechecking, and then rechecking again before you move, remove, insert, connect, or disconnect anything.

TWO

THE SYSTEM COMPONENTS

This chapter provides background information, identifying and describing components of typical microcomputer systems. Novices should pay particular attention to the presentations herein. Intermediate and advanced users—all you "old hands"—can treat them as quick reviews of things you probably know already.

A typical microcomputer system can be viewed as four distinct components, namely the CPU or MPU, memory, mass-storage devices, and I/O devices. These are shown in the simplified block diagram of Fig. 2-1.

THE CENTRAL PROCESSING UNIT

At the heart of every microcomputer system is the *microprocessor.* This is the electronic device that manipulates data, performs arithmetic and logical operations, and controls the flow of data and instructions between system components. In strict terms, the microprocessor is the *computer,* and without it there could be no system. Shown in Fig. 2-2, the microprocessor is an *integrated circuit* or *circuit chip* two inches or less long and less than an inch wide. With all the things this circuit chip can do, it's not surprising it has been called the "miracle device" of the twentieth century.

There are many types of microprocessors, each having a unique name or numeric designation. Some of the most popular are the 8080, 8085, Z-80™, 6502, and 6800, and these are just five of many. For my purposes, there's no need to describe the differences among the various processors or the ways in which they work. It's sufficient for you to know that the microprocessor is the "core" of your system and that there are operational differences that affect programmers and system designers.

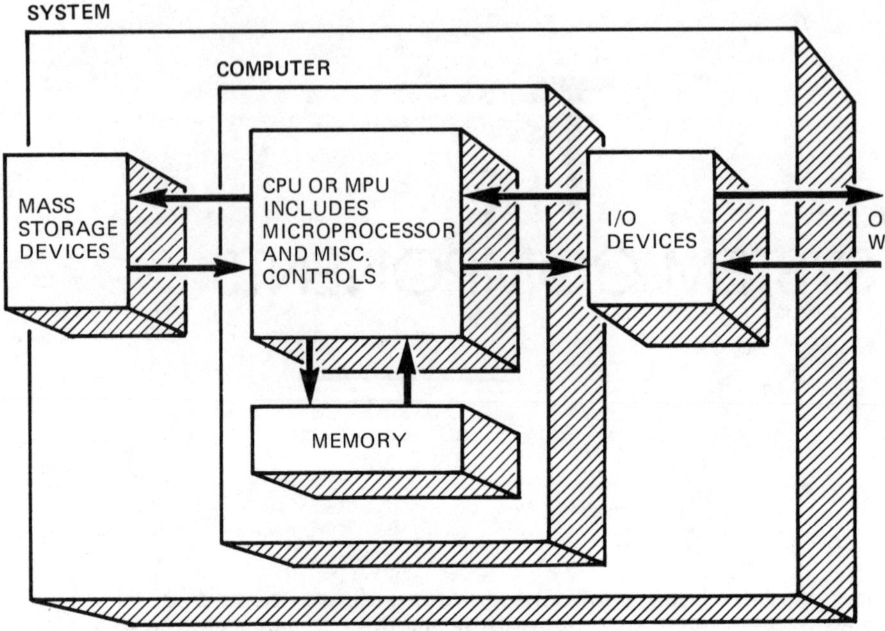

FIG 2-1 Typical microcomputer system block diagram.

FIG 2-2 Typical Z-80B microprocessor chip. *(Photo by author)*

By itself, the microprocessor does nothing. To perform its miracles, it must be connected to other devices and circuits. These are the controls that provide *clock* and *synchronization* signals, *status* indications, input and output *buffers*, and other supporting capabilities. Again, individual functions normally affect only advanced programmers and trained service technicians, although they are often mentioned in the instruction manuals that accompany systems. They can affect circuit-level maintenance but aren't critical to the higher maintenance levels with which this book deals.

Collectively, the microprocessor and control circuits are the *central processing unit* or *CPU*, though some people prefer the terms *microprocessor unit* or *MPU*. While there are some technical differences between a true CPU and an MPU, many manufacturers and suppliers have elected to use the CPU terminology. Often, one book or manual may refer to the CPU while another refers to the MPU, but both may be citing the same components. I'll be using the term CPU to keep in step with the trend.

The microcomputer industry uses two CPU styles. One has the microprocessor and its control devices on a plug-in circuit board that installs into a connector to contact a *bus*. This is typical of the *S-100 bus* computers such as the Morrow Designs' Decision 1™ and other *multiboard* computers. The bus is just a group of electrical paths or lines that convey signals from one device to another. Two typical cards are shown in Fig. 2-3; the larger card is an S-100 plug-in for an obsolete MITS Altair™ 8800b, and the smaller one is an Advanced Logic Systems' Z-Card™ for the Apple II. The connector permits the CPU circuits to contact the bus lines so that signals can be transmitted to and received from other circuit

FIG 2-3 Two typical CPU plug-in boards; S-100 and Apple Z-80. *(Photo by author)*

boards on the bus. Circuit-level technicians may have to differentiate among the *data bus, status bus, address bus,* and other line groupings, but few end users have to worry about internal signal paths. The two things that are important are (1) the bus structure permits easy replacement of boards and (2) the bus permits system expansion by adding new boards.

The second style is used in *single-board* computers such as the Apple II®, Alspa™ ACI-series, Xerox® 820, and many others. There, the microprocessor is on the same *main board* or *motherboard* that holds the memory, interface controllers, or other devices not part of the CPU. The microprocessor may be identified easily by its size and designation, but other CPU components may be difficult to identify. Usually, but not always, the CPU control circuits are those adjacent to the microprocessor chip. A single-board approach has both advantages and disadvantages—single-board computers are more compact and less subject to electrical noise and interference than bussed types, but lack easy replacement and expansion capabilities.

THE MEMORY

The computer's *memory* provides storage for information the microprocessor manipulates. The information can be program instructions telling the processor what to do, data supplied to or generated by the processor, or "addresses" of other memory locations that contain instructions or data.

In the book *The Applesoft Tutorial,* published by Apple Computer, Inc., computer memory is compared to a bank of "pigeonholes." Picture a huge wall of boxes into which you can insert or remove scraps of paper as you need them, and you'll have a grasp of the computer-memory concept. With the CPU playing the part of a clerk who fills and empties thousands of such boxes, you can develop a fair analogy for the overall operation of a computer.

The entire memory consists of electronic pigeonholes for storing data, addresses, and instructions. It's so much a part of the computer's operations that the system often is characterized first by the type and size of memory and only then by the type of microprocessor chip. The most common microcomputers at the personal and small-business levels are eight-bit machines, meaning that each memory address or pigeonhole holds a single *byte* of information consisting of eight *binary digits* or *bits.* The number of bytes available in the machine's memory then is a measure of the information it can handle at one time. Although computers based on 16, 32, or more bits are popular, there's no point in dwelling on differences, advantages, or disadvantages to memory structure since they won't affect procedures in this book. Therefore, I'll stick with common eight-bit microcomputers for my presentations.

By the way, I'm assuming you know enough about computers to recognize the terms "bit" and "byte." If you don't, you might want to purchase one of the many available introductory computer books.

A computer's "size" usually is represented as 16K, 32K, 48K, 64K, and so on. The "K" is an abbreviation for thousands, so the designations correspond to approximately 16,000, 32,000, 48,000, and 64,000 eight-bit bytes respectively. In computer terminology, 4K of memory isn't exactly 4000 bytes—actually it's 4096 bytes. As boards grew to hold larger memories, it was convenient to multiply 4K to obtain the new sizes. The actual sizes are 16,384 bytes in 16K, 32,768 bytes in 32K, 49,152 bytes in 48K, and 65,536 bytes in 64K. A few manufacturers have started to use 65K in the latter case. Don't be misled; a 65K memory is the same as 64K.

Too often, however, computers are compared solely on the basis of memory sizes. Since it seems logical for larger memories to mean more computing power, it's easy to assume that 32K does more than 16K, 48K does more, and 64K does still more. That's true when comparing computers of the same type or brand name. A 48K Apple II is able to work with larger programs and more data at one time than a 32K Apple II.

Factors other than "raw" memory size affect comparisons of different types or different brands. It's not strictly true that a 64K Morrow Designs' Decision 1 has a greater capacity than a 48K Apple II. In any cross-brand comparison, much depends on memory design, use of different types of memory, memory consumption by system software such as the programming language, and similar influences. Since I happen to operate both a 64K Decision 1 and a 48K Apple II Plus, I can use those two systems as illustrations. But before I can compare them, I have to define two types of memory.

Two principal memory types are *random access memory* or "RAM" and *read-only memory* or "ROM." There are others such as *programmable read-only memory* ("PROM") and *erasable programmable read-only memory* ("EPROM"), but I'll limit present considerations to RAM and ROM for simplicity.

RAM is memory used and manipulated by the computer for storing and retrieving information. ROM allows only retrieval of preprogrammed information; a ROM device normally cannot be altered or modified by the computer in which it is installed. Another distinction is that RAM is *volatile* and ROM is *nonvolatile.* Power interruptions originating on the line or caused by throwing a switch destroy RAM contents but don't affect ROM contents.

RAM and ROM use directly influences comparisons of memory capacity. To illustrate, the Apple II Plus puts the BASIC language known as Applesoft™ into preprogrammed nonvolatile ROMs where it's available when the computer is switched on. Being in ROM, Applesoft does not consume RAM locations, which remain available for programming use. A typical 48K Apple II Plus accesses Applesoft from ROM and leaves 47,100 bytes of available RAM memory with no disk operating system ("DOS") loaded. With DOS "resident" in RAM, available RAM decreases to 36,348 bytes.

Adding a 16K memory board to the Apple II and using any of several available *memory management system* software packages to move DOS into that memory board effectively provide a 64K machine with about 46,800 bytes of usable RAM. And that's with Applesoft and DOS available.

Many popular personal and small-business computers can have their RAM memories expanded. Achieving a 64K memory is usually easy, requiring only suitable plug-in circuit boards. Going beyond 64K on an eight-bit machine is also possible, but only with special programming considerations. Figure 2-4 illustrates a plug-in memory expansion for the Apple II or Apple II Plus. The one shown is a 32K Ramplus+™ card from Mountain Computer, Inc., and it features two independently selectable and controllable 16K memory "banks."

In comparison, a 64K Morrow Designs' Decision 1 requires that all system software be loaded from a disk and stored in RAM. With the CP/M operating system and Microsoft BASIC-80 (Revision 5.2) in RAM, it leaves only 31,046 bytes of free memory. That's about 5300 bytes fewer than the 48K Apple II. When Microsoft BASIC 4.51 is substituted on the Decision 1, free memory increases to 37,675 bytes, but it's still a gain of only about 1300 bytes over the 48K Apple. Therefore, a comparison based strictly on memory size is not adequate.

Another factor impacting on a computer's memory size and capability is the amount of memory devoted to controlling external devices. Yet another is whether it uses *memory-mapped video* where every screen location is controlled and continuously updated according to the contents of a reserved RAM area. All these and others can reduce the RAM available for a programmer's use, and all are variable from one system to another.

You cannot always judge the relative capabilities or performance of two computer systems by looking at total memory size. A 48K machine from one manufacturer may have more or less usable memory than a 64K machine from someone else. In any memory comparison, it's important that you know at least how much "free" memory remains after the system is "loaded" and ready to be used.

FIG 2-4 Typical memory add-on for an Apple II. *(Courtesy of Mountain Computer, Inc.)*

From a care and maintenance point of view, microcomputer memories aren't overly troublesome, although they do develop problems occasionally. Like most electronic components, they generally operate continuously and reliably after being properly burned in, with the highest failure rate seeming to occur within the first 100 hours of operation. Among three computers, I've averaged two memory failures a year over five years, discounting those occurring during initial 100-hour burn-ins. Of ten malfunctions, eight were RAM-chip failures fixed by replacing individual chips, and two were failures in the associated control circuits requiring the aid of a technician.

There is a difference between *static* RAM and *dynamic* RAM. In the first, the memory locations hold their contents until either changed by the CPU or disrupted by a power-off condition. In the second, the memory locations are "refreshed" periodically by the computer. There is a phenomenon known as "after-imaging" that occurs with some RAM devices, most notably in the dynamic type. That simply means that one or more memory locations burn in and retain an image of previously stored data bits, thus causing problems in trying to store new and different bit patterns. This can cause erratic system behavior in which programs "hang," erroneous computation results occur, or other operations become unpredictable. The solution is to isolate and replace the bad chip or chips, although it's not as easy as it sounds. This is the type of error that can be difficult to pin down because it's usually intermittent.

ROMs, PROMs, and EPROMs do require special handling, whether in the computer or in a connected system component. Their preprogrammed contents can be damaged or destroyed by static discharges, voltage surges, magnetic fields, and other adverse conditions. It's important that these devices not be handled carelessly. Static must be discharged before touching them. They should be stored with the "pins" pressed into insulating foam or similar material. They should not be handled in a carpeted area. A ROM, PROM, or EPROM failure should be easy to detect because the preprogrammed function isn't performed.

THE INPUT/OUTPUT DEVICES

Together, the CPU and the memory comprise what most people call the computer. It's necessary, therefore, to differentiate between the computer and the computer system. Although the word computer strictly applies only to the microprocessor and perhaps the other circuits of the CPU, it's commonly extended to include the memory and specialized connected devices such as automatic start-up circuits, power supplies, fans, and miscellaneous supporting items housed within the same box. That box and its contents are often called the *mainframe,* so the words computer and mainframe are sometimes used interchangeably.

Still, the computer or mainframe is of no practical use until it can communicate with the outside world to receive instructions and report results. Building a working and usable system around the computer requires adding the devices necessary for communication.

Interfacing is the fancy name the computer industry applies to connecting an external device to a computer. The process provides appropriate connections between the communications lines or input/output bus of the computer and those of the other device. Don't make the mistake of thinking that interfacing is easy. It can and often does turn into a complex and mind-boggling task to get two devices to "talk" to each other.

As a user, you probably won't have to worry about designing an interface. Prefabricated components are available for almost any purpose you're likely to encounter, so you'll have to worry only about whether particular components are "compatible" with your computer. Occasionally, you may have to design programs or "drivers" to access and use a component, but many manufacturers provide that programming for specific computers with which they intend their devices to be used.

To connect or interface any gadget to your system, you first must have the interface electronics, usually as a plug-in board for the computer and a matching electronic setup in the other unit. You'll have to determine whether you want a *parallel interface* or a *serial interface,* and they have to be matched between the computer and the external unit. Then you must determine whether the two ends will connect. For a parallel interface, there's an element of machine dependence—an interface designed for one computer won't necessarily work with another. For serial interfaces, there are matters of signal-line availability at each end as well as *hardware handshaking,* where signal lines control start and stop operations, as opposed to *software protocol,* where programming has to transmit specific signals to start and stop.

At least two external devices are required by any computer system. One is an *input device* that allows you to "talk" to the computer, and the other is an *output device* that allows the computer to "talk" to you. As a group, all such devices are known as *input/output devices, I/O devices,* or *peripherals.*

Peripherals include many types other than those with which you and the computer communicate. They include mass-storage units such as magnetic disk or tape drives, gadgets that enable the computer to control electrical circuits and turn equipment on or off, electronics that convert voltages generated by measuring instruments into numerical values for computer manipulation, and so on.

Since it's impractical and unnecessary to attempt a description of all possible peripherals, I'll limit my comments to those found on most recreational and small-business systems. You should recognize, however, that all peripherals are potential trouble spots in your system. Most either are mechanical or contain mechanical functions and are subject to wear, physical damage, and other ills. Overall, expect far more trouble from peripherals than from the computer itself.

The Keyboard

The keyboard lets you input instructions and data to the computer. Most are remarkably similar to the keyboards of conventional typewriters, but they often have more keys than a typewriter because computers use certain characters not needed in ordinary typing. Furthermore, the keys generate electrical signals instead of working through mechanical linkages, although the key mechanisms themselves are mechanical devices. All keyboards function in the same general manner—after you press a key, a numeric representation of the keystroke or character is transmitted electronically across the interface to the computer. The numeric transmission normally is an *ASCII* (*A*merican *S*tandard *C*ode for *I*nformation *I*nterchange) code.

While keyboards all serve the same function, there are differences among them. First, there's the physical location. Computers such as the Apple II, Apple III, Atari 800, Franklin Ace-1000™, and many others have the keyboard as part of the computer chassis as illustrated by Fig. 2-5. Other machines, including the BASIS-108™, IBM® Personal Computer, and Otrona Attache™, employ a "detached" keyboard similar to that shown in Fig. 2-6. In still other cases, the keyboard may be one part of a *terminal* device or *CRT* that also includes a display screen or printer for receipt of computer outputs.

There also are functional differences among keyboards—things aren't always standardized. Descriptions such as "ASCII keyboard,"

FIG 2-5 Franklin ACE-1000 with integrated keyboard. *(Courtesy of Franklin Computer Corp.)*

"conventional typewriter-style keyboard," and "typewriter-like keyboard" are common in the industry. As a result, the alphabetic, numeric, and space keys are usually in the same relative positions, while the Return, Control, Shift, Escape, Backspace, and other keys are displaced from one board to another. Frequently used characters such as the plus sign, equals sign, right bracket, left bracket, semicolon, colon, and others always seem to be in different positions. Another complication is that a character such as the equals sign may be uppercase on one device but lowercase on another. Just for the fun of it, take a close look at the comparative keyboard layouts of Fig. 2-7.

Keyboards also use different methods of generating electrical signals that are "decoded" into character or ASCII codes. For example, the Hazeltine™ 1500 terminal uses a mechanical "reed switch" arrangement in which pressing a key allows spring-metal contacts to come together. An Applied Digital Data Systems' Regent 25™ terminal (and many other devices) uses a Cherry™ keyboard in which pressing a key causes a metallic pad to contact and "short" two large-surface contact areas. The Atari 400 and Timex-Sinclair™ 1000 have touch-sensitive inductive keys much like elevator buttons. Of course, each approach has both advantages and disadvantages.

FIG 2-6 BASIS-108 with a detached keyboard. *(Courtesy of Basis, Inc.)*

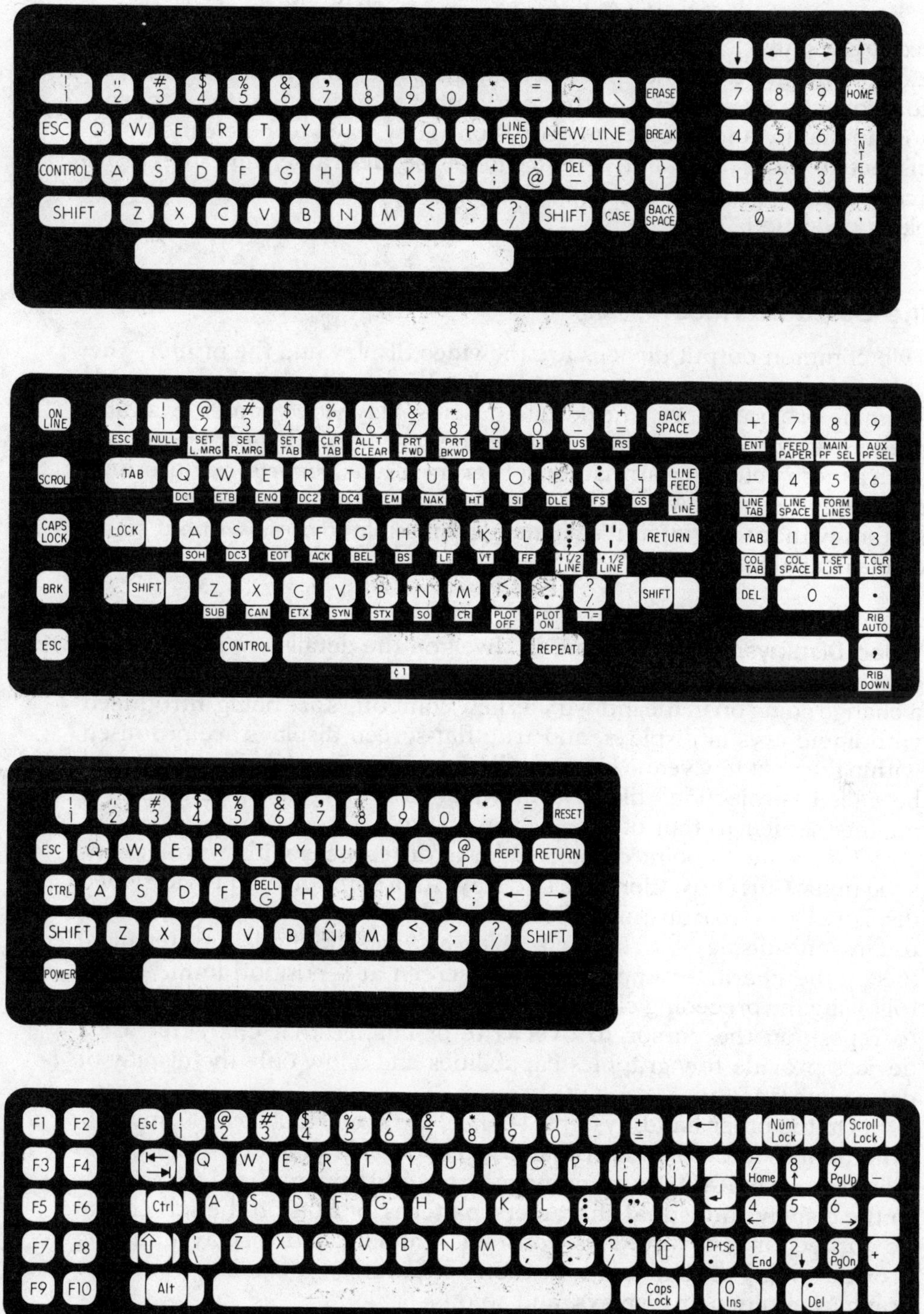

FIG 2-7 Typical keyboard layouts; from top: Adds Regent 25 terminal, Qume Sprint 5 KSR printer, Apple II computer, and IBM PC computer.

In most cases, keyboards turn out to be high-maintenance items requiring considerable attention to keep them functioning properly. Except for the touch-sensitive style, keyboards and their mechanical components are open to the atmosphere, accessible to airborne contaminants, and subject to corrosion. They have to be cleaned and inspected more frequently than might be desirable, and they can accumulate "dust bunnies" under the keytops that eventually could block operation.

The Output Devices

Two common output devices are the video display and the printer. The video display permits you to see what has been entered at the keyboard, examine program lines, check data outputs, play video games, examine preliminary reports, and so on. The printer provides *hard-copy* printouts such as complete program listings, program results, reports, manuscripts, or anything else you want to keep on paper. Although it is possible to use a system without a printer, it's virtually impossible to do so without some display capability.

Video Displays. I'm not going to dwell on the details of video-display capabilities, because there are too many variations available. There's also a change going on in the industry as new computers are being introduced with liquid-crystal displays, and true flat-screen displays are promised within the next few years. Instead, I'll be concerned only with what could be called "projection" displays in which the image is generated in a manner similar to that of a television picture.

I do want to point out a few basic differences within projection-style units. Currently, there are two ways for a computer to provide video displays. One is to transmit a character code or "stream" to a terminal for one-by-one display as received. With a typical cathode ray terminal (CRT), the character appears on the screen at a position immediately following the preceding character, and it takes special control characters to reposition the cursor to overwrite or change that character. CRT devices provide few graphics capabilities and allow only the display of defined characters.

On the other hand, systems such as the Apple II, Atari 400 and 800, Commodore VIC-20™, and other popular brands map every dot of the video screen in RAM. By scanning memory and transmitting the contents to the display, individual characters, patterns, or dots on the screen can be turned on and off. This constant scanning and display updating provide many useful and attractive features, including elaborate graphics, multicolor displays, and so on.

There's an almost unbelievable number of cathode-ray terminals, color monitors, and monochrome monitors from which to choose. Sometimes I think there may be more brands and models of video displays than there are computers. In monitors alone, the user has to decide between high-resolution or low-resolution, color or monochrome, green or amber display, and large or small screen, to name just the essentials. Most of the smaller computers can also be used with either color or black-and-white television sets. In short, the choices are overwhelming.

But video displays share a common trait: users should keep their untrained fingers out of the innards. All video displays should be treated as hazardous to your existence. They operate with internal voltages that could easily fry you if you don't know what you are doing. The worst are the color monitors and televisions. No one other than a qualified technician should open the case or poke around inside. Black-and-white monitors and televisions are somewhat less dangerous, but they can be deadly nevertheless. Since none of these normally has user-serviceable components anyway, there shouldn't be any reason to open them up.

Keyboard-equipped CRTs may be another matter. It's sometimes necessary to open one to gain access to the keyboard for cleaning and routine care. But anyone opening the case should exercise extreme caution. Open the unit only when there's no other choice and when you can't get a qualified technician. Unplug the unit and allow it to sit idle for not less than 24 hours to bleed off some of the charge from the internal storage capacitors. If you do open it, stay away from areas other than the keyboard itself. *YOU HAVE BEEN WARNED!*

Actually, video displays are dependable devices and give little trouble. If something does go wrong, it's usually beyond the average user's ability to locate and fix anyway. As I've said, the only exception is the keyboard, which is the weak link. The keyboards fail far more often than the video does, and they should receive some type of routine attention.

Hard-Copy Printers. Most small-business and professional users, and many recreational users, require permanent or semipermanent records of data, programs, and computed outputs. The *hard-copy* printouts for such records are obtained from peripherals known as printers.

Printer choices are almost as varied as those of video displays, and a user can select from character printers, line printers, dot-matrix printers, thermal printers, graphics printers, and others. Each type has its own characteristic speed, readability, interfacing requirements, and so on. Yet, printer selection often involves a compromise or tradeoff among various features. Figure 2-8 illustrates basic differences among the printouts from popular types.

Dot-matrix printers are probably the most popular for small- and intermediate-size microcomputer installations. They're fast, they offer many options, and they're available at moderate prices. They form individual characters from patterns of dots created by pins or wires striking a ribbon in specific arrangements. With prices starting as low as \$450 (1983 dollars), even inexpensive models can attain speeds from 50 to

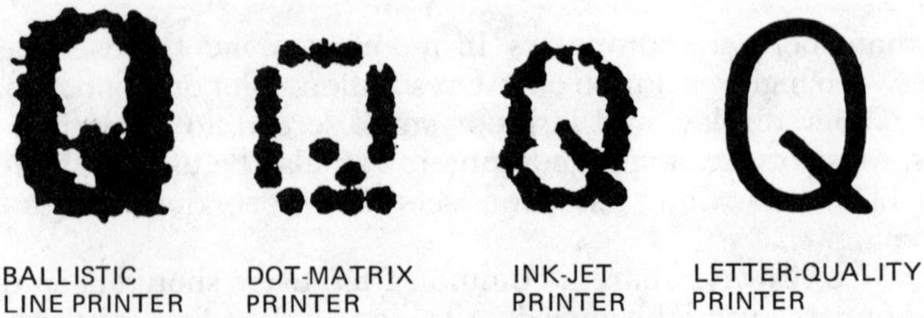

FIG 2-8 Comparative printer outputs. *(Courtesy of Qume Corp.)*

80 characters per second. The printout readability is a function of the number of pins or wires constructing the characters, so more wires mean a more readable output. A 9 × 9 matrix is more readable than a 5 × 7, and an 18 × 9 matrix produces better printouts than either of the others.

Any number of frills and options are available for dot-matrix printers. Some are proportional spacing, multiple type fonts, special graphics characters, bidirectional or unidirectional printing, text justification (flush-right margins), letter-quality simulation, and others. With the number of available features, the typical low price, and the acceptable speeds, dot-matrix printers are good for general-purpose printing. They may not, however, be well suited to specialized printing tasks. Usually, they are highly reliable, offering few problems. The most frequent care-oriented item is replacing an exhausted ribbon. On occasion, there may be a paper jam to clear, or a need to clean the mechanism. Infrequently, the printhead wears out and has to be replaced.

High-speed ballistic line printers, ink-jet printers, and similar types are rarely used with microcomputers and then only in special applications. These high-cost devices range to many thousands of dollars and are designed for high-volume uses where speed is the primary concern. Ballistic line printers can achieve speeds of several hundred lines per minute, far surpassing any character-by-character printer. However, the cost, complexity, and specialized application keep them from widespread use with typical microcomputers, so I'll not be discussing care and maintenance procedures for them. Even thermal printers, which use heat to create the character image on special sensitive paper, are special cases not widely used. I'll not dwell on them either.

Character or letter-quality printers are common system components for business and professional use, but somewhat less common for purely personal use. They print by positioning a "type element" and striking that element against a ribbon to produce a single, contiguous character image. The type element may be a spinning daisywheel, rotating ball, or turning thimble, but every printed character is a distinct character on the element.

Letter-quality printers are both slower and more expensive than the dot-matrix variety. Speeds range from 12 to 55 characters per second, and prices range from about $1000 to $4000 (1983 dollars). Various models offer options such as proportional spacing, bidirectional printing, interchangeable type elements, and either fabric or carbon ribbons. The high-speed, high-priced models offer the best performance, but they may be beyond the budgets of many businesses and most recreational users. Bluntly, it's possible for the cost of a good letter-quality printer to exceed the combined cost of the other system components. Granted, the new breed of low-cost letter-quality printers overcomes the price barrier, but only by sacrificing speed. A professional writer trying to print a 600- to 800-page manuscript on a 12- or 16-character-per-second printer could feel as if he or she is going to be old and gray before the job is finished.

Because letter-quality printers have more moving parts than dot-matrix types, they suffer more problems and demand more care. There are the usual problems of paper jams, worn ribbons, and worn print elements, but they combine with mechanical wear, breakage, alignment shifts, lubrication requirements, and others to necessitate extensive routine care and sophisticated remedial maintenance.

Combining lower price, higher speeds, and fewer care and maintenance requirements might make the dot-matrix printer seem a better choice than the letter-quality printer. Yet the choice isn't that simple. The printer can influence effective use of the system as a whole. A slow device, say a 12-cps character printer, may impose unacceptable waiting periods in applications relying on printed outputs—periods during which the entire system may be unavailable for other uses. A letter-quality printer may be unusable when most applications involve graphics such as bar charts or line graphs because the limited graphics capabilities of daisywheel, ball, and thimble printers often prove too slow and cumbersome to be effective.

Choose carefully! To illustrate, using a dot-matrix printer for word processing may be a mistake. Nearly every microcomputer is capable of being a word processor; all it needs is word-processing software. Wrong! Wrong! Wrong! A writer or an executive preparing manuscripts, writing business letters, preparing professional reports, or performing similar tasks could be in serious trouble.

Writers using dot-matrix printers could experience difficulties selling their work. Many editors and publishers resist dot-matrix manuscripts—often they are hard to read. Some have indicated that the works get less than preferential treatment, while others have said they wouldn't read such manuscripts at all. The result is a lost sale because the editors and publishers won't read the printing.

Businesses may have another problem, particularly affecting letters, reports, and other materials circulated outside the company. Dot-matrix printouts are easily recognized as being machine generated and are usually viewed as mass-produced "junk mail." They have little effective impact on potential clients or customers, probably get routed directly to the trash, and may create a negative image.

A Myriad of I/O Devices

I've only touched on the subject of input/output devices. There are hundreds, even thousands of devices. There are analog/digital converters, telephone modems, digitizers, graphics pads, speech synthesizers, display enhancers, digital clocks, plotters, light pens, printing spoolers, and other miscellaneous devices. Each has its uses, and each has unique care and maintenance requirements. I'll be describing some in later chapters, but I'll be ignoring others. Since a book covering every possible peripheral in detail would have much of its contents applicable to a limited number of users, I'll concentrate my efforts on those peripherals most widely used.

THE MASS-STORAGE DEVICES

The final component of Fig. 2-1 is the mass-storage device. On the most popular small computer systems, this may be a cassette tape, one or more floppy disks, or a hard disk. Regardless of the type, the device provides the means for permanently storing information such as programs, data, and text by recording them on a magnetic surface similar to the way sound is recorded on an audio tape. There is a tendency to include these as a subgroup of the input/output devices, but I prefer to treat mass-storage devices as a separate category.

As popular acceptance of microcomputers began to expand in the mid-1970s, there was a corresponding gain in the popularity of tape cassettes and floppy disks as mass-storage media. Both store large amounts of data, operate at reasonable speeds, and can be priced more affordably than devices used on bigger computers. As microcomputer sales boomed, efforts were made to incorporate other mass-storage devices such as magnetic card readers, paper tape punches and readers, large reel-to-reel magnetic tape units, hard disks, and so on. While hard disks have achieved acceptance and popularity, none has had the impact of cassettes and "floppies."

Many personal and business micros first were introduced with only the ability to record ("write") and play back ("read") from a tape cassette. Even as late as 1982, some new brands were still appearing in stores with only a cassette for data and program storage. The tape cassette cannot be distinguished from an ordinary audio cassette, and computers are often equipped with more or less standard audio recorders. While these are all right for recording and loading programs or data in strictly sequential order, they are slow and don't allow information to be accessed as easily as might be desirable.

Usually, only one computer program is stored on a cassette. With more than one program on a tape, locating the second or subsequent one is sometimes difficult and always frustrating. To get at programs beyond the first, it's necessary to advance the tape past unneeded ones, either by reading and ignoring the output or by using a fast-forward operation. With no reliable indication of where to stop searching and start reading, finding the start of the second program isn't easy. Furthermore, cassette-stored data are useful only if the entire set of data is needed at once or if sequential reading of the entire set can be tolerated. If you want to use only the 840th English word from a *file* containing 5000 words, you would either read all preceding words into memory or read, count, and discard words until you reached number 840.

The floppy diskette eliminates many problems associated with tape cassettes. The medium or diskette is a flat disk of plastic-like material coated with a magnetic surface and enclosed within a flexible plastic jacket. In a drive, the diskette spins at high speed, and a read/write *head* can record data or play data back. Most diskettes hold more data than cassettes, handle data transfers faster, and allow storage and retrieval in a nonsequential fashion.

Randomly accessing information on a diskette means numerous programs can be stored on a single diskette and retrieved without having to read past unwanted material. It allows written data to be verified and rewritten if necessary, preventing errors that later might interfere with the computer's operations. It also allows a single data item to be retrieved from hundreds or thousands without reading each item in sequence. Hard disks have further advantages in that they hold much more data and access it faster. A small hard disk often can hold data and programs equivalent to 100 or more floppy disks, and can retrieve data in only a small fraction of the time required by floppies.

While disk systems initially cost far more than cassette systems, the cost is usually offset by time savings and an improvement in the

FIG 2-9 Typical 8- and 5-1/4-inch floppy disk drives. *(Photo by author)*

computer's performance and capabilities. Of course, various computers can use different disk drives having different prices. Figure 2-9 shows typical 8-inch and 5-¼-inch floppy drives side by side. An 8-inch floppy disk drive costs considerably more than a 5-¼-inch mini-floppy but holds more information. A double-density drive costs more than a single-density drive but offers twice the data storage per diskette. A double-sided drive costs more than a single-sided drive, but again doubles the capacity. A particularly desirable setup is "dual quads"—two double-sided double-density drives equivalent to eight single-sided single-density drives. Although dual quads are expensive, the 8-inch variety provides nearly 2.5 million bytes (2.5 megabytes) of storage on line at one time.

Cassettes and floppy disks, including both drives and media, are perhaps the weakest links in any system. These components are likely to cause more problems than any others, partly because of the mechanical nature of the drives, cassettes, and diskette jackets, and partly because of the nature of the media. Virtually every possible hazard can cause trouble. Vibration, static, magnetic fields, heat, cold, and contamination all are hazardous to both drives and media. Mechanical wear is a problem within drives and on magnetic surfaces. Keeping heads in alignment and motors running at acceptable speeds sometimes is difficult. Power-line disturbances can be destructive. One slip-up in handling a diskette or tape can wipe out its contents.

Hard disks, particularly Winchester varieties, are less prone to problems, but they can fail too. Although Winchester disks are touted for high reliability, they must be treated with respect. Stray static discharges,

FIG 2-10 Apple Disk II compared to DSI-A506 Winchester hard disk. *(Courtesy of Davong Systems, Inc.)*

magnetic fields, and excess heat are the most likely causes of problems. Impact shock—jarring the unit by dropping it as little as an inch—is a major hazard during installation and system maintenance. The sealed environment of modern Winchester hard disks minimizes chances of contamination, but seals can break down. Meanwhile, unsealed cartridge-style hard disks still in common use are subject to contamination. In either case, if a high-speed hard disk crashes as a result of the head striking a dust particle, you can kiss the unit and the stored data goodbye. Figure 2-10 shows a standard Apple Disk II™ drive (a mini-floppy) next to a Davong Systems' five-megabyte (5MB) Winchester disk. Note the absence of openings in the hard-disk cabinet except for ventilation slots at the rear; unlike the floppy drive, the hard disk is sealed to prevent dust, smoke, and other contaminants from entering the mechanisms.

WHERE TO LOOK

In this chapter, I've identified the major components of a typical microcomputer system. I've also provided a rough indication of the ones that probably will show the most failures and malfunctions during the life of the system. To summarize, you can expect most of your problems to be in the peripherals, not in the mainframe CPU or memory. While there will be some infant mortality in the electronics, most of that should be eliminated by a thorough dealership burn of the equipment.

From the end of the infant-mortality interval, typically around 100 power-on hours, you should expect mechanical components to misbehave far more often than electronic ones. The magnetic media and associated drive mechanisms are likely to fail most often. Either the printer mechanisms or the keyboard are the next most frequent trouble spots, depending on whether you use a system more for printouts or for keying entries. At a much lower frequency, you'll still have some electronic failures such as a circuit chip burning out.

Through proper preventive care, you can minimize the effects of mechanical failures by cutting down on causes of unnecessary wear. By adopting good handling techniques, installing some protective devices, and taking other steps to safeguard your equipment, you can eliminate many potentially damaging conditions that could knock out your system. All these things will be covered in greater detail in the remaining chapters.

THREE

THE SEVEN DEADLY HAZARDS

This chapter elaborates on what I've chosen to call the seven deadly hazards. Introduced in Chapter 1, these are the things that contribute to excessive system malfunctions and high maintenance costs when ignored or neglected. As such, they are deadly hazards indeed—deadly to your system's hardware and software alike.

I provide parallel discussions of dirt and contamination, heat buildups, magnetic fields, static electricity, power disturbances, mechanical wear, and mishandling. For each, I proceed from sources and causes, through some notable effects, to some system-level preventive and remedial steps. The sections aren't comprehensive studies of the subjects; instead they provide background information and should get you started thinking in the right direction. Detailed examinations of individual components are deferred to later chapters, so consider the steps herein as top-level care, affecting the system as a whole and not just one or two parts.

DIRT AND CONTAMINATION

Everything gets dirty, and your computer is no exception. Dirt, dust, and airborne contaminants accumulate with alarming speed both outside and inside every component. While dirt on a chassis surface may be unsightly, dirt penetrating the inner workings can cause numerous difficulties.

Sources and Causes

The principal source of dirt is the atmosphere. Unless you're lucky enough to be in a controlled clean-room environment, your equipment is exposed to the ravages of dust, smoke, soot, chemical pollutants, "aerosols" (fine airborne particles), and so on. Exposure is unavoidable because contaminants exist everywhere. If you operate at home, you probably have an additional burden from cooking grease, food particles, pet hairs, and other household pollutants. Nearby industrial centers add byproducts of manufacturing processes, some of which are corrosive. Being near the seashore adds corrosive airborne salt spray.

You create some contaminants yourself: bits of hair, flakes of dandruff, cells shed by your skin, cigarette smoke, ash particles, carpet and upholstery fibers, and many others. The computer system even creates some of its own, including particles and fibers from printer paper, oxide particles from tapes or disks, fibers broken loose from printer ribbons, and so on.

Everyone's familiar with "dust bunnies," those accumulations of dust and grime under appliances, behind furniture, and in, under, or around household or office objects. Anyone who has lived near the ocean has seen the corrosive effects of "sea air" make cars rust out quickly. Well, what happens to other objects also happens to computers. Dust bunnies congregate inside the chassis, corrosive chemicals settle on and gradually consume metallic parts, and films of greasy sludge accumulate on surfaces. Over days or weeks, the effects may not be noticeable, but months or years of accumulation lead to trouble.

You must understand that most computer equipment is not airtight—it can't be! Electronic and mechanical components generate heat, and without cooling air, they would suffer damaging heat buildups. A flow of outside air is always necessary. Notably, there are two cooling methods; one relies on natural convection, and the other uses forced air. With convection cooling, rising warm air exits at the top of a unit and is replaced by cool air entering at the bottom. In fan-cooled units, a blower either pulls cool outside air in or pushes warm inside air out. Either way, air entering a device is far from clean, and the dust and other particles settle inside the box. Because more air flows through fan-cooled machines, they tend to accumulate more internal dirt than convection-cooled ones. Therefore, expect to devote more cleaning and care to components equipped with fans than to ones that are not.

Effects

The symptoms of a dirty installation can appear as anything from a gradual decline in system performance to a sudden component failure. Often, a problem builds so slowly it's unnoticed until a major malfunction occurs.

Surface problems are obvious. When a display screen gets dirty, it's hard to read. When key tops are dirty, they feel strange, often greasy or sticky. When covers get dirty, they're usually discolored. With any common sense at all, most people will exert at least minimal effort to keep outside surfaces and display screens clean as a part of normal housekeeping.

The serious problems, however, are hidden inside the equipment, where many users don't think to look. Contaminated disk drives and diskettes aren't readily spotted, but they are frequent and damaging dirt-related problems. At times, they may show up as data misreads ("I/O errors"), head "crashes," physical destruction of disk surfaces, or random intermittent errors while saving or retrieving data.

Additionally, dust bunnies block the flow of cooling air, thereby contributing to heat buildups, damaging delicate electronic and mechanical parts, and necessitating costly replacements. At times, contaminated contacts at cable connectors, circuit-board connectors, internal switches, and other points can fail to make good electrical contact or can start making and breaking contact intermittently during operation. Often, such problems may appear time or temperature dependent. Some show up only after the system has been switched on for an hour or more and is at operating temperature, usually called "temperature equilibrium." Others appear when power is switched on and disappear later when the affected components reach higher temperatures. Still others just go on and on.

A worse problem is that some contaminants are electrical conductors, allowing currents to pass where they are not wanted. Even if this doesn't cause a short circuit, it can lead to intermittent operating errors and system failures that are difficult to identify and correct. Particular problems are evident with soot, graphite particles from pencils, metallic chips, and the magnetic oxide worn from the surface of tapes or disks. All are conductors and can establish unwanted electrical paths.

Incidentally, bugs are conductive. No, not the computer bugs that plague programmers. I mean the living six-legged variety such as ants. In some parts of the country, particularly coastal areas, hordes of ants descend on crumbs and other food scraps, so it's important to keep those things away from computer systems. I've seen what armies of scavenging ants can do when they get inside electronic equipment in search of food. If they cross electrical contacts, they can short-circuit power supplies and other components. There have even been people reporting that ants developed a taste for wire insulation, waxes, and other things found in electrical devices, devouring them and severely damaging equipment. Again, cleanliness is the primary remedy and preventive step, but once an infestation has occurred it may be necessary to place insect traps inside the equipment or even freeze the units to kill the pests. However, don't spray or dust units with insecticide, both for your own safety and for that of the equipment.

Preventive and Remedial Steps

The best cure for dirt-related problems is to prevent accumulations. The only way to do this is to inspect and clean the installation regularly.

There are also some other preventive steps you can take. First, if you have a forced-air heating or cooling system in the building, its filters must be replaced at regular intervals. This is particularly important with gas-forced-air (GFA) heating systems—furnace filters should be replaced every two to three weeks. Additionally, you might consider adding either a furnace or room humidifier; humid air transports less dust than dry air and also relieves some problems with static-electric charges. However, you must not exceed the maximum humidity level specified for your equipment—condensation from humid air onto cool components can cause electrical and electronic problems and can interfere with the performance of magnetic tapes and disks.

You might also install a portable room-air filtration device near the computer installation. There are many brands available in department stores and even supermarkets. These can be placed on a table or desk where they circulate room air through a filter to remove particulates. Again, change the filters on a regular schedule and keep the units several feet from the computer equipment and magnetic media to prevent damage from electromagnetic fields.

I don't have any definitive data about ionization-type air cleaners that use "electrostatic precipitation" to remove dust from the air. Nor do I have any specifics about devices that claim to make the air healthier by ionizing the molecules and giving the air a slight electrical charge. Some people claim that ionization devices reduce static buildups in and around equipment installations, while others say that ionized air molecules may cause other problems, such as corrosion. Since I have no specific data, I can't comment either way. However, I have observed interference when electrostatic devices are operated near radio-frequency equipment, particularly cordless telephones, so I'd hesitate to put one close to the computer. I'd guess that an electrostatic precipitator on a forced-air furnace couldn't do any harm and probably would be beneficial, but I'd prefer a filtration unit instead of an electrostatic or ionization unit in the computer room.

Weekly Cleaning and Inspection. As a weekly routine, you should thoroughly clean the installation, system components, and surrounding area. Floors, baseboards, and window sills all must be vacuumed. Furniture surfaces and the outsides of all components must be vacuumed—use the soft-brush attachment on the vacuum cleaner and be sure you switch the system power off. Upholstered chairs, drapes, and curtains must be vacuumed. Don't use brooms, dusters, rags, or other cleaning tools because they only push the dirt from one place to another and raise dust clouds that resettle on or in computer components. You must capture and dispose of the dirt, and the only practical way is with a vacuum cleaner.

At the same time, wipe desk or table tops, component casings, and other exposed surfaces with a soft, damp cloth or a commercial cleaning product intended for computer use. Be sure the cleaning cloth is damp, not wet. You must not be able to squeeze drops of liquid from the cloth; a single drop penetrating the equipment can do more damage than all the dirt you'll ever see. Do not use detergents or solvents. Detergents leave powdery residues that cause more contamination later; unless you thoroughly rinse, they deposit a dirt-attracting film. If the solvents are not specifically approved for the item in question, they can harm surfaces and parts.

To illustrate, one of my display terminals was equipped with a screen to reduce glare with an etched plastic overlay. Without thinking, I used a commercial aerosol glass cleaner that must have contained a solvent, and then watched it literally eat the plastic, damaging the screen beyond use. On the other hand, alcohol sometimes is an acceptable solvent and is recommended by some manufacturers. For example, Amdek Corp. recommends it for cleaning the plastic-covered screen of their Video-300 monochrome monitor. However, check your manuals first, test a small area, and never use more than a damp cloth. Specifically, do not use "degreasing" solvents containing chemicals such as trichloroethylene, trichloroethene, methyl-ethyl ketone (MEK), acetone, or petroleum distillates unless specifically approved by the equipment manufacturer.

You may want to treat the display screen for static during the weekly cleaning. For this, you'll need a commercial anti-static kit made specifically for CRTs and video monitors. If you pass your hand in front of your display, you will probably hear a crackling noise. That's static—dust-attracting static which does more to dirty the screen than anything else. With proper treatment, you can minimize the static, thereby reducing dust and keeping the display readable for longer intervals.

Many useful cleaning products are available through catalog houses, specialty suppliers, and some computer retail outlets. I've come to rely on three suppliers for cleaning materials, namely Innovative Computer Products for several types of PerfectData™ cleaning kits; Inmac as an alternate source for a Clean Cycle™ Master Cleaning Kit (a private-label version of Innovative's PerfectData Micro Maintenance Kit); and Texwipe for assorted wet and dry cleaning cloths such as Texwipe® lint-free cotton cloths and Clearview Terminal Wipes®. There are other suppliers, but I rely on these three. I find that their products perform as advertised, do no harm to the equipment if used according to directions, and are "must have" items for every computer user. Catalogs are available from these suppliers (see Appendix A for addresses). Figure 3-1 illustrates Innovative Computer Products' Video Display Cleaning Kit with solutions and lint-free cloths.

During the weeky cleaning sessions, inspect all air vents and intakes. Examine all ventilation slots, filters, and fan housings for dirt or obstructions to the flow of cooling air. Fan-cooled units are particularly susceptible to blockages because most of them have a foam filter or wire screen across the inlet to trap large airborne particles. Clogging results in overheating. Follow the suppliers' recommendations for periodic replacement of filters. For units with fixed mesh screens or foam filters, use a vacuum cleaner to remove as much dirt as possible. If the screens are removable and reusable, detach them from the intake housings, clean them under clear running water (not a detergent), and let them dry completely before reinstalling. If filters are damaged, obtain new ones immediately.

Figure 3-2 illustrates a 4-inch diameter foam-filter insert from a floppy-disk drive. Note the dirt deposits and the hole in the material. I forgot to check and clean it for several months, and it became so clogged that the force of the cooling air drew the filter into the path of the fan blades. The blades ripped into the filter, causing a burst of collected dirt and rubber particles to spread throughout the drives. Contaminants penetrated the protective jackets of both floppy diskettes running at the time, and abrasive particles scraped oxide from the disk surfaces, immediately destroying them. All stored data were lost. I also lost several weeks of working time because the diskettes were the master and backup copies I was updating. Since the hole in the filter allowed passage of large dirt particles, this filter had to be discarded.

You'll also have to perform a few specialized procedures such as cleaning the magnetic heads of disk drives and tape transports, but those will be covered in chapters concerning the individual devices.

Monthly Cleaning and Inspection. Once each month, or more often in dusty environments, equipment should be subjected to a complete internal inspection. All boxes that can be opened should be opened and

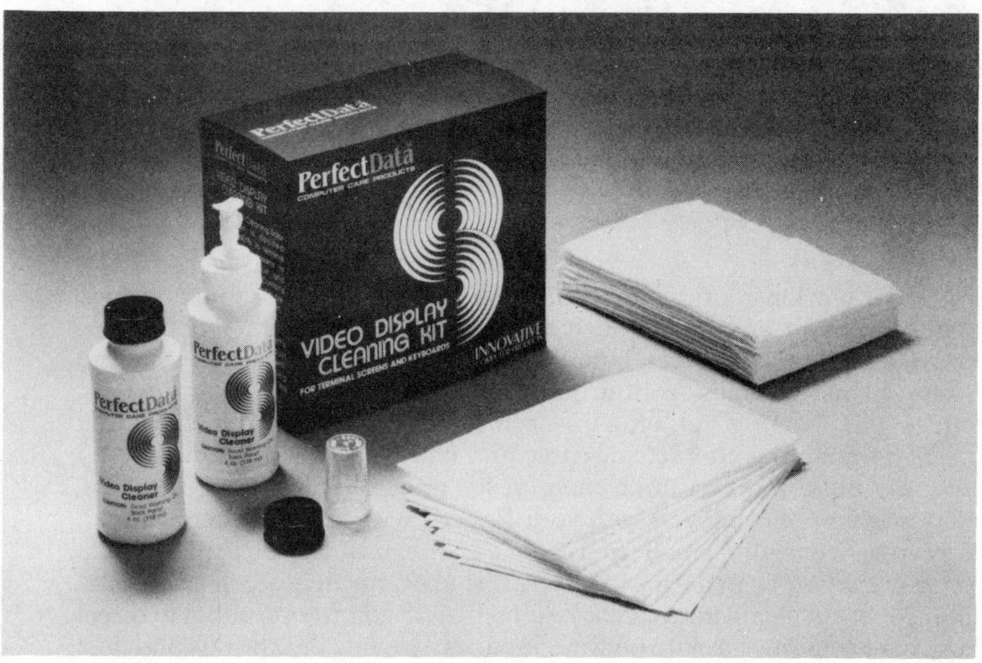

FIG 3-1 PerfectData Video Cleaning Kit. *(Courtesy of Innovative Computer Products)*

FIG 3-2 Contaminated and damaged air-intake filter. *(Photo by author)*

the inner workings examined for dirt accumulations. This must be done with power off and the power cords unplugged. Additional details are provided in other chapters, but for now just remember that you'll have to remove dust bunnies from around circuit boards and under keytops, check the "seating" of plug-in circuit boards and circuit chips, and perhaps clean the contacts of cable and circuit board connectors.

Do *not* use a vacuum cleaner inside any unit. Clumps of dust, dirt, and hair can be removed with your fingers, with long tweezers, or with forceps. Areas too small to reach can be cleaned effectively with pressurized air or inert-gas canisters designed for delicate instrumentation. Most such canisters can be equipped with adapters or tubes to direct a stream of air or gas into confined spaces, blowing out the dirt and dust without abrasion. However, use only a "clean" product intended for this purpose; the gas stream must be free of oil, grease, and other contaminants. Definitely do not do what some have done—do not reverse the hose on a vacuum cleaner and use it to blow air into a computer unit.

One useful product is Texwipe's Micro Duster™—a pressurized canister of laboratory-clean, fluorocarbon gas that is nontoxic, nonflammable, noncorrosive, and compatible with the materials in and around computers. I've also used "clean air" sprays intended for photographic applications such as cleaning cameras, darkroom equipment, and negatives. These are available under various brand names from camera stores and photographic supply houses. For home and most small-business users, the photo sprays should do the job at the lowest cost, with typical canisters priced at $2 to $6 each, depending on size. The Texwipe Micro Duster is more suitable for critical applications, although the initial cost is higher—approximately $20 for the first duster with its control nozzle, nearly $3 each for refills, and perhaps an additional $15 for an optional filter assembly for ultra-clean, ultra-critical installations.

Check mechanical components for wear. Printer mechanisms should be examined for evidence of worn spots on moving parts or bearing surfaces such as the fixed rails on which the printhead rides. Look for "burn marks" and abrasions on the magnetic heads of tape and disk drives, excessive oxide deposits in the drives, indicating possible wear on the diskettes, and any particles of worn material around the print hammer of a letter-quality printer. Be sure to clean paper chips and accumulated paper fibers from inside the printer. Check the guide rails supporting the read/write heads of the disk drives for dust and dirt that may interfere with smooth tracking.

If you use fabric ribbons with letter-quality printers, examine the printing element (daisywheel, thimble, or ball) for buildups of ink, fibers, and dust. Be prepared to clean the element at least once a month to achieve optimum printout quality. With dot-matrix printers, examine a printout for deterioration in the dot patterns which may indicate a need for printhead replacement. It's a good idea to run a reference printout with a fresh ribbon when you first acquire your printer. Each month, run another printout, using an equally inked ribbon, and check it against the reference. Since printer wear is a gradual process, you don't notice deterioration unless you have something for comparison.

Semiannual Cleaning and Inspection. Twice a year, be prepared to undertake the major process of stripping equipment, cleaning it, and reassembling it. No, I don't mean field-stripping it to individual circuit chips, nuts, and bolts. Instead, you remove plug-in cards and clean the edge connectors and sockets. Check the seating of all integrated circuits in their sockets. Check the seating of all cable connectors. Remove the keytops from the keyboard and clean out accumulated dirt; you might have to clean individual key contacts. Go through your manuals for mechanical devices and determine the appropriate lubrication points; then, clean and re-lubricate as necessary, using only approved lubricants.

In short, plan on a minor overhaul. You have to perform every task described in the preceding sections on weekly and monthly care, plus many more. Your approach must be systematic; the goal is to restore the equipment to as close to mint condition as possible.

I must qualify this somewhat. There are units you can't handle this way. It's easy on most S-100 bus machines, Apple II computers, and many others, but it's much more difficult on "sealed" units such as the Atari models that have not been designed for opening and servicing by users. For these, you may need to call a technician, and whether you want to spend the money for someone else to do the regular servicing has to be a personal decision. However, thorough preventive cleaning and inspection can reduce breakdowns and repair costs. Home and hobby users might not want to pay the price, and the equipment itself may not warrant such treatment. But business users whose operations depend on the computer should take every possible step to avoid downtime. For them, it is probably advisable to pay for semi-annual cleanings and tuneups.

HEAT BUILDUP

I've already commented on heat buildups, but I bring it up again because it's a sneaky hazard that can catch unwary users by surprise. Equipment manufacturers specify both operating and nonoperating temperature ranges. The nonoperating range applies to power-off storage conditions and should not be a problem for home or business users since the extremes are beyond the temperature range in most buildings. However, the operating range is of concern. Some typical specified operating temperatures are:

Morrow Designs Decision 1 Computer	50°F to 104°F (10°C to 40°C)
IBM Personal Computer	50°F to 110°F (10°C to 43°C)
Osborne 1 Computer	32°F to 85°F (0°C to 29°C)
Sanyo MBC 1000 Computer	50°F to 95°F (10°C to 35°C)
Quadram MX-700 Display Terminal	32°F to 104°F (0°C to 40°C)
Shugart SA850/851 Disk Drives	40°F to 115°F (4.4°C to 46.1°C)

Even when manufacturers do not publish the specifications (and many do not), limitations still exist. For example, the specification often does not state whether the temperature range is for the ambient air around the equipment or the temperature within the chassis; both methods are used in the industry. Internal temperatures often can be much higher than ambient ones, and I've seen reports of fully equipped Apple II computers reaching 120°F (49°C).

In general, personal and small-business computers and peripherals can operate successfully under ambient temperatures from 50°F to 80°F (10°C to 26.6°C); I don't know of any that can't operate in that range.

Besides, the limits on the operator's comfort are even more confining since they typically are 65°F to 78°F (18°C to 25.5°C). For my systems, the lower limit is never a problem, but the upper limit can be exceeded on hot summer days. Therefore, I keep a thermometer on a desk near the installation and shut down when it reaches 82°F (27.7°C).

Sources and Causes

Adverse high-heat conditions come from two principal sources. One is the ambient environment of the installation, which is subject to seasonal climatic changes and alterations by household or office heating and cooling systems. It's critically important for the operating environment to be maintained within the specified range. If the ambient temperature is too low, mechanical parts can be sluggish. If the air is too warm, the units achieve insufficient cooling, overheat, and may fail to operate properly.

The other source is the equipment. All electronic and mechanical components generate heat as a normal by-product of operation. If that heat isn't vented to the outside or if the flow of cooling air through the unit is obstructed, the internal temperature can be far higher than the ambient temperature around the installation. It's that internal temperature that causes difficulties, and it must be controlled so the equipment can function normally.

An Apple II computer is a good illustration. It's designed as a convection-cooled unit (no fan) in which warm air vents through slots along the sides of the top cover. The scheme works well when few plug-in boards are installed. The most common off-the-shelf configuration has only one plug-in, namely the disk controller, so seven of the eight available card slots are vacant. However, many users then fill the other slots with memory expansions, 80-column video cards, speech synthesizers, printer interfaces, and similar attachments. The electronics of each added component generate heat, the cards themselves obstruct the natural flow of cooling air, and problems of excessive heat can start occurring when as few as three or four plug-ins are in place.

For the Apple II, the situation is compounded when users place disk drives or video monitors on top of the computer. Those devices partly obstruct the venting of heat, and a video monitor can radiate heat of its own downward into the computer. The result is excess heat that can halt the computer, damage sensitive electronics, and cause innumerable operating difficulties. At one point, I had such a machine with all eight card slots filled and a monitor sitting on the top cover. Within two hours after turning the system on, the top surface of the Apple II and the bottom of the monitor would get so hot I couldn't hold my hand on the Apple's cover. Shortly thereafter, I'd start to see erratic malfunctions in data processing, disk handling, and printing operations.

With fan-cooled units, the most common cause of excess heat is blockage of the air intakes. This can result from installing the machine with insufficient space around it for free flow of air, or it can be caused by dirt and dust deposits on inlet filters or screens. It also can be caused by internal dirt accumulations that block the flow of air to and around critical components, even when the intakes are clean.

Other causes include installing the equipment above or near heat sources. Some of these are obvious, others less so. No equipment should be located within three feet of a forced-air heating vent or hot-water radiator. Similarly, keep at least six or more feet away from auxiliary space heaters, including electrically powered radiant heat panels, stoves, and similar devices.

Some auxiliary heating devices pose a double-barreled heat and contamination hazard, particularly kerosene heaters and wood stoves. While modern high-efficiency kerosene heaters minimize fume emissions, they do emit polluting hydrocarbons as aerosol particles of kerosene (a kerosene mist) that condenses as a greasy, electrically conductive film on surfaces, circuit boards, circuit chips, disks, tapes, screens, walls, furniture, and everything else in the vicinity. That film can mean a quick death for electronic components and magnetic media, so kerosene space heaters should not be used in the same room as a computer, probably not even in the same building if you want to play it safe.

Wood stoves may be a little better, but not much. They are "dirty" devices that contaminate entire buildings by spreading ash, smoke, and dust. You can't avoid spreading airborne ash and soot when fueling them, stoking the fire, or cleaning the ashes. Furthermore, should the stove or heater "smoke" when being lit, that smoke will settle on everything nearby, including the computer.

Perhaps the least obvious interior heat source is direct sunlight. Computers located near windows or under skylights may experience problems due to sunlight striking the machines and generating heat with which the normal cooling airflow can't cope. There's also a possibility of added heat radiation from window glass, drapes, furniture, or other objects exposed to sunlight. Although it may be pleasant to look out the window while working, it's just not a good idea to have a computer where it can be hit by the sun.

Effects

The effects of excessive heat are unpredictable. Often, the first sign of a problem is erratic operation, with a high incidence of "errors" occurring during data processing, disk accesses, and so on. Over extended periods, heat can cause irreparable damage to circuit chips and other components, after which errors appear frequently and under all operating conditions. Portions of memory may fail, the CPU may cease to function, a printhead or disk drive may lock up, diskettes may warp in overheated drives. It's possible for circuit boards to crack, connectors to make and break contact, and solder joints to break down. The cumulative effects can be both devastating and expensive.

According to one report, "Studies have shown that the life of electronics equipment is cut in half for every 10 Celsius degree rise in temperature. So if you keep your . . . computer 10 degrees cooler, you double its life and also increase its reliability during normal operation."[1]

A few, too few, computers are equipped with temperature sensors that shut the units off or sound alarms when internal heat reaches a critical level. As a result, equipment damage is minimized, but damage by an automatic shutoff to the work in progress could be troublesome. When such a unit shuts down, the contents of volatile RAM are lost, so a shutdown during something like a word-processing session could cost everything that had been written or edited during that session. However, the loss is only a few hours of the user's time, so automatic temperature-sensitive shutdowns are an effective form of protection for the hardware and the system as a whole.

Preventive and Remedial Steps

Heat problems can be prevented. In fact, there's no justification for any system ever being damaged by heat. If such damage does occur, it's due to the user's negligence; the effort and expense needed to prevent the problem are minimal.

First, keep units away from direct sources of heat. Don't install a computer near air vents, radiators, auxiliary heaters, stoves, or windows. Keep drapes, curtains, or other window coverings closed, even when the equipment is turned off. You might also consider installing a commercial reflective window film on the glass in the computer area. Bronze- or silver-tone reflective film is inexpensive compared to computer failures. It's easily installed, and it provides a substantial reduction in heat generated by sunlight if you accidentally leave the drapes open.

Second, keep the equipment clean, both outside and inside. Air intakes, vents, fan inlets, and other openings must not be obstructed by dust or dirt. Dirt must not be allowed to accumulate inside the unit. These preventive steps are accomplished easily during the routine weekly and monthly cleaning cycles previously described.

Third, allow sufficient space around each component for free air flow. Jamming a computer with rear-panel air inlets against a wall is asking for trouble. Similarly, placing a unit having bottom vents on a soft surface such as a piece of carpet or a foam vibration pad (or setting it on a carpeted floor) also is begging for problems. Many computer manuals contain an installation diagram that shows recommended clearances around the components, and you must not reduce or eliminate those clearances if you want the units to achieve the necessary cooling and operate properly.

Fourth, avoid stacking components vertically. It's common practice with some small computers to put the disk drives on top of the computer and then put a video display on top of the drives. While this may also

---

1 "Frequently Asked Questions about VENTOP," unpublished report (1982), Tovatech, 1903 Fordham Way, Mountain View, CA 94040.

FIG 3-3 VENTOP slotted cooling cover for Apple II. *(Courtesy of Tovatech)*

create other problems, it concentrates the buildup of heat in a vertical column. I'm not even fond of the stacking "work stations" available for small systems. Open racks may be okay, but some confined stations that hold the computer, drives, display, diskettes, and other devices may block the cooling air. Also, some prevent you from installing auxiliary cooling fans when necessary. Therefore, I advise caution in selecting and using such work stations, whether they be self-contained floor cabinets, tabletop stands, or homemade shelving units.

Fifth, install additional cooling provisions whenever possible. If we continue to use the Apple II as an example, auxiliary cooling should be added if you intend to expand the system beyond the simple addition of a disk controller. I recommend that extra cooling be installed immediately when purchasing the computer. The cost is relatively low, and it certainly can't hurt anything.

For the Apple II, there are two approaches to additional cooling; one is "passive," and the other is "active." Figure 3-3 illustrates a device using the passive approach, namely a Tovatech VENTOP™ cover. This is a slotted metal cover that replaces the standard Apple II cover. Slots extend across the entire width of the computer, providing vents for rising warm air above and between plug-in expansion cards.

According to the manufacturer, the inexpensive cover reduces internal temperature by at least 9°F (5°C) in a machine operating at an ambient temperature of 70°F (21°C) and lightly loaded with a 16K

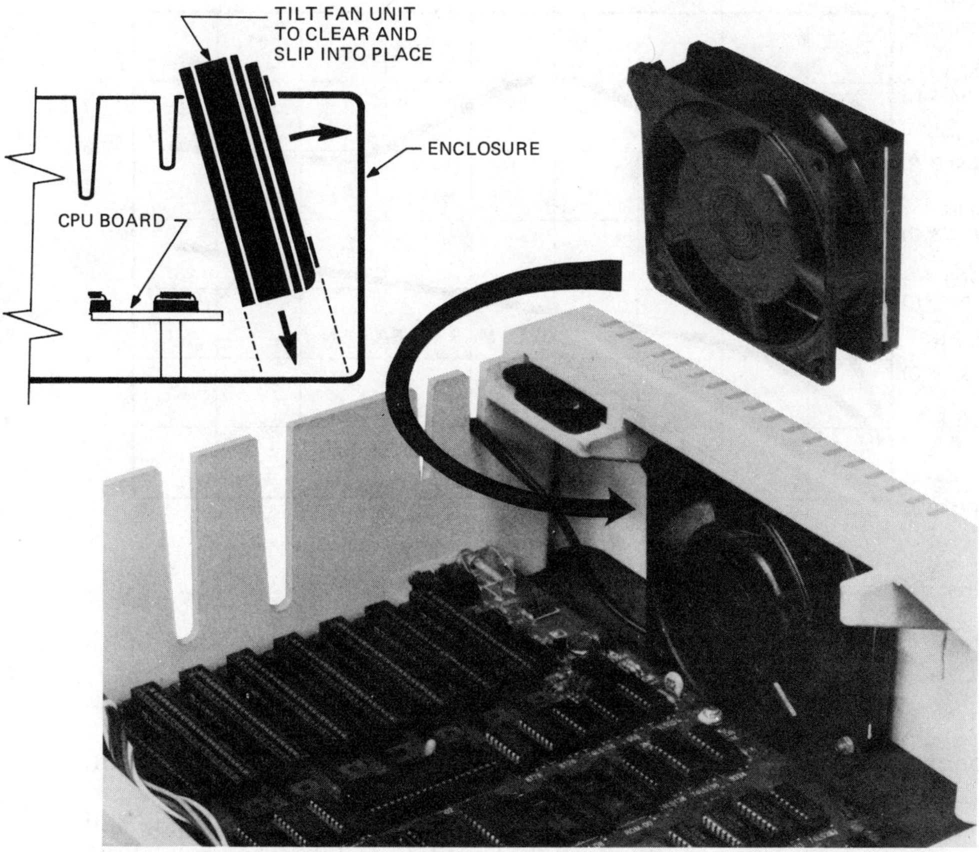

FIG 3-4 Cool-Mark II internal Apple II cooling fan. *(Courtesy of Mark Four Imports)*

memory card, a disk controller, and one printer interface. For a heavily loaded unit with seven of eight slots filled and the same ambient temperature, they report temperature reductions of 18°F to 19°F (10°C to 11°C) above the microprocessor chip, 8°F to 10°F (4.5°C to 5.5°C) around the motherboard RAM chips, and 5°F to 6°F (3°C to 3.5°C) at the power supply.[2]

The obvious advantage of the VENTOP cover is that it provides venting slots above the plug-in cards that are primary sources of excess heat. Thus, warm air rising from the cards exits easily. However, the best cooling is achieved when the venting slots are not blocked by disk drives or a monitor. Although Tovatech reports good results with a nine-inch monitor over the slots, a cover like this should not be obstructed. Besides, hot air vented directly under a monitor or disk drives raises the ambient temperature around them, possibly above their recommended ranges.

---

2 "VENTOP Temperature Test Results," unpublished report (1982), Tovatech, 1903 Fordham Way, Mountain View, CA 94040.

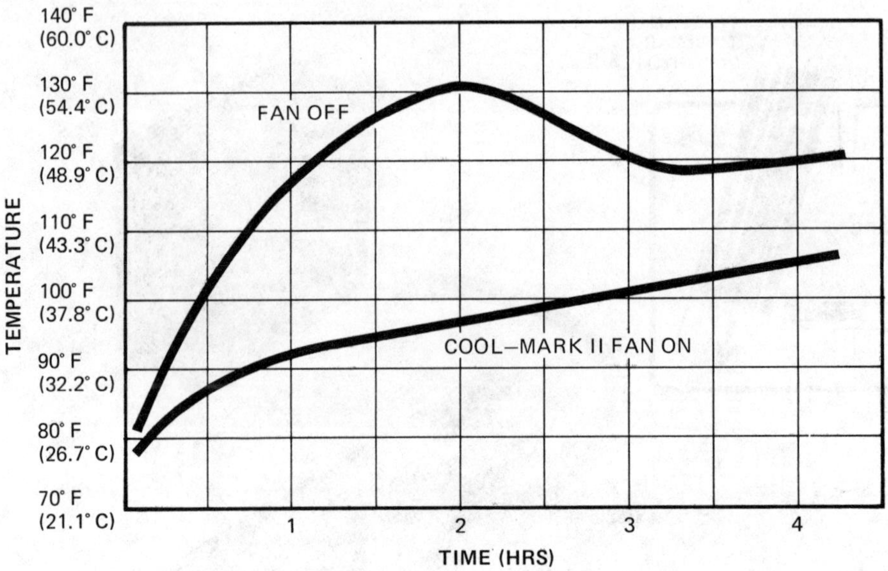

FIG 3-5 Thermal test data for Apple II with Cool-Mark II fan unit. *(Courtesy of Mark Four Imports)*

Active cooling for an Apple II is achieved by adding either an internal or external fan. The Cool-Mark II™, shown in Fig. 3-4, is an internal muffin fan available from Mark Four Imports. Held in place with adhesive mounting tape, it draws air in at the large flat face exposed to the inside and forces it upward and out through the ventilation slots at the side of the unit. Figure 3-5 illustrates some thermal test data obtained by Mark Four Imports as measured over the center row of motherboard RAM chips for a system with six plug-in cards and an ambient temperature of 74°F (23°C).[3]

According to the report, a 15°F (8.4°C) heat reduction is achieved by the third hour, when the computer has reached temperature equilibrium. Since the fan is quiet, noise is not a problem for the operator. There is little vibration if it's mounted securely, so it doesn't cause loosening of circuit boards and other components, although it's advisable to check circuit board seating periodically when any motorized device is in contact with the computer or work surface. One unanswered question is whether the magnetic field from the fan motor might interfere with delicate electronics located nearby, particularly a circuit card in slot 7 (nearest the fan). I've observed no obvious interference, but I also keep memory boards out of the slots closest to the fan.

Representative pull-type cooling fans include the System Saver™ from Kensington Microware, Ltd., and the Super Fan II™ models from

---

3 "Thermal Test Data of Apple II Computer with Cool-Mark II Fan Unit," unpublished report (1982), Mark Four Imports, P.O. Box A, San Gabriel, CA 91778.

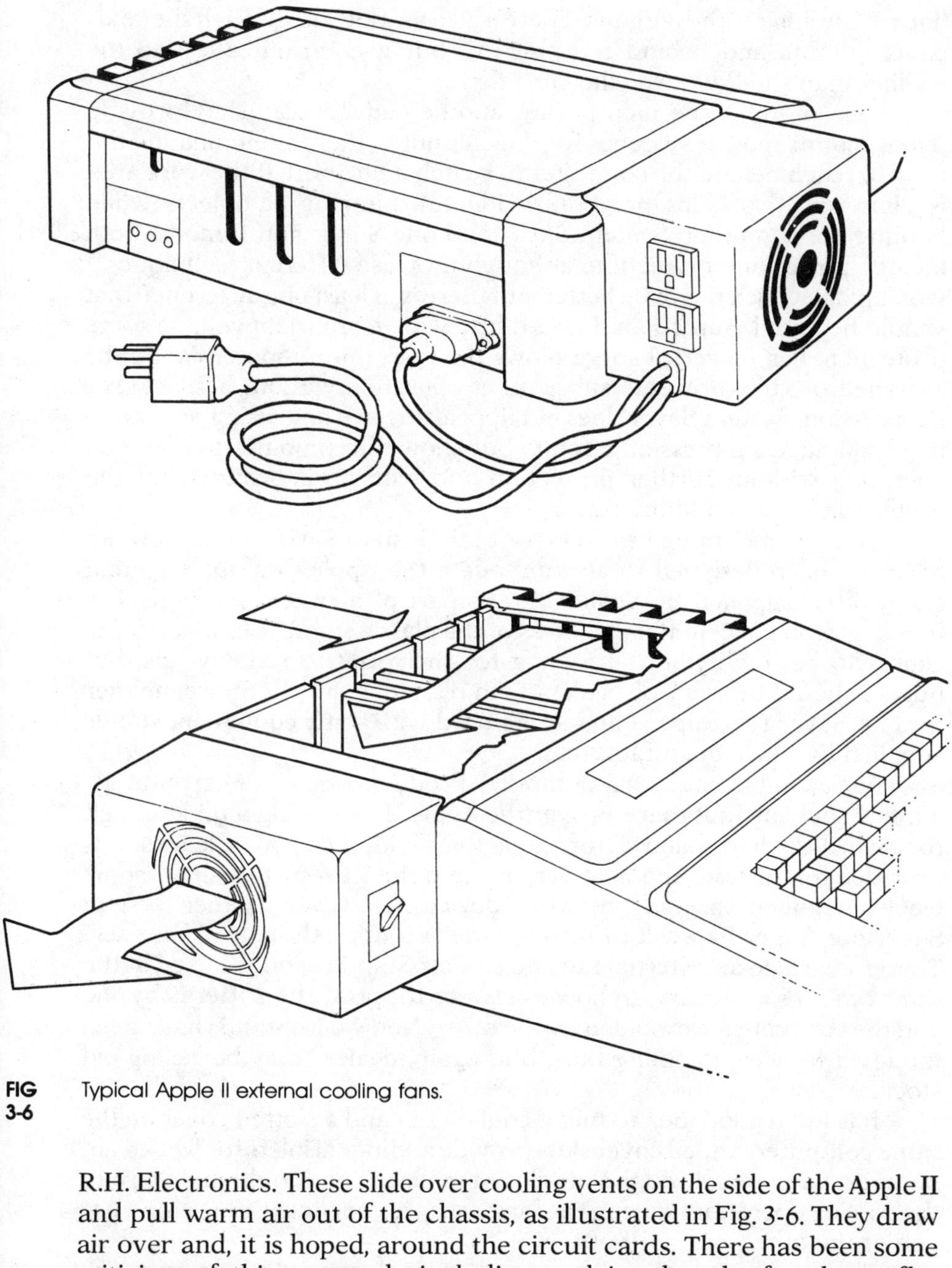

FIG 3-6 Typical Apple II external cooling fans.

R.H. Electronics. These slide over cooling vents on the side of the Apple II and pull warm air out of the chassis, as illustrated in Fig. 3-6. They draw air over and, it is hoped, around the circuit cards. There has been some criticism of this approach, including a claim that the fan draws flat against the first card only and doesn't cool the entire unit. I've injected a smoke tracer at the vents on the side opposite the fan, however, and have seen it ejected through the fan. Since there is clearance between the cards and the top cover, air does flow across the top of the cards to draw off heat as it rises. That's the important part—intercepting and removing hot air coming off the plug-ins. There's also air flowing through the rear-panel cutouts and behind the plug-ins, but it contributes less to the cooling than the flow over the card tops.

Fans of this type incorporate another advantage. They provide "front mount" power switches for the computer, thereby eliminating the need to reach behind the computer to switch it on or off. If the work area is cluttered, this helps prevent accidental dumping of objects when booting the computer. System Saver and one Super Fan II model both include power-line protection, although they use different techniques. I won't judge which might be better, but there is at least one difference that should be noted. Super Fan II uses a fuse with its transient voltage surge protection. If a powerful surge blows the fuse, the computer cannot be switched on; this prevents subsequent operation without active surge suppression. System Saver does not appear to have any fusing, so a surge might damage suppression circuits but allow the computer to continue operating without further protection and with no indication that the protection has been knocked out.

Notably, mounting brackets for both System Saver and Super Fan have not been designed to accommodate the Apple Computer system stand often supplied by dealerships as part of a system package. The brackets won't accept the thickness of the plastic stand. R.H. Electronics claims to be modifying the tooling for their unit to remedy this, but buyers should be wary of dealers with old stock. Furthermore, neither System Saver nor Super Fan can be used with some equipment stands supplied by other manufacturers.

For example, Standard Computer Products markets MicroStand™, a metal shelving unit that fits over the Apple II, providing a middle shelf for two disk drives and a top shelf for a video display. Clearance is provided for air flow and heat venting, and the steel surfaces give some electromagnetic shielding between devices. However, neither System Saver nor Super Fan will fit through the cutout on the side of the rack. Therefore, since an external fan and a MicroStand cannot be used at the same time, it's necessary to choose between the protection offered by one and the convenience provided by the other. New MicroStands have been modified to accept cooling fans, but, again, dealers may be selling old stock.

It is not a good idea to mix a cooling fan and a slotted cover on the same computer. Added cover slots provide additional inlets for forced air, but most air enters through slots closest to the fan and could short-circuit the cooling operation, leaving the farthest cards uncooled. Therefore, use one or the other, but not both.

The items cited are, of course, typical examples for just one computer. For other systems, you'll have to do some research into the availability of suitable products and cooling provisions. Don't neglect it, however. The more cooling you provide, the longer your equipment will last and the fewer problems you will have.

Electromagnetic Fields

Easily overlooked hazards around any computer installation are magnetic or electromagnetic fields surrounding everyday devices. They are hazardous because they can disrupt computer operations, alter data being processed, and erase magnetic storage media.

Sources and Causes

Every electrical current generates an electromagnetic field. These can range from slight, virtually undetectable fields to strong, disruptive, and damaging ones. If you wrap a length of wire around an iron or steel nail and connect the ends of the wire to a battery, you turn the nail into an electromagnet that can be used to attract other metallic objects. That nail is generating an electromagnetic field. If you place a piece of paper over the nail, sprinkle on some iron filings, and jiggle the paper, the filings assume a pattern following the field, thereby showing lines of "magnetic flux."

The same things happen inside most electromechanical gadgets we use every day. Motors, bells, buzzers, transformers, and similar devices contain powerful electromagnets. Some also contain permanent magnets. All have magnetic or electromagnetic fields. Even computer components generate fields, including some powerful ones such as the electromagnets used in ribbon-lifters of some letter-quality printers, head positioning and stepping motor mechanisms of disk drives, and transformers in video monitors and terminals. Furthermore, loose ferrous (iron-based) metal objects may be magnetized, including screwdrivers, pliers, wrenches, tweezers, scissors, paper clips, staples, and so on.

It's sometimes interesting to move a small magnetic compass around the computer equipment; a child's toy compass serves nicely. Often, you can see the needle jiggle and jog erratically as it moves through areas of high, low, and changing magnetic flux. Incidentally, this can be of some use in locating the extent of magnetic influence exerted by a particular device such as a CRT or a stereo speaker.

Effects

To demonstrate the effects of magnetic fields, consider a couple of tales—horror stories so to speak. In the first, an individual installed a new personal computer with twin disk drives. Shortly thereafter, he began calling the store where he bought the system—the drives wouldn't work right. He had booting failures, I/O errors, data misreads and miswrites, and a variety of other problems. The system was taken to the shop, not just once but a half dozen times, but the service technician could find nothing wrong. Everything functioned perfectly.

Finally, the store owner decided to visit the user's home to check the system on site. What did he find? The user liked to tinker with the system and had a habit of putting tools alongside the drives. One of those tools was a screwdriver with a magnet built into the handle to pick up screws and small objects. The magnetic field was strong enough to interfere with the read/write heads in the drive and was partially erasing the diskettes each time they were moved into or out of the drive doors. The solution: remove the tools several feet away, and the failures disappeared.

In another case, a user purchased an expensive color monitor for an existing system. The system wouldn't work right, and the monitor was swapped out by the dealer three times before they realized what was happening. The particular monitor contained a large transformer positioned in its base. The user was placing the monitor on top of the disk drives, which were, in turn, on top of the computer. The field from the transformer was sufficient to prevent proper magnetic read/write operation of the drives and damage data already recorded on the disks. It even penetrated to the computer memory, where it altered and erased memory locations. The solution: move the monitor two feet to the side of the computer and drives.

Like so many other things, the effects of stray magnetic fields are unpredictable. They can show up as drive failures, memory losses, garbled data, incorrect printouts, flickering or pulsating video displays, or any of a variety of other symptoms. The most damaging effect, however, is often an erasure or obliteration of magnetically stored data. Interference with electronic operation is transient and usually causes no permanent damage to the system. But loss of data from disks and tapes can be expensive, particularly if master and backup copies all are damaged so that everything has to be reprogrammed or reprocessed from scratch.

Preventive and Remedial Steps

Most problems associated with magnetic and electromagnetic fields are easily avoidable. All you have to do is remove the source of the field from the immediate area. The difficulty is in recognizing items that do or do not have such fields, and there's a tendency to overlook the obvious.

The worst offender is the telephone. It's a device we take for granted and tend to place in any convenient location. But since the bell or ringer operates with a powerful electromagnet, putting the phone next to a box of disks could easily damage the entire contents of the box the next time the phone rings. Similarly, locating it next to disk drives or memory circuits can interfere with data storage and processing operations.

Audio speakers are another often-overlooked source of trouble. If you like music while you work, you may be tempted to put speakers near the computer. But they, too, have powerful electromagnets (and permanent magnets) to move the speaker cones. They can damage diskettes, tapes, memory contents, and read/write operations.

The obvious solution is to move the offending devices at least three to four feet from the computer, to a position where you're not likely to walk through a field with a diskette or tape in your hands. As a rule, keep anything not required for operation away from the computer. That includes tools, flashlights, phones, speakers, intercoms, or anything else that has even the slightest chance of containing a magnet, being magnetized, or being attracted by a magnet.

Watch out for the "flyback" transformer in video terminals. Its field can "chew up" computer peripherals and magnetic media. Some tape and disk devices are particularly sensitive and cannot be run within two or three feet of a CRT or monitor. Similarly, multiple monitors may interfere with each other. On my Apple II installation, I use both color and monochrome monitors. However, they cannot be used at the same time within three feet of each other without the displays of one or both being unstable. When I first added the monochrome monitor, I thought it was defective. The video display pulsated wildly and jumped up and down by a full quarter-inch. By moving it toward or away from the color monitor, I was able to increase or decrease the erratic behavior, finally finding that a separation of three feet eliminated the problem.

If other considerations prevent removing an interfering device such as a CRT or monitor, some shielding may be possible. Often a thin sheet of ferrous metal, say a one-eighth-inch sheet of soft iron, placed between two devices will block interfering magnetic fields. Interestingly, some computer work stations or stands provide good shielding, and they don't have to be enclosed cabinets. The steel MicroStand rack for the Apple II (Standard Microcomputer Products) has demonstrated shielding effects for some monitors placed on the shelf above the drives. Plastic, wood, or aluminum racks do not provide effective shielding and probably should be avoided for vertical stacking applications where magnetic influences might be a problem.

Always protect your magnetic media. Tapes and disks should be in one of two places; either in a drive or in protective nonmetallic boxes at least three to four feet from any electrical or electronic device. Unless you are willing to lose stored programs and data, never leave disks on or near the computer, drives, monitor, CRT, printer, or any other system component. Never allow them near telephones, speakers, calculators, or similar gadgets.

ELECTROSTATIC CHARGES

Electrostatic charges—static electricity—are a constant problem around computers and other electronic installations. Depending on many factors, the problem may be mild or severe, but it's always present and always a potential source of computer malfunction.

Sources and Causes

The Static Control Systems division of the 3M Company offers a good description of the phenomenon:

> In scientific terms, it is an imbalance of electrons on the surface of a material. Whenever two materials that are in contact are separated, an imbalance of electrons occurs on each surface, resulting in a positive charge (deficiency of electrons) on one surface and a negative charge (overabundance of electrons) on the other surface. Because this charged state is "unnatural," each surface makes an effort to discharge, or return to its neutral state. A typical example . . . is a person walking across a floor (generating a static charge) and then getting a shock (discharging) as a door knob is touched. Quantitatively, when a person feels this shock, a charge of at least 2500 volts is involved, a charge level high enough to cause malfunctions of electronic equipment . . . charges well below 2500 volts can cause equipment malfunctions, so static protection may be needed even though "shocking" is not present.[4]

A common misconception is that static is a problem only in carpeted areas. Not true! All surfaces are potential problems, including vinyl tile, wood, and concrete. Furthermore, moving objects such as the flywheels and diskettes in continuously spinning disk drives are internal sources of static. Paper being fed through a printer, particularly a high-speed printer, can build and carry a charge into the printer and cause malfunctions.

Eliminating carpeting may reduce the buildup of electric charge but won't eliminate the problem. The 3M Company report just quoted cites some experimental work done at Western Electric Co., Inc., showing that the most common buildup for a person walking across a carpet was 12,000 volts, while walking across a vinyl tile floor under the same environmental conditions commonly accumulated 4000 volts. The highest readings reported were 39,000 volts for carpeting and 13,000 volts for vinyl tile. It shows that carpeting generates higher voltages, but solid floors still generate enough to be dangerous to delicate equipment.

Another common but erroneous belief is that high humidity eliminates electrostatic accumulations. It's true that high relative humidity reduces accumulated charges and reduces the danger to equipment by allowing charge dissipation through surface and airborne moisture, but it does not eliminate static completely. Besides, most homes and offices aren't maintained at high humidity levels, with 50 percent or less relative humidity being normal. In dry climates, humidity levels as low as 5 percent may be the norm.

Consider this! Exposed or unprotected electronic equipment such as circuit chips can be sensitive to static discharges as low as 10 volts. Encased end products such as major components of a computer system are partly protected to about 500 volts. Therefore, any of the previously cited levels are deadly to either bare components or finished products.

---

4 Robert J. Kunz, "The Solution to Static Caused Problems with Commercial Electronic Equipment: 3M Static Control Floor Mats," Report J-SFMP (501)R1, Static Control Systems/3M.

Effects

The visible effect of an electrostatic charge is a shocking spark arcing from one object such as a fingertip to another object such as a keyboard as the buildup is discharged. To a computer operator, this is an annoying, sometimes painful experience. But it's trivial compared with the damage the discharge can do inside electronic devices or to data stored on magnetic surfaces such as tapes and diskettes.

If a static discharge should penetrate the workings of a computer, it can alter or wipe out the contents of memory, create faulty data during printing or display, blank a video display, or cause unwanted printer carriage returns. Printers overprint or run wild. Disk drives read or write erroneous data. Programs are lost or yield incorrect results. Internal and external power fuses blow, shutting down components entirely. Worse, a static discharge can burn out circuit chips or entire circuit boards. A static discharge to or across magnetic media can permanently destroy stored data or damage the medium so it can't be used.

Interface cables connecting system components such as CRTs, printers, and disk drives to the computer are particularly vulnerable to static. I often have cables routed from corner to corner of a room or from one room to another. I even connect multiple computer systems so they can "talk" to each other from one room to another and thereby share programs and data. However, cables sometimes have to be routed where it's possible to step on them. If I'm not careful to avoid a cable when walking, I can and have discharged static into the cable, thereby "glitching" the computers. I've blown out many circuit chips on interface boards and two complete boards doing that.

According to the 3M Company, even equipment grounding isn't absolute protection. "When a static charge occurs, the charge always goes to ground. Assuming that the equipment is grounded, and assuming that the discharge path **by-passes** all sensitive circuitry, electromagnetic waves **will still be generated** by the discharge. These can couple into the circuits, thus causing malfunctions."[5]

In general, expect static problems to cause erratic computer behavior. However, similar external symptoms may be evident with other problems such as overheating, dirt, and magnetic fields, so you have to check for all possibilities if you see unwanted behavior or results. If you ever get a spark when touching the equipment, you've got a real problem on your hands and will have to take immediate steps to eliminate it.

Preventive and Remedial Steps

As usual, the best cure for static problems is prevention. The initial step is to make certain every component is electrically grounded, since chassis grounding is the only inherent defense the equipment has. Never, under

---

5 "Questions Commonly Asked by Static Control Floor Mat Prospects," Report J-SVQC-1 (128.07)R1, Static Control Systems/3M.

any conditions, operate ungrounded computers or peripherals—grounding not only protects the equipment from static but protects you from electrical shock if something should malfunction.

Actually, computers and peripherals require two grounds, each having a different function. One is the "logic" or "signal" ground and provides a zero-volt potential necessary for operation of electronic and electrical circuits. The other is the "chassis" ground that serves as static and shock protection. As a user, you normally won't be involved in the functional differences since most equipment ties the two grounds together to make them electrically the same. Rarely will you encounter a device that has provisions for separating the grounds electrically, and then it would be done only under circumstances extremely sensitive to electrical "noise" or interference. For nearly all personal and small-business computers, both grounds are provided through the grounding prong of the electrical plug you insert into a wall receptacle.

You must be sure that the third prong (the round one) of every line plug is properly grounded. Do not attempt to defeat grounding provisions! Do not break or cut ground prongs! Do not install three-prong to two-prong adapters! Some older buildings were constructed before codes required grounded electrical outlets and are, therefore, equipped with two-prong receptacles. Most people install an adapter to bypass the three-prong grounding and make use of existing outlets. They then either fail to connect the "pigtail" wire of the adapter to the center screw of the wall plate or connect it to one that is not grounded (many old two-prong receptacles do not have any grounded parts). Even new buildings may not have the third wire properly connected to ground. The only way to be sure of the system grounding is to have a qualified electrician check the outlets and electrical wiring before you install your computer system.

While grounding the system helps protect it from static, that alone is not sufficient. Additional steps are necessary. Others that help reduce static problems but still don't eliminate it include:

1. Remove rugs and carpets from the area, particularly those made of nylon or other artificial fibers.

2. Install and operate a room or furnace humidifier to raise the relative humidity in and around the installation.

3. Avoid rubber- or crepe-soled shoes. The soles are nonconductive, allowing a charge to be built up while walking but not allowing it to bleed off. Leather-soled shoes are the best choice.

4. Attempt to discharge to some large or grounded metal object before touching the computer. However, the object must not be electrically connected to the computer or be connected to the same power circuit.

5. Avoid excessive movement when operating the computer. Don't shuffle your feet, and don't slide around on a chair. Minimize actions such as standing up, walking around the room, and sitting back down at the keyboard.

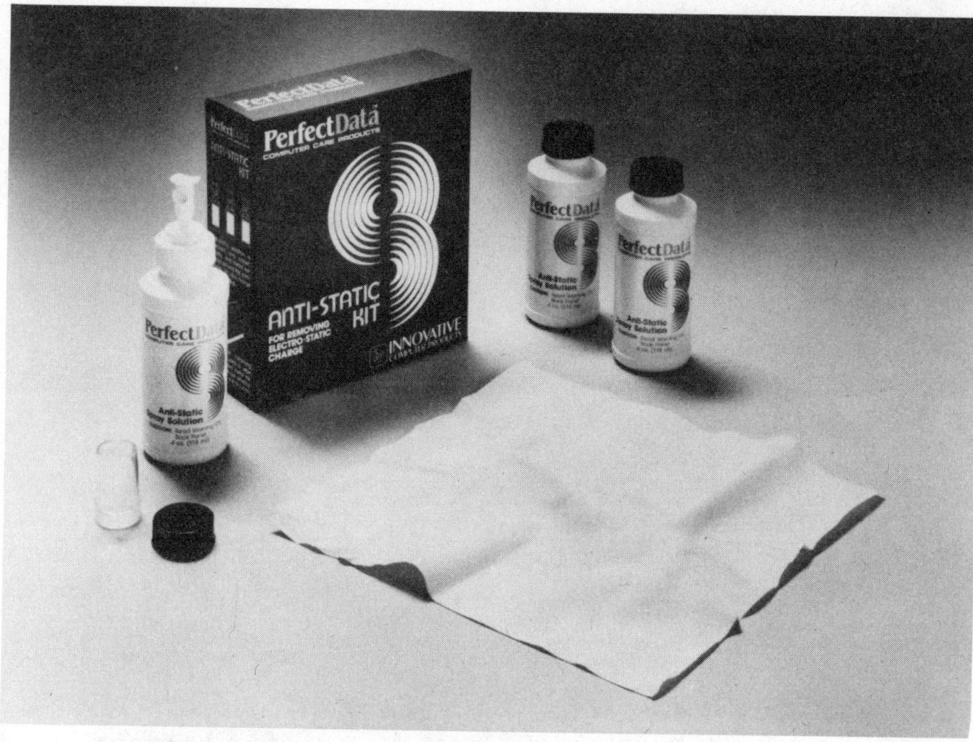

FIG 3-7 Typical anti-static spray kit. *(Courtesy of Innovative Computer Products)*

6. Route all interfacing and connecting cables where they can't be accidentally stepped on or touched. Putting them under a carpet is not sufficient—it improves safety since someone can't trip, but static discharges can penetrate the carpet and reach the cable and connected electronics.

7. Install and use protective anti-static products.

That last item needs additional explanation. Many anti-static products are designed specifically for computer installations. The simplest is something like Innovative Computer Products' Anti-Static Kit shown in Fig. 3-7. The kit contains three bottles of anti-static solution to be sprayed on floor and work surfaces around the equipment. It also contains an anti-static cloth for wiping the video screen. I've used this product, and it does provide a noticeable reduction in static problems by leaving a conductive film on the sprayed surfaces to discharge static buildups.

While anti-static sprays can be effective, avoid overspraying onto the computer equipment, keyboard, screen, or magnetic media. The residue left behind could cause later problems. Some sprays are also eye irritants (some may even be toxic), so be careful where and how you use them. Since some people may be allergic to the chemicals, test a small

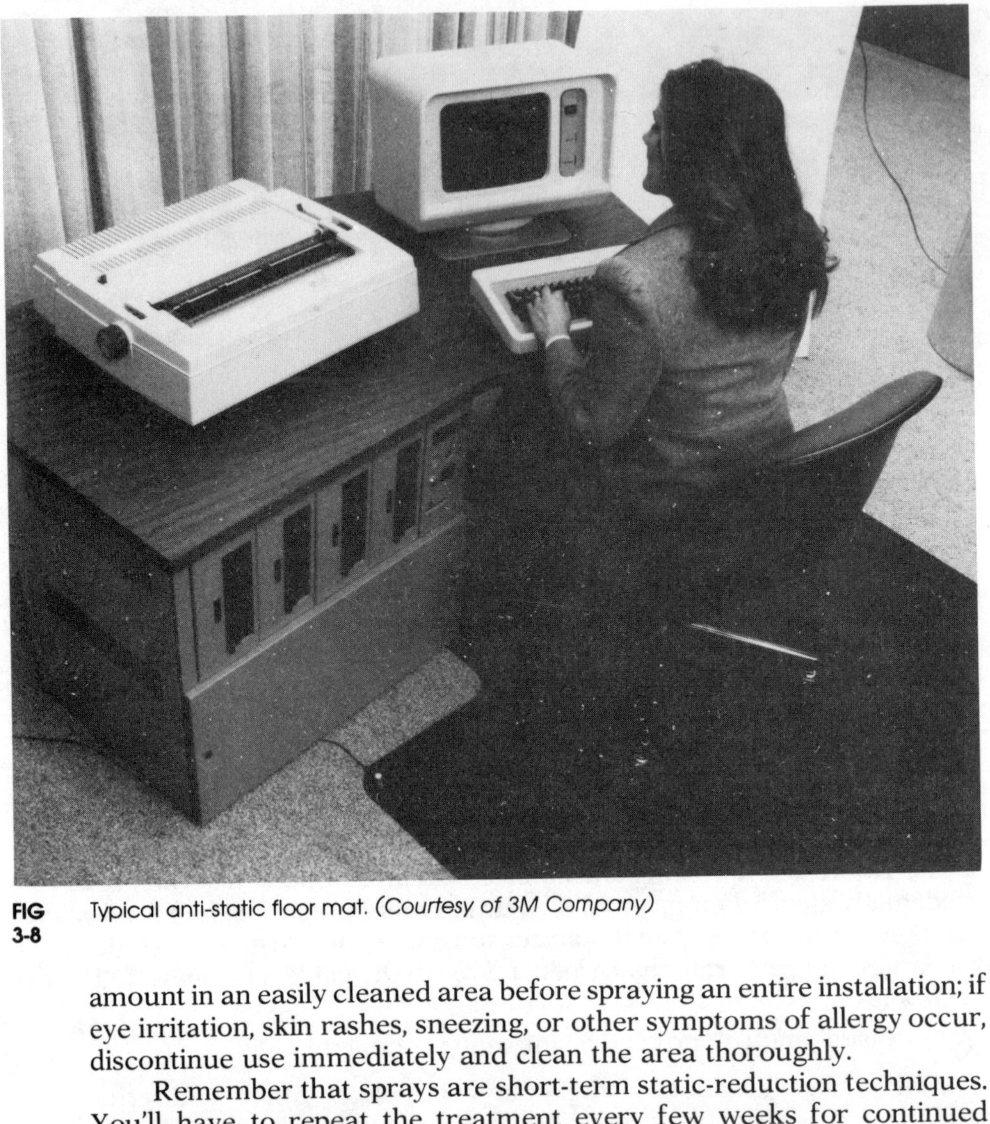

FIG 3-8 Typical anti-static floor mat. *(Courtesy of 3M Company)*

amount in an easily cleaned area before spraying an entire installation; if eye irritation, skin rashes, sneezing, or other symptoms of allergy occur, discontinue use immediately and clean the area thoroughly.

Remember that sprays are short-term static-reduction techniques. You'll have to repeat the treatment every few weeks for continued protection. Furthermore, normal housecleaning—vacuuming the carpet or wiping the desk surface—removes or degrades the anti-static protection. There also is some question whether the conductive residue contributes to dirt and dust problems as people walk across treated carpets; I can't prove or disprove this, but I raise the question so you'll be aware of the possibility.

Effective long-term solutions to static problems are achieved with anti-static floor mats such as the 3M Static Control Floor Mat shown in Fig. 3-8. Available from several suppliers, mats like this are installed under chairs, behind counters, and in other locations where people walk and come in contact with delicate electronic devices. The conductive mats are connected by a wire to an electrical ground—usually to the center screw of a grounded wall receptacle. Sitting or standing on such a mat provides grounding of any static charge built up while walking to the installation and prevents buildup of any charge while moving around at the equipment. Many mats also include a provision to protect users from accidental shock due to external electrical faults or malfunctions.

I recommend an anti-static mat for anyone using a computer. They're useful in any application, whether at home or in a business situation, and they do the job in any environment regardless of humidity, type of floor covering, amount of movement, and so on. The only restriction is that they must be grounded, but, since the computer must be grounded, there shouldn't be any problem.

There are also grounding mats or pads for use between a device such as a CRT and the desk surface on which it sits. They function the same way as the floor mats, but offer limited protection. First, only the device placed on the mat or pad is protected. Second, it's possible to use the CRT or other device without first touching and discharging to the desktop mat. Therefore, the protection of a larger floor mat, say a 4 × 5 foot or even a 4 × 8 foot version, is preferable.

Power Disturbances

Later in this book, I'll be devoting an entire chapter to power disturbances and their control, so I'll not go into great detail here. There are some things, however, that have to be mentioned by way of introduction.

Sources and Causes

To computer users, power disturbances are roughly comparable to the Black Plague (no pun intended). You can't escape them, and you rarely recover from them. Everyone knows what blackouts are—they're those nasty times when the power goes off and everything goes dark. Some last for less than a second, but others go on for minutes, hours, or days. Most people are familiar with brownouts—where the power stays on, but the lights dim. If you've spent any time at all around computers, you also know what blackouts and brownouts can do—after just a fraction of a second, you can kiss your program and data goodbye. What you may not know is that there are actually three major classes of disturbances, namely power outages, voltage fluctuations, and line noise. All three are disruptive at best and destructive at worst.

Another thing you may not know is that you are the one responsible for providing appropriate power to your equipment and installing any necessary protective devices. Furthermore, operating equipment with improper power and without protection against disturbances can be interpreted as negligence and used to void warranties or cancel service contracts. In short, every piece of equipment has specified power requirements, and neither the manufacturer nor the retailer is responsible for direct or consequential damages resulting from failure to meet those specifications.

Consider a Morrow Designs' Decision 1 computer. Under the power specification, it states, "110 VAC nominal (90V to 130V min/max) 60 Hz." The usual interpretation is that the unit can be plugged into any 110-volt ac wall socket. Not quite! That phrase in parentheses is a limitation to power between 90 and 130 volts and indicates that the unit cannot be expected to operate properly at voltages over or under that range. By comparison, the IBM Personal Computer specifies a nominal 120 VAC with a maximum 127 VAC and a minimum 104 VAC. Other devices specify other ranges. The important numbers are the minimums and maximums, not the nominal values.

It's not uncommon to have a home or office receiving power outside the range of a given device, and consistently high voltages tend to be more of a problem than low ones. I once lived in an apartment where I blew out an unbelievable number of light bulbs, sometimes six to eight in a single week, continuing week after week. Finally, I had the power lines monitored, and found I was receiving an average of 136 volts. Had I been running a computer, I would have been "out of spec," could have caused severe damage to the machine, and might have been stuck with the entire repair bill. Neither a store nor a manufacturer would be liable to repair, replace, or otherwise rectify damage caused by out-of-spec power.

Many installation and planning guides for large-scale computers mention that power obtained from utility companies may not meet specifications for particular equipment. Yet little is said about the problem in the world of microcomputing, probably because it might discourage potential buyers. After all, selling machines is the name of the game, and once the machine is in your possession, the problems are yours.

A 1974 study of commercial three-phase power sources used for large-scale computers was conducted by personnel from the System Development Division of IBM. They reported that typical computer facilities experienced an average of 128 error-producing power problems per month,[6] many of which had the potential for disrupting operations, losing data, causing hardware damage, or requiring reprogramming of computers. And that's on commercial power, often assumed to be "cleaner" than residential power.

I've not found a comparable report for residential power, but I do know that I've averaged about twenty computer-stopping power interruptions per month for the last four years. I've not even bothered to count the brownouts and flickers that didn't shut down the equipment. For two consecutive months during the summer of 1982, the utility company was hitting me with a one-second shutoff every morning

6 George W. Allen and Donald Segall, "Monitoring of Computer Installations for Power Line Disturbances," *Proceedings of IEEE Power Engineering Society,* Paper No. C-74-199-6, January 1974.

between 6:40 and 6:50, apparently while doing distribution network switching. It was sufficient to "dump" the computers and reset every digital clock in the building every morning.

The majority of power disturbances originate on the utility company's lines, although some may be caused by workmen digging up buried cables, lightning strikes on lines or transformers, auto accidents knocking out distribution boxes, and so on. Of course, you can overload a circuit and blow a breaker or fuse, create interference or noise with appliances or the computer equipment itself, or generate other problems, but most originate outside your installation.

Effects

Some effects of power disturbances have already been mentioned. The most common is immediate shutdown of the computer system, causing loss of programs and data in memory and whatever results have been computed to that point. Another is "glitching" the computer, giving rise to erroneous results, altering data or programs, causing a display or printout to miss or "garbage" one or more lines, and so on.

Yet there are worse things that can happen. A sudden surge of high voltage can wreak considerable internal damage, figuratively "frying" equipment as it burns out circuits and entire boards. Internal power supplies can fail. Printing and disk-drive mechanisms can jam, possibly suffering mechanical damage as they abruptly halt. Read/write heads can crash into disk surfaces, irreparably damaging heads or surfaces and costing hundreds or thousands of hours of reprogramming and reloading over and above the cost of equipment repair.

Even if heads don't crash onto magnetic media, the integrity of stored data may be jeopardized. If the drive was in the process of writing data onto a disk file when it was interrupted, that file and all data already written may not be retrievable when power is restored. On some computers, a single file error anywhere on the disk can make it impossible to recover any files at all, not just the one damaged.

In short, power disturbances are deadly to your system. Worst of all, you can't predict them, you can't prevent them, you can't control them, and you can't do much to protect against them without spending some money.

Preventive and Remedial Steps

Since I am devoting a separate chapter to power conditioning, I won't go into all the ways of protecting your equipment now. What I do want to emphasize is that you can only protect your equipment against the effects of power-line disturbances. You can't control when, where, how often, or how extreme those disturbances will be.

You are going to have to determine how much protection you can afford, how much your applications justify, and which of several

FIG 3-9 Panamax SS-120/4 (left) and SS-120/2 (right) voltage surge suppression products. *(Photo by author)*

alternatives are suitable. For instance, home users might protect only against devastating voltage spikes—a relatively cheap form of protection obtainable with "surge protectors" costing upward of $25. Others may protect against both surges and electrical noise, usually involving surge protection and line "isolation" and costing between $60 and $200. Guarding against short power interruptions and brownouts by using standby power supplies can cost from $250 to $1200 for small computers and several thousand dollars for larger systems. Business users with critical applications and larger installations may have to spend many thousands of dollars to achieve multipurpose protection against numerous disturbances.

Even though most retail outlets are reluctant to mention power conditioning and may even downplay its importance, the number of available devices is staggering. Just a few representative products are included here, with many more included in the chapter on power conditioning. Toward the low end of the price scale are inexpensive plug-in surge suppressors and noise filters such as the Panamax SS-120/4 and SS-120/2 units shown in Fig. 3-9. These guard against sudden increases in line voltage and against electrical noise that might be imposed on lines by appliance motors and other interfering devices. While they are effective on residential and commercial power lines subject to mild disturbances, they do not protect against outages, and most give limited protection against severe surges or extreme noise typical of industrial facilities.

Electronic Specialists, Inc., provides numerous power conditioning and protection products with various functions and prices, including the ISO-17 Magnum Isolator shown in Fig. 3-10. This heavy-duty device is more expensive than smaller units, but it's designed for controlling severe spikes and surges while eliminating potential electrical interactions among devices plugged into individual sockets.

FIG 3-10 ISO-17 Magnum Isolator. *(Courtesy of Electronic Specialists, Inc.)*

Standby power supplies are available in sizes from around 200 watts to thousands of watts and prices reaching from \$300 to many thousands of dollars. They provide automatic switching to temporary battery backup power during an outage or severe low-voltage condition. They typically include surge suppression and noise filtration with the standby power. One such unit is the Ramlok™ Standby Power System from Ladco Development Co., Inc., shown in Fig. 3-11.

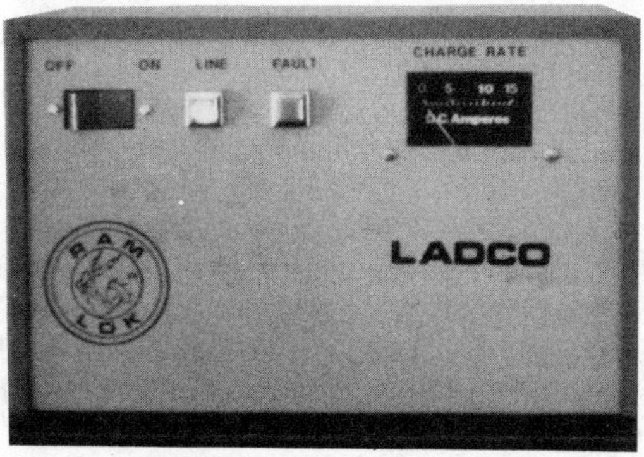

FIG 3-11 Ramlok Standby Power System. *(Courtesy of Ladco Development Co., Inc.)*

FIG 3-12 Line 2 Power Conditioner supporting a minicomputer installation. *(Courtesy of Topaz, Inc.)*

True uninterruptible power supplies, often called UPS units, continuously power the equipment from batteries and charge the batteries while the incoming line is active. When incoming power is cut off, the battery continues to power the computer without switch-over time that might disturb extremely sensitive circuits. These units also are available at many prices and in many sizes, although the price for any given size unit is typically higher than for a switching standby unit having the same output.

Usually, the power drain of the connected equipment and the characteristics of the incoming power dictate the size and price of the conditioning equipment needed. Although Topaz Electronics Division provides smaller, portable units, Fig. 3-12 illustrates their Line 2® Power Conditioner (the floor-mounted cabinet on the left) capable of supporting equipment requiring several thousand watts. Yet this is only an "intermediate" size unit; some companies can provide power conditioning equipment requiring cabinets several feet high, wide, and deep.

As a rule, assume you'll need some form of power conditioning no matter what your application or equipment configuration. Don't be lulled into a false sense of security by a few days or weeks of successful operation without evidence of disturbances. Don't be dissuaded by a salesman shrugging off the subject with a comment such as, "You don't have to worry about it." Sooner or later, your equipment probably will be hit by an interruption, a surge, or a noisy line, wrecking whatever operation is in process at that instant and possibly doing costly damage to the equipment.

WEAR AND TEAR

Physical wear, a normal sign of aging equipment, affects all moving mechanical parts. Your principal problems are going to occur in the printer mechanisms, disk drives, tape transports, keyboards, and switches. The component that wears the fastest will be the one most used, so a system requiring extensive keyboard inputs and few printouts most likely will have the keyboard go down far more often than the printer. If few inputs are required, but many printouts are generated, the printer probably will wear out faster and fail more often than the keyboard.

Sources and Causes

The culprit that causes wear is friction. Every time an object moves, it's subject to the effects of friction as it slides across some other object—even molecules of air. Gradually, bearing surfaces begin to suffer deterioration that, in turn, increases friction and accelerates further wear. Carried to an extreme, wear and the heat of friction can combine to cause bearings to seize, centerlines of rotating parts such as shafts and flywheels to shift and cause eccentric spinning or "wobble," electrical contacts to fail, and so on.

Another culprit is physical stress. You've probably heard the term "metal fatigue" used to describe the phenomenon that causes wings or engines to break off aircraft, bridges and buildings to collapse, or engine shafts to shatter. Well, the mechanical parts of computer components also are subject to stress and fatigue. This can lead to sudden, unpredictable failures, e.g. the drive shaft of a disk drive shearing off, the timing disk inside a letter-quality printer mechanism flying apart, the spokes of a daisywheel cracking or breaking off, and a host of other problems.

Effects

The effects of wear and stress are twofold. First, there is a gradual decline in the overall performance of the affected mechanisms. For instance, you might notice that some keys don't register while you're typing, and you have to go back and correct or edit missing letters. You might see output from your printer that isn't as crisp and sharp as it once was—perhaps the letters are dense and well formed on one edge but blurred or indistinct at another edge. You might notice that letters printed by a character printer don't line up properly in either the vertical or horizontal directions. Your disk drives may start giving intermittent read and write errors, particularly on disks you've used before. You may find that you have to cycle a switch several times before it makes proper contact. All these and similar occurrences are signs of wear and are your system's demand for attention.

Second, there can be an abrupt failure of a part, often causing an immediate halt to an operation. The printer might stop feeding ribbon or paper. The printhead itself might stop moving. A disk drive may cease to operate at all—it might spin the disk but fail to access any data or stored information. It may become impossible to turn a unit on or off with the power switch. Such total failures can indicate either outright breakage of a critical part, probably due to stress, or an extreme case of wear. The affected unit must be examined carefully to determine which.

Preventive and Remedial Steps

The best protection against wear is keeping equipment clean and within the specified operating temperature ranges. Dirt increases friction and accelerates wear. The dirtier the unit, the more the parts will wear and the sooner they will fail. Heat also contributes, since heated components expand slightly, further increasing the friction, wear, and probability of early failure. Therefore, periodic cleaning schedules and heat control provisions described earlier are your first line of defense.

Suitable lubrication in accordance with the schedules and procedures detailed in equipment manuals is essential. The purpose of lubrication is to decrease friction and thereby reduce wear. If you don't provide it, you're going to have costly repair bills. You do have to be careful to follow the manuals. Excessive lubrication is just as bad as no lubrication at all—heat can cause the excess to ooze or drip into adjoining components, and excess lubricant can attract and hold friction causing dirt. Furthermore, some parts must never be lubricated. Often, a manual specifies that the guide rails controlling positioning of a disk drive's read/write head are not to be lubricated—again because the lubricant attracts and holds dirt that would interfere with smooth positioning of the head.

You must use only the specified lubricant for a particular part. There are no universal, all-purpose oils or greases, and a device such as a letter-quality printer may require a half-dozen or more different lubricants. Granted, this can be costly, especially since many of the high-grade materials are expensive. Using the wrong lubricant is more costly, however, because it can contribute to increased wear, frequent failure, and high repair bills to replace damaged parts. A word of advice: throw away any all-purpose household machine oil or automotive oils and greases you have on hand. There's no place for them anywhere in your system.

Once a wear- or stress-related failure occurs, you have no choice but to replace the affected part or parts. Since such replacements often require major realignments of the entire mechanism, particularly printers and disk drives, all but the simplest replacements should be left to a qualified service technician. With mechanical devices, you can do more damage than you fix by trying to work without proper tools, gauges, and experience.

MISHANDLING

A final hazard is one I like to call "mishandling." That's a polite way of covering negligence, abuse, and overall mistreatment of the equipment, and it's a catchall for human blundering. I could, of course, take the next several hundred pages to list possible ways you might mishandle your system, but it wouldn't be of much practical use. Instead, I'll concentrate on just a few typical examples.

First, ignoring the preventive steps previously cited is, by my definition, mishandling. You are negligent and are mistreating your equipment if you don't provide regular cleaning and sufficient ventilation, if you don't eliminate sources of magnetic fields, if you don't take steps to eliminate electrostatic charges, if you don't provide protection against power-line disturbances, and if you don't lubricate equipment in accordance with the manufacturers' instructions.

Beyond that, carelessness is the single most frequent contributor to machine malfunctions. Dropping a component, even an inch or two, can cause impact stresses that do immeasurable damage. As I was working on this chapter, a friend who had been providing custom software attempted to move his hard disk from one room to another. One of his pet cats got underfoot, and he dropped the unit. A $7000 hard disk was destroyed, along with millions upon millions of bytes of stored data. Virtually every program this man worked on over four years was lost forever because he hadn't bothered to back up the hard disk onto floppy disks or magnetic tapes.

Perhaps the most common mishandling affects floppy diskettes. For one reason or another, people get sloppy about how they handle the diskettes, leaving them lying around the computer, forgetting to put them back into their protective dust jackets, stacking them up against the side of a drive or a telephone, or otherwise mistreating them. Somewhere, sometime, those same individuals wonder why they can't access a stored program or why the diskette won't record new data correctly.

FIG 3-13 Lightweight carrying cases for IBM PC and Apple II computers. *(Courtesy of Fiberbilt Div. of Ikelheimer-Ernst, Inc.)*

Other forms of mishandling involve accidentally spilling a drink into a keyboard, poking around inside a unit while the power is applied, touching magnetic surfaces (disk or tape) with a finger or other object, poking a foreign object into the innards of a disk drive, and on and on and on.

Another user fault, particularly with small "semi-portable" computers, is transporting them without protection. Too many people assume they can just toss their Apples, IBM Personal Computers, and other systems into the trunk of a car or set them on the rear seat to carry them from one location to another. Sure, it can be done that way but at substantial risk. It's far better to protect them in their original shipping cartons, although that's often too bulky and cumbersome for some users. An alternative is to acquire one or more custom cases for the components, thereby providing a safer traveling environment.

Several companies manufacture carrying cases. One is the Fiberbilt division of Ikelheimer-Ernst, Inc., which supplies custom cases for more than two dozen brands of computers and associated devices. Figure 3-13 illustrates their lightweight cases for the Apple III and the Apple II with two disk drives. Cases like these cost from $60 up, depending on the size and number of components held, but they offer good protection for carrying the equipment between work and home, in a car, as carry-on

FIG 3-14 Medium-weight, medium-duty carrying cases. *(Courtesy of Computer Case Co.)*

luggage for planes and trains, and so on. The same company also makes heavy-duty carrying cases and aluminum shipping cases for greater protection in luggage compartments of planes and trains, transcontinental shipping by common carrier, etc.

Another supplier is Computer Case Company, some of whose products are shown in Fig. 3-14. They provide medium- to heavy-duty cases for more than two dozen equipment brands. Most of these are constructed of mahogany plywood and are finished with high-quality luggage coverings and fittings. They weigh more than the lightweight Fiberbilt cases, they cost a bit more with prices upward of $100, but they offer more protection for equipment being transported under circumstances beyond the user's direct control. Although the cases are not recommended by the manufacturer for checked luggage aboard airlines and trains, they reportedly have survived such trips in good order. An interesting feature is that most of these cases can be used as permanent containers for the equipment. The covers can be closed and locked to prevent unauthorized tampering, without disconnecting interface cables and power cords. In fact, they don't appear to inhibit the operation of a computer in any way.

I frequently need to move my Apple II from one location to another, sometimes to a different room, sometimes to a client's place of business, and sometimes to a school where I'm lecturing. I'm also a bit accident-prone and have a nasty habit of colliding with furniture and other obstructions or tripping over my own feet. For that reason, I won't move a computer without the security of a carrying case. I like both the Fiberbilt lightweight and the Computer Case Company medium weight, but for different purposes. The light case is more convenient for driving around town, and it's somewhat less fatiguing when carrying the machine to different offices or classrooms during a day. However, I prefer the heavier case and the greater degree of protection it affords if I'm traveling by bus, train, or plane or anticipate a high risk of transit-caused damage.

I'm not going to go on and on with causes, effects, and preventive steps for mishandling. Most of what I might list is covered elsewhere in this book, particularly in cautions and warnings in descriptions of individual operations or procedures. The important points are to provide maximum protection for your computer investment and to persuade you to examine critically everything you do for potential damage to that investment. If you stop and think before you act, and if you use a little common sense, you'll be able to minimize unintentional damage.

FOUR

THE "MAINFRAME" COMPUTER

A logical place to begin describing care and maintenance of individual system components is the "mainframe" computer—the heart of the system. In keeping with Chapter 2, I include the memory, central processing unit (CPU), power supplies, and related components. I do not include input/output devices, mass storage, magnetic media, or peripherals and other external devices. A typical mainframe might look something like the Morrow Designs' Decision 1 desktop computer in Fig. 4-1. Those of you with a "unitized" system having disk drives, keyboard, video display, and comparable gadgets within one chassis or box may think they are part of the mainframe. However, such "built-ins" have characteristics of external devices and are treated in separate chapters.

Previously, I mentioned that electronic components have few failures after being burned in. Since the mainframe is electronic, it's reasonable to expect it to suffer the fewest time-dependent malfunctions. That is, once past the burn-in, the CPU, memory, and control circuitry should give reliable service for months or years.

That doesn't mean you can neglect or carelessly handle the mainframe. Although normal operation causes few malfunctions and demands little subsequent remedial maintenance, there are stringent requirements and restrictions regarding preventive care. Lack of preventive measures could lead to problems that wouldn't arise otherwise. In this chapter, I'll present information and procedures directly affecting the mainframe. I'll also identify some useful products, not necessarily as recommendations, but representing types you might consider for your installation.

FIG 4-1 Typical S-100 bus mainframe. *(Courtesy Morrow Designs)*

WARNINGS AND CAUTIONS

Before proceeding, I must issue a caution and some warnings. "Caution" is my term for recommendations that you may or may not choose to follow. Disregarding a caution can create problems, however, so ignore one at your own risk. Warnings, on the other hand, are mandatory and not to be disregarded. Warnings indicate high-risk procedures, endangering either the equipment or the person performing them. Also, since it's not possible to cover every contingency for every computer and peripheral, there may be risks beyond the ones cited. Always proceed carefully, and check your system manuals for specifics.

First a caution! Procedures described herein assume your mainframe can be opened. Most S-100 bus computers, Apple II computers, and numerous others are eligible. Some, however, are "sealed" devices not to be opened and possibly marked, in effect, ". . . no user serviceable components inside." Those require a qualified technician. At any rate, do not open or tamper with any unit while it's under warranty, typically for 90 days after purchase, or while it's under a service contract. Unauthorized tampering, even merely opening the case without specific instruction from the supplier, voids warranties and service contracts.

Now the warnings! Never open any chassis while power is on, unless the manufacturer instructs you to do so. Don't rely on a power switch—pull the plug so you can't power up accidentally. This protects you from dangerous electrical shock and protects the equipment from short circuits, electrical transients, and so on. Though a few peripherals

FIG 4-2 Right and wrong ways to pull a plug.

occasionally have to be operated with the case open, never power a mainframe while it's open. In particular, changing internal switch settings, inserting or removing circuit boards, and touching circuit chips are forbidden with power applied.

Incidentally, always grasp a plug firmly when removing it from a receptacle, as shown in Fig. 4-2. Never pull on the cord of any electrical device. Few cords have enough "strain relief" at the plug to tolerate the stresses of repeated pulls on the cord. Eventually the connections may separate, leading to a power failure or short circuit.

Avoid contact with the computer power supply. New computers often use solid-state switching power supplies housed in a metal box and protected against accidental contact. Older machines with "ferro-resonant" transformers often do not enclose them in protective casings or cages. If your unit has visible transformers, it probably has storage capacitors—the metal cylinders or "cans" near the transformer—and they are the things to avoid. Capacitors can and often do store dangerous electrical charges long after the machine has been unplugged. For safety, it's best to avoid any contact with the power supply, which usually is not user serviceable anyway. Instead, limit your activities to plug-in cards and the motherboard.

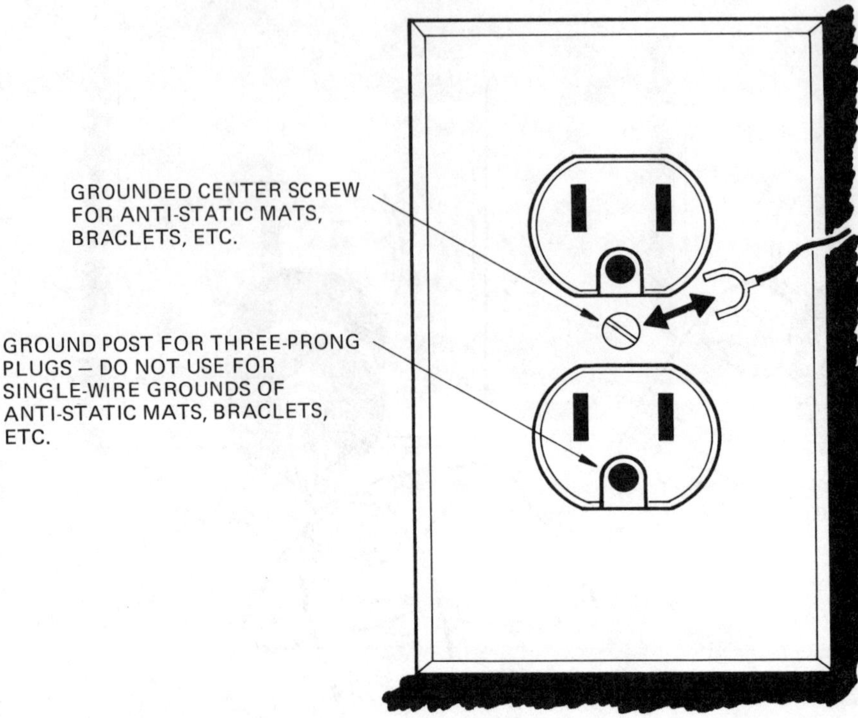

FIG 4-3 Ground locations of a standard three-prong, 110-VAC outlet.

I had to learn respect for storage capacitors the hard way. A few years ago, I was charging a battery pack and conditioning the storage capacitor of a photographic strobe light. After unplugging the cord, I accidentally touched the prongs with my thumbs—one thumb on each prong. The storage capacitor discharged through me, knocking me unconscious for half an hour and burning holes into my thumbs that took more than a month to heal. I now approach power supplies and capacitors with caution.

Do not work in high-static areas. A discharge into the innards of your computer or onto a circuit board can do immeasurable damage. The best protection is to work on a grounded anti-static mat. If you can't, at least stay away from carpeted areas, don't slide your body across a chair, and don't shuffle your feet.

One way to minimize static danger is to have some large or grounded metal object within reach. Before touching a component, touch that other object to discharge. Some instruction sheets advise discharging to the power supply casing, but it's effective only if the system is grounded. Since I've instructed you to unplug the unit, the power supply casing is not adequately grounded.

Alternatively, wear grounded bracelets on one or both wrists. Static bleeds off through the ground, while any electrical discharge from the equipment is grounded before it reaches your torso. You can simulate grounded bracelets by looping bare copper wire around your wrists and connecting the loose ends to a water pipe or some known ground. If electrical outlets have grounded boxes, you can connect to the center screw of the wall plate, but be careful. It's easy to stick a wire end into an outlet opening and hit a "hot" lead accidentally. Figure 4-3 shows the ground location.

An excellent working environment is provided by the Portable Field Service Grounding Kit from 3M Static Control Systems. Illustrated in Fig. 4-4, the kit contains a thin, flexible, anti-static work surface with a ground cord, plus a grounded wrist strap. The kit folds into a neat service bag for storage. Although it is intended for service technicians, any computer user who gets inside the equipment should have one. Owners of Apple computers or other units subject to frequent modification, alteration, and installation of additional chips and cards definitely should have this kit. It provides needed protection while installing ROM boards, RAM memories, or other sensitive plug-ins.

Finally, clear the area of clutter. Remove liquids, pencils, paper clips, tools, and similar objects. Spill any liquid into the mainframe, and you can toss the unit into the trash. A paper clip or staple falling unnoticed into the machine could short-circuit components when power is reapplied. Keep tools on a separate work surface; if they happen to be magnetized, they could erase preprogrammed memory devices and mass storage media just by being nearby. Keeping some small plastic foam blocks handy to hold circuit chips will prevent accidental bending of pins or static discharges during handling.

SYSTEM DIAGNOSTICS

Perhaps the most important software you can acquire is a good set of system diagnostics. Such packages are available for many popular computers—but regrettably not all—either from the original manufacturer or from an outside software house.

A few retailers stock diagnostics, but many are reluctant to do so. If a prospective buyer spots diagnostics on the shelf, it's natural to question the computer's reliability, and no sales person wants to jeopardize a sale by admitting that a machine might have reliability problems. Besides, stores and third-party service companies make money from minor repairs, preventive maintenance, and even routine checkouts of machines suspected of malfunctioning. They don't want to cut into their profits by giving the user a way to check out his or her own system. It's likely you'll hear any number of excuses when you ask for diagnostics, from a simple, "It's not available," to something like, "Only trained technicians can work on it." The excuse may or may not be true, so you'll have to do some research to find out what's available.

The Importance of Diagnostics

I can't overemphasize the importance of diagnostic programs, no matter what the system or application. Such programs are often the only means you have to determine what may be wrong. It's characteristic of

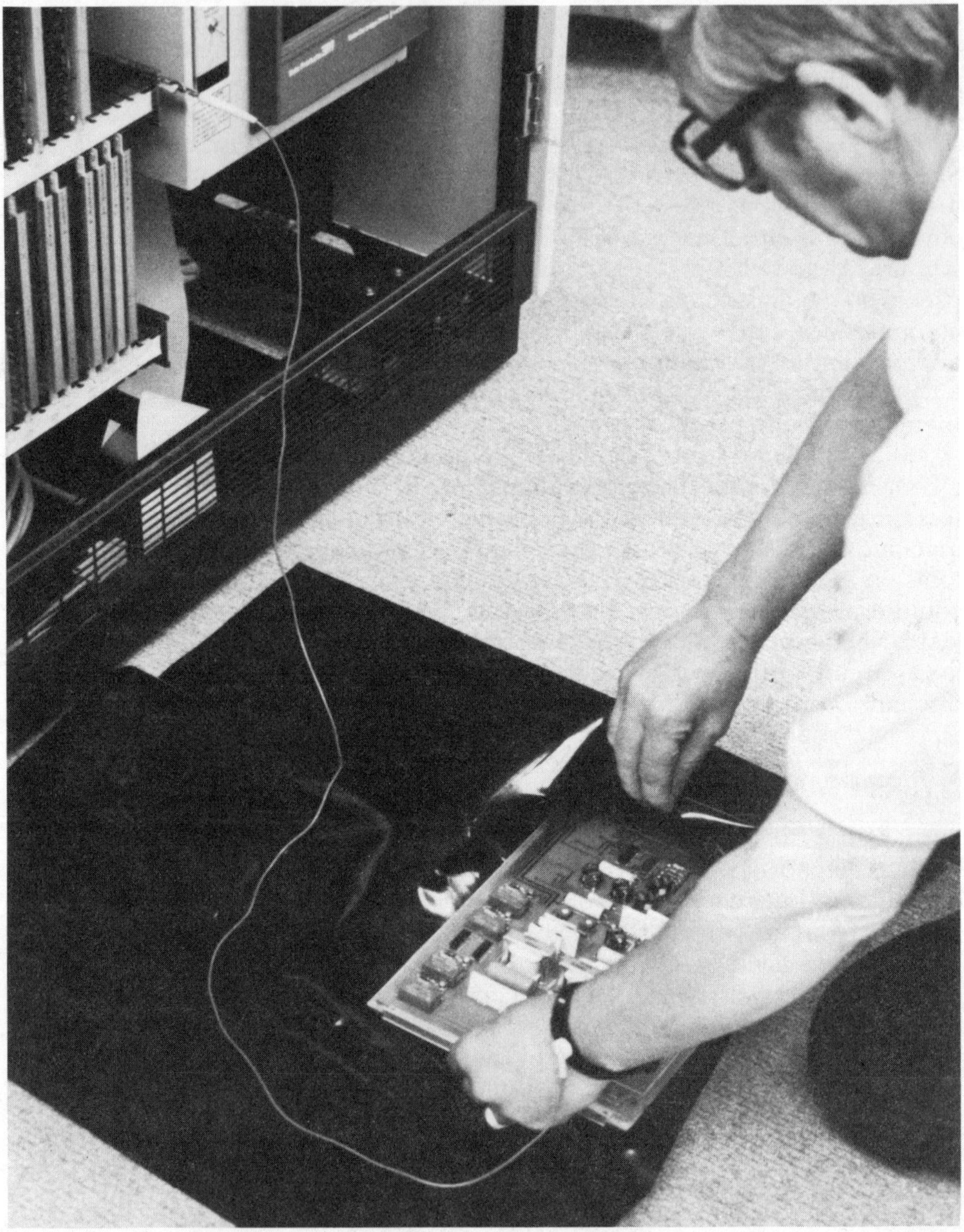

FIG 4-4 Portable Field Service Grounding Kit. *(Courtesy of 3M Company)*

computer systems that problems often can't be diagnosed from symptoms alone. A software error may look like a hardware failure, or a hardware failure may look like a software error. Within the hardware, a malfunction in one area may look like one in a different area.

As an example, consider the CP/M operating system's "BDOS ERR on x" message. According to the manual, this message is generated under one of three conditions: (1) a bad sector is encountered while reading or writing; (2) the system tries to access an uninstalled drive, say a third drive in a two-drive system; or (3) an attempt is made to write data to a diskette or file set to "read-only" status. The first may be an operator error, a software error, or a hardware failure. The second usually indicates an operator error or an improperly written program that "calls" a nonexistent drive name. The third may be an operator error such as not "unlocking" a file or leaving the diskette write protected, but it can be a hardware error when the write-protect detector in the drive or the associated electronics malfunctions.

I have seen this error message generated by conditions not immediately apparent from the manuals. Some less obvious causes include:

1. A disk is too full; either there are too few bytes remaining to record a new file or there are too many names in the disk directory. This is an operator error resulting from not checking the remaining disk capacity before saving a program or data.

2. A disk file is not intact. Often, this results from a system shutdown, power failure, or other disturbance during a disk access. A common cause is shutting down a system before disk operations are complete—bumping the power switch does it. Opening a drive door during disk activity is another cause. Incomplete files also result from a faulty disk controller, a faulty drive, a defective read/write head, a memory malfunction, a CPU failure, and even a timing error on internal communication lines (the bus).

3. The diskette isn't formatted correctly. Every system requires disks "initialized" for the particular drives and operating system; a failure during formatting or initializing can render diskettes unusable. Usually this is an operator error in specifying the wrong format on multiformat systems, using a disk formatted for another system, leaving the disk write protected during initialization, and so on. However, hardware errors in the memory, CPU, disk controller, or drive mechanism also can lead to improper formatting, followed by error conditions.

4. The diskette is physically defective. It may have bad sectors with poor oxide coatings, contaminants, scratches, abrasions, wear spots, and so on. However, an otherwise good diskette may be damaged by the system. For example, a failure in the hardware controller, drive mechanism, or other component can cause a head crash where the heads slam down onto the disk surface or a seeking error where electrically active heads scoot across the surface. A bad memory byte in a RAM area that controls disk operations can cause a head crash.

These are just a few potential causes of a single error message from one operating system. Notice there's usually a three-way possibility: operator error, software flaw, or hardware malfunction. The error message alone—the effect—is not sufficient to diagnose the cause.

Hence, it's useful to apply system diagnostics to isolate the cause or at least eliminate items from the list of possibilities.

Even failures known to originate in hardware can be impossible to isolate by symptoms alone. I had one such problem that put an old S-100 system out of operation for three months. Five technicians worked on it but were unable to locate the cause or fix the problem. Each saw the malfunction, each tried a different remedy, but none cured it.

This problem appeared after the system was more than three years old. Suddenly, I experienced symptoms that made no sense, At times, the computer refused to boot the operating system. Other times, the 64K computer accepted only 48K or 32K CP/M operating systems. Even after successful booting, the system could "go out to lunch" or "hang" at any time. Programs functioned normally for hours, then disappeared from memory. Entire memory blocks suddenly filled with garbage characters. Disk reads and writes that had worked hundreds of times entered error cycles in which data were misread and files written were full of garbage. Several times, attempting to write a new file erased existing files or damaged their contents. Long word-processing printouts proceeded perfectly through 30 or 40 pages, filled a page with garbage, and then resumed normal printing—even when disk files were intact and contained no extraneous data.

Try to make sense of that collection of malfunctions, any combination of which could occur at any time! I first thought it was disk-drive failure. I'd seen drive failures before, some demonstrating one or more of the symptoms. Two technicians agreed, so both drives and the controller were replaced. No improvement. The next possibility was a memory failure, so four 16K RAM boards were replaced, one by one. Again, no improvement. Every connector was checked, cleaned, and reseated. Every internal switch setting was checked and double-checked. Every socketed chip was removed and reseated. Outputs from the power supply and the incoming utility lines were monitored hour after hour. Nothing gave any improvement, and a $15,000 system remained too unreliable to use.

Finally, a technician came to check the system with his own diagnostic programs (I didn't have any of my own). For eight hours, he ran tests on the memory, CPU, disk drives, disk controller, and other components without finding a component-specific malfunction. By a process of systematic elimination, that left one possibility—an input/output interface board not tested by the diagnostics and not easily swapped out because it had long since been discontinued. Since the technician could not test or swap the board, he left me on my own from that point.

Examining the I/O board, I decided to try swapping out circuit chips. Since most were soldered into place, I chose to avoid those. However, eight were in sockets. I did notice one peculiarity: three identical chips near the center of the board could be identified as being associated with the RS-232C serial communications paths. Two were soldered, but one was socketed. It struck me as odd that one of three should be in a socket—perhaps in anticipation of frequent failures. A price check with a local electronics supply house also showed it was the least expensive of the replaceable chips on the board.

Wouldn't you know it! After months of playing games, I replaced that one chip at a cost of $1.35, and the problems stopped. I'm still not sure how that chip on that input/output board could cause all the symptoms I saw. I can understand its affecting the printer because that's the device it controlled. But nobody has been able to tell me how the failure fed back into the mainframe and disrupted other unrelated functions. But it did, and I've verified it as the culprit because the same chip has failed a dozen times since. Each time a random and unpredictable pattern of seemingly unrelated errors has been cured by changing the one chip.

The point I stress is that system diagnostics did assist in isolating and ultimately correcting the problem. Even though they didn't indicate the chip or I/O board as the cause, they eliminated other possibilities. Of course, by the time diagnostics had been obtained, costs had been incurred to replace two drives, a disk controller, and four memory boards. Although most of the parts and labor costs were covered by a service contract, there was a substantial loss of income through three months of not being able to use the system in my business. The unavailability of word processing alone cost me $9,000 because I couldn't deliver assigned projects by the deadlines, and several clients were lost when I had to turn down assignments.

Today, I won't run a system without diagnostics. I won't even wait for errors. Instead, I run diagnostics weekly, usually on Monday mornings, and I spend several hours a week checking and verifying system operations, cleaning components, and so on. If nothing else, the tests give me confidence in the system functions. I then can look to operator or software errors as probable causes of any malfunctions I encounter.

What to Expect of Diagnostics

A diagnostic software package must perform a thorough check of the principal components. A minimum is the CPU, RAM, disk controller, and disk drives. Without those, the software doesn't do any good. You might also want tests of preprogrammed ROMs, printer operations, keyboard functions, video displays, and other peripherals.

You must realize that diagnostics aren't perfect—they are not 100 percent cure-alls. Generally, they isolate major problems, particularly ones not of a transient nature. Yet, since many errors and failures are intermittent, finding the cause can amount to little more than pure luck. For example, of the thousands of memory bytes, each consists of numerous bits. Failure of a single bit can cause anything from a "soft" data error to a "hard" or "fatal" system stoppage. One or more bits may work part of the time but fail other times. Hence, a diagnostic may test a byte or bit when it's working, but the byte or bit may fail again later. To be effective, memory and other tests must be performed or iterated over and over, but always with the possibility of a bad location going undetected.

Diagnostic Approaches

There are two ways to obtain system diagnostics. One is to acquire a system with built-in self-tests performed either every time power is applied to the unit or under the operator's control. The other is to purchase a diagnostic software package.

Built-In Diagnostics. Many, but not all, peripherals and computers have built-in self-test functions. Often, switching a unit on is all that's necessary to activate the self-test. Depending on how the designers chose to set it up, the component might respond by printing or displaying a message such as "self-test OK," "RAM OK," "Check OK," or some variation. Alternatively, some units simply won't allow continued operation if the self-test fails; a computer might not display its sign-on message or operator "prompt" if internal tests indicate a malfunction. In other cases, the user might have to activate the self-test from a terminal keyboard or front-panel switches. In still others, self-testing is activated or controlled by switches inside the device.

First, consider a Morrow Designs' Decision 1 computer. This S-100 bus mainframe incorporates a multifunction "monitor" program with self-testing. My system is set up to boot directly into the monitor program, not to the CP/M operating system. Using the terminal keyboard, I then choose whether I want to progress to the operating system or use the special functions. With keyboard entries, I can direct a test of memory locations across a specified range, fill part of memory with a known constant value, compare or verify areas of memory using a known value, and move memory contents from one area to another.

The Decision 1 also performs an automatic power-on test of the CPU, disk controller, and direct memory access (DMA) channel. Furthermore, it provides switch-selected diagnostics for the CPU, including ones for the read and write registers, RAM operations, floating-point processor, and S-100 bus. However, the nonautomatic CPU diagnostics are recommended only for service personnel thoroughly familiar with microprocessor troubleshooting, and an oscilloscope with suitable probes is required. Nevertheless, the automatic tests and those activated from the keyboard provide a good indication that overall functions are intact and the computer as whole is operating nominally.

A device such as Compulink Corporation's SooperSpooler™ is worth mentioning because it's a hybrid serving both as a peripheral device and as a functional computer. It's a printing buffer that accepts outputs from a master computer, stores them, processes them, and then transmits them to a printer. To do that, it contains a Z-80 microprocessor, preprogrammed ROMs, and from 16K to 62K of RAM. Though used as a peripheral, it is a small mainframe in its own right. It also is equipped with a self-test feature. When you press two front-panel buttons or activate under software control, the unit performs a calculated "checksum" test of the total ROM and eight memory-test passes on RAM. On completion, it indicates the failed or passed status of ROM and RAM by outputting messages to the printer. For RAM failures, it also indicates the locations (circuit chip numbers) to facilitate replacement.

In a similar fashion, printers and other peripherals often contain a self-test. For example, a Qume Sprint 5™ letter-quality printer can be activated under software control or with its own keys (on a keyboard send-receive or KSR model) to check the internal electronics, printwheel movement, and carriage operations. This test is fun to watch. For a few seconds, nothing seems to happen as the electronics are tested. Then the printwheel starts to spin. Then the carriage exercise routine sweeps the printhead back and forth across a constantly narrowing path. Finally, if everything has gone well, a message is printed and, if switches are set properly, the machine starts printing row after row of the complete character set until stopped by the operator.

It's important to know what self-test capabilities you have, if any. To find out, read your manuals and check their indexes, not just for the mainframe but for all components. If the self-tests are activated automatically on powering the equipment, you don't need to do anything more. But if they require intervention, practice with them. Learn to use them frequently. You don't have anything to lose by performing the self-tests every day. It's better to spend a few minutes checking than to run into a problem in the middle of a critical operation.

Still, you must not become totally dependent on the built-in tests. As I've already mentioned, diagnostics are useful but not perfect, and these built-ins are no exceptions. They can miss some malfunctions, especially intermittent ones.

Software Diagnostics. Whether system hardware does or does not incorporate self-tests, it's good practice to run software diagnostics. Often, a diagnostic program can perform tests not provided by the built-ins, or it can be set to recycle or iterate for long periods, say overnight.

Not all systems have commercial diagnostic software available, but many do, sometimes from several different sources. I've found two packages I like—one for CP/M systems and the other for an Apple II. Both have proved useful and worth the investment.

For CP/M systems, SuperSoft, Inc., sells Diagnostics II™. It works on systems equipped with 8080, 8085, or Z-80 microprocessors, providing facilities to test the RAM, CPU, disk drives, CRT, and printer. Both "quick tests" and extended tests for the memory and disk drives are available, allowing either a fast verification or a slower, more thorough checkout. Diagnostics II includes a disk-drive alignment program, but it requires a special alignment diskette for the particular drives, an oscilloscope, and a knowledge of disk-drive operation. Since I keep my units under service contracts, I can't use the alignment program, but I use the other tests every week.

Unlike some programs, Diagnostics II allows choices in the extent of certain tests. Four separate, independently selectable memory tests are possible. One is a "quick test" of whether each bit in a specified range can be set to zero, then to one, and finally to a randomly selected value. A "walking-bit" test checks whether a bit change can be progressed through memory one bit at a time. This is a long test, and the manual advises that 16K could take up to 13 hours, while 32K might take up to 52 hours (proportional to the square locations tested). There's a "burn-in" test to ensure that memory locations aren't suffering from after-images left by previously stored data, and a "speed test" checks whether the CPU and memory are operating at the rated speed.

The quick test of the disk drives is a fast check for read errors without destroying data. A more thorough test overwrites and destroys data on a diskette, so it is used with fresh, formatted media. Under user control, the full test checks the read and write functions, the accuracy of track and sector seeking, and data integrity after a read. It detects faulty drives, bad diskettes, faulty memory, a defective controller, or other adverse conditions.

The CPU test checks the operating speed of the CPU and then tests every instruction the CPU is capable of executing; it checks the results of each instruction and various interactions such as one register affecting another. The CPU timing check even enabled me to find out that a system I purchased as a 4-MHz Z-80 unit had been strapped internally to 2 MHz, cutting its speed in half—I had a few nasty things to say to the supplier about that.

The printer test accomplishes some things that built-in tests often do not. It's particularly useful with letter-quality printers, where it checks forward and reverse printing, interleaved overprinting, horizontal tabbing, boldface overprinting, superscripts and subscripts, and vertical and horizontal page scaling.

The CRT test only exercises the output functions of the terminal. It includes a check of all printing characters in all fields, the clear-screen function, cursor addressing, highlighting modes, and the clear-to-end-of-line function. It does not check keyboard operation. Of the tests in Diagnostics II, I found all except the CRT test valuable; I'm usually well aware of a CRT problem from normal system use.

Non-CP/M systems pose more difficulties. Since diagnostics have to be programmed for just one brand, only the biggest sellers seem to have software available. The Apple II is a good example. Several companies provide diagnostics for it, but most wouldn't respond to requests for information. One company that did respond and does have an effective program is XPS, Inc., which supplies a package called Apple-Cillin II™.

I've been using Apple-Cillin II weekly. It's a series of menu-selected routines for testing motherboard and plug-in RAM, motherboard and plug-in ROM, the CPU and its registers, keyboard functions, the video display, the printer, the disk drives and controller, game paddles, a cassette deck, and selected peripheral cards. It's a fast, easily used program that gets at most standard Apple II components.

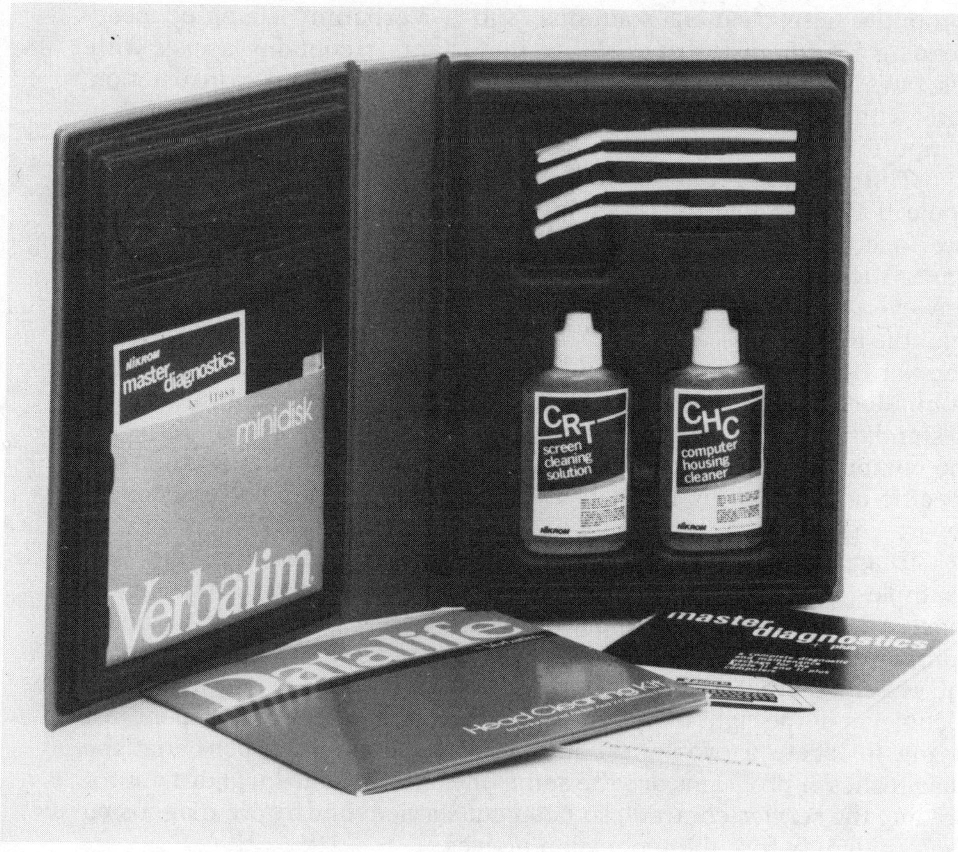

FIG 4-5 Master Diagnostics + Plus kit for the Apple II. *(Photo by author)*

I suspect, however, that the memory test is limited. The manual doesn't state what kind of test is performed, but from the speed at which it completes I would guess it puts a number into a byte, reads the number back, and makes sure it got back what it put out. For intermittent RAM problems, there's probably a chance of missing the bad location because the test goes by so quickly. The peripheral-card tests also seem a bit limited, but that's due to the overwhelming number of cards available for the machine. Since only a few have been preprogrammed into the routines, users find that some cards aren't fully checked or are listed as "unidentified."

The rest of the Apple-Cillin tests seem thorough. There are seven disk tests for reading, writing, and track seeking, with one routine specifically for checking and adjusting drive speeds. The CPU test reports each register, flag, and function individually. The video-display test even provides an assortment of test patterns useful for aligning and adjusting a monitor.

Another Apple II diagnostic is furnished as part of the "Master Diagnostics + Plus"™ kit from Nikrom Technical Products, Inc. Illustrated in Fig. 4-5, this kit contains some lint-free chamois swabs, screen and computer case cleaning solutions, and a Verbatim® Datalife™ head cleaning kit for disk drives. More important, it contains a disk with Nikrom's Master Diagnostics software for the Apple II and an instruction book with useful guidelines to the most important items of care for that computer.

The diagnostic routines include motherboard ROM tests (Apple II or Apple II Plus), Applesoft or Integer plug-in card tests, parallel printer interface card tests, motherboard RAM tests, various disk-drive tests, Hayes Micromodem II™ tests, and various monitor and game-paddle tests. However, the package lacks any means of testing the CPU itself (other than the ROM chips), add-on RAM cards, the keyboard, printers, or most popular interface cards provided by companies other than Apple Computer, Inc. The tests that are present provide a level of confidence for a "standard" 32K or 48K Apple having few enhancements. However, once the computer is built up into a full system using devices other than the specific ones called by Nikrom, either the add-ons remain untested or separate diagnostics have to be obtained.

Diagnostics II, Apple-Cillin II, and Master Diagnostics are just examples of programs to make your life easier. Owners of non-CP/M machines other than the Apple have to do their homework to locate comparable products. But remember, by knowing what's going on inside the system, there is a possibility you can fix it yourself or at least steer a technician in the right direction so that time and money aren't spent just trying to locate a problem. For my CP/M units, it happens that the Diagnostics II programs are the same ones used by the local distributor holding the service contract, so I can cut service time by pre-diagnosing the problem before the technician arrives.

CARD-LEVEL MAINTENANCE

Most care and maintenance procedures you're likely to perform are at the card level. That is, you install, remove, or replace entire circuit cards instead of individual circuit chips, resistors, diodes, and the like. That's also the most common maintenance level for warranty or contract repairs, with the technician isolating a problem to one or more cards and then swapping for new or rebuilt cards.

When a technician does this, the defective card either goes back to the shop or is sent to the manufacturer for testing and repair. Usually, this is the least expensive way to correct a malfunction because it minimizes the labor, and labor frequently costs far more than the parts.

When you do this yourself, you face two alternatives. To keep the computer fully functional, you have to obtain a replacement card, and that can cost hundreds of dollars. When the original card is repaired, you then have to decide what to do with two of them. Otherwise, you pull a card, return it to a service depot or the factory, and wait weeks or months to get it back so that you can restore normal operations. I recently received a ROM board for an Apple II from the manufacturer, had it fail two hours after installation, shipped it back under warranty, and then waited ten weeks for it to be repaired and returned.

The application determines which of the two approaches is best for your machine. As a hobbyist or recreational user, you may be able to tolerate downtime while a card is out for repair. As a business user, you need quick recovery with an immediate replacement of the defective board. For that reason, home and hobby users often do not sign up for extended warranties or service contracts, while business users almost always must have the added protection and fast response time they guarantee.

Isolating Problem Cards

In any malfunction, the biggest problem is isolating the fault to a specific card, assuming you are using a bus-oriented computer with plug-ins instead of a single-board unit. A good, step-by-step procedure is required—reconnecting, repowering, and retesting after each step. One approach is as follows:

1. Double-check all operating procedures and software. Be sure you aren't keying erroneous commands, haven't forgotten switches, aren't trying to access nonexistent memory or disk drives, and so on.

2. When satisfied that you do have a hardware problem, write down the symptoms. Keep a permanent log of failures, symptoms, and effective remedies. Figure 4-6 is a valuable aid in troubleshooting and fixing future problems. Try failed procedures several times and look for a pattern or repeatability. The easiest problems to solve occur consistently and demonstrate the same symptoms over and over. The hardest occur only occasionally or show a random pattern of behavior.

3. Check connecting cables and peripheral devices before opening the mainframe. Often, garbaged displays, trashed printouts, or disk-drive malfunctions are caused by a loose connector or a damaged cable.

4. Run system diagnostics against all components, but test the memory first. If memory is failing, most other tests will probably give incorrect results. If the diagnostics indicate a problem, concentrate on repairing or replacing that component first, then retest to see if the problem has been eliminated.

5. With the case open and power off, reseat the circuit cards by rocking them gently in their connectors. Rock them in the direction of the connectors' long axis; twisting or bending sideways can damage connectors and solder joints, loosen spring-metal contacts, or crack circuit boards.

6. Remove each board, clean the contacts, and reinstall. Connectors work loose or become contaminated by dirt, dust, grease, chemicals, and so on. Card-edge connectors that are not gold or gold plated can corrode.

TROUBLE LOG SHEET

System or Component: **Date:**

Symptoms:

1:	6:
2:	7:
3:	8:
4:	9:
5:	10:

Diagnostics and Results:

Attempted Remedies and Results:

1. Cleaning:
2. Check cables & connectors:
3. Reseat card(s):
4. Use alternate slots:
5. Replace card(s):
6. Replace chip(s):
7. Return to supplier:
8. Call service technician:
9. Other (detail):

Outside Service Required Date:

Circle One: Warranty Contract Paid

Service Company:
Address:
City, State, Zip:
Telephone:
Technician's Name:

Repairs Performed:

Cost:

Notes and Comments:

FIG 4-6 Sample trouble log sheet.

7. Try changing slot assignments. If you have vacant slots, use them. If none is vacant, change the installation order, but be careful not to put a card in an unusable slot. For instance, since the first language card (16K memory board) of an Apple II must be in slot 0, you have no flexibility there.

8. Remove the cards one more time and follow the procedures detailed later in this chapter to check and reseat all circuit chips on all boards. Once again, be sure cards are properly seated and all cable connectors are pressed down firmly.

Believe it or not, these simple steps are remedies to many common failures. With three systems, I've had frequent problems with things working loose. The vibrations of cooling fans, disk drives, and printers all combine to loosen cables, cards, and chips. Simple reseating usually is sufficient, though it's sometimes hard to identify exactly which component has worked loose.

Removing and Installing Cards

It may seem trivial to describe removal and installation of circuit cards, but the process is not so simple as it looks. There's more to it than "pull 'em out and stick 'em in." Improper removal or installation can keep a card from working and could do damage.

The procedures vary from machine to machine, depending on the design and plug-in connectors. For example, S-100 bus machines typically use slotted card guides like that shown in Fig. 4-7 to position the plug-in above an edge connector and provide support for the card.

Removing a card requires that it be pulled straight up and out, in the direction of the guide channels. It's usually necessary, however, first to rock the card gently along the edge-connector axis to free it. Installing a card requires positioning it in the guide channels and pressing downward into the edge connector, again rocking slightly to ensure proper seating and good contact. There are four critical points:

1. Cables or connections other than the edge connector should be undone before removal and reconnected after the card is installed or reinstalled. Note the orientation of connectors since some are "keyed" to prevent improper connection, but many are not and allow the connectors to be inverted. A wrong connection can prevent proper operation or damage sensitive circuitry. Scribe a mark on the connector if necessary.

2. Grip the card with both hands along the upper edge, but don't touch on-board components. The upper corners may have circuit chips, heat sinks, or other components that must not be damaged. Be sure of your grip; if the connector releases abruptly, your fingers may shift or press down reflexively, damaging adjoining components. Watch out for heat sinks, typically "finned" metal blocks or brackets around components. They can be hot enough to burn flesh, so touch nearby components tentatively before grabbing hold.

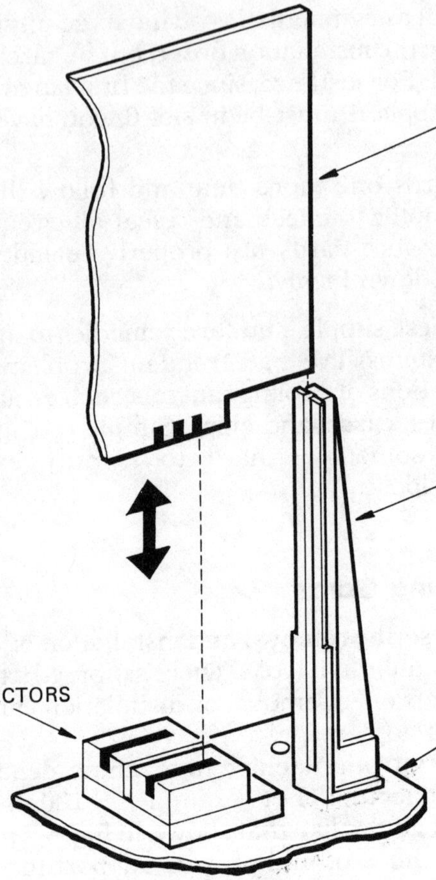

FIG 4-7 Typical S-100 bus plug-in card installation.

3. Never rock a card side to side to free it. That stresses the connector, card guide, and motherboard, possibly damaging contacts, breaking the guide, or cracking either the card or the motherboard. Do not use force. Cards should release and reinsert with minimum effort. With sensitive electronics, you cannot follow the principle "if it doesn't work, get a bigger hammer."

4. When installing, be sure the card is engaged in the guide channels along both vertical edges, and make certain it seats securely in the edge connector. A common mistake is leaving the card partly engaged with the connector, allowing it to work loose later. Rocking the card along the connector axis helps ensure tight seating and good contact.

There still may be a few computers around with "card lifters" on the guides, although they aren't widely used on micros. The pivoting plastic brackets at the top of the guides engage slots or tabs on the upper board edge. When the lifters are pivoted upward and outward, the card is freed from the edge connector and lifted a quarter- to a half-inch for removal. For installation, it's important that the lifters first be in the open positions. As the card slides down the guide channels, the lifters re-engage, returning to the closed position. In some, ingenious designs lock the boards into place so they can't loosen under vibration.

A machine such as the Apple II has edge connectors but no card guides. The preceding method applies to connecting and disconnecting cables, gripping the card, freeing it from the edge connector, and reinstalling it securely. The difference is that there are no guides to worry about. However, the absence of guides requires extra care to ensure card-to-connector alignment, and it's more difficult to be sure the card is fully seated. Since many plug-ins can be tipped forward in the edge connectors, making poor connection along the rearmost contacts, the card must be pressed down at the rear edge. Furthermore, because most Apple II cable connectors are not keyed, observe the positioning in the instruction manuals for each card type.

Other machines lock the plug-ins. An example is the IBM Personal Computer, which uses a screw to secure a retaining bracket to the chassis. Figure 4-8 illustrates the method for installing a new card, and removal is accomplished by reversing the sequence. An expansion-slot cover must first be removed, and the retaining screw saved. The card is held by the top corners and pressed firmly down into the edge connector. Then the hole in the retaining bracket of the card is aligned with one in the rear plate of the unit, and the retaining screw is reinstalled to lock the card into place. The method virtually guarantees proper positioning and seating since the holes are difficult to align if the card is out of position. Furthermore, it's unlikely the card will work loose under normal vibration.

Cleaning Card-Edge Connectors

Periodically, it's necessary or advisable to clean edge connectors to remove dirt, dust, contamination, and oxidation that interfere with normal contact. Though most edge connectors are gold plated to reduce corrosion, contaminants can and do accumulate. Cleaning is a recommended procedure when you are experiencing difficulties, particularly intermittent errors and failures. It's also good preventive medicine, and cleaning is advised at least once every six months even if the machine is not giving trouble. All plug-in boards should be cleaned, including peripheral controllers, disk controllers, CPU cards, and so on.

After removing a card, place it component-side up (solder-side down) on a static-free surface. Be sure there are no components on the solder side that might be bent or damaged, and be careful not to disturb any "jumper wires." Then proceed as follows:

1. Use an eraser to clean the contacts as shown in Fig. 4-9. Be gentle! Your touch should be as light as possible—you're trying to polish the contacts, not rub them off. Do not use an ink eraser such as one on a

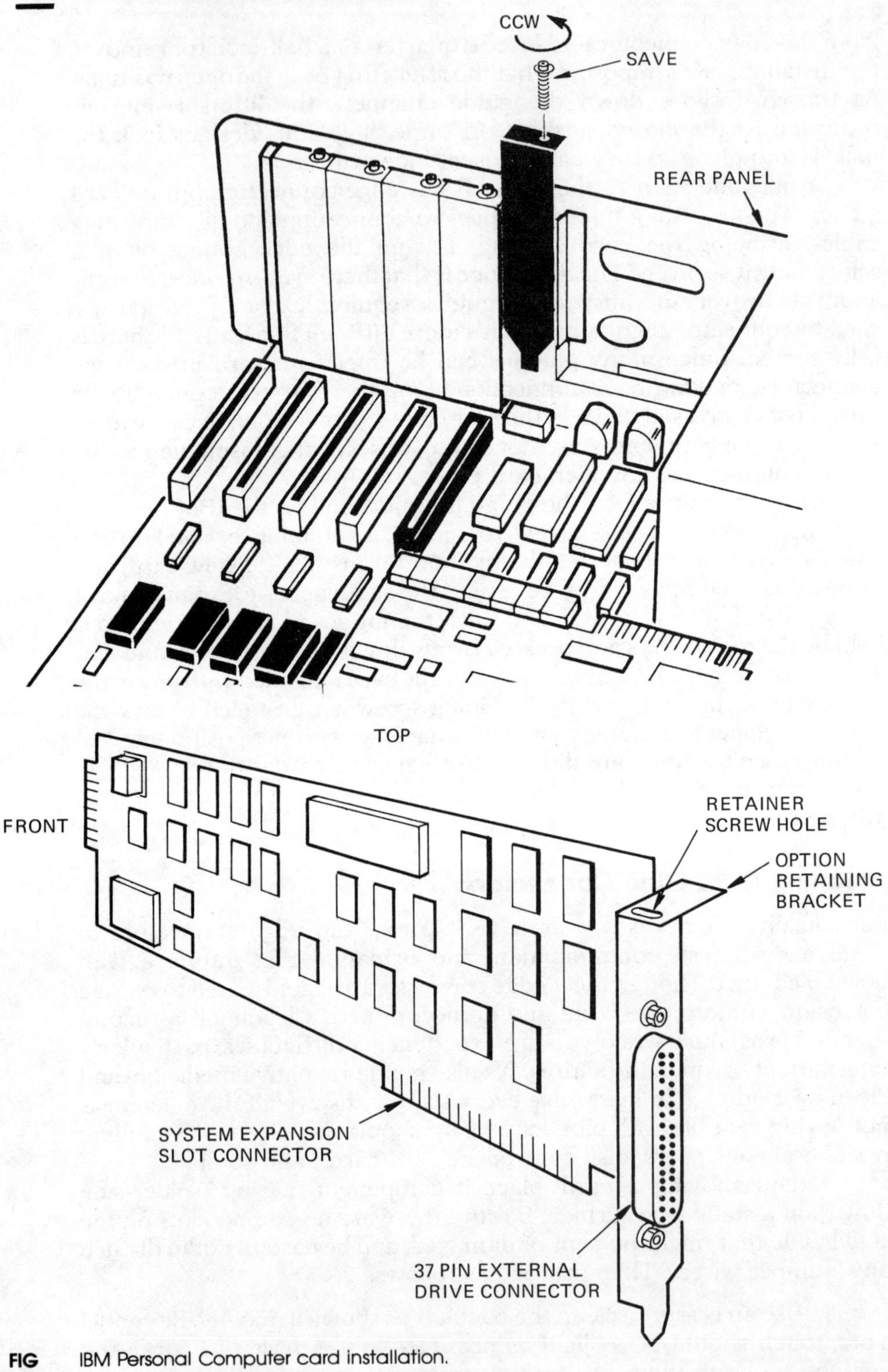

FIG 4-8 IBM Personal Computer card installation.

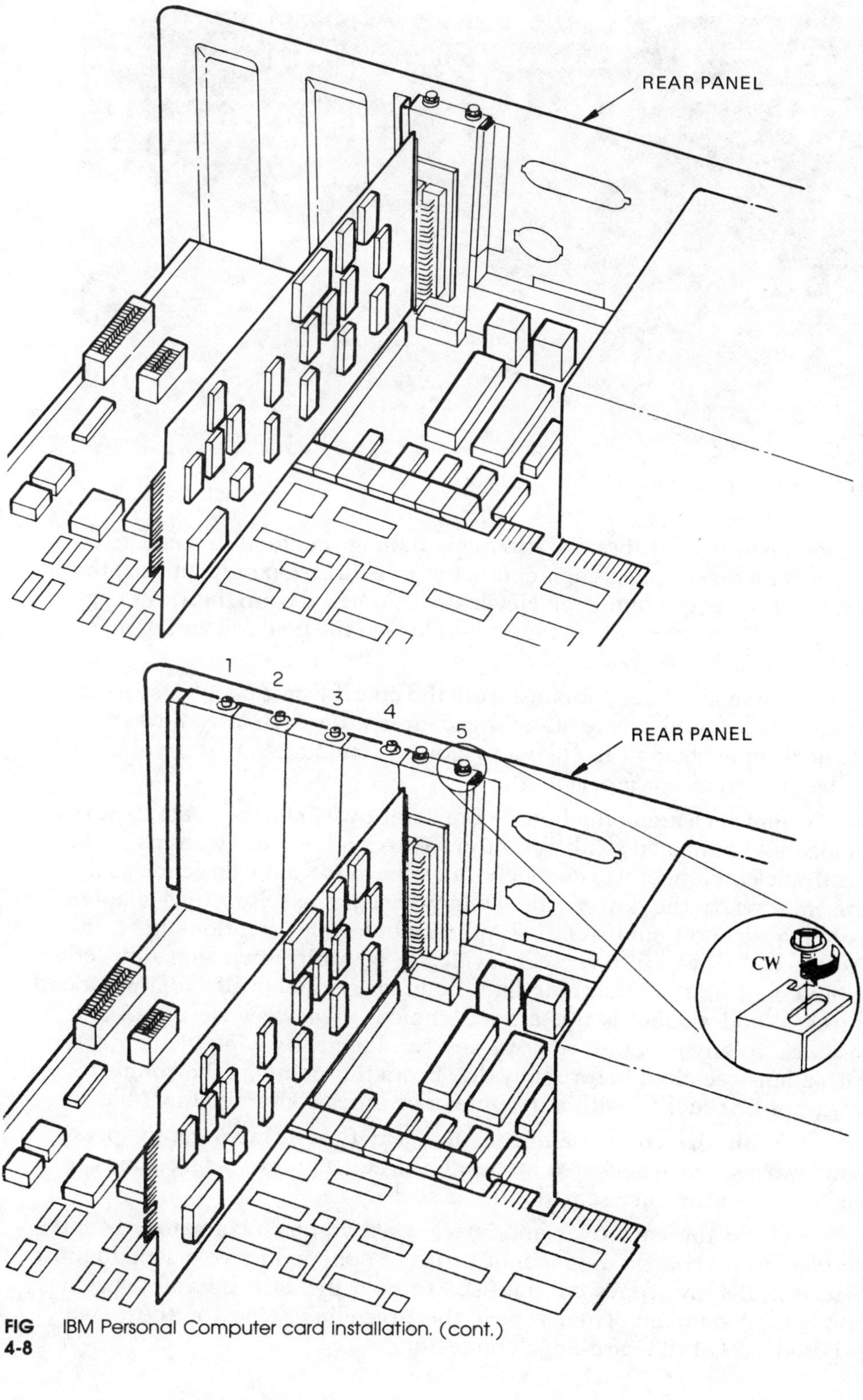

FIG 4-8 IBM Personal Computer card installation. (cont.)

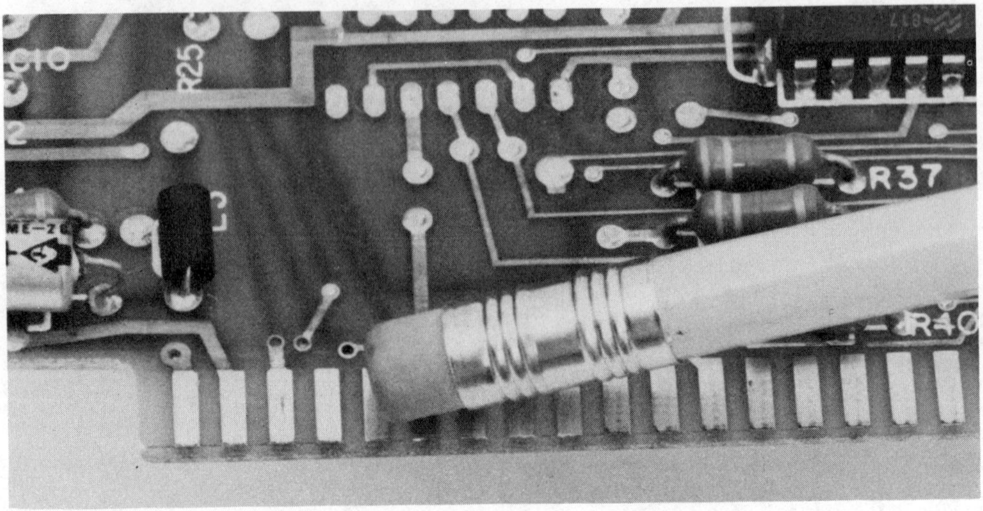

FIG 4-9 Cleaning edge connectors. *(Photo by author)*

ballpoint pen; it's too abrasive and might damage contacts. Instead, use a soft pencil eraser. Clean each contact in one direction only, toward the bottom of the edge connector. Never stroke upward from the lower edge or across the connectors as that might loosen the gold foil and damage the contacts.

2. Clean all eraser rubbings from the board. Some people use a soft brush, but it could create static. I recommend a pressurized air spray (clean air only), being careful not to blow the rubbings into the workings of the mainframe or a peripheral.

3. Finish cleaning the board connector by wiping the contacts with an alcohol-dampened swab. A cotton swab or a lint-free swab made for electronic equipment will do nicely, but wipe in the same direction as the eraser, toward the lower edge. Many people use isopropyl alcohol (rubbing alcohol), and many commercial cleaning solutions have the same base. However, I've seen evidence of a dirt-attracting film left behind, so I prefer something like the grain alcohol available at liquor stores. Wood alcohol is not a good choice, again because of possible residues. In any event, to remove any residue gently wipe the contacts with a lint-free cloth before they dry. From this point on, the connector must not be touched with bare fingers or other contaminating objects.

4. With the component-side up on a flat surface, gently press downward on each socketed integrated circuit, not the soldered ones, to make certain they are seated in their sockets.

5. Turn the card over and brace it above the surface to prevent damage to on-board components. Strips of nonconductive plastic foam placed under the edges can be used to hold the card up and prevent component damage. Then repeat the preceding steps for the newly exposed side of the card-edge connector.

6. Check any on-board cable connectors for signs of contamination or corrosion. While the card is out of the machine, these connectors might as well be cleaned, too. They are delicate, so limit your cleaning to using a damp (not wet) alcohol swab and a lint-free cloth. Be careful to avoid bending pins or dripping liquid onto components or into wire connectors.

7. Using a pressurized clean-air canister with a thin nozzle extension, blow any dust and dirt out of the motherboard connector slot. Inspect the slot to be sure there are no foreign objects lodged therein. Do the same for any connectors on the ends of cables. It's not a good idea to attempt any cleaning procedure other than blowing out contaminants; the space is far too small and the devices far too delicate for alcohol swabs.

8. Double-check all on-board switches and jumpers to make certain they haven't been disturbed during the cleaning process. If any have, restore them to normal before returning the board to the unit. Then, without touching the surfaces you've cleaned, install or reinstall the card and connect or reconnect any cables.

Amazingly, just cleaning connectors often eliminates annoying transient errors from the system. One problem I've noticed over and over again is that cards work loose, just from the normal vibration of disk drives and printers, becoming dirty in the process as surfaces are exposed. Gradually, the problem builds until one or more contacts doesn't carry the electrical signals properly, and the board fails to perform its function. A thorough cleaning then may reestablish connections and start the board running again.

Connectors should be cleaned before any new board is installed. There's no guarantee they haven't been contaminated in the package or on the shelf, so good electrical contact may be blocked from the first installation if they're not cleaned. Additionally, some computer stores repackage demonstrator or display boards and sell them as new merchandise, often with an added problem of oil contamination from the fingers of those who examined the boards or local sales personnel who handled them carelessly.

Miscellaneous Card-Level Procedures

There are several other card-level procedures of which you should be aware. These include setting internal switches and changing internal jumpers. Virtually any plug-in may be affected, but the procedures commonly affect memory boards and interface controllers.

Internal Switch Settings. Almost every computer and peripheral is equipped with internal switches to control features and operations not changed frequently. The switches are provided in small blocks known as digital in-line packages or "DIP switches." Another common name is

FIG 4-10 Typical DIP switches. *(Photos by author)*

"pencil switches," indicating that they are just the right size to be repositioned with a pencil point, although that's not an advised procedure. Figure 4-10 illustrates several DIP switches, showing some different designs used in modern microcomputers.

The pencil points in Fig. 4-10 are shown for scale only. You should not use pencils to change switch settings. Since the graphite is an electrical conductor, broken points, graphite chips, and powdery residues can cause all kinds of trouble. Pieces of graphite can work into card connectors and other vital circuitry, shorting out the signal lines. Even the particles left on the switch can work into the switch casing, again shorting contacts.

What can you use? Not ballpoint pens! The electrical properties of the ink are unknown, so there is a danger of electrical problems; besides, ink makes an ugly mess. I prefer a wood or plastic stylus, especially since I don't like to poke around with metal objects. Some companies recommend items such as bent paper clips, but there's always the possibility of doing damage or dropping the clip into an inaccessible area. Since wood and plastic are nonconductive, however, they don't do damage if dropped, and they leave no residue behind. I've even used wooden toothpicks and plastic hors d'oeuvre spears as styli, preferring them to pencils and pens.

There are three points to remember when changing switch settings. First, the change may result in an unwanted function occurring or a desirable function being lost. Check your manuals and record all original settings before making any changes. Second, switches are delicate devices and can wear out. You should not tamper with them unless necessary. Often the switches set up "default" conditions, so set them to your most common needs and let software override the settings for less frequent needs. Third, since the switches don't always make good contact and are subject to the same contamination and degradation as any other electrical contacts, it sometimes takes several tries to get an old switch to open or close properly. I make it a habit to exercise the internal switches whenever I'm experiencing machine malfunctions, usually as part of the overall connector cleanup.

Unlike card connectors, DIP switches cannot be cleaned. Don't even think about getting close to one with alcohol swabs or other liquids—that's the fastest way I know to ruin a switch. If they aren't self-cleaned by cycling a few times or by being blown with a clean-air canister, you're not going to be able to clean them at all, and they'll have to be replaced.

Internal Jumpers. Throughout the mainframe and peripherals, internal jumpers often serve functions similar to those of DIP switches. The difference is that the features controlled by jumpers require fewer changes than those controlled by switches. There are three general types of jumpers. One is the soldered type, where a wire is soldered between two contacts or two solder pads on the board are "bridged." These are considered permanent jumpers and may be changed only with considerable risk of damage to the equipment and voiding of warranties or service contracts. The second type is a modular jumper block which may be changed by the user, if needed. The third type might be called a "modification wire," since it typically connects two seemingly unrelated devices to modify the operation of the machine.

To illustrate, the Apple II contains several jumper pads, one group of which is illustrated in Fig. 4-11. These happen to be part of the "mod" to use the Apple with European monitors. The pad at the top with the triangular solder shape is a "cut" type, where the connection is broken by cutting through the solder at the thinnest point with a sharp instrument. The other two are "bridge" points, at which connection is made by soldering over the separations. However, all such modifications involving solder joints will probably void warranties or service contracts, even if done by an authorized dealership or service technician.

Similar solder jumpers exist everywhere. The Apple II has a set known as the "USER 1" jumper; when bridged it changes the characteristics of input/output device usage. The Videx Videoterm™ 80-column board for the Apple has several locations for normal/inverse

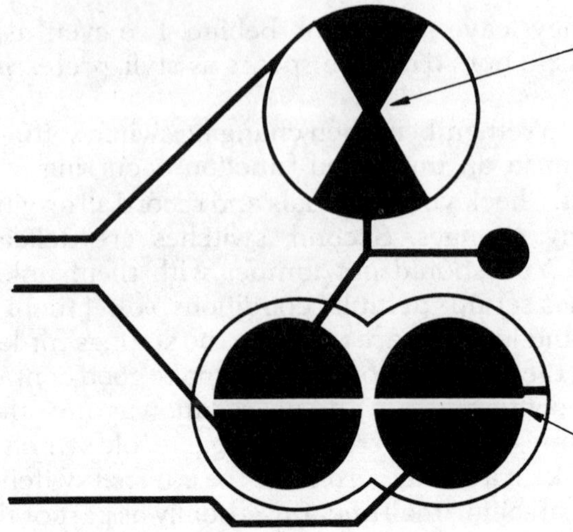

FIG 4-11 Typical soldered jumpers.

operation, EPROM selection, and so on. The Qume Sprint 5 printer has one to disable the out-of-ribbon halt operation. The list goes on and on, but the common thread is that meddling with these is done at your own risk.

Alternatively, there are jumpers that can be changed, typically provided on a block similar to one shown in Fig. 4-12. The block on the left is a "wire" type, where short wires route from a socket on one side to a socket on the other side. The block on the right is a "modular" type with small plastic-encased jumpers that fit snugly over a pair of pins. Variations of the modular approach allow jumpers to fit horizontally or vertically, changing the characteristics of the circuits according to which pins are connected to which others.

FIG 4-12 Typical jumper blocks. *(Photos by author)*

Normally, jumper blocks require little attention once set up the way you want them. If you do have to change them, be careful not to break the wires or bend the pins. With either type, it's best to remove and replace the wires or modules with tweezers; it can be delicate work in a confined area, so trying to get your fingers in there could damage nearby boards or components. It's a good idea to remove and reset the jumpers once a year, just to ensure solid contact by breaking through any buildups of dust or corrosion.

Modification wires are similar to jumpers, connecting two electrical points. They usually run between different devices, however, not on a pad or block. Often, you'll find jumper wires installed on the solder sides of circuit boards, where the supplier has made a change or product improvement. Some you may have to install yourself. Two examples come to mind: one is the Videx Enhancer II™ keyboard modification for an Apple II, and the other is a single-wire shift-key modification for the Apple.

Installing an Enhancer II is a complex job requiring almost total disassembly of the computer. Part of the process involves installing modification wires from one pin of one circuit chip to some pin of another circuit chip. The affected chips have to be removed from their sockets, the wire must be inserted into a specified contact, and the chip reinstalled to lock the wire into place. It's not a difficult process, but it runs the risk of damaging chips, bending pins, and possibly doing some electrical damage if you get the wires connected to the wrong "legs" of the chips and then power up the equipment. Yet without the modification wires, many useful functions of the Enhancer II aren't operational, so you're caught between the proverbial rock and hard place. To activate functions, you have to risk some damage. To avoid any possibility of damage, you have to live without features. Of course, you could pay a dealership or service technician to do the installation, but it takes time, and time can be expensive.

Another example is the so-called single-wire shift-key modification that activates the shift key for lowercase typing on an Apple II. Usually, a wire is run from a pin of the gameport socket to a pin of the connector between the keyboard and the "decoder" board located below it. The gameport socket isn't difficult since the wire may be inserted into the connector. If game paddles or other plug-ins to that socket aren't used, there's no problem. However, many manuals then instruct you to solder the other wire end to a pin of the keyboard "outrigger." That immediately voids any warranties or service contracts.

A few software suppliers have started to distribute packages with solderless test clips on the shift-key mod to prevent voiding the warranty. It's a good idea, and I recommend it for any modification wires on any machine. "Alligator clips" and test clips are inexpensive and serve well for many wiring applications. A pair of Radio Shack's Mini Test Clips (part No. 270-372) cost only about $1.49, so there's no reason to take the unnecessary risk of soldering wires if there's a place to attach a clip.

While I'm on the subject of Apple shift-key wires, I might comment that I'm not fond of the idea of sticking a wire into the gameport socket. It works, I'll grant that. But some of the wires provided are too thick and can damage the contact so that it won't connect well with other devices later. Besides, any time it's necessary to disconnect the modification or connect paddles, joysticks, light pens, and other peripherals, it's necessary to get inside the computer. That's something I don't recommend at all. Each entry poses a risk to the computer, and the gameport connector is particularly difficult to get at.

I damaged several connectors doing this, until I installed a gameport extender allowing connection from the outside. The extender I chose was a Model GS-1 from Happ Electronics, Inc., and it's worked nicely. With the shift-key mod wire routed out the side of the Apple, the wire or any other devices can be connected or disconnected at will. I chose the Happ connector because it features a locking lever that enables the socket to clamp down on the mod wire or an inserted plug, giving a firm connection yet a quick release to change something.

CIRCUIT-LEVEL MAINTENANCE

Most users won't be involved with circuit-level maintenance. Fixing something at this level usually requires a high degree of technical expertise and an assortment of sophisticated test equipment such as multimeters, oscilloscopes, and signal generators to identify the circuit chip or other component at fault. I've already mentioned that even service technicians avoid this level, preferring to replace entire boards then returning the defective boards to the manufacturer or fixing them on a fully equipped test bench.

Nevertheless, you must occasionally work at the circuit level, even if it's not remedial maintenance. Some computers make it necessary to get down to the nitty gritty to install various devices, and the Apple II serves as a good example once again. With this machine, you have to go inside to change a chip for lowercase display capability. You have to remove a chip to add a memory expansion board. You may even have to remove and replace chips to install certain types of shift-key modifications. I've already mentioned that a near-total stripdown is necessary to install a Videx Enhancer II, and there are many similar situations.

Of course, there's always the possibility you'll be able to isolate some specific problem with diagnostics. If you can identify a specific memory chip as faulty, you can save time and money by installing a new one yourself. If the microprocessor chip fails, it can be replaced in a matter of minutes. Similarly, any component that fails, or can be isolated as the failure, and can be replaced without soldering is a candidate for a do-it-yourself fixup. I do not recommend that you ever touch anything with a soldering iron; in fact, I recommend you get rid of your soldering iron to remove the temptation. Nor should you pull and replace components at random. Yet there are situations when simple remedies suffice.

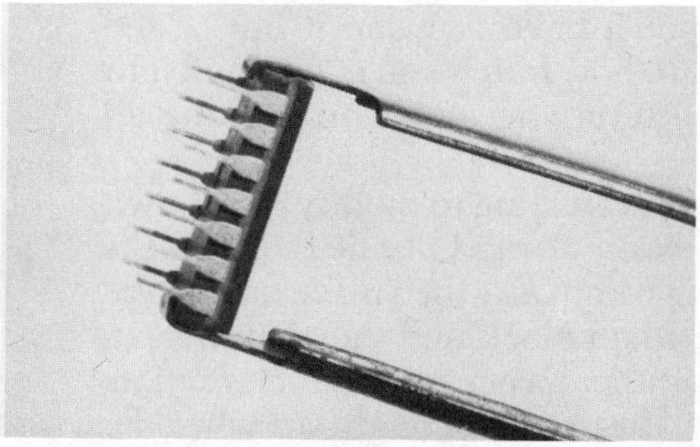

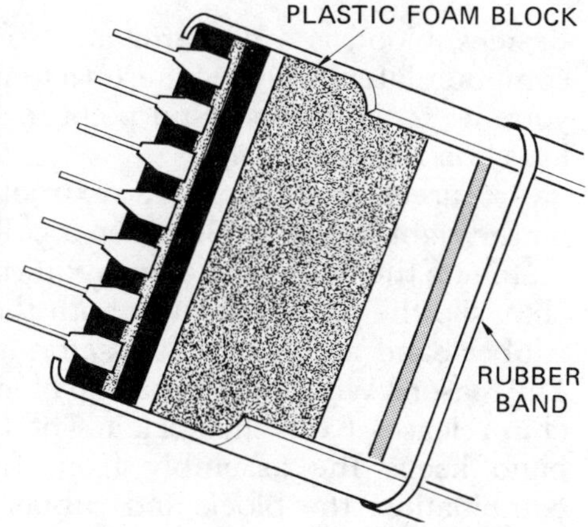

FIG 4-13 Simple chip extractor. *(Photo by author)*

Chip Removal

Chip removal, whether from a motherboard, a plug-in mainframe board, or a peripheral device, is a delicate matter. If you don't do it right, you risk damaging circuitry, bending or breaking pins, or pricking a finger.

I'll assume you know which chip you need to remove. I have to make some assumptions, and you shouldn't be attempting this anyway unless you have isolated a chip you want to pull. You should have the power off, preferably with the unit unplugged, the chassis open, and an uncluttered static-free work surface. You also should have a few small plastic foam blocks and a "chip extractor" handy.

You're asking, "What's a chip extractor?" Well, it need be nothing more than a fancy set of tweezers with bent legs, like the one in Fig. 4-13. The hooked ends slip between a chip and its socket, allowing you to pull more or less straight up for removal. There are other, fancier types of extractors, but this one serves the purpose for most users. They're not always easy to come by, however. The one shown was included with a Microsoft 16K RAMCard™ expansion for an Apple II computer. Since installing the RAMCard required removing a memory chip from the motherboard, Microsoft was kind enough to provide the tool, although they have been the only ones to do so among the many plug-in suppliers who require chip removals.

Several instruction manuals recommend other techniques for pulling chips, among them slipping a knife blade or screwdriver between a chip and its socket and then prying upward. That will get the chip out, but at the cost of bent pins and possibly a cracked socket. Even alternately prying one end and then the other risks bending or breaking something. Furthermore, since knives and screwdrivers might be magnetized, they could damage sensitive components.

The most important thing is not to use your fingers. Chips are seated firmly and require some effort to remove. When they come free from the sockets, they tend to do so abruptly, making it difficult to hold onto them. The pins are needle sharp, and it's easy to drive them into a finger, while also bending them out of shape. Fingers will heal, but the chip may not.

Besides, blood is a contaminant, so you'll have to clean it out of the computer later. Anyway, there's a limit to how much you need to put into your work, and there's no point in suffering an injury and risking an infection unnecessarily.

I rarely use a "bare" chip extractor, preferring to modify it as shown on the right in Fig. 4-13. I keep a collection of rigid plastic foam blocks matching the lengths of chips requiring removal. I then place one on the chip, slip the extractor over both the foam block and the chip, wrap a rubber band around the extractor, and then proceed to the extraction. The reason? Without the bracing block, the extractor might slip when the chip releases from the socket. The block adds rigidity, and the rubber band keeps the assembly from flying apart if I lose my grip. In combination, the block and rubber band make it less likely that I'll damage a chip by losing control of the extractor.

The step-by-step procedure to remove a chip is as follows:

1. Note the orientation of the chip in its socket. Most have a "dimple" on one end, and the replacement must be installed with the dimple on the same end. The most common dimple is a notch or depression on one end. However, some have paint spots, raised dots, or something similar. If you can't find the dimple, then at least note the orientation of chip markings such as the identification number.

2. With the board on a secure surface, install the extractor onto the chip. While you can remove chips from a secure motherboard without disassembling the unit, plug-in boards should be removed and laid on a flat surface. Be sure the gripping edges of the extractor are between the chip and socket. It's easy to get between the socket and board, where you could rip the socket assembly completely off.

3. Gently rock the extractor to loosen the chip. Movement should be in the direction of the chip's long axis. That's in the direction of the non-pin edges. Never rock toward or away from the sides with the pins.

4. Gradually work the chip up and out of the socket, being sure both ends are free. Then pull straight up and out. If you've done it right, there should be little pin bending, although some distortion is unavoidable. If you've done it wrong, the pins are likely to look as if someone hammered them over on their sides.

5. Release the chip from the extractor and immediately press the pins into a foam plastic block to prevent further damage.

Chip Installation

Putting a chip back into a socket is not the reverse process of taking it out. Don't try to use an extraction tool for installation. Instead, begin by examining the new chip carefully. All pins should be straight and parallel. If they are not, fix them by gently adjusting with tweezers or small needle-nose pliers.

FIG 4-14 Integrated circuit chip with a bent pin. *(Photo by author)*

Test the pin alignment by setting the chip on the socket, but don't press it down. The dimple must be toward the correct end. Examine the pins carefully, making sure each is resting into the depression for its socket contact. Keep adjusting the pins with the tweezers or pliers until you get an exact match between them and the socket contacts. With new chips, you may have to widen or narrow the gap between the two rows, but do so carefully.

When you are satisfied everything lines up, double-check to be sure the chip is oriented the right way, and press it down into the socket. Try to press straight down on the center, not to one side or another. If you shift the chip accidentally, the pins may collapse and you'll have to start over. The chip should "pop" into place with only a little effort. Once it's down, carefully examine all pins for any that might have missed the connectors. A pin that misses by slipping down the outside of the socket or collapses to the left or right is easy to spot. One that bends to the inside, as shown in Fig. 4-14, is much more difficult to spot, especially if it's not on the end. It's also possible for a pin to break off and yet appear intact. Therefore, be sure you examine the chip under good lighting, and pay particular attention to anything that looks like a hairline crack.

An important point in installing a new chip is that it must be of the same type as one removed. There are users who assume they can mix and match, sometimes putting a dynamic RAM chip in a static RAM slot or vice versa. Some will try to replace a 2-MHz Z-80 microprocessor with a 4-MHz or even a 6-MHz version. These generally don't work, and all removed chips must be replaced with ones bearing the same number. Static and dynamic RAMs cannot be intermixed. For microprocessors, there are CPU and memory timing considerations involved, so speeding up a system usually requires more than just using a faster processor, to avoid internal signal conflicts and a complete breakdown of operations.

Chip Cleaning

Occasionally, it's necessary to clean the pins of integrated circuits. Most often, pins are silver or silver plated, with good conductivity but subject to tarnishing. Once they are installed into a socket, the contacts keep air from reaching the silver, so tarnishing is minimal. However, new chips purchased from a supply house often have black pins instead of shiny ones, and it's advisable to clean them up before installing them.

The procedure is similar to that described for cleaning card-edge connectors, but it is far more delicate because of the ease with which pins may be bent or broken. Alcohol and cleaning solvents do not cut through silver tarnish. Commercial silver polishers may clean up the pins, but they leave a residue that must not be allowed to enter the computer. Furthermore, the anti-tarnish treatment provided by silver polishing leaves a coating on the metal that can degrade electrical contacts.

Instead, brace the chip with the pins supported on a flat static-free surface. I usually hold chips with long tweezers and secure the tweezer legs with a loosely wrapped rubber band. Then, I carefully clean the pins with a pencil eraser, rubbing only along the length of the pins, never across them. With care and a light touch, the pins are cleaned without bending or damage. During installation, contact between fingers and chip pins should be avoided to prevent contamination. It's a good idea to wear thin, white cotton gloves. Photo stores often stock such gloves intended to prevent fingerprints when slides or negatives are handled, and the same gloves work well for protecting electrical contacts.

UNCLASSIFIED THOUGHTS ABOUT MAINFRAME CARE

Microcomputer mainframes, like the mythical Pandora's box, are full of surprises that pop out when the box is opened. As a result, not all care-and-maintenance thoughts can be so neatly classified. The rest of this chapter discusses some of these areas, though not necessarily in any logical or procedural order.

Memory Testing

Sometimes, if you're lucky, memory problems can be diagnosed from symptoms. However, isolating the bad board or bad chip requires some systematic approach, one of which might be termed "rolling the memory." This involves reassigning memory boards or chips to new addresses and seeing if the symptom follows the relocation. Where memory is housed on several separate boards, the process begins with rolling the board locations, and then rolling the chips on the boards. Where memory is on a single plug-in board or on the motherboard, only the chips are rolled.

Rolling Memory Boards. Assume you have a 64K S-100 system with four 16K memory boards. Also, assume you run a full-memory CP/M operating system, typically configured to something like 62K or 64K according to its sign-on message. It's common for a memory failure occurring in an area used by the CP/M system to cause a specific symptom, namely refusal to boot. One way to check this is to try a smaller operating system like 48K or 32K; I prefer 32K to begin testing. Often this gets you past the booting problem by not using one or two of the four 16K boards (or a 32K bank). If it doesn't, try rolling the memory, as I'll explain later, to locate a usable 32K segment.

Since you can't reconfigure CP/M if you can't boot it, keep a disk with a minimum system configuration of 32K on file for those times when the full-size version refuses to boot. From the 32K version, you can reconfigure another disk to 48K or to maximum memory as needed.

A fast, slick test involves reconfiguring the operating system. CP/M systems usually include a utility program called MOVCPM.COM, which sizes the system, and the keyboard command "MOVCPM* *" reconfigures for maximum available memory. If a RAM location or board is bad, the highest usable location is often the one just below the problem, so the system sizes itself to something less than full memory and indicates that size on the display. By altering bank-select DIP switches to roll the boards as shown in Fig. 4-15 (power off each time), the maximum reconfiguration size should vary. If this happens, the problem board can be isolated and located as the highest bank or address group. Once isolated, chips may be rolled to locate a failure, the board may be pulled for repair, or other steps may be taken. Meanwhile, the computer system remains at least partly operational, though with a reduced memory capacity and a reduction in the sizes of programs and data that can be run.

It's often useful to roll memory this way even if diagnostic software is available; check to see whether the error follows the reassignments. If it does, either the board's control circuitry or a RAM chip is bad. If it does not, the problem probably is somewhere other than the memory. On systems with selectable memory addresses, I like to roll the boards every six months anyway. It distributes the memory usage and helps eliminate some problems of after-image retention.

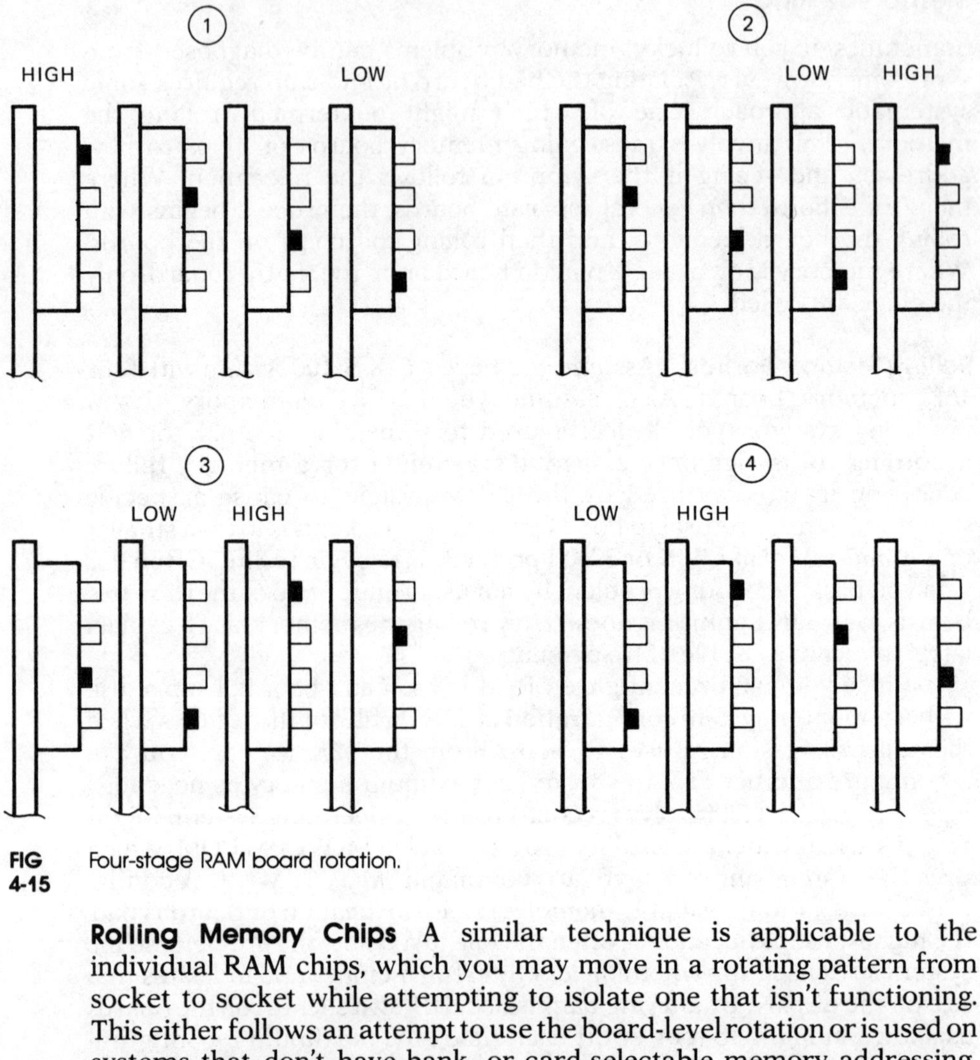

FIG 4-15 Four-stage RAM board rotation.

Rolling Memory Chips A similar technique is applicable to the individual RAM chips, which you may move in a rotating pattern from socket to socket while attempting to isolate one that isn't functioning. This either follows an attempt to use the board-level rotation or is used on systems that don't have bank- or card-selectable memory addressing. The important thing is to follow a uniform pattern, rotating chips either upward or downward through memory in the same direction each time. Again, diagnostic software or operating system reconfiguration at each step provides a useful test.

Rotating chip by chip is a long, tedious process, with the number of steps determined by the number of memory chips. It's generally reserved as a last resort, when nothing else works to isolate the problem. A popular variation combines testing with a simultaneous effort to eliminate a bad chip. A single new RAM chip is used to replace one in the system, and the tests are performed. If the malfunction still exists, the previously removed chip replaces the next higher chip, and the test is repeated. By proceeding in this manner, a failure due to a single chip can be eliminated at minimal cost when the rotation reaches the bad one.

However, multiple-chip failures aren't solved this way, and it may be necessary to repeat the procedure with groups of two, three, or more chips at a time. Even that doesn't work if several bad chips are at separated memory addresses.

On a system like the Apple II, the motherboard RAM and the first 16K expansion RAM board are treated as a contiguous block of memory, so the rotation must include the chips on both. Do not, however, treat memory locations other than the normal expansion from 48K to 64K in this way. In particular, don't include "RAM disks" such as the 128 KDE Soft Disk™ from Legend Industries, Inc., as a normal memory expansion. Such a board is not a part of normal memory and isn't tested as such. It may be possible to rotate chips on that board alone, using special software to test the functions, but diagnostics like XPS' Apple-Cillin package do not recognize the Soft Disk as memory.

Circuit-Board Bracing

One problem with a computer like an Apple II is that the only support for plug-in circuit cards is the edge connector. Nothing guides or supports the ends of the cards. For most plug-ins, that's not a problem, but a few are oversize cards, which extend several inches forward of the connector. Typical of this type are Personal Computer Products' Appli-Card™ (Z-80 with 64K memory), Novation's Apple-Cat II™ communications modem, and SSM Microcomputer Products' AIO-II™ serial/parallel interface.

The difficulty is that the cards are "front heavy" and tend to tilt in the edge connectors, especially if there's any vibration from a nearby printer or from people bumping into the supporting desk or surface. When the cards tilt forward, the contacts at the rear of the edge connector loosen and may even separate. The Appli-Card alleviates the problem by having an extension tab near the forward edge, keeping the card from tilting so far that it disconnects. With others, it sometimes helps to install a nonconductive foam or wooden block, slotted to fit the card edge and resting on the motherboard.

Circuit-Card Incompatibility

Occasionally, it's possible to encounter some system configuration that just won't work, sometimes because plug-in cards aren't compatible. Often the symptoms make no sense at all, and a solution may not be found.

It happened to me with an Apple II Plus. I had equipped the system with a Microsoft SoftCard and 16K RAMCard, giving me a 64K computer capable of running CP/M. Months later, I acquired a PKASO™ printer interface from Interactive Structures, Inc., to drive an Epson MX-80™ printer. I chose the interface for its outstanding graphics capabilities and used it without any problems for two months under Applesoft. Then, I needed to work under CP/M and Microsoft BASIC for a while, but I started to have problems.

Errors occurred at random. The most typical one was difficulty in booting the CP/M system from disk, either failing to boot at all or getting garbage characters in the sign-on message. After eight or ten tries, I'd finally be able to boot, load BASIC, and then load a program into memory. Minutes or hours later, the program would "bomb." On listing the program, large sections might be missing, characters in statements and instructions might be changed, or the program might not list at all. Other times, CP/M utilities for copying or debugging would fail part way through an operation or after several successful operations. Several times, saving a program to disk recorded erroneous data, erased or damaged other files, gave a "disk full" error message on an empty disk, and so on. I also saw a scattering of weird error messages such as an "illegal command" for a simple LIST, or a "reset error" when there had been no attempt to reset the system.

I went through months of trying to isolate the problem, with the help of technicians and various manufacturers. The first approach assumed a defective memory board, but tests showed nothing wrong and three replacement boards of the same brand behaved the same way. Then the Z-80 RAMCard was replaced, in the assumption it might have failed. No improvement. An alternate PKASO board was tried in combination with several Microsoft RAMCards and SoftCards, but the errors persisted. The system was run with every possible installation of cards in every allowable combination of slots, and from a minimum number of cards to a maximum number. Again, the errors. On the advice of one service department, all the Apple's DMA chips were replaced, without effect.

There was only one consistency. The system would run properly without the PKASO printer interface. If the interface was plugged into any slot, whether using the printer or not, CP/M would self-destruct in anything from three minutes to two hours. Yet no problems were occurring under Applesoft, Apple Integer BASIC, Apple PASCAL, or any time the Microsoft CP/M card wasn't in use. Later, I also acquired Advanced Logic Systems' Synergizer™ kit and Personal Computer Products' Appli-Card as alternate CP/M systems. Under test, the PKASO board did not cause failure of the operating system with either of those. I also tried various combinations of plug-in memory expansions from different manufacturers. Similarly, the Microsoft cards were tried with various other printer interfaces, all combinations of which operated perfectly.

Eventually, it came down to one simple fact: the one interface card would not work with the Microsoft SoftCard and its version of CP/M. Those two cards, and only those two, somehow were incompatible within my system (though not on all Apples that I tried at the dealerships). The cause never was pinpointed, in spite of numerous replacements, returns for repair, and dozens of long-distance phone conversations. The only cure was to avoid using the printer interface with that Z-80 plug-in.

This points to important considerations for any computer user. First, make certain you have the right to return a plug-in for full refund within a stated interval. If you can't return it, don't buy it! Second, immediately test the card under all conditions you expect to encounter. My mistake was using the card under one operating system where it worked well and not testing the alternate operating system until weeks later when I had lost the right of return for refund.

Mechanical Components

There are a few mechanical components in the mainframe that may demand attention from time to time. These include cooling fans and front- or rear-panel switches. Fans must be kept operational, so you should replace a fan immediately if it fails. Also, the blades must be kept clean.

Front- or rear-panel switches can fail or work loose. Whenever the computer chassis is open, check switches to be sure they are mounted tightly. Retaining nuts and screws should be tightened if there is any evidence of their having worked loose. If a switch fails, even once, replace it immediately. Cam-to-spring switches such as key-operated power controls are a particular problem. The cams loosen and don't press the spring-loaded switch contacts properly, the spring-metal weakens with age and use, and the mounting screws work loose. Since switches often aren't accessible without dismantling the system, any slippage or failure that isn't readily fixed by tightening an easily reached screw or nut should be brought to the immediate attention of a service technician.

Many locking connectors have a limited number of opening/closing cycles. These plastic connectors typically join wires; they are not the card-edge connectors or cable-to-electronics connectors. Often, you'll find them on wires coming from the internal power supply. They usually feature some kind of molded locking device to keep the two parts attached. Such devices should not be disconnected unnecessarily because some have a life of only 20 to 30 disconnect/connect cycles.

Ground leads should be checked whenever you open the box. The chassis and electronics must be properly grounded for personal safety, static protection, and normal operation of the circuitry. Often, there is a braided wire attached to a metal rail or chassis bolt. Make certain the securing nut or screw is tight. If necessary, trace the connections from the incoming power line. It's not difficult to follow the third wire or ground through the incoming power connection and on to its branches reaching the chassis or possibly to solder "lands" on the motherboard. All connections must be secure throughout the system.

Conclusion

I've shown that there are many things you can do to extend the life of your mainframe. The procedures aren't particularly complicated, assuming your equipment allows you access to perform them. You can extend the life of the equipment through routine preventive care, you can often diagnose your own problems, and you may even be able to fix many of the most common failures. All it takes is some thought, patience, and the willingness to do something.

Yet there are many things you won't be able to do. Things such as troubleshooting individual CPU circuits or repairing a damaged power supply are better left to the authorized service technician. I don't recommend that you tamper with the equipment while it's under warranty or if you are paying for a service contract, but the procedures I've detailed can be valuable once the unit is out of warranty, the service contract elapses, or the service organization refuses to work on your equipment.

FIVE

KEYBOARDS, DISPLAYS, AND TERMINALS

To communicate with your computer, you need two devices, namely a keyboard and a video display. A few users still try to get by with a keyboard and a hard-copy printer, but the cost of wasted paper often drives them to a video display within a short time. Some small systems such as the IBM Personal Computer, Apple II, Apple III, Franklin ACE-1000, and BASIS-108 use separate monitors and keyboards. With these, a user can pick almost any monitor from any supplier, but the keyboard is obtained as part of the computer (built in or attached). Other systems such as the KayPro™, Osborne™, Otrona Attache™, and Epson HX-20™ have both keyboard and video display built in. Many larger systems, including S-100 bus computers, need a separate terminal or CRT (cathode ray terminal) combining both display and keyboard.

Regardless of the configuration, the keyboards, displays, and terminals are peripherals, not parts of the mainframe computer. They have to be interfaced to the computer electronics. Sometimes that interfacing is invisible to the user, as in Apple computers, and other times it requires one or more special plug-in cards. Whether you can see and control the interfacing makes no difference; it's there.

Each keyboard, display, and terminal requires certain attention. First, the devices have to be set up correctly. Second, they demand adequate preventive care. Third, they fail more often and require more remedial maintenance than the computer mainframe, though less than some other devices such as disk drives.

KEYBOARDS

Keyboards are notorious troublemakers, whether they are stand-alone devices, are built into a computer, or are part of a terminal. Except for touch-sensing keypads on a few recreational computers such as the Atari 400 and Timex-Sinclair units, they are electromechanical devices. The accent is on mechanical, and that's where most trouble occurs. Even though the keyboard generates an electrical signal and is packed with sophisticated electronics, the keys themselves are moving parts subject to wear and contamination. The more you use them, the more they wear. The longer you let them sit idle, the dirtier they get. It's a no-win situation. Either wear or contamination can degrade performance.

There have been many efforts to get around keyboard problems. The sealed touch- or pressure-sensitive keyboards are one approach. They don't have moving parts that wear out, and, since they are isolated from the environment, there's no interior dirt or dust contamination. But they're virtually impossible to use in professional applications because they lack the "feel" of a conventional keyboard. Secretaries, data-entry technicians, and others who do a lot of typing rely on both audible and tactile feedback to know that they've struck the key properly. With practice, most typists can tell when they've made mistakes because something does not feel or sound right. Touch-sensitive keyboards don't provide that feedback, and even "beeping" the computer each time a key is pressed doesn't suffice.

I'm not going to pay any further attention to touch-sensitive keys in this chapter. Since they are sealed, there's nothing you can do to prevent failures or fix them anyway. The only care needed is an occasional wipe with a damp cloth to remove surface dirt and accumulated oils from fingerprints. Just be sure to use a damp cloth and avoid detergents or solvents. There's no danger of dripping liquid into the keys, but there are often other openings around the keys for things such as cable connectors, power switches, and so on.

Other approaches to eliminate the problems of conventional keyboards have included light pens, touch-sensitive screens, and so on. The intent is to use high-reliability electronics to minimize or avoid mechanical gadgets. A light pen projects a beam of light onto a screen, and the beam can be detected by electronics. If the computer is properly programmed, it can recognize the screen coordinates where the light strikes as menu selections, instructions, et cetera. Touch-sensitive screens are similar in that the screen divides into electronic zones. Each zone then has a specific meaning to the programming. Both techniques assume the computer is programmed accordingly, however, and they often limit choices to selections from preprogrammed menus of operations. They are not suitable for writing programs, doing word processing, entering data, or doing other tasks not involving simple yes/no or multiple-choice selections.

So that leaves the conventional keyboard for most serious computer use. It also leaves the problems associated therewith, and the need for certain procedures to protect the keyboard and fix minor malfunctions.

Keyboard Setup

In setting up a keyboard, you're in one of three situations: (a) it's built into the computer chassis as on an Apple; (b) it's detached from but cabled to the computer the way it is in an IBM Personal Computer or Osborne; or (c) it's part of a combined terminal device that also includes the video display. Specifics on connecting and setting up terminals are included later in this chapter. For now, you need be concerned only with the first two types.

Built-In Keyboard. If the keyboard is built into the computer chassis, there's little to worry about. Connections are internal, and normal interfacing requirements have been established by the manufacturer. However, you should be aware of possibilities that might affect keyboard operation, depending on the equipment.

A good example is the Apple II keyboard. It's characterized as a typewriter-like, uppercase-only keyboard. Normally, it generates only part of the ASCII character set used by computers, and it lacks lowercase letters and many special symbols normally required for applications such as word processing. As a result, many users modify the Apple keyboard to obtain the missing functions.

Usually, the first modification installs something known as a lowercase adapter. This special circuit chip provides lowercase characters for screen display (not necessarily for printing), and it replaces the regular character generator near the front edge of the motherboard. Installation requires disassembly to get at the chip socket, and it is a warranty-voiding operation. Since the modification is desirable for word processing and many other applications, it's best to have the chip installed by the dealer before taking delivery of the unit.

Lowercase adapters aren't expensive, usually around $50, and a dealer can install one in less than a half hour. Be careful of two things, however. First, look for a chip with "descenders"—the tails of the lowercase letters g, j, p, q, and y extend below the line of displayed characters. Many chips do not have descenders, placing bottoms of the tails even with the line, raising the body above the line, and giving a display that's hard to read. Second, be sure to acquire the necessary programming or software for the adapter. Not all programs for an uppercase computer recognize or use lowercase letters.

This leads to a need for the single-wire, shift-key modification described in Chapter 4. A single wire runs from a pin of the Apple's gameport socket to a pin on the encoder board below the keys. As I said previously, soldering the lead immediately voids all warranty coverage, even if done by a dealer, so use only a test-clip for the connection. Be careful to follow specific instructions furnished with the lowercase chip or software requiring the modification wire. The usual shift-key mod for a newer Apple runs from gameport pin 4 to encoder board pin 24; running it between other pins or allowing bare wire to cross and short two pins not

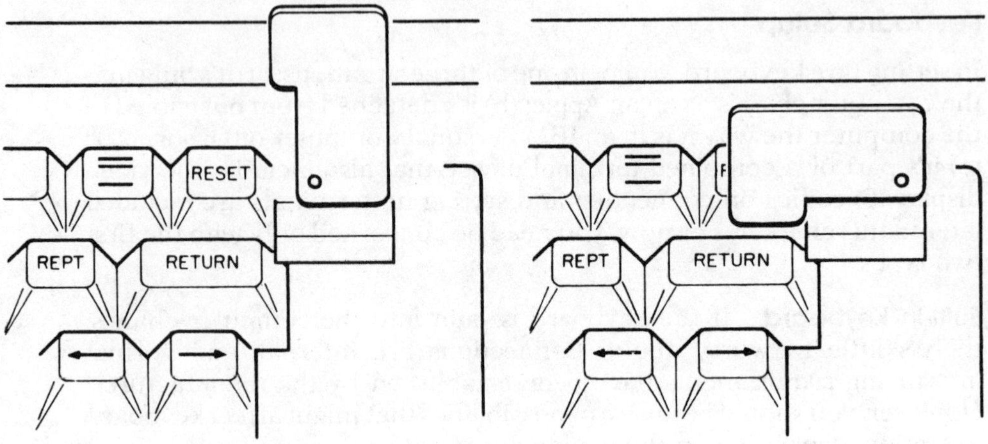

FIG 5-1 Reset Guard for the Apple II.

only prevents the modification from working but may damage electronics.

There's more! The Apple II keyboard encoder has a switch to change the RESET key operation. It's about the only modification that doesn't void the warranty. With the top cover removed, the switch is visible on the rear edge of the encoder board (hanging down into the computer below the keyboard). One position allows a computer reset by the RESET key alone, the other forces combined use of the CTRL and RESET keys. Instructions advise using single-key reset while learning the system, and changing to two-key operation later. I think two keys should be required from the start. Since CTRL and RESET are at opposite corners of the keyboard, two-handed operation prevents loss of programs and data due to inadvertently missing the carriage return and striking RESET.

For machines incapable of setting up a two-key reset, the RESET key can be blocked. For example, Compdent makes an inexpensive Reset Guard shown in Fig. 5-1. It fits onto the Apple and has a pivoting shield to prevent accidentally pressing RESET. Personally, I prefer setting the internal switch for two-key resets, but older Apples and some other machines may not have that feature.

There are, of course, numerous other modifications to add buffers for storing keystrokes and allowing faster typing, implementing self-repeating keys, altering the keyboard layout, and so on. One such device is the Videx Enhancer II, which provides those features, sets up shift-key modification without the separate wire, converts the Apple to a fully functional ASCII keyboard, and adds other functions. The device is not compatible with all commercial software, however. Installation requires complete disassembly of the computer, replacement of the encoder board, removal and installation of several chips, and running modification wires throughout the machine. At best, installation is time consuming. At worst, it is risky if not performed carefully and correctly. The detailed instructions help, but the procedure again voids the warranty, so users who don't feel comfortable playing around inside their computers should consult dealerships or qualified technicians.

These examples have dealt only with the Apple II. Since other machines may have different requirements and capabilities, it's important to study the manuals carefully. Follow procedures step by step without shortcuts. And don't be embarrassed to ask your dealer for advice and help before undertaking any kind of modification or alteration.

Detached Keyboard. Machines using detached keyboards may or may not have modifications available for keyboard operations and functions. If they do, follow the instructions carefully. They do have an added problem, however. The connectors at the keyboard and computer are weak spots, no matter what type of connection is used.

A few manufacturers use short, rigid cables to connect the keyboard and computer. Early Osborne computers were typical, and users began reporting problems of excessive cable wear, connectors dislodging, and so on. Other manufacturers use longer, flexible cabling that allows the keyboard to be moved farther from the computer and reduces strain on the connectors. A typical connection is like a coil-cord on a telephone receiver. In fact, several machines use telephone cords, complete with modular jacks. The advantages are that strain on the connectors is relaxed, connectors can be installed only one way, and replacements can be obtained from many sources, including telephone retailers.

Regardless, there always is the possibility of a bad connection between the keyboard and computer. Often this results from pulling the cord and damaging connectors or wires. Dropping a keyboard off the edge of a table and letting the cord take the strain is a common problem. Another is moving around with the keyboard and fully extending the cord to its limit. It's not a good idea to sit back in a chair with the keyboard in your lap. If you tip backwards or fall, you might rip the connectors free, not to mention breaking your neck.

Dirt and wear also interfere with connections, particularly in portable computers, which may be assembled and disassembled frequently. Anytime connectors are exposed to the air, there's the possibility of contamination and pin bending. Each time they are connected or disconnected, there's wear on the contact surfaces. Two steps can minimize the problems. One is to wrap the connectors in plastic or foam to prevent contamination during transit. The other is to clean the contacts periodically. However, don't use alcohol or other liquids on these connectors. I don't recommend using erasers to clean the metal, particularly with telephone-style modular jacks, since the contacts are delicate and easily damaged. You can use pressurized clean-air canisters to remove dirt and dust. Beyond that, inspect the cords and connectors frequently, and replace cords anytime they exhibit evidence of damage.

Keyboard Protection

A major concern has to be protecting the keyboard. It's also the best method for guarding against unnecessary problems. This means keeping liquids from spilling into the works, keeping objects from between keys, and providing a barrier against dust and dirt when not in use.

There are some basic ground rules. Never keep coffee, soft drinks, or other liquids near the computer. In particular, don't set drinks or cleaning solutions on any component, whether it's near the keyboard or not. I'm always surprisied to see managers allow employees to have coffee and drinks at their desks, particularly when the employees discover that heat rising from a video display makes a good place to keep coffee warm. It doesn't take much to dump liquids, and if they spill into a keyboard or other device, that's about it for the equipment.

Paper clips, staples, coins, nail files, and other objects are almost as bad. They should be kept away from the computer. If it is necessary to have stapled or clipped papers around, keep them on a surface separate from the computer and keyboard. It's easy to pull a clip from a sheaf of paper or extract a staple and have it drop into the machine, where it then can short out electrical circuits.

One habit is particularly bad: jamming an object into a keyboard to hold down a key. Sometimes, a key must be held for a long time, often to repeat something like a carriage return over and over again while scanning data. Users quickly discover the key can be pressed down and something wedged between it and another key to keep it down. Among the objects used are coins, pencils, matchbook covers, and folded papers. That's bad news for the system! If the object slips between the keys (and there often is enough separation to allow slippage), a conductive material could short the circuitry. If a pencil point breaks off, it also could short the system. I'm as guilty as anyone, but, if I have to wedge a key, I at least use something nonconductive such as paper, plastic, or wood. Obviously, soft materials are better than hard ones because they can't scratch or break keytops.

Keyboards should be covered while not in use, and covers serve two purposes. One is to keep from accidentally spilling something into the equipment while walking past or setting up for a day's work. The other is to keep airborne dust and contaminants from settling into the unit. Most small computers, at least those in business, are used about eight hours a day. The other two thirds of the time, they're idle but are accumulating dirt, so covering them should provide a substantial reduction in accumulations. There won't be a two-thirds reduction in dirt, however, because the idle time occurs when people aren't around filling the air with smoke and stirring up dust.

Many types of covers are available for different machines, varying from loose-fitting, soft-plastic slip-ons to custom-made gadgets for individual brands and models. Figure 5-2 illustrates soft-vinyl anti-static covers from Inmac that protect against spills and contamination while,

FIG 5-2 Soft anti-static dust covers. *(Courtesy of Inmac)*

according to the supplier, dissipating static. These covers are available for several keyboards, terminals, and printers.

Figure 5-3 illustrates the approach taken by Last Electronics with inexpensive Plexa-Lok™ keyboard "shields." Available for the Apple II, Apple III, Xerox 820, and TRS-80 Model III, these rigid acrylic shields are not dustproof covers. They are open on three sides, so some dust does penetrate, although there is a significant reduction. Unlike tight covers, they have the advantage of allowing a flow of cooling air, making it possible to keep the unit turned on and shielded at the same time. They also guard against unauthorized tampering with the keyboard which sometimes happens in offices or schools when the user is away from the installation—the shield has to be removed first, and that's far more obvious to observers than someone just walking past and tapping a key. On the other hand, there is one possible disadvantage. The supporting "legs" that hold the shield above the keys can scratch or mar the computer while sliding on or off. That's easily cured by gluing strips of felt or cork to the contact surfaces.

A tight-fitting, semirigid cover for the Apple II, called the Qwk™ cover, is available at low cost from Hutton Industries, Inc. (Fig. 5-4). It fits snugly over the keyboard. The contact points are padded with soft rubber to prevent scratching. Since all edges are turned downward or wrapped,

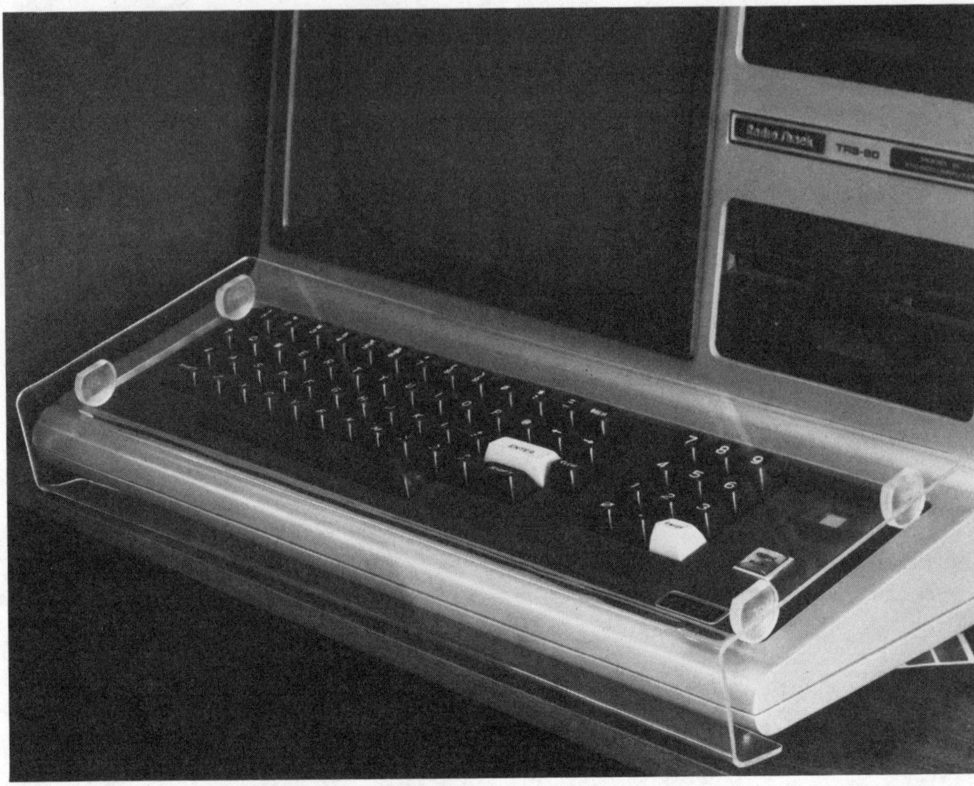

FIG 5-3 Rigid acrylic keyboard shield. *(Courtesy of Last Electronics)*

FIG 5-4 Form-fitted keyboard cover. *(Courtesy of Hutton Industries, Inc.)*

there is little dust penetration. It provides good dust and spill protection, although it's not advisable to run the computer with this cover in place because it does cut off the air flow. Again, there is some protection against tampering, although this cover can be popped off with a single finger under any edge.

The choice of covers is one of personal taste, and many people choose on the basis of appearance instead of function. Actually, they all serve the same purpose, and any cover provides protection. It's just that some give more protection against specific things than others. I don't know of any commercially available cover that I consider unusable. The important thing is that the keyboard be protected when left unattended. Since covers are available at prices as low as $10 to $20, there's no reason not to use them.

Keyboard Cleaning

No matter how much care you take to protect your keyboard, you still have to do some cleaning. How frequently and how extensively depends on the kind of covers you use, on how dry the climate is, on how much airborne pollution is around, on whether you smoke cigarettes, and on a host of other factors.

Include the keyboard in the weekly cleaning mentioned in a previous chapter. While vacuuming around the installation (power off, of course), put a narrow "crevice wand" on the vacuum and carefully run it along the separations between keys. Do this vertically and horizontally. It's not advisable to blow pressurized air into the keyboard, as that only forces dirt deeper, where it can do more harm. Having vacuumed what you can, inspect between the keytops for loose dirt or ends of hairs. Since a single hair crossing contact points can block operation of a key, manually extract any you can find, using tweezers if necessary.

Once every six months, remove the keytops for a thorough cleaning. Most keyboards have removable tops that can be pried off, but check with your dealer to be sure. As shown in Fig. 5-5, a thin lever can be inserted between keys, catching one under its edge and using an adjoining key as a fulcrum. Protect the fulcrum from scratching by inserting an open, empty matchbook cover or other thin cardboard between it and the lever. A metal fingernail file works well, but be sure it's clean. Pry upward on the key gently, supporting the edge opposite the lever with your other hand. It should pop loose and can be lifted straight up. Some keys, notably the space bar and return key, may have two or more attachments. Space bars are often further complicated by having hidden stabilizer rods. Be sure to release all attachments of oversize keys, and avoid removing the space bar unless necessary. Watch out for loose springs! Generally, there is some kind of spring mechanism to push the keys up, and the springs are often loose after the keytops have been removed. Don't lose any, and remember to reinstall them later.

With the keytops off, clean out the dust bunnies. You're likely to find accumulations of dirt around key posts and in corners, and hairs may be

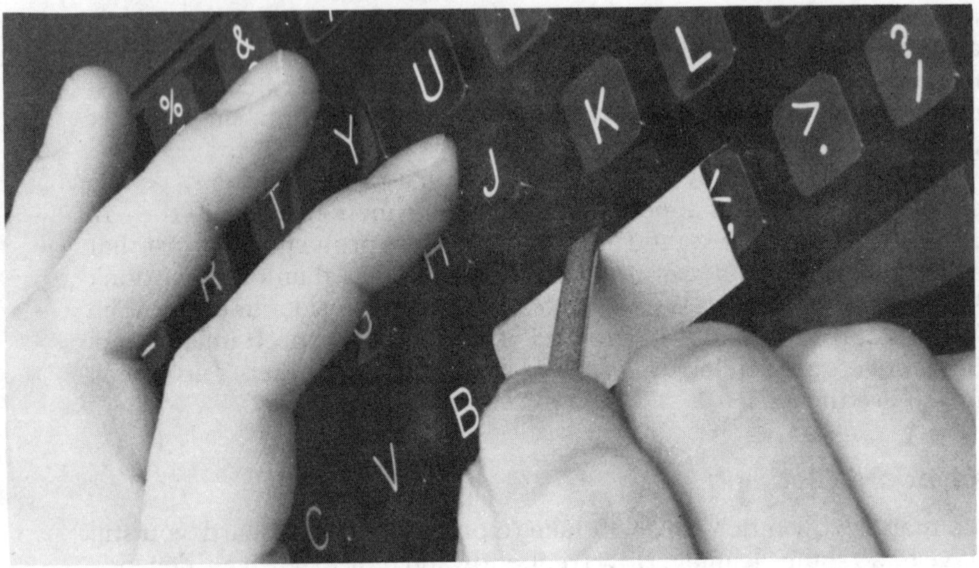

FIG 5-5 Keytop removal. *(Photo by author)*

wrapped around key mechanisms. If there are no loose parts, you can use a vacuum cleaner with a soft brush attachment. Otherwise, pick out the dirt by hand. Then clean the keytops before reinstalling them. I use a cloth dampened with alcohol to clean the keytops, rubbing vigorously to remove oils, grease, and smoke deposits. It's surprising how much can accumulate on the sides of the buttons in a few months. Be sure to test the alcohol on the bottom of a key first, just to be sure it won't dissolve the plastic. Also test it on a small area of a key letter—some letters are silk-screened or printed onto the plastic and can be dissolved by alcohol. If you see any rippling in the plastic or smudging of the lettering, don't continue with the alcohol. Try a soap solution instead.

When reinstalling keytops, be sure you get them in the right places and turned the right way. Refer to your system manuals, and don't rely on your memory. Be sure you reinstall any loose springs under the tops. For most keyboards, all you have to do is place a keytop on the post and press downward. It should pop into place with little effort.

This cleaning is about all you can or should do as a matter of routine care. As I'll describe in the next section, cleaning individual contacts is possible, but it is meticulous work and somewhat risky. As a result, cleaning contacts should be a remedial procedure instead of preventive care.

Keyboard Repair

Keyboard failures can be and usually are a disaster. Without the keyboard, you have no way to communicate with your system and give it instructions. When a failure occurs during a processing run—say the editing of long text with a word processor—there may not be a way to exit the program in a logical sequence that will save changes or text entered to that point. Shutting down is less than satisfactory because that probably will lose anything already entered, and it might even damage previously recorded files or disks. There's not much you can do about it once the failure happens, but if you are using backup disks, you should be able to hold your losses to just the work done during one session. The original then can be retrieved by recopying the backup.

The symptoms of keyboard failure cover a wide range. At worst, there's a complete failure to communicate—nothing typed reaches the computer. The cause can be an electronic failure that disables the keyboard. Or, it can be a loose connector between devices. For a detached keyboard, it's worthwhile to check connectors before shutting down. Sometimes reseating a loose connector will restore communications. Do not, however, disconnect and reconnect any cables while power is on. That can cause electrical transients, which might further damage the keyboard or mainframe. Instead, just press down on the connector, and see if that cures the problem. Be aware, however, that lack of communication does not always indicate a keyboard problem. It can also result from memory or CPU failures, power interruptions, or a "hung" computer.

Limited failures are far more common, typically appearing as the loss of one or several keys, but not complete loss of the keyboard. Most often, this is due to a chip failure in the keyboard circuitry, usually an encoder chip, or some contamination affecting one or more keys. I've had failures where a vertical row of keys stopped generating characters. About half the time, a service technician had to replace the encoder chips. But the other failures were due to a hair working into the keyboard and lying across a column of contacts, preventing the affected keys from making contact.

Another typical symptom, is "keyboard bounce." Pressing certain keys might transmit a character one time, not transmit another time, and transmit numerous characters at other times. If you were entering a program in BASIC, and the "O" key were bouncing, you might see entries intended to read "GOTO" actually reading "GOT," "GOOTO," or "GOOTOOO." Again, there can be many causes, including the encoder, a memory problem, or a CPU failure, but the most frequent is dirty key contacts. The obvious step after ensuring that connectors are intact is cleaning the key contacts.

WARNING: Cleaning key contacts is a high-risk procedure. It should not be attempted as part of routine preventive care but only to fix a problem. Even then, cleaning should not be attempted on any unit under warranty or service contract unless you have no other choice. Disassembling a keyboard will void any warranty and most service contracts. Consider the procedure a last resort, best attempted only if you can't get a service technician or absolutely cannot live with equipment down until a technician arrives.

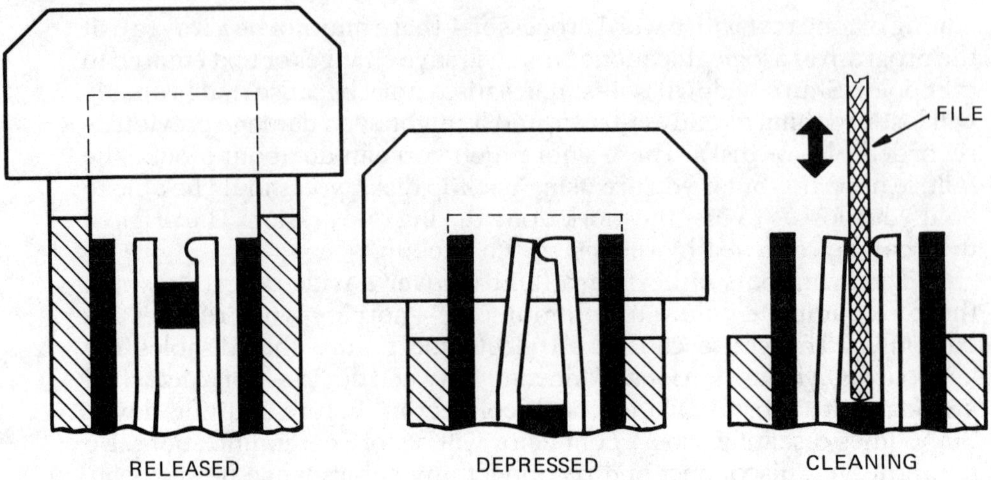

FIG 5-6 Key-contact action and cleaning for reed switches.

CAUTION: Contact cleaning should be attempted only on equipment having easily accessible contacts, and then only after having observed a qualified technician doing it. Most often, detached keyboards and those contained in terminal devices are accessible and pose few problems. Keyboards built into a computer chassis generally are too difficult to reach, may require a complete computer disassembly, and should be left to a technician.

To demonstrate what's involved, I'll describe the procedures for two types of keyboards. One uses "reed switches" as contacts, while the other uses "contact pads."

Cleaning Reed Switches. Keyboards with reed switches are the easiest to clean, but they seem to become contaminated faster than other types. Therefore, they require more frequent cleaning. In this type of keyboard, spring metal contacts extend up into the key housings or stems as shown in Fig. 5-6. When the key is depressed, the contacts are allowed to come together, establishing the electrical path that registers the character. When the key is released, the contacts separate, and the connection is broken. To clean the contacts, it's necessary to get between them, using something like the following procedure for the keyboard of a Hazeltine 1500 terminal:

1. With power off and the cord disconnected, use the procedure previously described to remove the keytop from the affected key.

2. Visually inspect the key stem for large particles of dirt or hairs. Carefully remove any dirt or hairs found.

3. Carefully check the operation of the switch. Press down on the sliding part of the key stem, and make certain the reeds come into contact. If they do not, stop here, replace the keytop, and call a technician.

4. With the key released (contacts open), insert a thin file between the contacts. The preferred device is either an electronic burnishing tool or a clean diamond-dust metal fingernail file. It's a good idea to wipe the file with an alcohol-dampened cloth before using, just to avoid any possibility of added contamination. Do not use an emery board or other device from which abrasive particles may detach.

5. Gently move the file straight up and down three or four times, making certain the reeds stay in contact with the file surface and that the touching surfaces are as "square" as possible.

6. Remove the file. Then use a canister of pressurized, clean, dry air with a narrow-tube nozzle to blow out any residual dust.

7. Reinstall the keytop, reconnect the equipment, power up, and retest the affected key. If it still bounces, repeat the preceding procedure. Then do any other affected keys the same way.

The trick to cleaning contacts is to wield the file gently, keeping it vertical and aligned with the contacts. Do not twist sideways or tilt the file, since that could bend the reeds. Be careful that the file doesn't slip abruptly.

Cleaning Contact Pads. Keyboards with contact pads are more difficult to clean because they require disassembly. However, since the construction that makes them difficult to clean also minimizes the dirt and contamination that reaches the contacts, cleaning is needed less often than with reed switches.

Contact-pad keyboards are recognized easily. When keytops are removed, there are no visible contacts. Instead, there is a spring-loaded plunger that slides down the stem into the assembly. The Cherry keyboards used by Applied Digital Data Systems' terminals, Qume send/receive printers, and other units are typical. The problem is to get the keyboard assembly out of the unit so that it can be disassembled. In a terminal such as the ADDS Regent 25, it's necessary to remove the top terminal cover. The keyboard rests loosely on four support posts and connects to the rest of the terminal through a single multi-wire connector. After you disconnect (noting the connector orientation), the keyboard lifts out easily.

Following Fig. 5-7, you disassemble and clean the keyboard as follows:

1. Turn the board upside down, resting the keys on a protective surface of plastic foam or other nonabrasive material.

2. Mark the positions of screw heads so that they can be reinstalled in the same locations. Some people scribe the board with a pointed instrument, but care must be taken not to cut or damage solder lands. The preferred method is to use a felt pen and put a small dot near each screw head.

FIG 5-7 Dissassembling a contact-pad keyboard for cleaning. *(Photos by author)*

3. With a small screwdriver, remove all mounting screws securing the circuit board to the metal housing. Be careful the screwdriver doesn't slip—it could slash across the board and cut solder lands.

4. Lift the circuit board off the housing, separating contact pads on the board from the plungers. Notice that the plungers have a layer of foam covered by metal foil. That foil may be dented, scratched, and marred, but don't try to do anything about it. In fact, don't touch the foils on the plungers at any time.

5. Examine the plunger assemblies and circuit board for accumulated dirt and hairs. Carefully remove any you find. Tweezers or a wooden toothpick work well for removing large contaminants, but be careful not to damage plunger foils.

6. Note the large, circular solder pads on the board. They are split into two semicircles. As plunger foils are pressed down onto the halves, contact is made, current flows, and a character is registered.

7. Carefully clean the solder pads. This is similar to cleaning card-edge connectors as described in Chapter 4. First, burnish the pads lightly

with a pencil eraser (not an ink eraser). Then wipe them with a clean cloth dampened in alcohol. Finally, wipe with a clean, dry cloth to remove any residue. Repeat this three times to ensure that the contacts are clean.

8. Replace the board on the housing, with the solder pads in contact with the plunger foils. Then reinstall all mounting screws to the same holes from which they were removed. This is important. If you get the screws into the wrong holes, slightly warped boards may not make good contact across the entire set of keys. Again, be careful that the screwdriver doesn't slip and damage solder lands.

9. Reassemble the equipment, reconnecting the keyboard in the process. Double-check the orientation of the keyboard connector. When you're finished, apply power and test every key. If problems persist, you probably need a service technician.

Obviously, this keyboard is not easy to clean, and most users prefer to let someone else do the job. Luckily, cleaning isn't needed often; I average one per year on my terminal, and then only if the keyboard isn't behaving properly.

Miscellaneous Keyboard Repairs. Aside from dirt and contamination, the other principal cause of keyboard failure is a fault in the encoder chip that converts electrical signals to character codes. Although this can appear as a total failure, I've almost always seen it as the loss of a group of keys, usually in a contiguous cluster. For example, I might lose two vertical columns, eliminating the 1, 2, Q, W, A, S, Z, and X keys.

The solution is to replace the encoder chip. I've had enough troubles over the years to justify keeping a half-dozen encoders on hand for each terminal. On one terminal, I average one encoder a year, but on another, I've used as many as eight in a two-week period. I even had that second terminal rebuilt four times trying to find out why it burns up chips, but never have solved the problem.

Be alert to possible retrofits authorized after a keyboard is released to the market. For example, two years after I acquired an ADDS Regent 25 terminal, I had a service call and was informed that a "bounce kit" modification had been authorized at no charge for all such terminals. The technician then installed a piggyback circuit board, thereby eliminating about half of the bounce problems I had been attributing to dirt and dust.

There also may be unauthorized modifications that can be performed after equipment is out of warranty. As an example, several technicians and service firms have told me there's a wire that can be soldered into the keyboard of a Hazeltine 1500 to ground out static discharges and reduce the number of encoder chips destroyed.

VIDEO DISPLAYS

Video displays are little more than specialized television sets. Many recreational computers are designed to use televisions for video displays, providing adequate monochrome or color video without the added cost

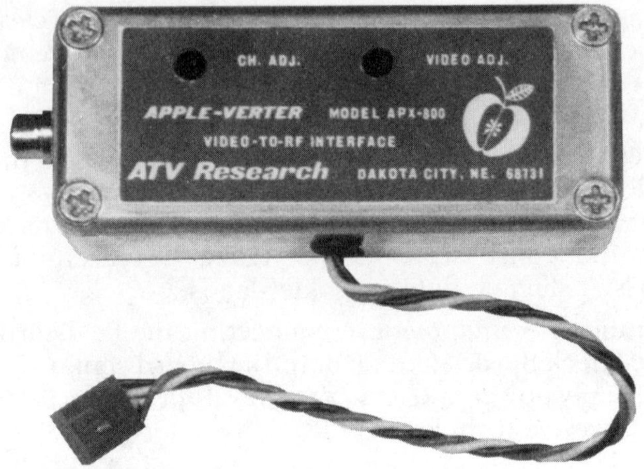

FIG 5-8 Typical video-to-RF converter. *(Courtesy of ATV Research)*

of a special monitor. Yet, for all but the simplest recreational applications, there usually are several choices to make concerning the type of video display.

Monitor Types and Setups

The obvious and easiest way to obtain a display for small computers is to use an existing television, either a black and white or a color set. Many low-cost computers such as the Commodore VIC-20 and Timex-Sinclair models are designed with that in mind, containing built-in connectors that cable to the antenna input jack of the TV. All necessary circuitry to provide an acceptable signal has already been provided within the computer. A user has only to connect a video patch cord between the computer and TV jacks.

Some machines, however, do not output a radio-frequency (RF) signal directly usable by the TV (the Apple II, for example). The video output jack on the back panel is intended for monitors, not conventional TV sets. If a color or monochrome monitor is used, all that's necessary is to run a video patch cord between the jacks. If a TV is used, a special video-to-RF modulator is needed. The ATV Research APX-800 Apple-Verter™ shown in Fig. 5-8 attaches to a motherboard video connector inside the Apple II and then connects to the TV. Similar converters are available from many manufacturers, using either VHF or UHF frequencies. The APX-800 shown is a high-range VHF unit claiming improved image stability by operating with tunable channels 7 through 10. Channels may be selected and tuned for optimum image quality. Some converters allow switching between computer and antenna inputs; others such as the one shown are not switchable and are intended for use with TV sets "dedicated" to the computer and not normally used for regular broadcast viewing.

Regardless of how they are connected, conventional televisions aren't adequate for most professional or business users. They don't have the image quality necessary for long sessions of data entry and processing, word processing, and similar uses. The user then must seek a better video display, often through a high-resolution monitor. Here again, choices have to be made. There are color monitors and monochrome monitors, with the monochrome versions subdividing into black and white screens, green-phosphor screens (green and black), and amber screens (yellow and black). Some are designed for use with light lettering on a dark background, while others are better with inverse displays of dark lettering on a light background.

Often, the choice is one of personal preference, although the application should be considered carefully. Color monitors are beautiful for graphics in business and professional presentations or for game playing. A good color monitor makes virtually any conventional television look shabby, but even cheap ones cost several hundred dollars. Yet color monitors often aren't a good choice if applications involve text, such as word processing, programming, or extensive data entry. Since the color display often causes raggedness and "bleeding" of letters, text can be hard to read. That leads to fatigue and subsequent inefficiencies. Conversely, monochrome monitors are less expensive than color ones, doing well with text but causing problems if a program using color graphics is being run. Often, monochrome monitors convert colors to line patterns, making it difficult to differentiate between the patterns and, thus, the "colors" in graphs and pictures.

With a monochrome monitor, the choice between black and white, green screen, and amber screen depends for the most part on which is comfortable. Of the ones I've looked at, the newer amber displays seem to have excellent resolution and quality. I'm not particularly fond of green screens because I have a vision problem that makes green difficult to see clearly. Far more important is whether the monitor is set up for light lettering on a dark background or inverted dark lettering on a light background. I have either capability throughout my own systems but find the inverted display is too hard to use for long sessions. The large field of intense light background causes fatigue and leads to errors. I don't even like inverted blocks of text for emphasis, finding them distracting, and I take great pains to modify software to eliminate the "highlighting" functions.

Once you select a monitor style, your decisions still aren't complete, because there are several types available. In the United States, two types of monitors are available, namely NTSC and RGB, with others available in other countries. NTSC monitors are the easiest to connect and use, normally requiring only a video patch cord between a computer and monitor. Some also offer a degree of flexibility, being usable on normal video hookups by changing a switch setting. I have an NTSC color monitor that is connected sometimes to a computer and other times to a video recorder for soundless monitoring of a program being taped or a tape being duplicated.

RGB monitors offer the best color displays—at a price. An NTSC monitor costs only a few hundred dollars, but an RGB version often costs well over a thousand. Furthermore, RGB monitors do not use regular video transmissions, instead accepting bit-by-bit data transmissions and using that data to control individual red, green, and blue projections on a dot-by-dot basis. Therefore, the computer must be equipped to send its display data in a form acceptable to the RGB monitor. Usually, this requires a special interface and cabling. Some computers have an interface already built in; others such as the Apple II require a special and possibly expensive interface board.

Monitor Care

Regardless of the monitor in use, there are some common care requirements, primarily in the areas of installation and routine preventive care.

Monitor Installation. Initially, you have to be sure the monitor is what you want. If you're not comfortable reading green letters, then don't get a green-phosphor monitor. If your emphasis is on text instead of graphics, stick with a monochrome monitor and don't spend the money on a color monitor that may not do the job. If you have a computer that outputs a signal for an NTSC monitor, don't purchase an RGB monitor. Don't try to use a television set without a video-to-RF converter.

Assuming you have acquired a suitable a monitor and feel comfortable with that acquisition, there are several installation considerations you should observe.

1. Keep monitors away from sources of direct heat. You shorten the useful life if the monitor is close to a radiator, fireplace, or wood stove. Similarly, keep monitors away from windows or direct sunlight. If you use a light pen for on-screen data entry or program control, be especially careful to keep away from bright light sources that might interfere.

2. Avoid placing a monitor on disk drives or a computer chassis. Keep it away from your disk storage. Electromagnetic fields, particularly those from a "flyback" transformer, can inhibit read/write heads, alter memory, or erase tapes and disks. If you must put it on top of other devices, at least shield things by inserting a sheet of soft iron or carbon steel between the monitor and the other devices. Heat buildups caused, in part, by blocking vents in equipment beneath a monitor can contribute further problems.

3. In multiple-monitor installations, keep monitors two to four feet apart to prevent interactions between electromagnetic fields. If you notice image instability, separate the monitors to see if interactions are the cause. If they are, move the monitors around until you minimize or eliminate the problem.

4. Place the monitor on a secure, stable surface where it's not likely to fall or be knocked off. Don't put it where someone walking by could

bump into it or hit the screen. Cathode ray tubes are fragile and can break, with disastrous results. If the tube cracks for any reason, even a bump, it could implode under the force of its own vacuum. The glass flies first inward then outward, posing an extreme hazard to the user.

5. Make certain all connections follow manufacturer's instructions. For monitors using video patch cords, be sure to use shielded coaxial cables. Attempting to jury-rig your own cable from bell wire or other unshielded wire only causes electromagnetic interference problems, both for the monitor, which receives interference from outside sources, and for external devices that receive interference from the monitor.

Care of the Monitor. Monitors generally do not require much care or preventive maintenance, and they provide long operational lives with minimum attention. The principal requirement is to keep them clean. Of course, cleaning must extend to both the screen and chassis ventilation slots. Cleaning should be performed at least once a week, and more often if the environment is particularly dusty.

Cleaning a screen is easy, though there's a little more to it than just spraying on some glass cleaner and wiping it off. Window cleaners are not the best choice for video displays since many screens have an etched or plastic overlay to reduce glare. Some window-cleaning solvents can react with the plastic and mar it, or they can leave dirt-attracting residues. Detergents, ammonia, and degreasing solvents should be avoided.

Check your monitor or terminal instruction sheet for a suitable cleaning agent. Some, such as the Amdek Video-300, specify alcohol. Others say nothing at all, and you have to guess whether they will tolerate alcohol or only water. Commercial screen cleaners such as the ones in Innovative Computer Products' Video Display Cleaning Kit (Fig. 3-1), their Micro Maintenance Kit, or the Inmac Clean Cycle Master Cleaning Kit are about 20 percent isopropyl alcohol and 80 percent "inert" ingredients. All such products should be tested on a small area in a corner to be sure the surface doesn't react adversely. The odds are against an adverse reaction, but it is possible that a manufacturer is using a coating that won't tolerate alcohol or some other ingredient.

Avoid spraying cleaning solutions directly onto a screen, no matter what the instructions say. The spray can accumulate into large drops and travel down the screen, entering the unit at the lower edge. Since you have no idea what, if any, electronics may be there, it's always dangerous to allow liquid to enter. Instead, have three clean, lint-free cloths available. Spray the first with solution until it's damp, not saturated, and wipe the screen. Be gentle; dust is abrasive, and rubbing vigorously could scratch the surface. Wipe off the solution with the second cloth. Now, dampen the third cloth, and rewipe the screen, giving special attention to corners and edges. Finally, use the reverse side of the dry second cloth to wipe a fourth time.

If you wish, finish the job by wiping the screen with an anti-static cloth. Do not spray with any anti-static solution as that will leave an unpleasant residue and could damage the surface. Anti-static sprays are intended for use around the installation, with the emphasis on the word around. They must not be sprayed directly onto any equipment chassis, magnetic media, screen, or keyboard.

With a water-dampened cloth (again not saturated) wipe all case surfaces to remove dust. Check ventilation slots on all sides to be sure they are not clogged. Pay particular attention to slots in the top, since these are vents for hot air and must be unobstructed. If you see any deposits, use a vacuum cleaner with a narrow crevice wand to clean them.

Check all connections between the video display and computer. Be sure video jacks and plugs are secure, and remove any kinks from cables or patch cords. If there's evidence of cord wear, particularly at the connector, replace it immediately. If a video jack is loose, it can be tightened by gently pressing on the sides of the plugs, or rolling the edge of the plug on a tabletop with light pressure. As with electrical cords, never pull on a video cord—always grip it by the plug and minimize any twisting as you remove or install it. Often the video jack built into a computer or monitor is a weak point, and excessive twisting of cable connectors can break internal connections. If the jack rotates as the plug is twisted, either replace it or have it replaced; sooner or later, internal connections will break, and it's better to do the replacement when convenient instead of after losing your display capability in the midst of a run.

Consider adding your own screen overlay. If your screen does not have an anti-glare surface, you could purchase and install one. You also might prefer a tinted overlay that alters the color or contrast. Personally, I don't care for these, but it's a matter of preference. Most overlays are thin plastic films that contact the screen surface. If your screen does have any anti-glare etching, you'll get light-interference patterns known as moiré patterns. You can get them even when putting a film on a plain glass. Besides, screens are curved and overlay films are flat—they never fit right and leave wrinkles, bumps, and other visual distractions. If you do install a film, clean and dry the screen first so that you don't trap any dirt between it and the overlay. Be prepared, however, to have later problems when you try to clean the overlay, since it probably scratches easily and there's always a chance of moisture penetrating between the overlay and screen surfaces.

One add-on may be of special interest if you worry about x-ray exposure from video tubes. For years, there's been a running controversy about radiation from television sets and video display devices. One side says that government standards for television sets are adequate for computer displays; the other says they aren't, claiming the government standards would allow too much exposure. One side says FDA (Food and Drug Administration) and NIOSH (National Institute of Occupational Safety and Health) tests found no dangerous emissions in properly operating video units, and the other counters that units emitting dangerous levels were considered to have been improperly operating and were excluded from the data. I could go on and on, citing numbers and extracting from reports and counter-reports, but it turns into a bottomless can of worms.

I won't attempt to advise you one way or the other. Besides, I don't know and wouldn't want to guess which side might be right. However, if you worry about x-rays, you might consider an inexpensive product called I-Protect™ from Langley-St. Clair Instrumentation Systems, Inc. This is a sheet of rigid acrylic which attaches over the screen with self-adhesive fabric grippers so it's easily removed for cleaning. The acrylic is impregnated with "microfine lead dust," giving a radiation shield equivalent to 0.15 millimeters (0.006 inch) of lead. The acrylic is made by a Japanese company that manufactures window materials for nuclear power plants, and the supplier claims it blocks all x-rays that may radiate beyond the screen. It also is supposed to block ultraviolet emissions, thereby reducing eyestrain and user fatigue.

While I can't report on the effectiveness of the I-Protect shield because I've no hard data of my own, there is one observation I should make. The current version is a smooth, flat acrylic and does give some problems with glare. In a darkened working area, there does seem to be some reduction in fatigue, as the manufacturer claims, but I can't be sure whether that is due to reducing ultraviolet or is just a subjective response because I expect it. In a normal room, however, there are enough reflections and glare to possibly offset any advantage. Supposedly, a future version with a nonglare surface will be available soon, and that should eliminate the only specific objection I've had.

Monitor Repair. A warning! Keep your fingers out of your monitor. All televisions and video monitors contain high voltages and deadly electrical currents. Unless you are a qualified TV repairman, don't attempt to open the case or do any work inside. If someone's going to get fried, let it be a repairman who gets paid for it, not you.

What can you do? Well, a few minor adjustments are possible using external controls. For example, most monitors have external adjustments for vertical size, horizontal and vertical holds, brightness, and contrast. Color monitors add adjustments for hue and tint, and they may or may not have others for sharpness and the relative intensity of the color beams or "guns." Beyond adjusting those in attempt to stabilize an image or improve visual appearance, there's little you can or should do.

You should have a usable test pattern for adjusting the monitor. The master system disk that accompanies an Apple II computer has a program that places color bars on the screen. With that, the hue, tint, contrast, and brightness controls can be adjusted for optimum color. If necessary, and only as a last resort, individual-beam controls may be used to adjust the image. Diagnostics such as Apple-Cillin II (XPS, Inc.) also provide some dot and line patterns that indicate "pincushion" or "barrel" distortion where the lines dip in from the edges or swell out from the corners. The fix for alignment problems, however, is usually internal and requires the aid of a technician. Similarly, color alignment problems where colors overlap, bleed into each other, or leave large gaps between areas all require a technician.

A few cautions. First, be careful with the rear-panel controls of a monitor. A few have knobs you can turn, but some have recessed screws you have to reach with a small screwdriver. I have a color monitor with recessed screws, and it uses metal screws instead of plastic. I've been zapped! It didn't take long to find out the adjustments aren't insulated or isolated, so sticking a screwdriver into the access hole while touching the tool's metal shaft earned a swift jolt. The most dangerous procedure is sitting or standing in front of the monitor to see the image and reaching around to twist a screwdriver. If I slip, I get a shocking reminder. A better way is to stand behind the unit, where the controls are, and view a reflection of the screen in a mirror. That way, I can see what I and the screen are doing.

Never put anything on top of a video unit. Spilled liquids entering the ventilation slots can "smoke" the unit and carry dangerous electrical currents outside the case. Solid objects block the flow of air, causing heat buildups, which shorten the useful life or create a fire hazard. Papers, drawings, and other flammables on the monitor could overheat, ignite, and burn you out. Don't leave a terminal or monitor switched on while it is covered; make it a point to check the power switches before covering the unit. Again, the rule is nothing on top of a video display. No exceptions!

Well, maybe one—some people working at home have pet cats. It doesn't take a cat long to discover the video display is a source of warmth, so there may be a four-legged critter parking itself on the equipment. It's not good, but arguing with a cat is an exercise in futility. Just be aware that the vents may be blocked and that pet hairs could get into the computer. At least move the cat every twenty minutes or so to allow the display to cool down. Incidentally, there's a special hazard here, since the cat may be annoyed by your work at the keyboard and suddenly leave claw marks in the back of your hand. Above all, don't let the blood drip into the computer.

One final note. Keep an eye on service technicians. The one thing you don't want a technician to do is touch the magnets on the video tube's "yoke"—the thin neck extending toward the rear of the chassis. Those magnets aim the electron beams so that they strike the tube properly. If misadjusted, the magnets can keep the entire unit from displaying properly. Most magnets are "locked" to the yoke by the manufacturer in preset positions, and few technicians have the capability of adjusting them correctly.

I had a $1500 video terminal ruined by a technician. He couldn't get the unit adjusted by normal means. Before I could stop him, he reached in and twisted the magnet housing, rotating it around the yoke. Then, he couldn't get it back the way it had been, so after five hours of playing with it, he threw up his hands in despair and walked out, never to be seen or heard from again. The terminal ended up with a "squishy" display—big, fat letters on the edges and little skinny ones at the middle. From then on, the display was virtually unreadable, could not be realigned by other technicians, and eventually had to be scrapped. Touching those magnets or getting anywhere near the yoke should be treated as a final option, to be resorted to when nothing else works and then only on the assumption it may do more harm than good.

TERMINALS

A terminal, more popularly known as a CRT (cathode ray terminal), is a combination device containing both keyboard and video display. It may be a "dumb" terminal that only transmits keystrokes to the computer and displays characters received back. It may be an "intelligent" or "smart" terminal that has its own memory, microprocessor, and other electronics for pre-processing keystrokes before transmission to the computer and post-processing data received.

Most microcomputer systems for recreational, business, and professional applications work with a dumb terminal, letting the computer do all processing of keystrokes and data. In that application, they are exactly what the name implies: terminals at which the data entry and display are the ends of an electronic track. You get on the track by typing at the keyboard, and you get off by reading the displayed return.

In general, the considerations concerning keyboards and displays already presented in this chapter are applicable to terminals. The keyboards must be protected against dirt and contamination, keyboards and screens must be cleaned periodically, ventilation slots must be kept clear, the terminal should not be on top of other units or next to magnetic media, and so on.

There are some important differences, however. A terminal is a sophisticated device requiring special interfacing to the computer. It doesn't use a simple video signal the way a monitor does. It transmits coded signals, which the computer then decodes for usable information. It receives back coded signals, which the terminal then must decode for display on the screen. Usually, terminals have little or no graphics capability and are reserved for serious applications where most work involves text.

Terminal Setup

Before you can use a terminal, it must be interfaced to your computer, usually through an I/O plug-in card installed in a mainframe expansion slot. A cable must connect that card with the terminal, providing the appropriate number of leads required for the specific interface. Most CRTs have what is called a "serial" interface requiring at least two wires, sometimes more. I'll be discussing interfacing at greater length in Chapter 10, but for now you simply have to be aware that specific hardware needs must be met.

Assuming you have the terminal correctly installed, there are several switch-selected features that establish communications between the devices. Usually, these are switches on DIP packages accessible from the back panel or under an access cover on the front or side of the unit.

Baud Rate. The baud rate is the single most important communication feature, determining the speed at which the computer and terminal communicate. Don't let the fancy word throw you. Baud rate simply indicates the maximum number of bits that can be transmitted in a second, so a 300-baud device can send or receive a maximum of 300 bits per second. With eight bits in a character, that's 37.5 characters per second. Typical terminal speeds vary from 110 baud to 19,200 baud, with 9600 baud being the setting used most often and achieving a display rate of 1200 characters per second. Since an 80-column by 24-line screen holds 1920 characters, 62.5 percent of the screen can be filled each second.

The baud rate at each end of the communication line (computer and terminal) must be the same. If it is not, one device sends faster than the other can receive, and "overrun" causes lost or garbled data. The usual symptoms of mismatched baud rates are a blank screen, a screen full of garbage characters, or a computer malfunction appearing as though the machine is "hung."

To fix the problem, turn everything off and check the settings at both ends. Because it's possible to bump a switch while installing or cleaning a card, start with the computer. If its baud rate is set correctly, check the terminal. If both are set to the same rate, the problem is elsewhere.

Some computers set baud rates for I/O devices via software. A typical example is a Morrow Designs' Decision 1 with a Morrow Mult-I/O board. The board has a default setting for each of three ports determined by hardware jumpers, but any port or combination of ports can be reset under program control. Therefore, it is possible that new software, particularly a new disk operating system, may reset the rate without your knowledge.

Table 5-1. **Baud Rate versus Cable Length**

Transmission Speed	Max. Cable Length
300 baud	4000 ft (2000 m)
1200 baud	1000 ft (300 m)
1800 baud	650 ft (200 m)
2400 baud	500 ft (150 m)
4800 baud	250 ft (75 m)
9600 baud	125 ft (38 m)

It's also useful to know the length of the interface cable between the terminal and computer. To some extent, maximum baud rate is a function of that length, and long cables require slower transmission rates than short cables. At least one manufacturer recommends the baud rates of Table 5-1.

Exceeding the recommended baud rate for a given length or exceeding the length for a given baud rate can cause garbled data transmissions looking much like improperly matched transmission speeds. It's also necessary for some leads to be twisted pairs at high baud rates or long cable lengths, usually having a signal lead and its ground return run as such a twisted pair. The manuals on specific terminals often have the necessary information on cable lengths, cable construction, and transmission speeds, so all users should read and follow the directions to achieve reliable communications.

Line Mode. The line mode may be either full- or half-duplex. Again, these are fancy words, but only indicate the path followed by signals. In the half-duplex mode, characters generated by the keyboard are "echoed" to the screen display regardless of whether they are transmitted to the computer. In the full-duplex mode, characters are sent to the computer, and the computer echoes them back to the terminal for display.

Again, there may be switch settings in the computer as well as the terminal, and the settings must be matched. Most modern microcomputer installations require a terminal set for full-duplex operation, where the characters are sent from the keyboard to the computer and then transmitted back from the computer to the terminal for display. The half-duplex mode then is useful for testing a terminal because anything typed at the keyboard should be echoed back to the screen even when it is disconnected from the computer.

The most common symptom of mismatched line modes is the appearance of doubled characters on the screen. This results from a terminal being set to half-duplex operation when full-duplex is required. A character typed on the keyboard is echoed to the screen by the terminal, and then echoed a second time by the computer. Conversely, a blank screen may indicate full-duplex operation when half-duplex is required, with no echo back from the terminal and none from the computer. Usually, changing the switch setting on the terminal eliminates the problem.

Parity. The communications feature known as parity is not often used by small computer systems. On some larger systems and older minicomputers, a special bit was assigned as a parity bit in each "word" of data. That bit could be either one or zero, on or off, "odd" or "even." Both the computer and terminal were set up to transmit and receive only data with the parity bit at the preselected value, and any data having improper parity bits were assumed to be in error.

The 8-bit microcomputers cannot, however, afford to waste a valuable data bit on parity checking and therefore have no parity provision for data transmissions. Therefore, most micros require that both computer and terminal be set to "no parity," "zero parity," or "mark parity" to ignore the error checking. If the devices are mismatched, communication between them is impossible.

The symptoms of a parity mismatch are somewhat unpredictable. On some systems, data transmission occurs, but data are incorrect. On others, no transmission occurs. On still others, strings of identical characters such as asterisks are displayed on the screen. Check your manuals to see if they address the matter of parity. If they do, set the computer and terminal accordingly. If nothing is said, try the "no parity" or "mark parity" setting on the terminal—it should work even if the computer is transmitting a parity bit, since the terminal may ignore the bit.

Automatic Line Feed. An improperly set auto line feed is a common problem. When strings of data are transmitted, they usually end with carriage returns. Unlike a typewriter, however, a return alone doesn't move the display to the next line, but moves it only to the left edge of the screen. A separate line feed is required as a distinct character to move down, and that line feed must be provided either by the computer or by the terminal, but not both.

If the computer and terminal both generate line feeds, everything typed appears as though it's double-spaced because the sequence is return, line feed, line feed. If neither generates a line feed, characters never move down but just keep overwriting the same line.

Since most microcomputer systems operate on the assumption that the computer generates the line feed, the terminal should have the automatic feature switched off. Some computers allow a switch selection, however, and some software overrides the switch settings, so there may be times when the terminal must be reset. Particular care is needed with word-processing packages for personal computers, and the software manuals should be consulted to see if the software assumes one function or the other. In general, if you see double-spaced displays when you want single-spaced, check that the auto line feed is off. If you see everything being typed on the same line, set the auto line feed on.

Miscellaneous Terminal Settings. Many terminals have other switches to control features not related to the communications. These are items of user preference and don't affect data transmissions between the terminal and computer. For example, there's often a switch that selects light letters on a dark background or vice versa. Another might switch an audible beeper on or off, allowing the terminal to beep each time a key is pressed and provide feedback to the typist or eliminate that feedback if it's annoying. Other options might include selecting alternate foreign character sets, reconfiguring the functions of a numeric keypad, changing the type of on-screen cursor (position marker) from an underline to a square block, and so on.

For these functions, there are no right or wrong settings, only preferred ones. Since they aren't matched between the terminal and computer, picking a wrong setting won't block transmission, generate garbage characters, or demonstrate any other errors.

Terminal Repair

As indicated earlier, terminals are combination keyboards and displays. Therefore, the same preventive and remedial steps are used as though the devices were housed separately. Since the procedures for cleaning and care have been described in earlier sections, there's no point in repeating them here. Refer to the sections on keyboards and displays, and apply the information or procedures therein.

One exception. Terminals do have to be opened to work on the keyboards, and this violates the rule I laid down about not opening display devices. If you are careful, you shouldn't have any trouble. Just remove the terminal casing, usually by releasing four to eight screws, and lift or tilt it off the base. Be sure power is off and the cord is unplugged. Be careful of short internal wires attached to the case, usually by clips. Since you don't want to break the wires, lift the cover gently and visually examine it for attached wires as you lift. If you see any in clips, they can be removed easily, or the cover can be tipped in the direction of the wires to avoid having to remove them.

Once the unit is open, you have access to the keyboard and decoder board, without having to venture near the tube or the power supply. If you limit your activities to the front of the chassis near the keyboard, there shouldn't be dangerous electrical currents. If you feel uncomfortable with the idea of opening the terminal, then don't. Call a technician instead.

It's often an advantage to observe how a technician works on a terminal. In fact, I recommend that you watch a technician at least once before you attempt to get into any part of your system. Don't be afraid to ask questions, particularly about the procedure for opening and closing the cover. Also ask for guidance about what you can or cannot do on your own to keep the unit operational. A good technician will tell you the best procedures for your equipment.

CONCLUSION

The devices by which you communicate with your computer and it communicates with you are sophisticated, delicate components. They do require attention, sometimes frequently. With reasonable care and attention, you can minimize problems caused by common hazards, and often can perform some limited remedial procedures after a failure.

Most actions you can and should take are limited to "surface" procedures such as cleaning cases and screens, positioning away from other sensitive components, and avoiding sources of heat, static, or magnetic fields. To a lesser extent, you can get below the surface and undertake the simpler forms of maintenance such as cleaning key contacts, checking cable connections, and so on.

SIX

PRINTERS

To receive outputs from your computer, you need either a video display or a hard-copy printer. From a functional view, video provides rapid access to information such as computed results, program listings, word-processing text, and so on. Such displays can be scrolled rapidly on the screen for examination or alteration. However, video is a transient thing, not an output suitable for sitting back and examining at your leisure. Furthermore, a screen allows you to see only a small section of information at a time.

On the other hand, hard-copy printers provide outputs on paper—a physical medium that can be examined, stored, handed to others, or thrown away. The printers provide a "permanent" record of computed information, programs, text, and other outputs, either for your use or for someone else's. Few serious computer users can get by for long without a hard-copy printer. After all, the results justify the means, and the most important results are those that can be used by people—on paper.

Since printers are, by nature, mechanical devices, they require some special care and maintenance. The electronic circuitry generally poses few problems once past the burn-in period, but the mechanics require almost continuous attention throughout the life of the unit. I'm going to deal here with the two most popular and widely used printers, namely the dot-matrix and letter-quality printers. Much of what I present will be applicable to other types as well, but regardless of the printer used, you should check the instruction manuals for specifics before launching into any but the most simple procedures.

Incidentally, few user manuals for printers contain sufficient care and maintenance information, yet not many manufacturers supply "service" manuals with the printers. Therefore, it's to your advantage to contact the manufacturer, requesting or purchasing the appropriate service manual. Read it, and follow its recommendations carefully. Be aware, however, that service manuals are written for technicians and contain many instructions you can't apply yourself, usually because you lack certain tools and test equipment. On the other hand, those manuals also contain necessary guidance for proper setup, cleaning, lubrication, and minor adjustments you can perform without outside help.

PRINTER SETUP

When you acquire a printer, regardless of the type, the first critical step is to set it up properly. Too many users get in a hurry, unpacking the unit, plugging it in, and switching on the power to see if it works—all without reading the manual first. The result can be a severely damaged printer.

Setup requires planning and logical procedure, starting with selecting where the printer is to be installed. There's more to it than just clearing an area of a tabletop and plopping the unit down in some convenient location.

First, the support surface should be separate from the one holding the computer and disk drives. Printers of any type cause vibrations, but letter-quality printers are the worst. Those vibrations result from the motion of the printhead, the impact of the print hammer or pins, and the drive mechanism that propels the paper. In turn, vibration can contribute to disk-drive malfunctions, loosened circuit cards in other components such as the mainframe, life-shortening filament vibration in cathode ray tubes, loosened interface cables, and so on. Therefore, printers are best installed on their own tables, preferably on special printer tables.

Second, the installation location must be within easy reach of the cable that connects the printer to the computer, while providing an unobstructed path for paper to feed into and out of the machine. Figure 6-1 illustrates a common way of setting up a printer to use continuous or "fanfold" paper. Typically, paper is acquired in a carton of 2000 or more sheets. That carton must be placed directly below the printer so that paper can be fed upward and into the machine without rubbing across corners or sharp edges that could stall the paper and rip the perforations between sheets. Most printers have special racks or paper guides as either standard or optional equipment, and instructions for their use should be followed exactly.

On leaving the printer, the paper should have an unobstructed path to the "accumulation point," which may be a box or stack on the floor or a rack attached to the back of the printer. I prefer a rack on the printer because it makes accumulated printouts easier to retrieve. But the most important consideration is that both paper supply and receiving rack be "square" to the printer itself. If the front and rear edges of the supply are skewed at an angle from the printer platen, or if the stack is shifted even an inch or two to one side or the other of a straight vertical rise, the paper can buckle, rip, and jam.

Another point! Paper must not be allowed to rest on ventilation slots along the upper rear surface of the printer. Many printers, especially

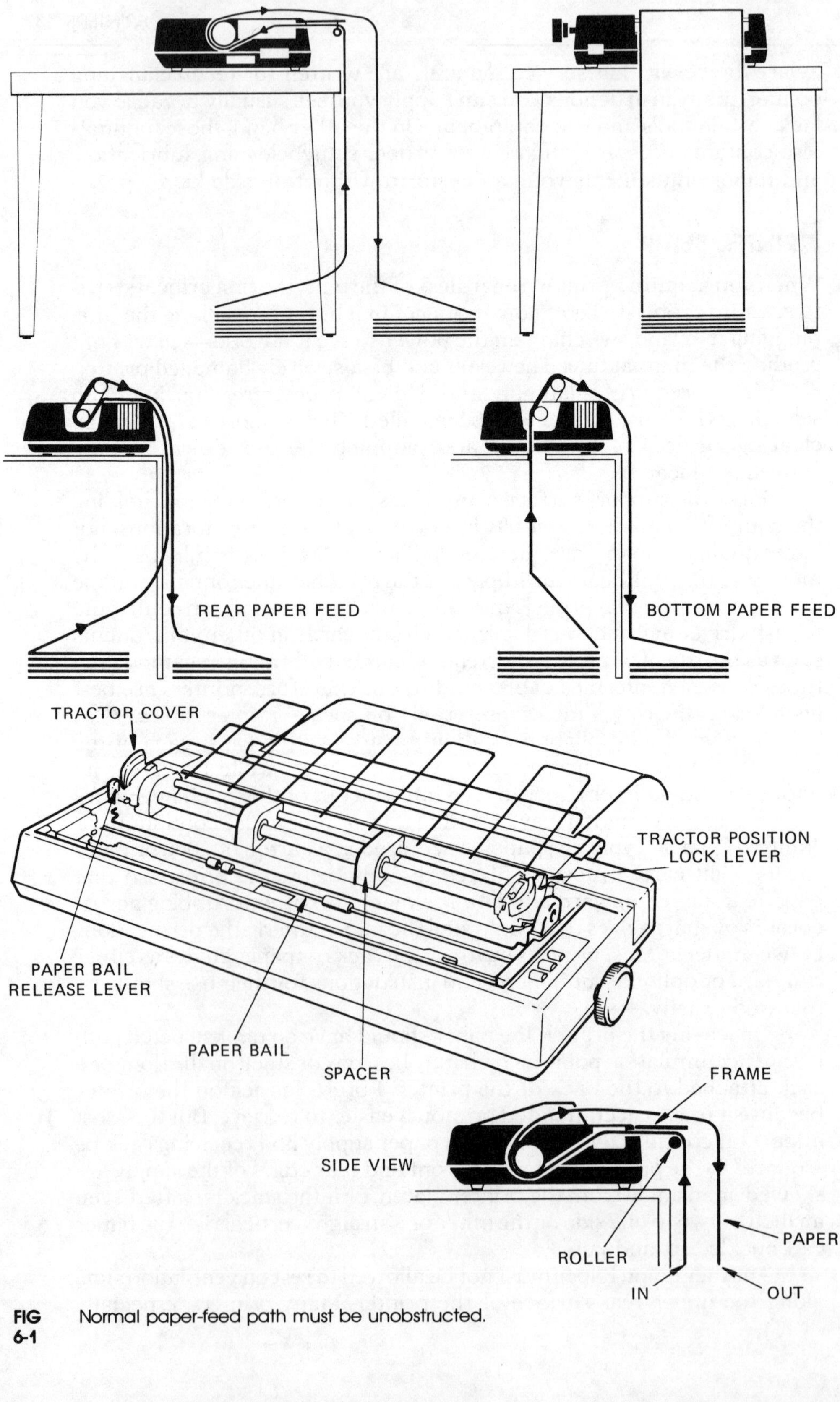

FIG 6-1 Normal paper-feed path must be unobstructed.

letter-quality types such as a Qume Sprint 5, have power supplies inside or attached to the rear of the chassis, venting below the paper path on a rear-feed arrangement. Such printers must be equipped with racks to guide the paper above the vents, allowing a sufficient flow of cooling air.

Let's jump ahead and assume you have a printer set up and running. You've installed a forms tractor to pull perforated, continuous paper through the machine but notice that perforation holes are ripping open, usually more on one side than on the other. There could be several possible causes such as something jammed in the mechanism or a misaligned tractor, but the most common is that the paper supply is shifted out of position to one side or another or is twisted as it enters the printer. As paper feeds, the printer tries to straighten it out, further twisting or skewing sheets and straining one edge. The result is damaged perforations, and the solution is to adjust the position and alignment of the supply so that the paper rises without twisting and binding.

Be sure you allow sufficient room around the side of the installation to change paper. It does no good to have everything correctly aligned and then find you can't get a new carton into position without moving the entire setup.

Assuming you have a suitable location and printer stand, check your manuals and the printer for any tie-downs and shipping screws. If the printer has been burned in by a dealer, this should have been done for you, but double-check anyway just in case the dealer says it was burned in but wasn't. Mechanical components are generally secured to protect them from damage in shipping. Most often, the printhead is secured with wire or plastic ties that hold it to one side of the carriage path. Meanwhile, shipping screws are often installed in the bottom of the case to keep the chassis from "floating," much as an audio turntable is locked down to prevent it from floating while being moved. Remove any such lockdowns *before* connecting the power cord, and keep them for future use if you ever have to transport or ship the printer.

If you fail to remove tie-downs and shipping screws, powering the printer could literally tear it apart. Rails can bend, belts can break, pulley shafts can shear off, and gears can strip if the printer tries to move the printhead while mechanical components are secured. It's a case of an irresistible force meeting an immovable object—something has to give, and it's costly when it does.

Read the rest of the setup instructions in the printer manual, and follow them to the letter. Improper setup is a frequent source of trouble, sometimes appearing as a machine malfunction or shortening the life of the unit. Pay particular attention to interfacing requirements, switch settings, ribbon loading, and "impact" adjustments.

Printer Interfacing

The interfacing requirements for printers are similar to those for terminals described in Chapter 5. Usually, there must be special interface electronics installed in the computer, either as a standard feature or as an added plug-in. Furthermore, the interface must be compatible with printer requirements. The most popular interfaces are either parallel or serial communication links, and within those two categories there are variables for which you must account.

Most printers impose an "either/or" situation—the printer is either a parallel type or a serial type. Parallel printers pose the least difficulty in interfacing, providing the interfaces are designed for compatibility. Different types and configurations of parallel interfaces are usually designed by OEMs (original equipment manufacturers), who obtain components from outside vendors and then combine components into a working system. Such designs are "machine specific" and could lead to situations where a given computer works with only one type or model of printer, or a given printer connects to only one host computer. These are often the least desirable arrangements because the two specific machines are tied together for their entire working lives.

Alternatively, there are "standard" parallel interfaces, widely used through the industry for machine portability and interchangeability. For example, many printers are provided with a "Centronics-compatible" interface. At the same time, suppliers of interface boards for machines such as the Apple often make their boards Centronics-compatible so they supposedly work with numerous printers such as the Epson MX-series, Okidata Microline™ series, and so on. There is a qualification you must recognize, however. Such printers often have some graphics capability requiring special controls from the computer. Furthermore, the graphics controls vary widely from one printer to another, unlike the straightforward printing of letters and numbers. As a result, even a "standard" parallel interface may not be fully compatible with a printer brand and model.

Serial interfaces are another matter. Most are designed to something called the RS-232C standard, which supposedly defines the signals used to communicate among devices. Many popular printers can be obtained or modified with circuitry using RS-232C interfaces, thus claiming to be universally compatible. However, as I'll show in a later chapter, the RS-232C standard is anything but standardized, and just trying to get all the wires of a serial interface connected and working properly is a chore. Much depends on how the printer or interface manufacturer chose to view a particular device, whether it's a sending or receiving unit, whether it's an originating or answering unit. In short, there's a question of whether a device is intended to be a DCE or DTE device—that is, data communications equipment or data terminal equipment.

Since I'll get into this subject in more detail elsewhere, let's assume you have a suitable interface that you've either set up yourself or had a dealer construct. The next problem is setting the printer's control switches.

Printer Controls

Almost all printers offer some control over basic operating functions. There may be external switches on the front panel or DIP switches inside the unit, but those switches are crucial to proper operation. Again, check the manuals for locations and settings of switches, but bear in mind that an erroneous setting could prevent proper printer operation.

Baud Rate. Baud-rate settings are used with serial-interface printers, not parallel units. The transmission speed of a parallel interface is preset, allowing the user no control. However, serial printers can be set to various speeds.

As with the terminals mentioned in Chapter 5, the baud rate of the printer is the most important communication feature, determining the transmission speed between the computer and printer. Again, there are usually several choices of speed, ranging from a low of about 110 baud to a typical high of 1200 baud or more. Probably the most common setting is 1200 baud (1200 bps, or bits per second), even when the printer itself is much slower.

For example, a 45-cps letter-quality printer might be interfaced at 1200 baud. At 8 bits per character, that's 150 characters per second. This doesn't mean the printer can exceed its 45-cps print speed or that information flows continuously from the computer at 150 cps. Instead, it means that data are transmitted in "bursts" at a maximum rate of 1200 baud for temporary storage in buffers until processed. Many printers are equipped with a first-in first-out (FIFO) buffer of limited size, say 256 or 512 bytes. The computer fires data into the buffer until the printer notifies it that the buffer is nearly full. The transmission then halts until the printer has processed and output enough characters to clear part of the buffer and accept more, after which the computer is notified to send another burst. Therefore, the "peak rate" is 1200 baud, but the average rate may be more like 300 to 360 baud.

As with terminals, the baud-rate setting at both printer and computer must match to prevent transmission errors. An indication of mismatched rates is garbled printouts, usually containing meaningless characters, losing margins, performing random form feeds, and so on. Anytime you see trashed printouts, check transmission speeds at both ends of the communication line. If the transmission speed of an I/O port is set via software, as it is with the Morrow Designs Mult-I/O board, be aware that commercial software may require modification. Also, check the cable lengths connecting the printer and computer; they must be within the ranges specified for terminals in Table 5-1.

Line Mode. Many serial-interface printers are equipped with a half-duplex/full-duplex mode switch, especially "keyboard send-receive" printers that may be used as complete communication terminals. As usual, the settings at both printer and computer must be matched so that the devices can "talk" to each other. A wrong setting shows as either no printout or characters being printed twice in succession. If odd printouts are noted even after baud rates have been matched, check the duplex switch and try the opposite setting. Often that's sufficient to start printing correctly.

Parity. Most printers with serial interfaces have a parity switch. As described for terminals, few modern microcomputers use the parity bit. Most printers should be set to the neutral position, called "zero parity," "no parity," or "mark parity." Check the printer and computer manuals first, however, just to be sure parity checking isn't required.

Often, a printer contains an internal switch called "parity disable." That switch overrides the settings of any other switches for odd or even parity. If your printer has a disabling switch and parity checking isn't required by the computer, set this switch to the disabled position.

The usual symptom of improperly set parity is incorrect printed data. If you see errors and can't eliminate them by adjusting the baud rate and line mode, try the parity switch. If it's set to anything other than no parity, disable parity checking and retest the system.

Automatic Line Feed. The auto line feed function must be set correctly, regardless of the type of interface. If the computer outputs a line feed command with each carriage return, the printer should be set to not feed automatically. On the other hand, if the computer does not output discrete line feeds, the printer should be set to provide them for every carriage return.

The symptoms of an improper setting are identified easily. If auto line feed is enabled and printouts have too many blank lines between printed lines, the printer switch should be moved to the off position. This would be something like a double-spaced printout where only a single-spaced one is desired, or quadruple spacing instead of the expected double spacing. Conversely, lines piling on top of each other without moving down the paper indicate that the auto line feed is off when it should be on.

Users of word-processing software have to be especially careful about this. Most such packages contain an installation parameter that tells the software whether to output line feeds with carriage returns. If the software is instructed not to output line feeds and the printer is not set to provide them automatically, lines will overprint one another. If the software outputs line feeds when the printer also is providing them, everything will be spaced twice the normal separation.

For most users, the printer should probably be set to disable automatic line feeds, and all software then should be set up to output a complete carriage return and line feed sequence. Whatever you do, be consistent. It gets far too complicated to remember alternate switch settings when you jump between software packages set up to function differently.

Modem/No-Modem Operation. With serial interfaces, there is often a switch selection for either modem or no-modem operation. The function may also be designated as handshaking or protocol communication. It is essential that this feature be properly matched to the computer for reliable communication.

This goes back to stopping and starting data transmissions when a printer buffer fills or empties. There has to be some communication between printer and computer through which the computer can be informed to halt its transmissions. The communication may involve either of two approaches, depending on how the computer has been set up. Often it is a function of the operating system software as much as of the hardware.

One method is known as hardware "handshaking," wherein special signal lines in the interface are used to designate printer and computer status. When the printer is able to accept data, it sends a signal on the appropriate line to the computer. When it's not ready, it removes that signal. The computer is programmed and wired to halt or begin transmission in accordance with the received signal, and it may also provide a signal of its own to indicate when it has data ready to send.

The other method is software "protocol," where signal lines are not used. Instead, the printer and computer communicate their respective functions by sending defined codes (ASCII characters) on data lines. This situation is similar to the classic representation of a two-way radio conversation, where the operators signal each other when they're finished by saying "over," "go ahead," or some other special word. In computer jargon, this is "acknowledge/negative acknowledge," "start of text/end of text," or "transmit on/transmit off" protocol. Often the terms are abbreviated "ACK/NAK," "STX/ETX," or "X-ON/X-OFF" respectively (or some variation).

The handshaking or protocol must be matched between printer and computer. If a printer is sending an electrical signal to halt communication while the computer is looking for an ASCII character command, the computer is not going to know when to stop transmitting. It will, therefore, continue to send data, overrunning the printer capabilities and garbaging the printout.

If both units are set for software protocol, they must be matched for "ACK/NAK," "STX/ETX," or "X-ON/X-OFF" functions. The functions denote specific ASCII characters with certain codes. Again, if the printer transmits one code while the computer expects another, the computer fails to heed the printer's demands, and the outputs are garbled.

It's usually not easy to change the computer's functions without major modifications to the operating system software. Instead, the printer is set to the desired handshaking or protocol. In a machine such as the Qume Sprint 5, the modem setting establishes hardware handshaking, while the no-modem setting establishes software protocol.

Note, however, that protocol and handshaking often are not required for slow transmission speeds. With printers operating at any reasonable speed, serial communication at 300 baud and slower is often accomplished successfully without concern for protocol. For example, 300 baud works out to approximately 37.5 characters per second, well within the printing rate of a 45-cps letter-quality printer without overrunning. However, interfaces operating at 1200 baud and faster almost always require handshaking or protocol for all but the highest-speed printers.

Some new, inexpensive letter-quality printers handle only 12 to 16 characters per second. If we work backwards, that means transmission rates faster than 96 to 128 baud require handshaking or protocol. It may be possible to run a 110-baud interface without special considerations, but not any of the higher rates.

Miscellaneous Printer Settings. Many printers have other switches for noncommunication features. Some items of user preference include character fonts on dot-matrix printers, page length in number of lines, amount of space to skip over perforations on continuous paper, stop or continue after detecting an out-of-paper condition, and so on.

There are no right or wrong settings, only preferred ones. Since they aren't matched between printer and computer, picking a wrong setting won't block transmission, generate garbage characters, or demonstrate errors other than possibly an undesirable format on the page.

PRINTER CARE

Printers are extremely complex devices, both electronically and mechanically. Open almost any dot-matrix or letter-quality printer, and you'll find an overwhelming assortment of parts and mechanisms. There are parts that slide, parts that rotate, parts that push or pull on other parts, and parts that are firmly fixed in place. It's the moving parts that generally cause the most trouble, yet they are the ones a user is least likely to be able to fix, adjust, or align.

Most printer adjustments and repairs are difficult to perform since alignments, distances, pressures, and other factors all are critical to achieving a quality impression on paper. Special tools and gauges are required for even minor adjustments, and attempting to alter one setting may disturb a dozen others. To protect your investment in the equipment, all but the simplest procedures should be left to trained technicians who have the experience and tools for the job.

Nevertheless, there are a few things you can and should do to ensure the best operation of a printer.

Printer Cleaning

Naturally, printers are subject to the usual problems of airborne dust and contaminants. In fact, they may be more of a problem than other devices because they contain moving parts subject to wear and are more exposed to the environment. Since paper must feed through the mechanisms, printers have large openings through which dust and dirt enter.

Furthermore, printers create their own problems with dirt. Simply feeding paper through the roller introduces fibers that detach from the surfaces and cut edges. Continuous-form paper—the kind with the perforated edges and fold lines—introduces more fibrous material than single sheets because the fibers detach and shed easily from the perforations. Furthermore, the punch holes for pin feeding the paper are often not cleanly cut, leaving small circular cutouts that are carried into the printer, where they detach and settle into the machinery.

Inked fabric ribbons add more fibrous materials worn or broken off under the impact of pins or print elements. Clumps of ink-permeated dust and fiber accumulate on printwheels and printheads. Fine particles of ink are spread throughout the mechanism, particularly when a new ribbon is first used. Carbon or film ribbons are less trouble, but they, too, can shed particles and contaminants.

With the combination of all dirt sources, the interior of a printer gets to be a dirty place. Since the affected areas are usually out of sight, most users pay them little attention. Yet those areas may be bearing surfaces for moving parts, where the dirt increases friction, contributes to increased wear, and could jam the parts. Therefore, thorough and regular cleaning of accessible printer parts is mandatory.

Carriage Cleaning. The entire area around the carriage or printhead assembly should be cleaned at least once a month (every two weeks under heavy use). This includes the card guide that holds the paper against the roller, the carriage rails, the printhead itself, and the floor and walls of the carriage chamber. Ribbons should be removed before attempting any cleaning. For letter-quality printers, the printing element also should be removed to protect it from possible damage. For dot-matrix printers such as the Okidata or Epson models, it may be necessary to remove the printhead assembly to gain adequate access.

Metal and plastic parts can be cleaned with a lint-free cloth moistened with a low-residue cleaner. The cloth must not be so wet that cleaning solution drips into the interior of the machine. Some printer manuals recommend using so-called "spray and wipe" all-purpose household cleaners, specifically the ones that don't require rinsing. If wiped off, they generally don't leave damaging films or residues, and they are effective at cutting through ink and oil deposits.

Do not use abrasive cleaners, not even the "mild" scrubbing compounds advertised for scratch-free cleaning of household fixtures. Those leave abrasive residues that quickly destroy bearing surfaces. Use alcohol on printer parts only when and where specified by the manufacturer.

Pay particular attention to removing accumulations of "sludge" on the carriage rails at the extreme ends of the carriage path. In printers where the carriage rides on oiled felt pads, be sure to remove the sludge from the leading and trailing edges of the pads, but be careful not to damage the felt in the process. Sometimes, those accumulations are difficult to remove, so you may have to go after them with a wooden toothpick or a swab, again being careful not to damage bearing surfaces, bushings, or felt pads.

Confined areas that can't be reached with a cloth should be cleaned with compressed dry air, dampened swabs, or both. Gears and similar mechanisms should be cleaned with compressed air.

Be sure to clean and examine areas around all interlock switches and optical sensors. There is usually some kind of detector to check whether the unit's cover is closed, and there may be others to detect an out-of-ribbon or out-of-paper condition. Switches and detectors must be unobstructed. I've been hurt by a letter-quality printer where the optical sensor for cover closure was blocked. When I was installing a new ribbon, the ribbon interlock engaged, the printer recognized the blocked sensor as meaning the cover was installed, and the printhead activated before my hand was out of the way. The printhead slammed home to the side of the machine, with my hand between it and the case. Ouch!

Finally, examine all parts for jammed paper fragments, cutouts from pin-fed paper, and other foreign objects. If any are found, remove them. Often, small tweezers can be used to grasp and remove such objects, or the end of a wooden toothpick can be used to work them loose. Be extremely careful with tweezers and avoid using other metal objects because they can scratch plastic and metal parts, causing more problems than the object being removed might cause.

Print-Element Cleaning. The printheads of most dot-matrix printers usually cannot be cleaned more than superficially. Since they do tend to build up deposits of ink-soaked fibers, you may be tempted to try. However, there is a danger of damaging the small pins if you attempt to scrape the deposits from the area, and liquids pose a distinct threat.

On occasion, a heavily used printhead may accumulate so much sludge that it starts pressing the ribbon against the paper and leaving smudges. You then have no choice but either to replace the printhead or to attempt a cleaning. Figure 6-2 shows a printhead from an Epson MX-80. Notice that the pins are recessed slightly from the front surface that contacts the ribbon. When you have removed the printhead following instructions in the manual, the front surface can be cleaned by carefully using a lint-free swab dampened with a low-residue cleaning solution, but the recess in which the pins sit should not be cleaned. The deposits in the recess around the pins generally won't cause problems anyway.

Print elements of letter-quality printers are another matter. Daisywheels, thimbles, and balls all require cleaning if used with inked-fabric ribbons. Those used exclusively with carbon (film) ribbons don't need cleaning because there's nothing on the back side of the ribbon to contaminate the elements. However, fabric ribbons build accumulations

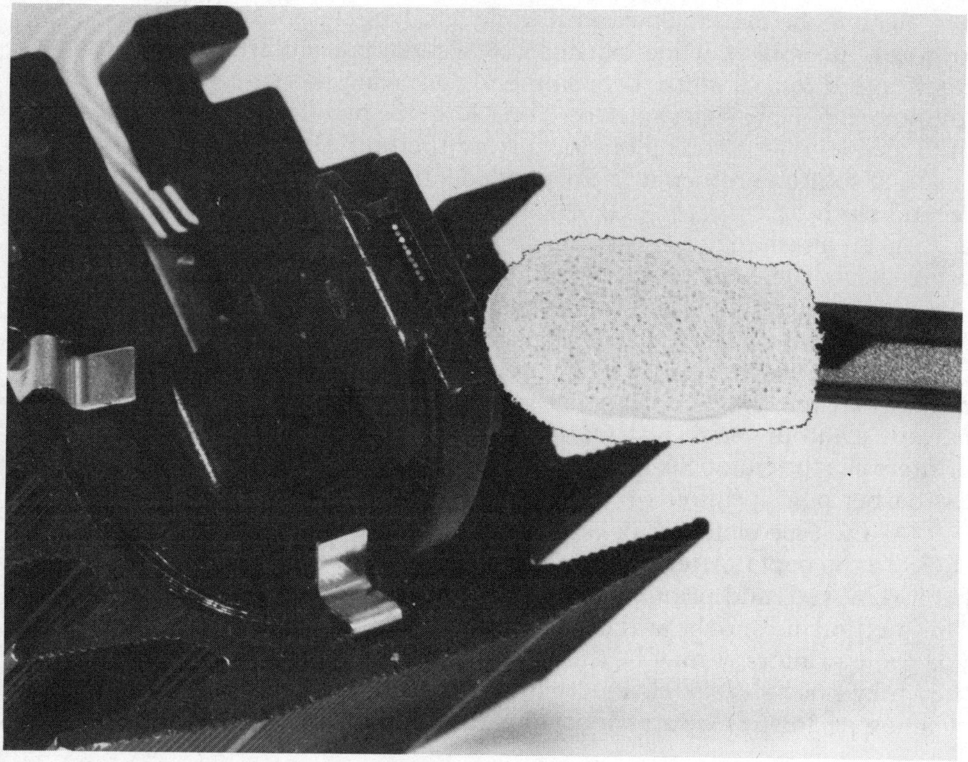

FIG 6-2 Cleaning a dot-matrix printhead. *(Photo by author)*

of ink and fiber sludge around and in the opening of letters, eventually "plugging" the letters and producing poor print quality.

I use carbon ribbons for final printouts of manuscripts, letters, and documents being sent to others, but I use fabric ribbons for rough drafts and internal documents such as accounting records. I usually stock three daisywheels of each font. One is for carbon ribbons only, another for fabric ribbons only. The third is a backup in case either of the others breaks. That way, daisywheels used for high-quality outputs never come in contact with fabric ribbons and never require cleaning to produce optimum print appearance.

Elements used with fabric ribbons require frequent cleaning. They may be immersed in a shallow bowl filled with the low-residue cleaning solution used for the carriage area. Soak them about five minutes; you will thereby dissolve most ink deposits. Using a typewriter brush (a "soft" or "medium" toothbrush also works), gently remove any undissolved accumulations. Finally, wipe or pat gently with a lint-free cloth.

Two cautions! First, brushing a type element is a messy job. Ink spatters freely, so this job should not be done while wearing good clothing, nor should it be done near any objects that might be ruined by the resulting ink spots. Once clothing has been stained by ink, it's virtually impossible to clean.

Second, be extremely careful while handling daisywheels. It's easy to break the spokes while brushing or wiping, particularly if a spoke catches in a fold of cloth. I recommend removing the wheel from the solution and laying it flat side down on a lint-free pad. Then lightly brush the type element, stroking outward from the hub. Dip it back into the cleaning solution, return it to the padded surface, and pat it dry with a second cloth.

As an alternative, it's possible to clean type elements in all printers using special "cleaner paper." A product called Typeface Cleaner from Inmac is typical. It's a box of fanfold material that runs through the printer the way normal paper does. However, the surface is coarse, fibrous, and absorbent. All that's necessary is to remove the printer ribbon, load the typeface cleaner as you load regular paper, and run a test pattern printout. Such test patterns are provided internally by some printers like the Qume Sprint 5, or they can be generated by the computer as "barber pole" printouts from system diagnostic software.

As the type elements or printhead strike the cleaning surface, ink sticks to the paper. After a few minutes, most sludge and deposits have been removed, and printout quality has been improved substantially. This method may not be as thorough as others, but it is more convenient. For some printers, it may be the only cost-effective solution; otherwise they may not be easily cleaned without calling a technician. And type cleaning performed by a technician is expensive.

Platen Cleaning. The platen or roller also requires periodic cleaning, usually once every six months. No matter how careful a user may be, there are always times when the printer activates without having paper loaded, thereby printing on the platen. Over time, ink or carbon deposits build and can transfer to the reverse side of printed sheets. Users who feed single sheets and print both sides also transfer ink or carbon to the platen when the sheet is turned and struck from the reverse.

The general procedure is to remove the platen from the machine, following the manual for the individual printer. Once removed, it then may be wiped with a soft cloth dampened with an approved platen cleaner. Alcohol, detergents, household cleaners, and similar substances are not approved cleaners. The Qume manual recommends a product called FEDRON™, but it's not always easy to find. Users should check local typewriter and office machine stores or service companies for a suitable platen cleaner.

Use extreme caution! Platen cleaners must not contact any plastic parts, or the parts will dissolve. Since such cleaners also are toxic and flammable, they may be used only in well-ventilated areas and in places where pets and children can't get into them. With any such substances, it's always a good idea to take precautions against accidental ingestion, eye contact, or excessive skin contact. Wear eye protection, and wash thoroughly after using chemical solvents.

Printer Lubrication

Lubricating a printer is a touchy subject. Some manufacturers specify lubrication of specific parts at regular intervals. Others say parts are not to be lubricated. Others hide the information in technical manuals not normally provided to users. Yet the simple fact is that all moving parts require lubrication of some kind to reduce friction. Furthermore, lubrication inhibits rust, so it may be crucial under humid conditions or for units operating in coastal areas. The trick is to find out where, when, how much, and what kind. One thing to remember is never use household or all-purpose machine oils in, on, or around computer equipment.

Consider a letter-quality printer such as the Qume Sprint 5. The maintenance and training manual, normally provided only to service technicians, stipulates a rigorous schedule of lubrication at six- and twelve-month intervals. Most procedures are easily performed by the user, but there's one for the print hammer that should be done only by a technician. I should point out that I've not found anyone willing to include regular printer preventive maintenance as part of a service contract, and it's definitely not covered under warranty. Most service firms won't be bothered with cleaning and lubrication, preferring to have users run the machines until they break.

Anyway, Qume recommends certain actions at six-month intervals or 1000 printing hours, whichever comes first. Specifically, they recommend the following:

1. Saturate oiler pads (felt) at both sides of the ribbon lifter and the inner bearing surface of the paper-feed gear. Refer to Fig. 6-3 for the locations. Qume recommends a medium-grade oil equivalent to Shell's Tellus 25™. This is one of the few times something must be saturated, but these pads provide a constant supply of lubrication to the parts between service sessions. A single drop of the same oil should be applied to the pivot point of the carriage-pulley lever, also shown in Fig. 6-3.

2. After cleaning the carriage rails with alcohol and a lint-free cloth, use a cotton swab to apply a thin, uniform layer of grease (Shell Darina-AX™ is recommended) to the lower bearing surfaces. Figure 6-4 shows the locations. The grease is applied over a distance of six inches by positioning the swab between the bearing and the rail while rotating the swab and moving the carriage. The lower bearings on both rails are done this way; take care to avoid excess buildups of grease. Oddly, Qume does not recommend lubricating the upper bearings that ride on the same rails.

Both preceding items can be accomplished without disassembling the printer or disturbing any adjustments. However, Qume also recommends that the print hammer be disassembled, cleaned, and oiled every six months or 1000 printing hours. That is not a user function, because careful and complete alignment is required during reassembly. The alignment can be performed only with suitable gauges provided by

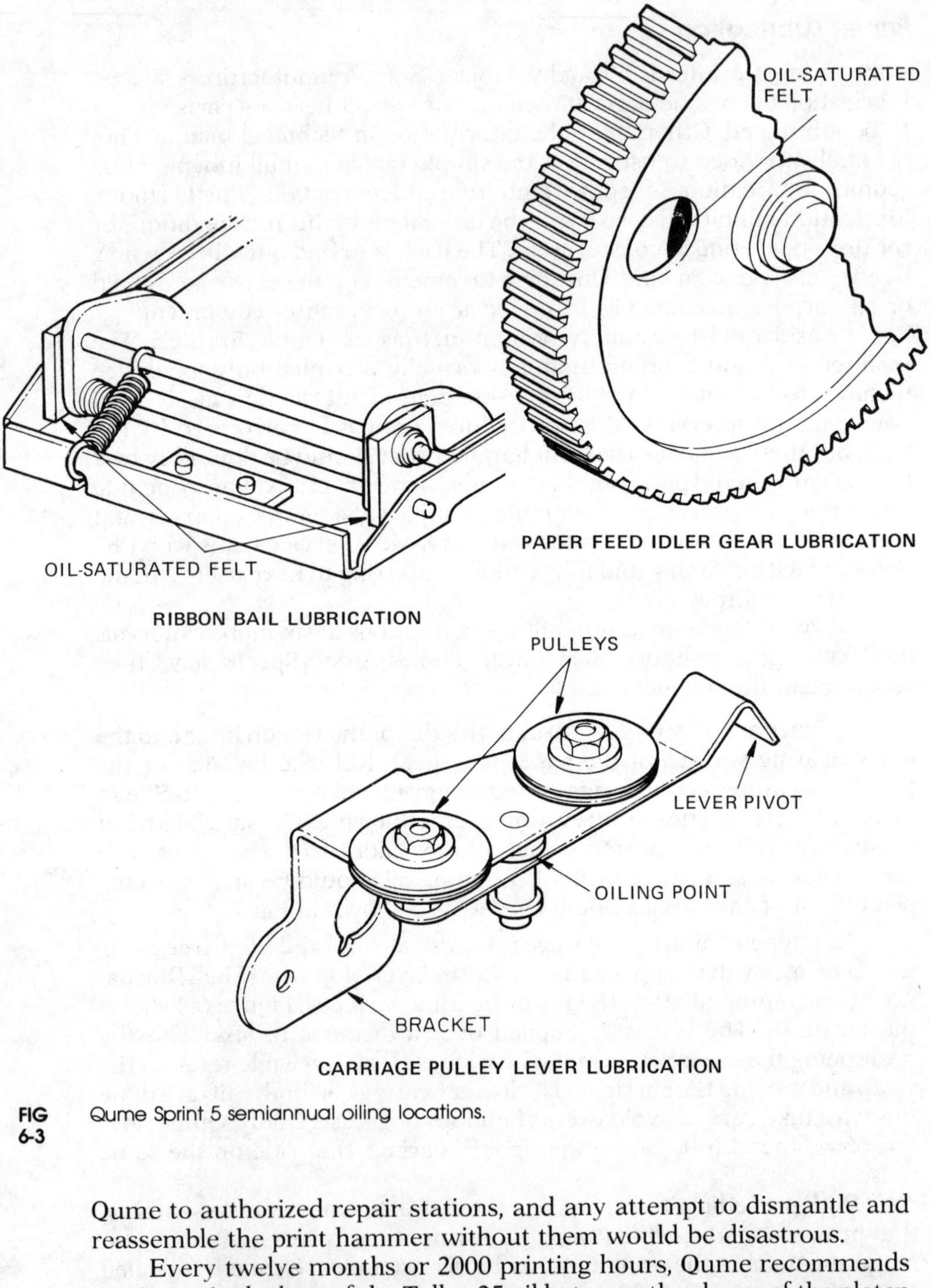

FIG 6-3 Qume Sprint 5 semiannual oiling locations.

Qume to authorized repair stations, and any attempt to dismantle and reassemble the print hammer without them would be disastrous.

Every twelve months or 2000 printing hours, Qume recommends putting a single drop of the Tellus 25 oil between the sleeve of the platen and the drive gear for the paper tractor. At the same time, single drops of the same oil should be applied to the ends of the platen shaft assemblies. These locations are shown in Fig. 6-5. The only disassembly necessary is

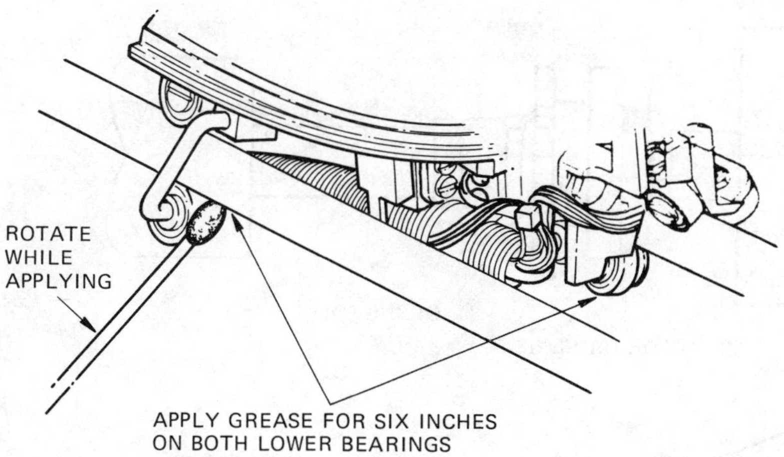

FIG 6-4 Qume Sprint 5 rail lubrication.

removing the platen roller, which the user can do easily with no effect on adjustments or alignments.

In contrast, the maintenance manual for the Okidata Microline 84 states that the dot-matrix printer is "maintenance-free, and no oil is necessary during normal operation." It adds, "Apply oil after disassembly, reassembly or cleaning." Since the manual does not specify an interval for overhauls, it seems to indicate that the unit should be run until it breaks down, taken into a shop, and fixed and lubricated at the same time.

The manual for the Epson MX-80 indicates, in an appendix, that two lubricants are recommended, with something called O-2 to be used on the carriage shafts and platen bearings every six months. The regular printer manual does not, however, identify other lubrication points or intervals, and refers the user to technical reference manuals.

Because of the sensitive nature of such lubrication procedures, I cannot and should not attempt to describe them. If I did, there would probably be something overlooked or misinterpreted, either by me or by readers, leading to potential problems and damage to equipment. Instead, I advise all printer owners to contact the manufacturers immediately. Beg or buy a maintenance manual for your specific machine and study it carefully. There's valuable information about how the machine works and what it needs—information you won't find in the user's instructions. Once you have the manual, decide what you can and cannot do for yourself, and make arrangements with another party to take care of items you can't handle.

Static Protection

Have you ever seen a printer with metallic fringe installed where paper enters or exits? Some people call them "fuzzies," but they're actually static brushes, and they serve a purpose. In simplest terms, paper fed

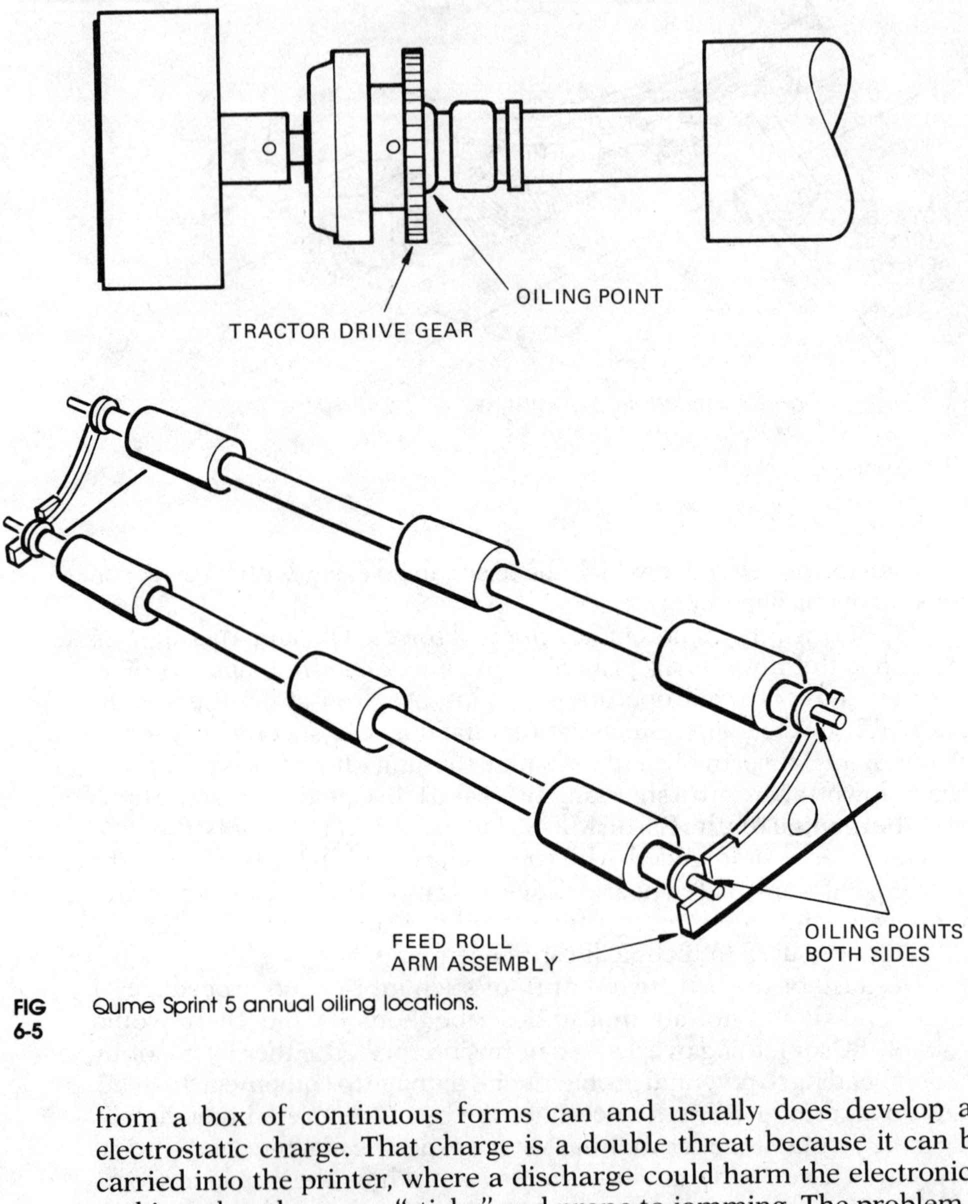

FIG 6-5 Qume Sprint 5 annual oiling locations.

from a box of continuous forms can and usually does develop an electrostatic charge. That charge is a double threat because it can be carried into the printer, where a discharge could harm the electronics, and it makes the paper "sticky" and prone to jamming. The problem is most noticeable with high-speed printers used on large computer installations, but it can be a nuisance to microcomputer users as well.

Both hazards are serious. A discharge within the printer can damage electronics, erase buffers, glitch printouts, and so on. A paper jam can damage mechanical parts, especially if paper wraps around the platen, bunches up, and gets in the way of the printhead.

By installing a grounded brush, usually on the input path, the static charge is neutralized before it can discharge to the electronics and without interfering with the paper feed. Most of these devices, such as the

Static Eliminator Brush from The Texwipe Company, are inexpensive and easy to install. They usually attach to the printer or paper rack, with one or two ground leads connected to a good earth ground.

Vibration

I've mentioned it before, but it bears repeating. Printers cause vibration! Some cause more than others, but they all vibrate. Therefore, they should be placed on surfaces separate from the rest of the computer system so that vibrations aren't transmitted to disk drives and other components.

It's also a good idea to place a rubber vibration mat under the printer. Actually, it serves two purposes. One is to dampen the vibrations and reduce physical stress on the printer. The other is to lower the noise level around the installation. Some printers shake so violently they "walk" across a tabletop or desk surface, sometimes moving several inches an hour. A vibration pad can eliminate that problem as well.

Even with the pad, there may be enough vibration to eventually loosen components inside the printer. Having had the problem of circuit boards working loose in one printer, I now check my units thoroughly every month. All cable connections are checked. The units are opened, and all circuit boards are reseated. Then, all mounting screws and bolts are checked and, if necessary, tightened. I find one or two loose items each time I check, with the letter-quality printer showing the most problems because its vibrations are much more severe than those of the dot-matrix printers. If a printer suddenly begins to act strangely or fails to operate at all, the first thing I'll look for is a loose connector or circuit board.

PRINTER REPAIR

There's very little a user can do to repair a printer once it fails. The procedures for disassembly, reassembly, and readjustment are complex enough that a service technician is almost always needed. Without tools and gauges specifically designed for a particular printer, the average user stands little or no chance of restoring an inoperable unit to usable status without outside help.

There is one exception. Worn printheads on some dot-matrix printers can be replaced with little effort. On an Epson MX-series printer, the head is accessible after removal of the lid and ribbon. By turning the locking lever clockwise, you release the head from its mounting and it can be lifted straight up and out to the limit of the ribbon cable. Securing the cable connector with one hand, you can grip the cable in the other hand and pull it free. The cable of the new head is then inserted into the connector, the head is positioned on the mounting bracket, and the locking lever is turned counterclockwise. After reinstalling the ribbon

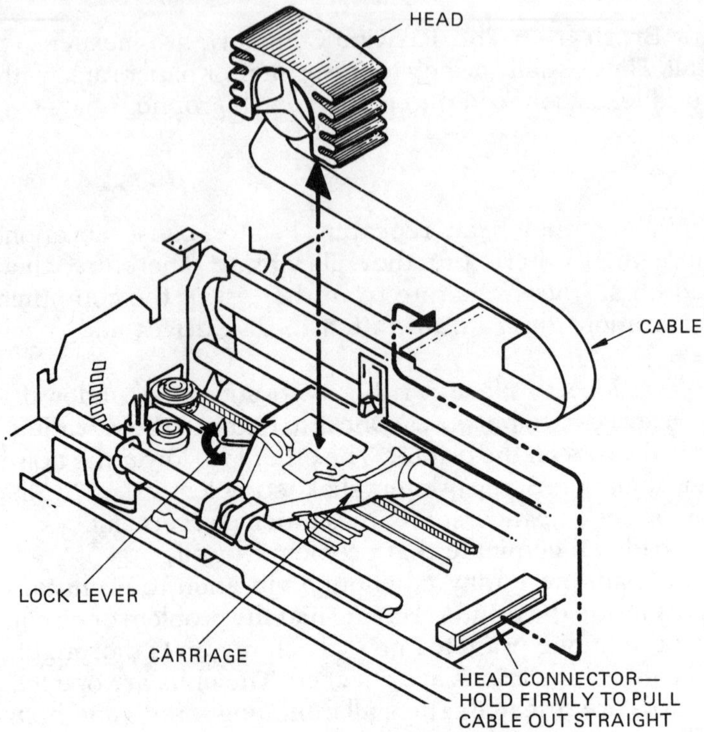

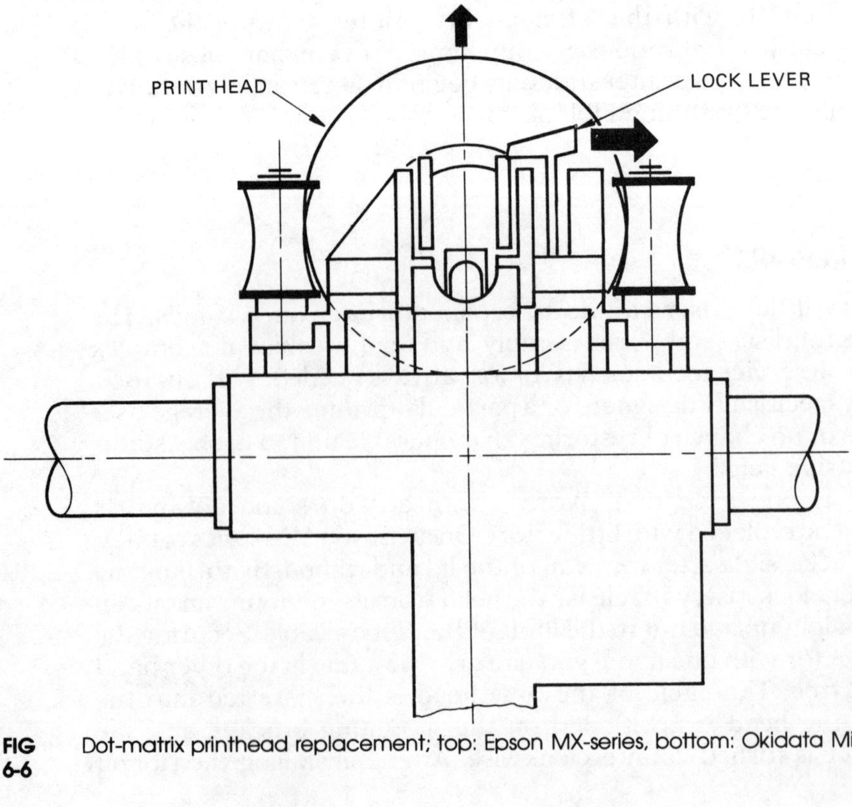

FIG 6-6 Dot-matrix printhead replacement; top: Epson MX-series, bottom: Okidata Microline 84.

and lid, you have an operational printer. This process is illustrated in Fig. 6-6.

The same procedure applies to Okidata's Microline 84, and to many other dot-matrix printers as well. The whole repair job can be done in less than a minute.

Use caution, however! Allow the printer to cool before changing a printhead or doing anything else that would get your hand close to the housing. While in use, these printheads get hot—very hot. They can leave some nasty burns if you're not careful.

OTHER PRINTER CONSIDERATIONS

Admittedly, the preceding descriptions of printer care are sketchy. I had hoped to be able to provide more information of a universally applicable nature, but it turned out that there are few consistent things about printers. Anything approaching a reasonably thorough examination of printer repair would occupy several volumes, each much larger than this book.

Before I leave the subject of printers, there are a few random considerations to present in the interest of lowering your costs and improving the performance of your installation.

Ribbons

Did you know that virtually all cartridge-style ribbons can be recycled? There are companies in most major cities that specialize in reloading printer ribbons. You turn over used cartridges or shells, and they install new ribbons and return them to you. The cost is usually less than one-quarter of what you would pay for a new ribbon, and the quality is usually as good as or better than ribbons provided by the printer manufacturer.

You also can buy recycled ribbons, though not at the same savings as having your own shells reloaded. Typically, purchasing a recycled ribbon costs from one-half to three-quarters the price of a new cartridge, but you still get a break. Then you can have those recycled when they're exhausted.

Some computer stores, repair companies, and others insist that running recycled ribbons will damage a printer. According to them, the ribbons jam, contain inferior parts, and so on. Nonsense! I've had ribbons recycled for five years, including Qume carbon, Qume fabric, Diablo carbon, Diablo fabric, and Epson MX-80 fabric. Some Qume cartridges have been reloaded 25 times. Rarely have I had a problem with any binding, jamming, or other mechanical defect. I actually see fewer problems with the reloaded cartridges than with factory-fresh ones. The only trouble I did run into was a bad load of carbon ribbons in one batch—the carbon wouldn't stick to paper. But the company took them back and reloaded them again at no charge, using a perfectly satisfactory stock.

You'll have to do some calling to locate a company in your area that specializes in ribbon reloading, but it shouldn't take too long. Ask around at computer stores (the professional kind, not the hobby shops) and office supply centers. Even if you're not immediately successful, don't throw away the used cartridges, because a recycler may open shop in your area next week.

I don't recommend re-inking fabric ribbons or rewinding carbon ones. There are machines available to perform both functions, and there are also companies that do the jobs. If you look at a used ribbon, you'll find that it's not just a matter of being out of ink or carbon. There's also physical damage. Fabric ribbons are especially troublesome because they stretch and distort during the many passes they make through the machine. Just re-inking them does nothing for the damage, and running such ribbons could lead to jamming and serious mechanical problems.

The Ribbon Lifter

Letter-quality printers often have a mechanism known as a ribbon lifter. It's the device by which the ribbon is raised into position between the print element and the paper from an idle state as much as a half-inch to an inch lower. The lifters can be real troublemakers on some machines. On a Qume Sprint 5, I've never been able to get the lifter adjusted properly. It's moved by an electromagnet, and the amount and speed of movement is a function of magnet position, tension on the return spring, and lubrication of pivot points.

I've always had one of two problems. If the ribbon doesn't rise fast enough or far enough, I lose all or part of the first word typed on each page. If the ribbon moves too fast or too far, it flips over the top of the daisywheel, lodges between the spokes, and breaks either the ribbon or the wheel.

Finally, in desperation, I wired the lifter into position. I held it so the ribbon centered on the print element, moved the electromagnet up against the bar it pulled, and used baling wire to secure the assembly rigidly in that position. No more missing letters! No more stripped daisywheels! All I lost was the ability to change between half-inch and quarter-inch ribbons. Since I use only quarter-inch ribbons, that wasn't any loss at all.

Impression Setting

Almost all printers have some means of adjusting the impression on the paper to accommodate various form thicknesses. Usually this is a lever to one side of the platen, and moving it allows single sheets or multiple-sheet forms to be inserted. It functions by a slight altering of the distance between the platen and the print hammer or pins, giving a harder strike to penetrate multiple copies.

It's important that the impression setting be returned to the single-sheet setting when you are not using multiple-page forms. Some users like to darken printouts by leaving the machine set for multiple copies, but it imposes unnecessary wear on the print element or pins. If you fail to position the lever correctly, you'll see an abundance of broken print elements or inordinately fast wear on dot-matrix heads.

Forms Tractors

Most popular printers can be equipped with a forms tractor. That's the device that sits on top of the unit and pulls paper through by the perforated edges. The device also can be removed when single-sheet feeding is desired.

Take care when attaching or reattaching the tractor. It's easy to misalign the gears, and subsequent activation could strip those gears. Follow instructions for your particular tractor, and rotate the platen a few turns by hand. Watch for binding or misalignment. Also, make sure the tractor drive rotates. If you feel resistance or the drive doesn't turn freely, you haven't installed the unit correctly. Do not apply power to the printer until you have corrected the situation.

Unattended Operation

It's not a good idea to let a printer run unattended. During long print runs, it sometimes seems convenient to walk away from the installation and let the printer do its thing for the next few hours. That's a dangerous maneuver! Suppose the paper leaving the machine doesn't fall correctly and bends back into the supply path! A closed loop forms and grows tighter and tighter around the platen, until the platen jams and the gears strip.

Suppose a ribbon binds in its cartridge! The ribbon drive continues to turn, tightening the ribbon against the guides and printhead until something gives way. If you're lucky, the ribbon will give first. If you're unlucky, guides bend, ribbon lifters collapse, and printhead alignment is destroyed.

If you do have to leave the computer while a printout is in progress, at least stay close enough to hear the operation clearly. Usually, a paper or ribbon jam alters the sound of the printing process, so you can hear when something goes wrong. If you do hear a change in sound not attributable to something like overstriking for boldface or underlined type, get to the printer immediately. If paper or ribbon jams are apparent, halt the printout and correct the problem. If there's no printed image on the page, halt the printout and check the ribbon.

SEVEN

MASS STORAGE

Of the components needed to make a working computer system, mass storage devices and magnetic media used therein comprise the most sensitive, most vulnerable, and most critical subsystem. Without magnetic media and the devices used to record and play back the media, the entire system is nothing more than a fancy calculator. It is mass storage that allows you to store programs for future use, create and save data for further processing or reprocessing, develop accounting records for a business, write and edit text files for letters and manuscripts, and so on. If you did not have a way to store such things for future use, you'd have to reenter everything every time you wanted to use the system, something far too difficult and time consuming to be practical.

In short, some form of mass storage is crucial to successful and efficient use of any system. Yet those devices are delicate. The tape or disk drives are electromechanical devices; that is, they combine both electronics and mechanics. Therefore, they are sensitive to each of the seven deadly hazards. Specifically, dirt and contamination, heat, magnetic fields, static electricity, power disturbances, mechanical wear, and mishandling all are mortal enemies of mass-storage subsystems.

To describe adequately the care-and-maintenance requirements, mass storage can be divided into two broad categories, namely tape and disk subsystems. Those are subdivided into other categories such as size, type, and technology used. I'll not go into the details of each possible category, but will concentrate on the most popular forms of tape and disk approaches, covering the drives in this chapter and media in Chapter 8.

There are many kinds of mass storage other than tape and disk. Some are punched cards, paper tape, and magnetic cards. Newer technologies, such as bubble memories and laser recording techniques, are on the horizon. But most of those are of limited application. The paper-based approaches are old technologies, suffering from slow speeds and cumbersome handling. They are gradually being phased out, even for the big computer systems, and are rarely, if ever, encountered on microcomputer systems. Bubble memories and laser recordings are too new to have gained a major foothold in the market, and they will be of limited interest until the technologies have been perfected and are available for widespread use at reasonable prices. Since limited subjects aren't applicable to a book of this scope, there will be no further mention of them in this chapter. Instead, I'll dwell on the magnetic media for the most popular recreational and small-business systems.

TAPE SUBSYSTEMS

Of the two popular approaches to mass storage, the most elementary is magnetic tape. It's a technology not unlike audio and video recording, where a ribbon of plastic-like material is coated with an oxide layer sensitive to changes in magnetic "flux." Just as sound can be converted to electrical signals and recorded on tape, digital data already existing as electrical on or off signals can be recorded. In fact, some tape subsystems for microcomputers use an audio signal that almost sounds like music when played back through a speaker.

There are three types of tape subsystems, specifically cassette, cartridge, and reel-to-reel. The most popular and most likely to be encountered with microcomputer systems is the cassette. Yet all three operate on similar principles, differing primarily in the packaging and the mechanical drive assemblies used to move the tape from the "supply" to the "take-up." All are available in various sizes. Cassettes can be obtained in the conventional audio sizes offering from thirty minutes to an hour or more of recording time. Microcassettes also are available, using tapes originally intended for dictating equipment and offering storage capacities as high as two hours each. Cartridges—basically elaborate cassettes specially designed for data storage—come in regular, mini, and micro sizes, again offering various recording times. Reel-to-reel tapes can be obtained in 3-inch reels, 7-inch reels, and even 15-inch reels, along with variations in availability for audio recorders or data recorders.

As a rule, reel-to-reel computer tape drives are limited to large-scale fixed or permanent minicomputer or "mainframe" installations. They are expensive devices not often used with microcomputers. Some micro owners do, however, like to use reel-to-reel audio recorders, substituting them for the cassette recorders for which the computers were intended. Cartridge drives also are expensive, although they can be obtained in portable versions suitable for microcomputers. However, high cost and a lack of operating flexibility limit them to sophisticated applications, often business or scientific, requiring higher data reliability than can be obtained with cassettes. To an extent, tape cartridge drives are finding a place in the micro market, but most often as backups for hard disks.

That leaves conventional cassette drives as the typical low-cost medium for micros. Many micros, especially those for home, hobby, and

FIG 7-1 Epson HX-20 computer. *(Courtesy of Epson-America, Inc.)*

recreational markets, are designed specifically for tape cassettes and often appear first with only that capability. Disk facilities are usually added sometime later. The Apple II was such a machine, as were the Atari units, the Commodore VIC-20, the Epson HX-20 pictured in Fig. 7-1, and many others. Sometimes, special hookups are possible to other devices like reel-to-reel tapes, but cassettes are the initial "standard." The Epson HX-20 is somewhat unique because it can accommodate its own microcassette module inserted at the upper right corner, or it can be wired to an external audio cassette unit through three connectors along the right side of the case.

Tape-Drive Setup

Depending on the tape drive, connecting to the computer can be anything from extremely complex to extremely simple. The more elaborate digital reel-to-reel and cartridge recorders usually require their own special interfaces, much the way a terminal or printer does. Since these devices are designed specifically for data storage, they often incorporate many "high-tech" features such as automatic stopping and starting, formatting data into pre-sized "blocks," verifying recorded data to make sure what got onto tape is the same as what was sent by the computer, controllable searching for specific data sequences or "file marks" that indicate starting and stopping points, automatic read-after-write verifying with unattended backup and rewrite operations if a data error is encountered, and so on.

The interfaces are often designed for individual tape drives, and the computer must be able to support the required functions, through special electronics, special software, or both. Of course, all the control electronics and mechanics involved push the cost up, often to a level where such devices are beyond the budgets of individuals and many small businesses. Furthermore, the units are subject to all the setup requirements affecting terminals and printers, including matching baud rates, parity, start and stop bits, and so on.

For micro users, a simple audio-style hookup usually suffices, especially for computers working with conventional audio cassettes. There often are no fancy features like automatic starting and stopping, verifying, or searching, but the units do work well for sequential recording and retrieving of programs and data. Although the strictly sequential read and write operations get to be tedious and annoying for any serious computer user, they're a lot better than the old punched-card and paper-tape methods. Those same inconveniences lead most users, even hobby and recreational types, to seek disk-drive capabilities for the machine eventually. Once disk facilities are added, cassettes are relegated to backup status or are discarded entirely. Yet until that time, it's essential that tape units be properly connected, operated, and maintained to ensure maximum reliability.

General Installation Guidelines. Assume you are installing and connecting a cassette recorder. The first problem is to find a suitable location. Like other electronics, the unit must be positioned away from heat sources, preferably on a static-free surface. It must be several feet from sources of magnetic fields such as tools, telephones, and speakers, and it should be located so that the drive is accessible for cleaning. It does no harm to connect the power cord through some kind of power-conditioning equipment, even if just a surge protector.

Be aware that voltage fluctuations can affect the motor speed, thereby changing the speed of tape movement across the head. Such variations in tape speed often are sufficient to garble data during recording or playback. Similarly, audio recorders operated from batteries have distinct and possibly disruptive speed variations. Since new or freshly recharged batteries run the drive motors faster and more smoothly than old or rundown ones, recording with new batteries and then playing back with old ones will cause data-reliability problems. Just as the sound of an audio recorder deteriorates as the batteries run down, the quality and "integrity" of the data read back or recorded will decline. In extreme cases, severe data misreads or miswrites occur, leading to trashed and unusable data or programs. For computer use, recorders should not be run from batteries. Use the power cord if one is provided, or purchase a suitable ac/dc adapter—either gives far better performance than batteries.

For the same reason, only capstan-drive recorders should be used. Some recorders simply rotate the take-up spool, using it to pull the tape across the heads from the supply spool. They generally have poor speed control, as evidenced by distortion even in audio use, and they can stretch and distort the tape itself. Either causes data problems, and the latter can cause permanent damage to the tape and all recorded contents. Capstan drives, on the other hand, not only turn the take-up but have motor-driven shafts that drive the tape at a more uniform speed across the heads, thus providing more uniform data recording and playback with far fewer problems.

Similarly, the drive speed itself is of some concern. Some recorders, particularly microcassette types for dictating equipment, are being sold with two- or three-speed operation. With such units, it's crucial that the fastest available speed be used. That's comparable to audio and video recordings, where higher speeds yield better sound or image reproduction. The same holds for data recording—the higher the speed, the more reliable the data will be.

The Audio Hookup. The audio hookup itself is usually simple. Either two or three wires connect the computer to the recorder. With a computer like the Apple II, only two wires are used. One connects the MIC (microphone) input of the recorder to the computer output, while the other connects the EAR (earphone) recorder output to the computer input. Some recorders have an AUX (auxiliary) input that may or may not work in place of the MIC connection, so check the computer manuals. AUX input is electronically different from the MIC input, and connecting the wrong one may result in improper data recording. With a two-wire system, ignore any REM (remote) connection on the recorder typically used to start and stop under control of a switch on a microphone. Since machines like the Apple II do not support remote start/stop operations, tape motion must be controlled with the recorder switches.

A few computers such as the Epson HX-20 use a three-wire hookup. The MIC and EAR connections are handled just as in the two-wire setup, but now the REM lead also is used. With the REM wire in place, the recorder switches can be set at the start of the recording or playback session, and the computer then starts and stops the tape motion just as with a microphone switch.

Figure 7-2 compares the two-wire and three-wire approaches. It's essential that the MIC and REC wires be shielded (coaxial cable) to prevent electromagnetic interference from affecting data transmission. The shielded cable also prevents data transmissions from interfering with radio and television reception, and the shielding provides some protection against static discharges into the wires. Two-wire shielded audio patch cords are available from most radio and electronic supply stores. With the three-wire setup, the MIC and REC leads also must be shielded, but the REM wire need not be. When necessary, an audio patch cord can be used for the MIC and REC leads, and a separate wire for the REM connection.

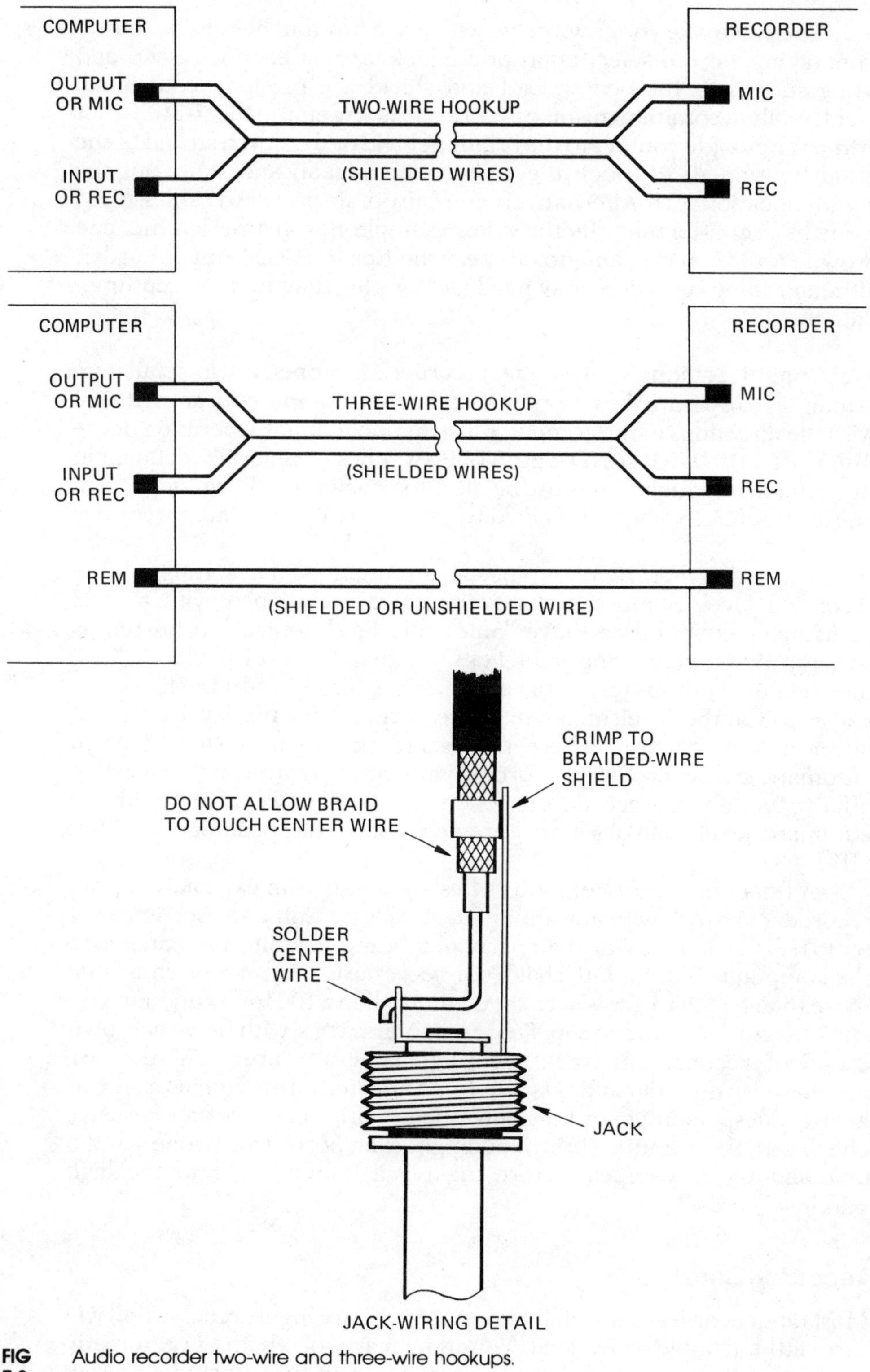

FIG 7-2 Audio recorder two-wire and three-wire hookups.

You can make your own cable with just a few touches of a soldering iron, taking care to select appropriate jack sizes at each wire end and being sure both the center lead and shield are properly connected. Incidentally, a common mistake in wiring a jack (detail in Fig. 7-2) is to not crimp the outside contact to the braided shield or to allow a strand of the braid (grounded) to touch the center wire (signal) and short out the communication path. Alternatively you can obtain prewired cables, often from the computer manufacturer. For example, Epson America, Inc., can provide a three-wire cable to connect the Epson HX-20 to a recorder, although some recorders may need jack or plug adapters to accommodate the differing sizes.

The Control Settings. Once the recorder is properly wired, all that remains is to operate the recorder switches and computer in accordance with the directions in the computer instruction manual. Operation of the PLAY, RECORD, REWIND, and STOP switches is generally detailed in the manuals, though you must be alert to procedural differences from one computer to another and between the two-wire and three-wire hookups.

A matter that requires special attention is the setting of the recording level. Some cassette recorders are equipped with a level adjustment knob; others have "automatic level control." Adjusting is largely a matter of trial and error. For the adjustable-level machines, have the computer output test data such as a long program to the recorder, and monitor the level meter to make certain that the level does not hover in the red area where the recording can be distorted. With automatic level control, try recording with the control on and then with it off. I've found most recorders function better and more reliably with the automatic level control set on, but one recorder has been better with it off.

A final note. Most computers designed to use an external cassette recorder can work with any audio-quality device. Some salespeople may try to talk you into buying their particular brand, claiming it's matched to the computer. Watch out! That's not necessarily true and often is little more than a ploy to get you to spend more than $100 for a function you could acquire for under $30. Few computers work with only their own brand of recorder. In fact, recorders generally are OEM devices, purchased in quantity and relabeled with no internal modification. If you hear a salesperson claim that only one specific recorder can be used, check with the manufacturer. You might even borrow someone's audio unit and try it yourself before making a commitment to the high purchase cost.

Recorder Care

Most tape recorders, especially cassette types, are highly reliable and will give little trouble—provided you take care of them. I've already mentioned that you must keep them away from heat (including direct sunlight), magnetic fields, and static. You also have to keep them clean—lack of cleanliness is the single biggest cause of recorder failures.

The Cassette Chamber. Always keep the cassette access door closed. Whether the unit is in operation or is sitting idle, you want to keep airborne dust out of the tape path and mechanical components. Keep the case clean, wiping it down weekly with a damp cloth to remove surface dust, dirt, and grease accumulations. At least once a day, inspect the cassette chamber, recording heads, capstans, and rollers for accumulations of oxide. If they are discolored by oxide, they must be cleaned. Actually, it's to your advantage to keep a rigorous schedule according to the number of operating or system power-on hours. A good schedule for operating all tape devices is:

1. Clean the recording heads after every 8 to 16 hours of operation. This can be done with a commercial cleaning tape, cotton swabs, or lint-free nonabrasive swabs. When using swabs, dampen one with alcohol or a commercial head-cleaning solvent, wipe the heads, capstan, and non-rubber tape-contact surfaces thoroughly. Use as many swabs as necessary, throwing each away when contaminated. Be sure to wipe all surfaces dry with yet another swab to minimize residue left by the cleaning solution. The top photo in Fig. 7-3, shows a cleaning in progress; the bottom shows the heads after cleaning. Notice the contamination along the guide edge below the swab and the smear of oxide across the head on the left.

2. Clean the capstan drive roller (rubber) after every 16 to 24 hours of operation. Use a lint-free swab dampened with commercial rubber-drive cleaning solvent or a solution specifically identified as safe for rubber parts. Alcohol isn't always a safe solvent for these parts. Be sure to wipe the roller dry to minimize residues.

3. Clean the entire unit thoroughly at least once every 100 hours of operation. Remove dust, oxide particles, and lint accumulated inside the drive chamber. Use pressurized clean air or a soft brush, taking care not to touch the heads with any object hard enough to scratch or mar them or with your fingers. Be sure to clean any ventilation slots, speaker grilles, and other openings. At the conclusion of the cleaning, demagnetize the heads with a commercial device intended for that purpose and available from audio or electronic supply houses. Be careful to avoid passing the demagnetizer anywhere near your stock of tapes or disks or near the sensitive electronics of the computer. It's preferable to disconnect the recorder and move it to another room for demagnetizing.

4. If moving mechanical parts begin to squeak, they may be oiled, but only sparingly and then only with an approved lubricant. Before attempting this, check with the store that sold the recorder or with the manufacturer for a list of lubricants. Oil parts carefully, making certain lubricant doesn't drip onto other parts, contaminate tape-contact surfaces, or accumulate where it can attract additional dirt and dust. One good way is to dip a sewing needle into the lubricant; the point of the

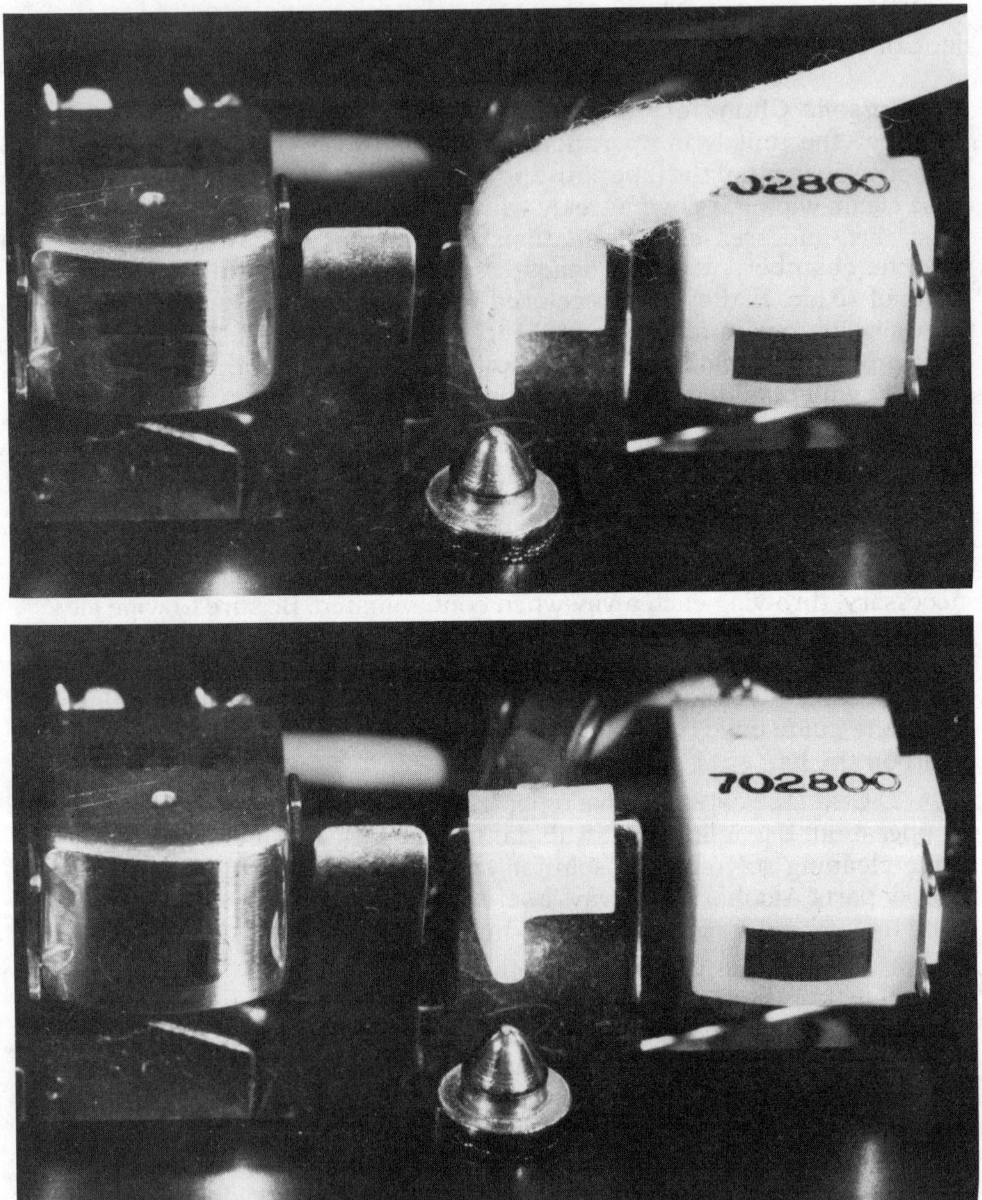

FIG 7-3 Cassette head-cleaning operation. *(Photos by author)*

needle may then be positioned on a part, allowing a minute quantity of oil to enter the part.

Throughout, take special pains to avoid touching magnetic heads, tape guides, rollers, capstans, or the tape with your fingers. Oils from your fingers can and probably will damage the data reliability, if not the equipment and tape themselves.

FIG 7-4 Cassette drive belt. *(Photo by author)*

The Drive Belt. Another problem in most low-cost cassette recorders and many reel-to-reel recorders is the drive belt. Few inexpensive units are equipped with direct-drive motors, relying instead on a rubber belt between the motor and the drive mechanism. Over time and with extensive use, that belt wears or stretches, allowing slippage. A severe shock to the unit, such as dropping it or slamming it down on a tabletop, may even dislodge the belt. In any event, it's often necessary to tighten or replace the belt.

Figure 7-4 illustrates a typical belt-and-pulley arrangement in a cassette recorder. The drive mechanisms are accessed by opening the recorder case, but the procedure differs from brand to brand. Usually, the way is obvious—remove four or more screws from the bottom of the case and separate the halves. However, you have to be careful to note how various parts fit together. Some parts, like the cassette-chamber access cover, may be spring loaded, so disassemble slowly and note the orientation and proper positioning of all components. Do not force the case open—if you feel resistance you can't identify easily, reassemble the unit and let a qualified technician do the job.

Once the case is open, the belt and pulleys are located easily. If there is evidence of rubber shavings and particles in the area, the belt is worn and probably needs to be replaced. Otherwise, it may be possible just to tighten it by repositioning the "idlers." In Fig. 7-4, notice the center pulley (white). Just above and to the right are three holes in the mounting plate, with a small metal brace inserted in the center hole. By lifting the end of the brace out of one hole and locating it another, you can adjust the idler position to either loosen or tighten the belt. In this example, moving the brace away from the idler increases belt tension, so the unit shown can be tightened one more "notch."

Be sure the area around the belt and pulleys is clean. Occasionally, it may be necessary to lubricate the center shaft of the idler, but sparingly and only with the approved oil used inside the cassette chamber. Do not—I repeat—do *not* oil the shafts of the fixed pulleys at the motor or main-drive pulley. Furthermore, do not allow any oil to get onto the belt or pulley surfaces, as it would cause additional slippage and could cause the belt to disintegrate while in use.

FLOPPY-DISK SUBSYSTEMS

By far the most popular mass-storage media are magnetic disks, either the so-called "floppy" diskettes or "hard" disks. They offer distinct advantages over tape storage. Even with floppies, which are slow compared to hard disks, the time required to read or write data is only a fraction of that needed for tape. Furthermore, disks allow random reading and writing from anywhere on the magnetic surface, instead of requiring sequential read-through.

However, floppy drives and diskettes are extremely sensitive to all seven deadly hazards. They are easily disrupted or damaged by dirt and contamination, excess heat, static, magnetic fields, power disturbances, mechanical wear, and careless mishandling. Hard disks, whether removable-cartridge or "fixed" Winchester disks, are less subject to these hazards, but not completely free of their influences. The Winchesters have the fewest problems, largely because they are assembled as sealed units under ultra-clean conditions, thereby eliminating dirt, dust, and contamination. They are extremely sensitive to shock and vibration, however, so the units require particular care in handling.

Floppies, named for the flexible nature of the diskette and jacket, come in three major types, determined by size. The regular floppy is an 8-inch diskette, and the drives are generally powered from AC current. A principal characteristic of the 8-inch floppy is that the drive rotates continuously, whether data are being transferred between the computer and diskette or not. The "minifloppy" is a 5-1/4 inch diskette used in a drive normally having dc motors that receive power from the computer mainframe. Typically, these drives start and stop for each sequence of disk accesses. The minifloppies provide less on-line data storage than comparable 8-inch units, and they usually have a longer access time because of the interval required to bring the disk up to speed when an operation is required. For a size comparison between typical 8-inch and 5-1/4-inch floppies, refer to Fig. 2-9.

"Microfloppies" are new additions to the line. These use hard-cased disks measuring between 3-1/2 and 3-3/4 inches (the standard hasn't been established yet). While preparing this book, I received no responses

FIG 7-5 "Thin" Shugart SA200 drive (left) compared with conventional drive (right). *(Courtesy of Shugart Associates)*

to inquiries for information from microfloppy suppliers, so I can't comment in this edition on the mode of operation or the care and maintenance requirements.

Within a size category, there are numerous differences. Variations include single- versus double-sided, single- versus double-density, and hard versus soft sectors. There also are "thin-line" models designed to fit in less space than conventional drives. An example is the Shugart SA200 minifloppy shown on the left in Fig. 7-5, compared to a conventional unit on the right.

Hard disks, which are more expensive than floppies, offer the advantages of increased speed, greater amounts of data on-line at any one time, and decreased sensitivity to environmental and operational hazards. As already mentioned, the principal types are the removable cartridge drives and the fixed Winchesters. There is a third version now appearing on the market—an interchangeable Winchester drive in which a sealed disk pack can be removed and replaced by another. However, no specific information is available at present on the reliability of the seals. Figure 7-6 compares a Shugart minifloppy having up to 1 Mbyte (1 megabyte or 1,000,000 bytes) of storage with an equal-size Shugart fixed Winchester providing up to 10 Mbytes in the same physical space. Notice the absence of any front-panel openings in the Winchester drive on the right, as well as the housing around the disk platters that keep them free of airborne contamination.

Removable cartridge drives have been popular for many years among sophisticated business and professional users, though removability causes problems. Cartridges can be dropped, set near heat sources, zapped while walking across a carpet, stored within the influence of a magnetic field, and so on. Worst of all, the cartridges have openings

FIG 7-6 Shugart SA410/460 Minifloppy (left) compared to SA600 fixed Winchester (right). *(Courtesy of Shugart Associates)*

through which air and contaminants can pass, allowing particles to settle on the disk surfaces where they can cause head crashes capable of destroying the drive, the cartridge, and all stored data. Since they are fixed and sealed, Winchesters are less likely to be moved and are therefore less likely to be dropped, exposed to heat sources, damaged by static charges, etc. The sealed environment inside the drive protects them from the adverse effects of airborne contamination, so they will probably not suffer head crashes.

Disk-Drive Setup

All disk drives require certain common setup procedures, whether they are floppies or hard disks. Of course, if drives are built into the computer chassis, as many are, you have no control over these matters. On the other hand, if the drives are external, observe the following points:

1. Keep the drives away from all heat sources, including direct sunlight. Magnetic media usually consist of oxide coatings on a plastic or plastic-like base. Excess heat can soften and warp the media, thereby destroying them, possibly damaging the drives, and causing loss of stored data.

2. Make certain air intakes and outlets are unobstructed. Manuals often recommend minimum clearances between the sides of units and the nearest objects; don't attempt to reduce those clearances. This is especially important with hard disks and 8-inch floppies that run off ac power and spin continuously. If no clearances are specified, allow 6 to 12 inches between the drives and adjoining walls or components.

3. Keep drives away from sources of static and electromagnetic fields, either of which can severely degrade the performance or

damage magnetically stored information. Pay special attention to positioning of telephones, audio speakers, reserve power supplies, and video displays—they generate potentially disruptive fields.

4. Allow room to work around the drives. Most ac-powered units contain ventilation fans, so allow sufficient room to clean or replace filters on a regular basis. Removable cartridge hard-disk drives usually contain filter packs which must be replaced frequently. Floppies often have screen, foam, or woven-fiber filters on the back panel which need to be either cleaned or replaced.

5. Position drives where they're unlikely to be bumped, jarred, or otherwise "shocked" during operation. A common but potentially dangerous practice is to place drives at or near the edge of a desk or close to a walkway. Someone walking by accidentally bumps the drive—if a read or write operation is in progress, the shock can be sufficient for the heads to crash with disastrous results. Similarly, disk drives should be on a solid surface separate from other major sources of severe vibration such as printers.

6. Read and understand the installation and operation manuals before connecting the drives. Pay attention to the cabling instructions and the orientation of cable connectors at both the drive and computer ends. If a connector is inverted or positioned even one pin out of alignment, applying power can and often does cause severe damage to the computer, the disk controller card in the computer, the drive, or some combination thereof. This is a common problem with machines like the Apple II, where cable connections are unkeyed, making it easy to misalign them. Some people even manage to get the connectors backward, as shown in Fig. 7-7, damaging both the controller and the connected drives when power is applied.

7. If drives are ac-powered, the third-wire ground must be connected properly. Spinning disks generate electrostatic charges, which must be bled off to ground. Attempting to defeat the grounding provision allows static to accumulate on disk surfaces and drive elements, ultimately interfering with data communications and possibly damaging magnetic surfaces and electronic circuits.

8. Check the manuals for internal switch settings that affect the device assignments. A unit may have a DIP switch package that assigns a device number for access by the controller, and it's important that disk assignments be made in sequence. It's also important that two disk drives not have the same device numbers. Since computers almost always boot from the first drive in a chain (the lowest numbered or lettered unit), you must know which is the boot drive.

On receiving new floppy drives, check the diskette chamber for a transport "shield" or "shipping disk." Typically, this is a cardboard sheet shaped like a diskette and inserted in the drive to keep the head from smashing into the pressure pad or an opposing head during transit. The shield must be removed before powering the unit. If the drives have been

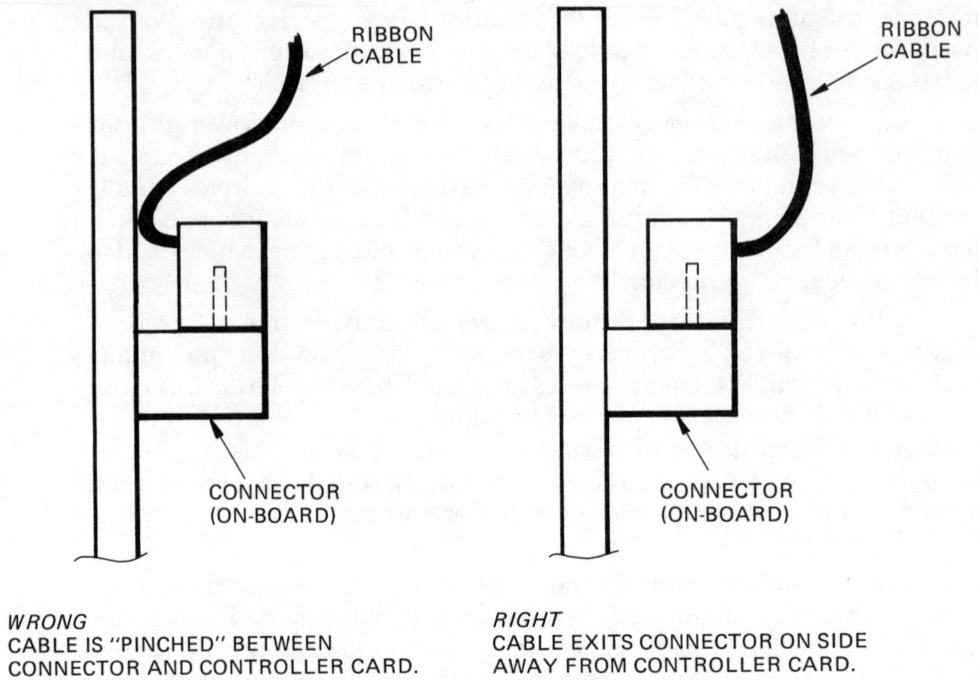

FIG 7-7 Wrong and right ways to attach disk cables to "unkeyed" Apple II controller.

burned in by the supplier, the shield should have been removed to enable the burn-in. However, some suppliers reinsert the shield before delivery, while others do not. If the shields are missing, ask the supplier to give them to you since you need them if you ever have to ship drives to the manufacturer for repair.

When first using the drives, take special note of diskette removal. Some drives require that you open the access door and then use your finger to lift and disengage the front edge or one corner of the diskette. Other drives have spring-loaded ejection mechanisms that pop the diskette out a sufficient distance to grab it. When I changed computer systems recently, I went from drives requiring manual manipulation to ones having spring-loaded ejection. The first few times I opened the doors on the new drives, the diskettes were ejected onto the floor. I had to learn to hold my hand in front of the doors when releasing the diskettes to catch the leading diskette edge as it came shooting out. Eventually, the springs weakened under use so the diskettes now eject only part of the way, but the first week or so required a radical readjustment of my operating procedures.

Disk-Drive Care

As extremely sensitive devices, disk drives other than Winchesters generally require more attention more often than other system components. Since disks are the primary storage for programs and data essential to the system as a whole, an unnecessary failure poses the double-barreled threat of damaged components and the loss of stored information. The components can be fixed or replaced with comparative ease, but restoring lost data can take hours, weeks, months, or even years at a high cost in lost time.

Disk-Drive Diagnostics. In Chapter 4, I mentioned system diagnostics for the computer mainframe. Diagnostics are just as important for disk drives and are, I think, the most valuable software you can purchase. If not acquired with the system purchase, they should be obtained as soon thereafter as your budget will allow.

Programs such as SuperSoft's Diagnostics II for CP/M systems, XPS' Apple-Cillin II for the Apple II, Nikrom's Master Diagnostics for the Apple II, and similar programs for these and other systems all contain disk-drive testing and verification routines. It's characteristic of malfunctions that they often build slowly, going unnoticed until a major failure occurs and stops the system dead in its tracks (no pun intended). It's also true that drive problems often look like other things such as memory or CPU failures. A good set of diagnostics used regularly (once a week) often can detect disk problems early enough to prevent serious data losses.

At a minimum, the software should check read/write operations by recording data and then reading it back to verify that what is retrieved is the same as what was output. All three programs cited have that capability. A few, like Diagnostics II and Apple-Cillin II, include track-seeking tests wherein head movements are exercised while the program verifies that the head ended up at the proper place each time. Apple-Cillin even includes variations that test the user's choice of sequential or random access to tracks, completing the check of operations by verifying smooth transitions from one track to another and "jump around" transitions that stress the drive mechanisms.

Computer-specific software such as Apple-Cillin and Master Diagnostics for the Apple II often contain special routines for adjusting most routine settings in a drive. Both of these contain speed-calibration routines that allow checking and adjusting drive speed. This subject will be covered later in this chapter.

Caution is necessary, however. Any but the most cursory disk tests are "destructive"—users must be careful not to have a disk with valuable data in the drive during the test. The tests write data to the diskette, overlaying or destroying anything already recorded. Therefore, use a freshly formatted diskette for the tests. Another caution! The drive tests assume that the diskette being used is "good." If the diskette itself contains one or more bad sectors, they're likely to register as drive errors. I've made it a point to reserve particular diskettes for each of my systems and use them only for drive tests. They have been checked and rechecked for data integrity and are known to be free of flaws or defects. They're never used for normal data or program recording and are labeled as test disks only. This ensures that any errors detected by the diagnostics are system errors and not just flaws in the magnetic surface.

If the diagnostics detect drive failures that can't be remedied by simple cleaning and care procedures outlined in the following sections, the aid of a technician is required. Aside from the few items I identify, drive problems tend to be too complicated and require too much test equipment for the average user to fix.

The Importance of Drive Cleanliness. As with other system components, the paramount consideration for disk drives is cleanliness. But here, keeping things clean is even more important than in any other component. With floppies, the read/write heads contact the oxide surface. Most high-grade diskettes use a lubricated oxide coating to minimize wear and friction, but dust and other airborne contaminants settling on the surfaces are abrasive to both the media and the heads, shortening the useful lives of both.

With hard disks, a "flying head" hovers 20 to 100 microns (0.0008 to 0.004 inch) above the rapidly moving magnetic surface. The relative linear speed in a hard disk approaches 60 miles per hour, so imagine what happens when the flying head collides with something too large to pass beneath it. The situation is similar to driving a car into a brick wall at 60 miles per hour, with much the same result. The head generally deflects, causing a crash onto the disk surface. Since the surface is still moving at full speed, the head is bounced around relentlessly. Oxide coating is stripped from the disk surface, disks and heads crack under the strain, often fragmenting explosively. In short, both the drive and the disk platters are destroyed.

At best, it's an expensive failure since the disk platters have to be replaced and the drive has to be rebuilt or replaced. Furthermore, all stored data, usually millions of bytes, are lost forever. At worst, the disk and drive mechanisms can fly apart, posing a distinct personnel hazard since some have been known to go off like shrapnel. A spinning disk is like a flywheel—a device capable of storing tremendous amounts of mechanical energy. When a head crash occurs and the disk screeches to a halt, stored energy has to go some place, and that place may be into high-velocity pieces that can pierce equipment casings or even walls.

To illustrate the phenomenon graphically, Figure 7-8 shows the size relationship between a hard disk's flying head and some common airborne pollutants. Variations on this illustration appear in many catalogs and articles, but the source is unknown. Figure 7-9 shows some additional size relationships among other contaminants, based on information contained in handbooks on industrial pollution control and including pollutants commonly found around metropolitan areas and industrial developments. There are some conflicts between Figs. 7-8 and 7-9 in the sizes of certain pollutants, so the illustrations should be viewed as approximations only. However, most drive manufacturers seem to consider anything larger than 3 microns (0.0001 inch) hazardous to high-speed disks, and anything larger than 20 microns (0.0008 inch) extremely dangerous. Those ranges include virtually all common particles in the visible and microscopic ranges.

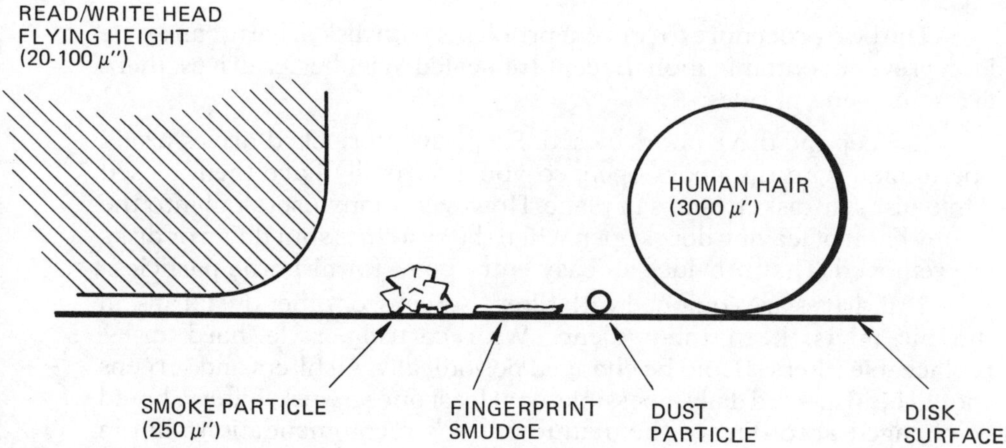

FIG 7-8 Relationship between disk-head and common contaminants.

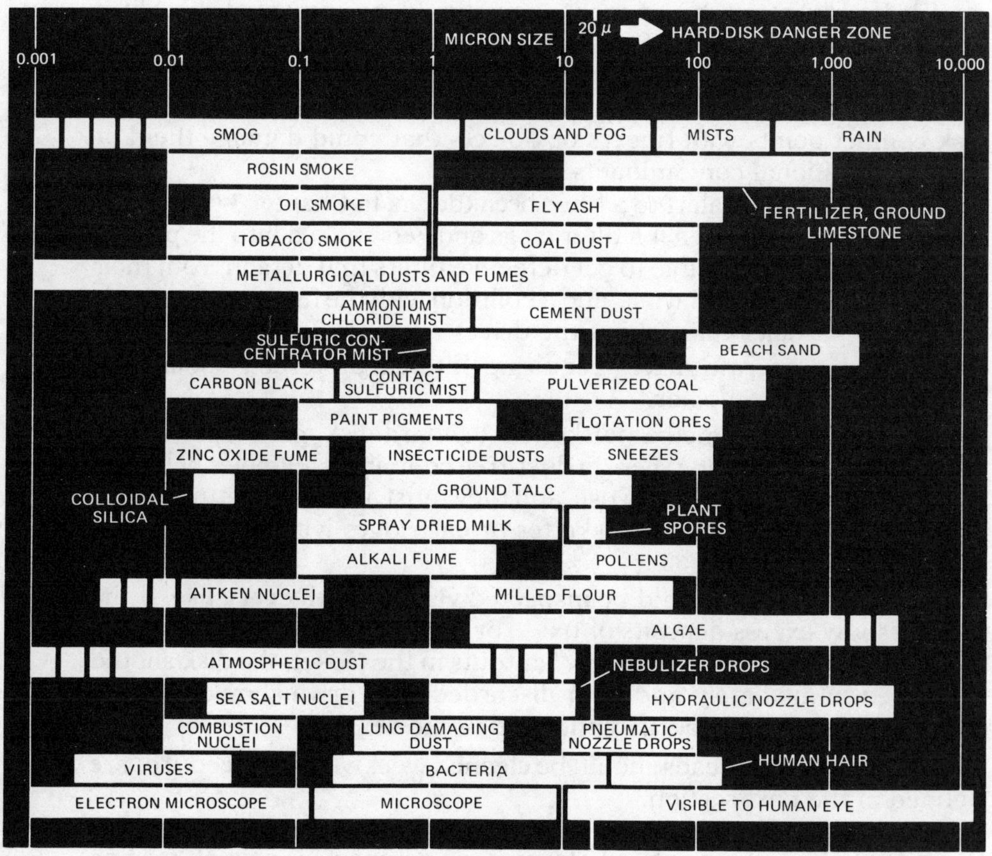

FIG 7-9 Size comparisons of common airborne pollutants.

The best procedure to prevent problems with disk drives of any type is to prevent contamination. Except for sealed Winchester drives, there are some general rules:

1. Keep the drive doors closed. Properly interlocked drives aren't operational with the doors open, so you'll normally have them closed while disks or diskettes are in place. However, many users fall into the sloppy habit of leaving doors open when the system is shut down or disks are removed. That provides an easy entry point for airborne particles.

2. If drives are equipped with filters, screens, or other dust traps on the air inlets, keep them clean. With cartridge-style hard disks, replaceable filters should be changed periodically. All filters and screens should be inspected daily if possible, or at least once a week. Filters should be changed according to the manufacturer's recommendations, but in extremely dusty or dirty environments halve the expected life of the filters. Cleanable filters and screens such as the ones commonly found on ac-powered floppy drives should be cleaned with a vacuum at least once a week, or removed and washed in a low-residue cleaning solution if possible.

3. If drives can be opened, they should be inspected weekly if possible, but not less than once a month. Accumulations of oxide, dust, filter fibers, or other foreign materials must be removed carefully with lint-free swabs or pressurized clean air. Avoid touching heads or other disk contact points with fingers or objects that could damage them or transfer additional contaminants.

4. Be especially alert to a filter breakdown. In Chapter 3 (Fig. 3-2), I showed what can happen if a filter clogs and gets sucked into the path of the fan blades. It is possible to get defective filters that detach from their mountings during normal use, and a collision with the fan blades spreads dangerous particles throughout the drives.

5. Never operate drives requiring filtered or forced cooling air without the filters in place.

6. Protect the media (diskettes or hard-disk cartridges) from contamination by storing them in dust-free containers. Floppies belong in their dust jackets when not in use, and they must always be returned to a protective box. Never leave diskettes or cartridges lying around in the open.

7. Floppy disks should be inspected visually with every use. If the jackets show excess deposits of oxide or if any damage or excess wear can be seen through the "window" cutouts in the jacket, the disk should be copied immediately and then discarded. The drive should then be cleaned thoroughly, especially the read/write heads.

8. Read/write heads should be cleaned weekly. The procedures are defined in the next section.

Head Cleaning. Proper head cleaning is an important part of keeping your disk drives and your system operating reliably. Of course, there's no provision for this on a Winchester hard disk, and the procedures vary from system to system with cartridge-style hard disks. All floppy drives, however, follow much the same procedure, which is defined in this section. Owners of hard disks must check the manuals or contact manufacturers for recommendations.

Cleaning should be performed on a regular schedule, preferably once a week. On my own three systems, I clean heads every Monday morning, whether the system has been used heavily or lightly during the preceding week. Furthermore, I clean the heads after every use of a diskette other than the brand I run as a standard. I've made it a habit to run only premium-grade diskettes of one brand—diskettes I know are top quality and have few problems with oxide peeling, flaking, or contamination. However, diskettes obtained or purchased from other sources are usually of inferior or at least unknown quality. Therefore, when I finish making the working copies, I clean the heads to remove contamination or oxide that may have been left behind where they might damage my own diskettes.

One of the worst things that can happen to floppy drives is building an oxide accumulation on the head. A gradual buildup is normal and easily taken care of with routine cleaning. But sudden adhesion of an oxide flake left by a defective diskette can be a disaster, allowing the flake or chip to act like a plow on other diskette surfaces. I've had it happen, so I know! I once wiped out 180 successive 8-inch diskettes before realizing that a bad one had flaked onto the heads. When it finally occurred to me to inspect the bottom side of the diskettes, I found they were grooved like audio records. Naturally, I lost all data stored to that point, since both master and backup copies were destroyed while I was trying to find the cause of the problem. I no longer take any chances. Running any diskette other than the brand I use regularly mandates an automatic cleaning procedure to minimize any possibility of that happening again.

The easiest and most popular way to clean heads is with a commercial cleaning diskette. These are available in at least two types through computer dealers or by direct mail. The major advantage is that the drives don't have to be opened or disassembled, thereby eliminating the likelihood of voiding a warranty or service contract.

One type is included with the Nikrom Master Diagnostics Plus package cited in Chapter 4 (Fig. 4-5). The item is the Datalife™ Head Cleaning Kit by Verbatim (the same people who manufacture floppy disks) and can be obtained separately as well. The kit contains a special jacket or cleaning-disk carrier in either a 5-1/4-inch or 8-inch size, plus two cleaning-disk inserts. An insert presaturated with an alcohol and fluorocarbon solution is removed from its protective foil pouch and inserted in the carrier, and the combination is inserted into the disk drive like a normal data diskette. The drive then is activated for 30 to 60 seconds; this places the head or heads in contact with the spinning treated surface. The carrier then is moved to each additional drive in the system, cleaning each for the same 30- to 60-second interval. When the cleaning is

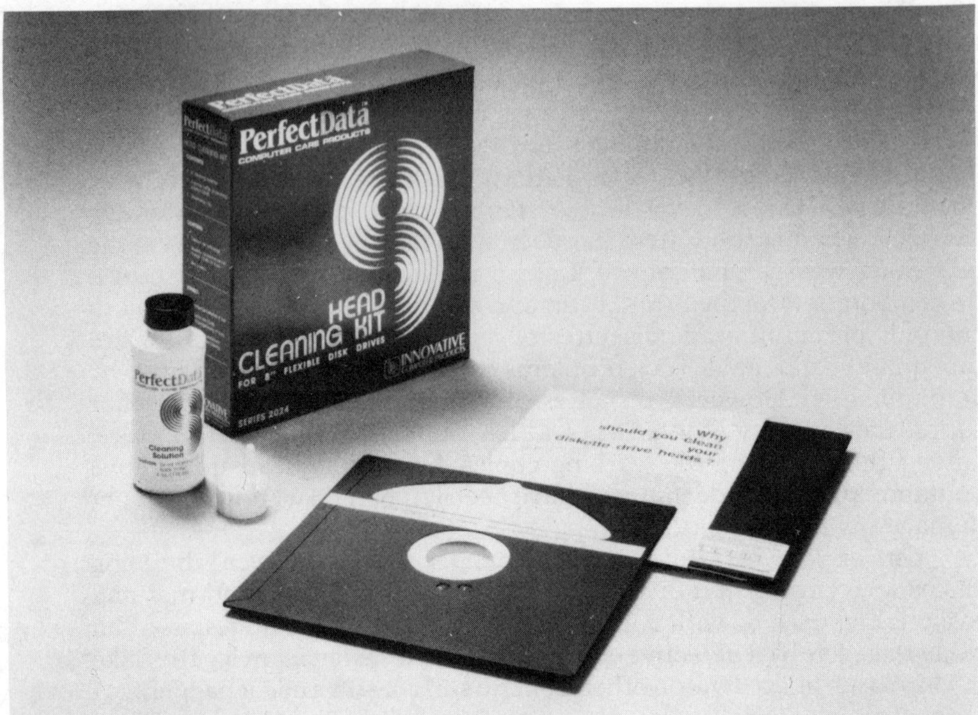

FIG 7-10 Typical head-cleaning kit with reusable diskettes. *(Courtesy of Innovative Computer Products)*

done, the insert is removed and discarded, while the carrier is stored until the next use.

The one possible disadvantage to this approach is that replacement inserts have to be purchased for each cleaning. If you clean once a week as I advise, the cost can add up. The instruction book that accompanies this package recommends cleaning once a month, but I've found this insufficient for the heavy use I impose on the system. It might work for a system used only an hour or two a day, but I much prefer weekly cleaning if for no other reason than to minimize the chances of undetected damage to my diskettes. I've also had trouble locating the replacement inserts in computer stores, although most do carry the entire kit with the carrier. That means you may have to order inserts from the manufacturer, keeping a working stock on hand and ordering well before any anticipated need. On the other hand, there is a distinct advantage in having a fresh cleaning surface each time you need it. It prevents any possibility of carrying over contamination from one cleaning session to another.

A different approach is used by Innovative Computer Products in their PerfectData Head Cleaning Kit shown in Fig. 7-10. This kit also is included in the PerfectData Micro Maintenance Kit shown in Fig. 7-11 and is available under private label from other sources such as the Inmac

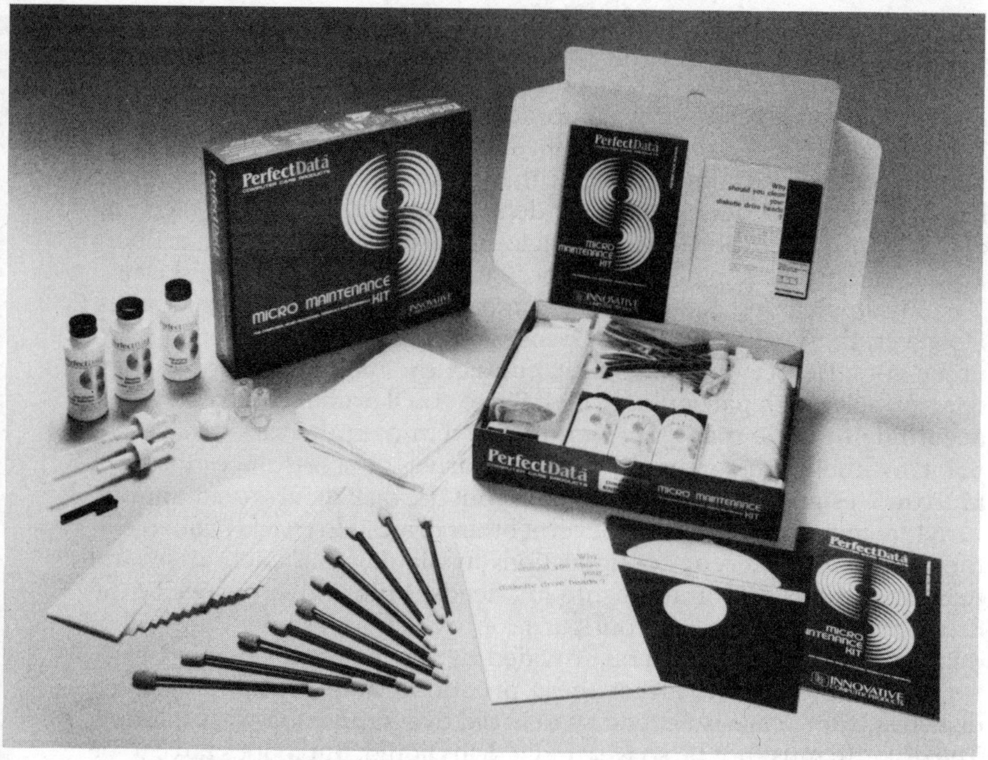

FIG 7-11 Typical maintenance kit including a head-cleaning diskette. *(Courtesy of Innovative Computer Products)*

mail-order catalog. It contains two reusable, lint-free, wet/dry, fiber diskettes permanently housed in a carrier (the Micro Maintenance Kit contains only one diskette). Approximately one-third of the diskette is exposed through a large opening, and that portion is saturated by the user with a cleaning solution in the kit. Ordinary alcohol also could be used, but the solution provided contains an additional fluorocarbon for efficient cleaning. The disk is then run through each drive for 30 seconds, resaturating the exposed disk portion for each drive and hitting each head with alternating wet and dry surfaces as it spins.

With this approach, one diskette has a recommended life of 13 cleaning sessions. The manufacturer advises discarding the diskette after 13 uses, even if it does not show visible signs of contamination. This is to minimize transmission of microscopic particles that can't be seen with the unaided eye. I've found that 13 uses begins to abrade the lint-free fiber diskette, and trying to push it beyond that runs the risk of adding fibrous contaminants to the disk environment. The obvious advantage is the ability to reuse the cleaning kit, possibly at a lower cost than the throwaway approach. The disadvantage is the possibility of carrying contaminants over from one cleaning to another or having the diskette get dirty during storage in an improperly closed environment.

Both versions are capable of cleaning single- or double-sided drives, although the procedure is different for the two configurations. With single-sided drives, a plastic blank on the opening in one side of the carrier must remain in place to prevent abrading the fibrous pressure pad that holds the diskette in contact with the head. For double-sided drives, the blank is removed to allow contact with both heads at the same time. If the blank is removed accidentally or deliberately, however, the cleaning diskette must not be used on single-sided drives—the coarse fibers abrade the pressure pad, and the pressure pad damages the diskette.

These cleaning diskettes are compatible with most floppy drives. However, the Verbatim Datalife package excludes Vydec™ 8-inch word processors. Before obtaining a kit, contact the manufacturer to verify compatibility with particular drives. Since you'll probably have to verify according to drive manufacturer, not system manufacturer, make it a point to know who manufactures the drives. For instance, I own a Morrow Designs' Decision 1 computer, but the disk drives are manufactured by Shugart Associates. Several other drives also were available at the time, with different configurations available from each of several manufacturers. To communicate my needs, I must always specify the drive make, model, and configuration, which is not in the system documentation and had to be provided by the local dealer.

Two other points affect these products. With reusable cleaning diskettes, some care is necessary to avoid oversaturating with solution. The diskette must not be so wet that it drips liquid, but it does have to be thoroughly saturated.

Furthermore, it's necessary to activate the drives so the heads contact the disk surfaces. Just turning them on and letting them spin doesn't do the job. My approach with a CP/M system is to insert the cleaning diskette and have the computer "initialize" it with the CP/M FORMAT.COM utility. The computer doesn't register an I/O error until it has made the entire formatting pass and then goes back to verify the sectors. That takes almost exactly 30 seconds, during which the heads are stepped across the disk surface in constant contact with fresh cleaning solution. With an Apple II, I use any of several available disk-cleaning routines that are part of system or disk diagnostic programs.

An alternative and less desirable approach is to play technician. The object is to get inside the drive and clean the head with a swab. A caution—for most external drives, it's not difficult, but it is time consuming and does void warranties and service contracts. Many computers having built-in drives don't even allow access to those drives without a near-total disassembly of the computer itself, and this approach should never be attempted where there is a need for extensive disassembly. Furthermore, the procedure is suitable only for single-sided drives where there is one head opposed by a pressure pad; never attempt it on a double-sided drive where there are opposing heads.

Another caution—it's wise to watch a qualified technician perform this procedure before you try it. Although it's often easy to do, you have to be careful to reassemble the drive exactly as it was, and you must not do anything that will disturb mechanical adjustments or alignments. The information I provide is just that—information—and is intended to complete the discussion. It is not a recommendation, and I prefer the cleaning-disk approach whenever possible. About the only time I'll get into a drive is when I suspect some major contamination adhering so tightly to the head that the cleaning disks can't dislodge it. Then I have no choice other than to go into the drive and clean the head manually despite the risk to the equipment.

If we assume you have external drives or drives that slide out of the computer chassis, a typical procedure is:

1. Open the drive case. Usually the case can be opened by removing as few as four screws along the sides or on the bottom. Other configurations may require loosening screws on the bottom of a main chassis and sliding the drive forward, or merely slipping a drive chassis forward on its own mounting rails. Regardless of the configuration, take care to avoid straining or breaking internal wires. If you feel any resistance to opening the case, look for wire clips or other attachments that may prevent the cover from moving.

2. Once the case is removed or opened, most drives require that a circuit board be removed from above the drive heads. Never touch the drive motor area or any circuit boards surrounding it. The only candidate is a top board, usually secured by several screws to the drive chassis. Carefully loosen the mounting screws (don't drop any into the drive) and lift the board slightly. Usually, it's possible to tilt the board back or to one side to expose the drive mechanism without removing any cables. If that's not possible, note the positioning and orientation of all cable connectors before disconnecting anything.

3. Once the head mechanism is exposed, it should look something like Fig. 7-12. The entire assembly must be moved to a position where the pressure pad and its supporting arm can be raised to provide working clearance. This is done by slowly rotating the large drive screw connecting the "stepper" motor to the head. Generally, moving the head to the extreme forward position will allow the pressure pad arm to lift far enough for cleaning.

4. With the head now accessible, dampen a cotton or nonabrasive, lint-free swab with alcohol. Do not saturate the swab so it drips. While gently lifting the pressure pad arm, lightly rub the head in a circular pattern. Severely burnished deposits may require several repetitions and slightly increased pressure on the swab.

5. Once the head is clean, wipe it dry with a fresh swab, thus removing any residue left by the alcohol. Inspect the head for wear, burn marks, and abrasions, which usually can be spotted by holding a flashlight at an angle to the head surface. If the head appears damaged or worn, arrange to have a technician examine and possibly replace it.

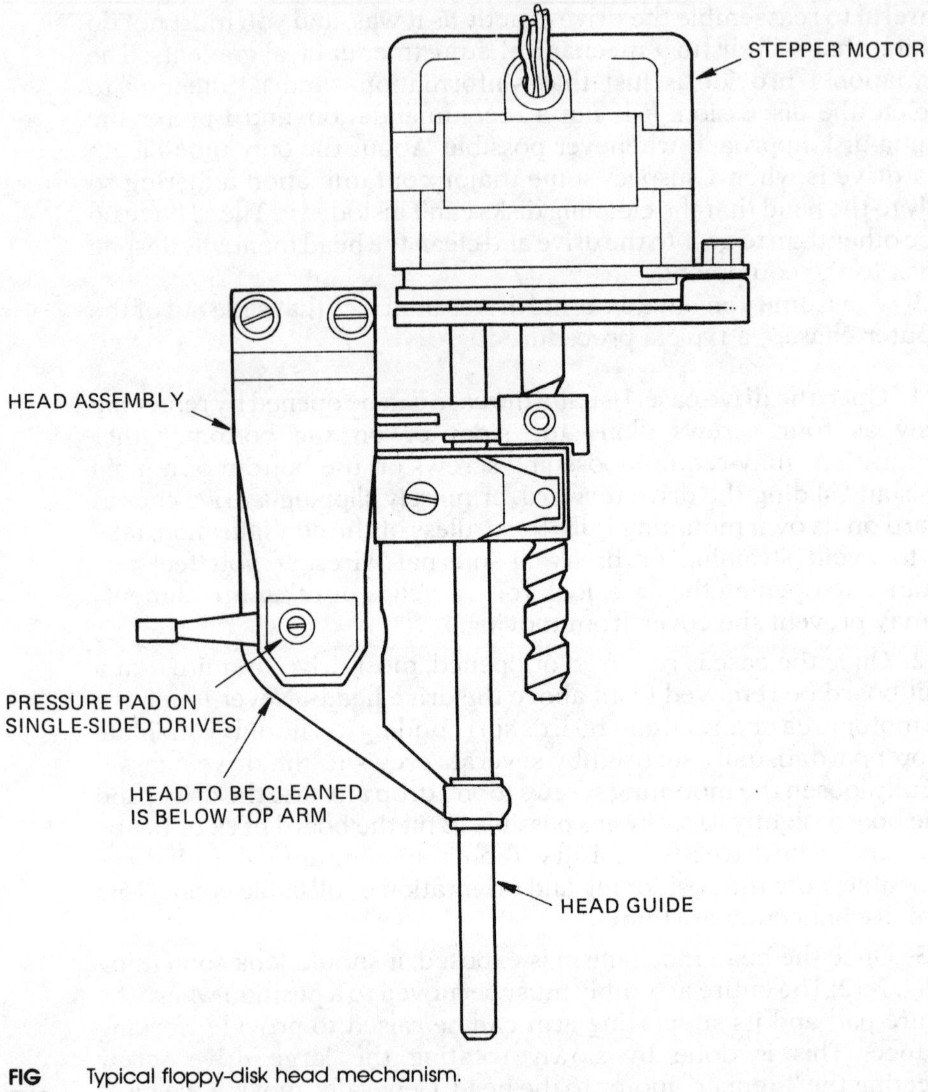

FIG 7-12 Typical floppy-disk head mechanism.

6. Clean any dirt, dust, and oxide deposits from the drive, using either a soft brush or pressurized clean air.

7. Reassemble the drive in the reverse order of your procedure for taking it apart. When reinstalling the circuit board above the drive mechanism, make certain the screws are seated firmly. Since these screws are often ground connections between the board and the drive chassis, they must be tight to provide an adequate electrical ground.

The method used to clean drives and read/write heads is less important than cleaning them on a regular basis. While the cleaning generally is beneficial to the drive and helps prevent head crashes that could be costly to fix, the advantage lies in protecting magnetic media and, most important of all, the stored data. It may cost a hundred dollars or more to replace a damaged head, and you may be able to replace damaged disks for $5 to $10 each, but the loss of valuable data can be a disaster. For business and professional applications, important files and archival materials could be lost forever. Even if the materials can be restored from hard copies, hundreds or thousands of hours of working time and costly computer time could be spent trying to correct the effects of just one badly contaminated head.

Head Demagnetizing. None of the service manuals I've examined has addressed the matter of head degaussing or demagnetizing. The whole subject of residual magnetic fields in the heads is rarely mentioned, and then only superficially. Personally, I've had no problem, and haven't yet attempted to demagnetize a head on drives as much as five years old. I generally recommend that users not attempt to degauss their own units anyway. The procedure requires using a device that throws an extensive magnetic field too close to other system components, which might easily be damaged by the field.

Pressure Pad Replacement. Single-sided drives almost always have a fiber pressure pad, sometimes called a "head-load button," opposing the read/write head (Fig. 7-12). When inserted into the drives, the diskette is between the head and the pressure pad, so the magnetic surface is held in contact with the head surface. When the pressure pad becomes worn, as it will eventually, contact between the magnetic media and the head becomes erratic and unreliable. At some point, the wear may be so extreme that the floppy disk "floats" over the head, causing numerous reading and writing errors. Usually this shows up as erroneous data at first, followed by a high incidence of "I/O error" messages, and it eventually leads to a total failure. The same can happen if a defective pressure pad breaks away from its mounting.

Make it a habit to examine pressure pads of single-sided drives every week. Note the thickness when the drive is new. When that thickness decreases to less than half the original, replace the pad. Assuming you can open the drive, all you have to do is access the pressure arm as outlined for manually cleaning the read/write head. The pad or button mounting is usually held to the arm with a small screw (often plastic), so remove the screw, replace the pad and mounting with a new assembly, and reinstall the holding screw. If the mounting is secured with an integral retaining clip, compress the clip with tweezers or needle-nose pliers to remove it. It's a simple operation and doesn't require any subsequent mechanical or electronic realignments. It does, however, void warranties and service contracts.

Drive-Belt Replacement. Most floppy drives are belt driven. That is, a rubber belt connects pulleys on the drive motor and center hub for

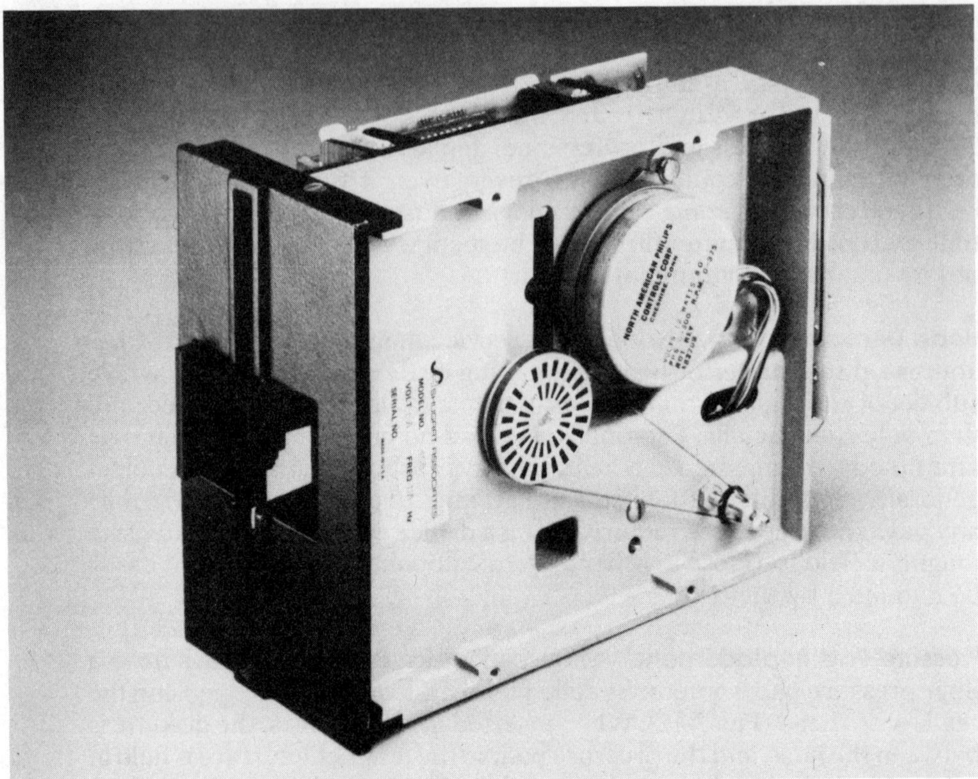

FIG 7-13 Typical floppy-disk drive belt. *(Courtesy of Shugart Associates)*

spinning the diskette. Occasionally, the belt slips off the pulleys, breaks, or wears out. Slippage or breakage is almost immediately identified by the fact that the drive ceases to work. Since the disk won't spin, nothing can be read or written, and the sound of the drive changes dramatically. Excessive wear is harder to spot, demonstrating the same symptoms as other drive malfunctions; it begins with a high incidence of reading or writing errors with "I/O error" messages and gradually increases to a point where no disk operations are possible.

Figure 7-13 illustrates a typical drive belt and its pulleys. It's located on the underside of the drive chassis and is accessible by removing the drive case or sliding the drive out of its mounting slot. The area should be inspected every six months or so; look for burn marks on the pulleys, which would indicate slippage or binding as well as particles of worn rubber.

If the belt slips, breaks, or wears out, it can be replaced easily. Just loop the loose belt or a replacement over the large pulley and stretch it over the smaller one. Be sure the belt centers on both pulleys; otherwise, it could slip right off again. An easy way to center the belt is to rotate the pulleys by hand, and the belt should center itself.

If there are burn marks on the pulleys or if the belt slips or breaks frequently, there may be other problems. The usual cause is something binding, probably the shaft connecting the large pulley with the center hub. Burn marks, repeated belt breakage, or frequently detached belts are indications of a major mechanical malfunction, possibly worn bearings or bushings, and require the assistance of a technician.

Usually, belts can be replaced or remounted without electronic or mechanical readjustments. However, motors, pulleys, bearings, bushings, and such cannot be replaced without major realignment and retiming of the entire drive. Therefore, anything beyond the simple reinstallation of a new belt should be done by a technician. One note of importance: the pulleys, hubs, and belt should be cleaned before the belt is mounted or remounted. Residual particles of rubber, grease, oils, fingerprints, and other contaminants adhering to the contact surfaces can degrade the reliability of the drive. Pulleys and hubs can be cleaned with lint-free swabs dampened with alcohol or some other approved solvent. The belt should be cleaned only with a rubber-roller cleaner or other approved solvent to prevent softening or marring the contact surface.

Static Wipers. Some drives are equipped with "static wipers" under the large drive-belt pulley shown in Fig. 13. The most notable are 8-inch floppies driven by ac power and spinning continuously. The static wipers ground the pulley and, through it, the center hub and diskette. The purpose is to bleed off electrostatic charges that build up as the diskette spins, preventing spontaneous discharges into drive mechanisms, through heads, or onto magnetic surfaces.

At least one drive brand uses a graphite block held against the rotating pulley by a spring-steel bar. Such static wipers are subject to wear, reducing their effectiveness and contaminating the drive with graphite particles. They should be inspected and, if necesssary, replaced every 6 to 12 months.

I've had particular problems with these on a pair of older drives. As the graphite blocks wear, they begin to "squeal" loudly while the drives spin. One technician caused problems with his remedy. His "cure" was to soak a cotton swab with silicone lubricant and rub the upper pulley surface where the wiper made contact. Within a day, the drives were squealing again. Furthermore, the lubricant got onto the pulley edge where the belt rides, causing the belt to slip and the drive speed to become erratic. Finally, the lubricant attracted additional contamination from airborne dirt and graphite particles wearing off the wiper, creating a black sludge on the pulley.

Such a remedy may be useful as a stopgap measure, but it's advisable to replace worn static wipers instead of trying to lubricate them. Once a lubricant has been introduced, it's necessary to repeat the procedure often, thereby increasing contamination and causing a multitude of other difficulties.

Lubrication. As a rule, nothing inside a disk drive should be lubricated by the user, and rarely by a technician. Since oils and greases attract contaminants, they eventually increase friction on moving parts and can destroy drive performance. Most instruction manuals advise against any lubrication, and users would be smart to follow that advice.

Other than the experience with the static wipers described in the previous section, there's been only one other time when lubricant was introduced into one of my disk drives, and that was in desperation. I had an Apple II disk drive that jammed regularly. Virtually every time I started a day's work, and often during the day, the drive would refuse to position the head. I could free the head and return to normal operation by repeated attempts, but within a short time it would bind again. Diagnostics showed nothing wrong—the speed test itself would free the head so the problem wouldn't be evident. Six trips to a service center failed to cure it—the technicians would run diagnostics which showed nothing wrong, clean some cable contacts, reseat circuit chips, and so on, but the drive would soon hang up again.

One day, I had an inspiration. Suppose the guide rail for the head assembly had a sticky spot I couldn't see. If the head hit that spot and stopped on it, perhaps it couldn't get moving again. Figuring I had nothing to lose with a drive that wouldn't work and appeared unrepairable, I decided to lubricate the rail—against every known recommendation. Using a lint-free cloth lightly treated with a high-quality watchmaker's oil, I wiped the rail. Then I wiped it as clean of oil as I could with another lint-free cloth. A miracle! When reassembled, the drive ran perfectly, and the problem has not occurred since.

Notice four things. First, I violated my own advice about not using lubricants, but only after there seemed to be nothing else to do. Second, I used a high-grade oil designed for delicate mechanical parts, not a universal machine oil. Third, I oiled sparingly, using a cloth to deposit only the thinnest possible film. Fourth, I wiped the components clean to minimize any dirt-attracting residue. It just goes to show that you sometimes do have to break the rules.

Drive Connections. Normal vibration inside a drive is capable of loosening cable connectors, circuit chips, and other components. Any time drives are open for other maintenance, all connections and all mountings should be checked. Among the most important items are:

1. Check all mounting screws and nuts, particularly ones securing components to the chassis. They must be tight. If a screw or nut works loose and starts bouncing around, it can cause massive destruction.

2. Clean and reseat all cable connectors, paying special attention to cleaning any edge connectors on circuit cards. Use the procedure already described under "Card-Level Maintenance" in Chapter 4.

3. Gently press down all socketed circuit chips to be sure they are seated. Be sure to discharge any static before touching a chip or circuit board.

4. Locate and check any ground leads connecting the electronics to the chassis. Good grounding is essential, and many ground wires are equipped with "spade clips" which work loose from the mounting posts.

5. Verify internal switch settings. It's easy to alter a DIP switch accidentally, and leaving a switch set improperly is a frequent cause of malfunctions.

6. Check the connections on the disk controller in the computer. These are just as likely to work loose or become contaminated as the ones in the drives.

Drive Adjustments. Disk drives, floppies and other types, are full of adjustments for things like speed, timing, and alignment. These are off limits to all but qualified technicians equipped to deal with them. Normally, adjustments require an oscilloscope, special-alignment diskettes from the drive manufacturer, and a knowledge of electronics and drive operation. In fact, I'll issue a warning—with one possible exception described in the following paragraphs. Keep away from all adjustments inside a disk drive. That includes potentiometers, funny little dials, set screws, cams, and so on. Limit your activities to the items already described in this chapter.

The exception is the speed adjustment on certain minifloppy drives. The most notable is the Apple Disk II drive or Shugart Associates Model SA400. These have a potentiometer on the motor control board that can and should be adjusted. The location is shown in Fig. 7-14. This is the only adjustment that can be changed by the user. However, adjustment does void any warranty or service contract. Proper speed adjustment does require some special timing software that you must obtain first.

Timing-calibration software for a machine like the Apple II spins a drive, writing and reading information to and from a diskette while displaying the detected timing graphically on the video screen. Each available program has its own unique form of display, and each defines an acceptable range for some type of indicator. If the detected speed is within the indicated range, the drive can be assumed to be operating nominally. Otherwise, it's necessary to adjust the potentiometer (Fig. 7-14) until the speed is within range. The procedure is about as simple as you can get. The only disassembly is to remove four screws and slide the casing off the chassis.

There are a couple of hitches, however. First, of several timing-calibration programs I've tried, no two have been in exact agreement. One program might show a drive operating acceptably, while another program shows it "out of spec." Since there's no way of knowing which, if any, programs are exactly right, I work through several programs in cycles until some indicate an acceptable speed—even if only marginally. I've just been through that procedure, for the thousandth time. When I used the timing-calibration features of several programs to adjust two Apple Disk II drives, XPS' Apple-Cillin showed both drives way off, with one too fast and the other too slow. Nikrom's Master Diagnostics showed

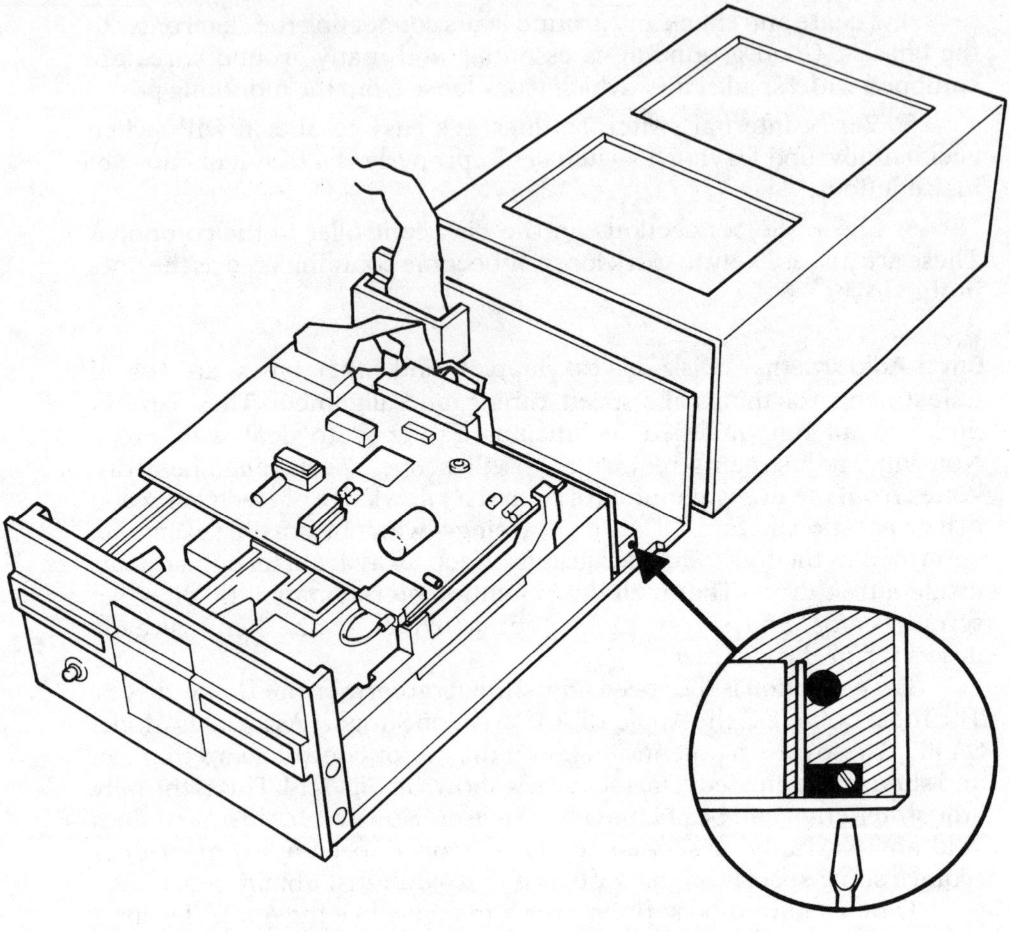

FIG 7-14 Speed adjustment on Apple Disk II (Shugart SA400 minifloppy drive).

both drives within tolerances, with one dead center on the recommended setting and the other slightly slow but acceptable. Meanwhile, Omega Microwave's Locksmith™ indicated both drives were fine, with the slower one being "on the money" and the faster one just within tolerance. See what I mean about inconsistency? When I add the timing tests available under Computer:applications' Nibbles Away II™, Central Point Software's The Filer™, or ALF Products' PenultiCopy™, I sometimes get different results again.

Second, there's some argument about what constitutes a correct speed. I had purchased a commercial game program that was disk-intensive and kept "bombing out" on me. After the sixth replacement, I started doing some checking. The game supplier told me they recorded at a speed setting of zero according to a diagnostic furnished by Apple Computer, Inc. But the dealer from whom I bought the machine insisted that his instructions from Apple were to set the speed at six "notches" fast or slow with the same timing program, never at zero. That started me thinking, and I soon discovered that many software suppliers record their diskettes at different nominal drive speeds. Therefore, if a diskette is recorded at one extreme of an acceptable range while the user's drives are set at the other extreme, the operations may be marginal at best.

Similarly, my drives are subject to considerable speed "drifts." It's necessary to reset both drives every two weeks. If I go longer, the operating speed differs so much from the speed at which a diskette was recorded that the operations fail. The first step I take when a purchased or previously recorded diskette fails to boot or read properly is to check and reset the drive speeds. Sometimes, I've been able to access a seemingly bad diskette just by temporarily kicking one drive way off speed, leaving the other drive at the recommended speed, and copying the diskette to the correct drive. I'll be presenting more information on disk copying in Chapter 8.

There is a danger in readjusting drive speeds or otherwise meddling with drive alignments, whether you do it yourself or have it done professionally. There's always a possibility diskettes recorded on a badly timed or aligned drive won't read on a drive that's set up correctly, especially if the drives were marginal when the recordings were made. Suppose, for example, you've recorded diskettes with a drive running more slowly than normal—so slowly the drive is marginally operational. Now, a technician resets the speed and leaves it slightly faster than normal. There's a good chance the previously recorded material won't be readable at the new speed, and you could lose your programming or data.

To prevent this, you follow a particular sequence of events for all diskettes you suspect were recorded on a marginal drive, assuming you have two drives with which to work and both drives are operational. The recommended procedure is:

1. Format or initialize a blank, receiving diskette on the drive to receive a copy. Don't format it on the marginal drive used for the source. This ensures that track and sector marks are recorded on the diskette with the same timing and alignment as the data files, and it's an important step in avoiding possible alignment and timing conflicts that could cost you your data.

2. Place the original diskette in the marginal drive (the one in which it was recorded), keeping the blank preformatted diskette in the other drive.

3. Use whatever copy utility program you have to copy the files from the original to the new diskette. If the utility has a "verification" option such as the "[V]" parameter in CP/M's PIP.COM utility or the verification selection on an Apple's FID program, use it. This will ensure that you obtain a good copy. Label the new diskette as a "temporary copy" and include the drive designation used.

4. Have the marginal drive adjusted as necessary. That's the drive used as the source of the preceding copies. Don't have the other drive adjusted yet.

5. Reverse the procedure, copying back from the temporary diskettes to either new or the original diskettes. Again, be sure to format or reformat the diskettes on the receiving drive that has been adjusted, and make all copies from the second drive to the correct one.

6. Repeat this entire procedure for the other drive, copying the doubtful diskettes, adjusting the drive, and recopying the diskettes back to the original drive.

With this procedure, you should eliminate or at least minimize any difficulties resulting from drive incompatibilities. You always have the needed files on a diskette specific to a working drive.

Users with single-drive systems obviously cannot do this and have few alternatives. Of course, it's possible just to take one's chances and hope the readjusted drive will be able to read the old diskettes. However, you might be able to talk a dealer into loaning or renting you a second drive or allowing you to use "demo" drives right in the store to make the backup copies. Even if you have to pay for the service, it may well be worth it to protect your stored information.

Incidentally, single-drive systems should be subjected to diagnostic tests more frequently than dual- or multiple-drive systems. Whenever I have a drive out of service for repair, leaving only one active, I automatically switch to a daily diagnostic run, checking the remaining drive's performance and timing immediately on firing up the system for a day's work.

HARD-DISK SUBSYSTEMS

Care and maintenance of a hard disk is somewhat different from that of floppy disks, although much of what has been presented in previous sections may be applicable. There are some similarities in that hard disks are sensitive to stray magnetic fields, static discharges, power disturbances, and other normal hazards. It's the user's responsibility to practice the normal preventive care for these devices just as with any other system components.

Hard disks seem particularly sensitive to "shock," either thermal or physical. The paramount rules seem to be (1) avoid rapidly changing or extreme temperatures, staying close to the middle of the specified operating ranges, and (2) avoid unnecessary jarring or vibration that could cause the heads to contact the spinning platters and result in a head crash.

Cartridge-style drives also seem susceptible to dirt and dust, perhaps more so than the floppies. Cartridges must be handled carefully, including storage in dust- and dirt-free environments. The seals and dust barriers are not foolproof and can be penetrated by airborne contaminants. Again, this can lead to a disastrous head crash and the loss of large quantities of data—plus the destruction of expensive magnetic platters and even the drive itself. Of course, there also are specialized aids including different models of an automatic Disk Cartridge Cleaner available from Innovative Computer Products. As a rule, these devices may appear expensive, but if you can afford to use cartridge-style hard disks, you probably can afford to purchase the cleaning units as well. In fact, saving yourself a single head crash will justify the costs of most cleaning units.

With a little investigation, you can turn up some other useful products like the Protective Bottom Cover provided by Innovative Computer Products for certain types of cartridges. Some front-loading cartridges are open to the environment on the bottom, allowing contaminants access to the magnetic surface. There also may be a possibility of scratching and otherwise damaging cartridge parts by physical contact with foreign objects, a physical shock and subsequent unseating of rotating parts, or lateral movement of the disk platter within the housing. A product like the Protective Bottom Cover is designed to prevent these adverse effects, locking the platter, centering and securing the moving parts, and covering and sealing the open bottom.

Cartridge-style disk drives often have special filter packs installed to clean air at the cooling intakes. These packs get dirty, cutting down the air flow and eventually causing overheating problems. The packs must be replaced frequently and regularly, and all users must keep careful track of the filter condition and replacement cycles to prevent serious damage. Furthermore, filters are not something on which you should pinch pennies. Bargain filters are no bargain if they allow dust and dirt to penetrate the drive. If you once knock out a drive, have to spend thousands of dollars for repair, and devote hundreds of hours to recovering lost data, you'll quickly be convinced that it just isn't worth it to save a few dollars by buying off-brand, generic, or inferior filters.

Fixed Winchester disks don't have all the dirt and contamination problems, but most of the manufacturers to whom I've spoken have admitted that the units are extremely sensitive to both temperature and physical shock. In short, you must operate within the temperature specifications to prevent minor or major malfunctions, and you must not drop, bump, or otherwise jolt them either while they are in operation or while they are idle.

Some Winchester models, such as the Shugart Associates SA600 Fixed Disk Drive, have a designated "shipping zone" on the magnetic media. This is an area of the disk that is not used for data. Instead, the read/write heads can be positioned to the area before power is turned off so that any shocks incurred during moving or shipping the drive affect only the particular zone, not the valuable storage areas of the media. If a drive is so equipped, the heads should be positioned to the shipping zone before any attempt is made to move the unit. Don't even slide the drive forward in a rack or across a tabletop until the heads have been positioned where they can't harm the data. Definitely don't carry the unit from room to room, or transport it to another location without locking the heads to the shipping zone or taking whatever other steps the manufacturer advises.

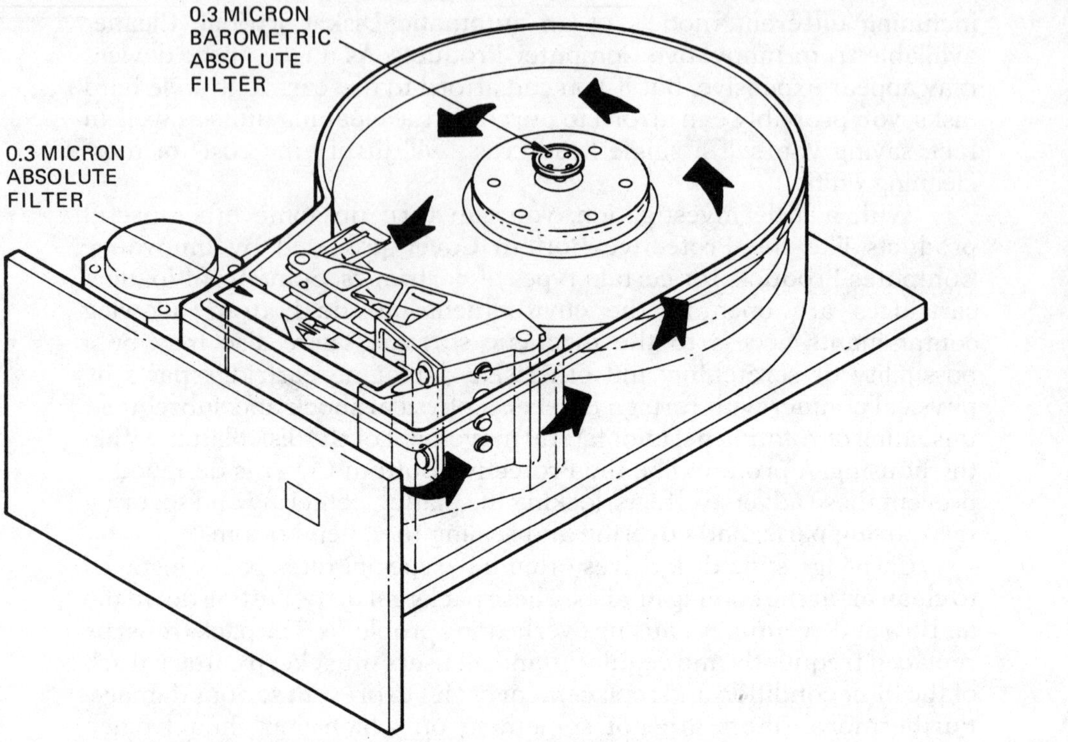

FIG 7-15 Typical Winchester air filtration. *(Adapted from Shugart Associates)*

A final note: all models of Winchesters are not necessarily maintenance-free, contrary to what many people believe. As shown in Fig. 7-15, some like the Shugart Associates SA600 are equipped with an "absolute breather filter" that allows pressure equalization of the internal recirculating air system with the outside air. Since the filter traps all particles 0.3 micron or larger, the equalization can take place without contamination. Ambient air pressures change continuously—that's what the barometric pressure on the evening weather report is about. As ambient pressure changes, internal pressure equalizes through the filter. That means some air flows, which traps airborne particulates in and on the submicron filter. Eventually, the filter gets dirty and requires replacement, although the manufacturers don't say how often and don't provide any procedure in the service manuals. Most likely, the job should be left to a qualified technician, and I have a feeling that the filter should be professionally checked at least once a year (more often in dirty or dusty environments).

Supposedly, submicron filters within the sealed housing are used only to clean the recirculating air. There should be little or nothing for those filters to capture, so the life should be quite long. Most manufacturers don't mention the filters, and they are not accessible to users. The sealed casing around a Winchester drive may be opened only by the manufacturer in a clean-room environment. If your manual states that the internal filters have to be replaced, then assume that shipment back to the factory will be necessary.

CONCLUSION

Disk and tape drives, though effective and popular mass storage, are vulnerable areas of any system. They are adversely affected by anything and everything that can affect any part of the system, although problems associated with dirt and contamination are the most common. If the drives are given appropriate care, protection from destructive external influences, and routine preventive maintenance, most problems can be minimized. Users should expect these devices to cause most of the downtime encountered during the life of a system.

Disk drives, especially floppies or flexible-media types, are particularly prone to dirt and contamination because they are not sealed or otherwise protected from the environment. Users of all magnetic media should be prepared to purchase auxiliary supplies and equipment in addition to the basic drives and controllers, including diagnostic software, cleaning kits, and similar products. Though costly at first, these products do contribute significantly to the continued long-term use of the drives and to their overall cost effectiveness.

Above all, users must recognize that preventive care is primarily for the benefit of the magnetic media and the data stored thereon. Even the most expensive hardware failures are repaired cheaply when compared to the cost of lost software, damaged or destroyed information files, and the expenses of restoring software to a system once it has been lost.

EIGHT

MAGNETIC MEDIA AND SOFTWARE

Proper care of magnetic media and the software (programs and data) stored thereon is closely allied to drive care and maintenance. These are also areas often neglected or ignored by novice and experienced users alike, out of either ignorance or carelessness. There's no way I can overemphasize the importance of good media and software care, since a computer system is useless without the programs and data that make it do its thing.

You're probably getting tired of hearing about the seven deadly hazards, but it is necessary. Dirt, heat, magnetic fields, static, power disturbances, wear, and mishandling are no less important in regard to media and software because each is potentially destructive, and each can cause major problems in lost software, added expenses for replacements, lost time to restore damaged data, and so on. Even if you ignore the previous chapters, don't ignore this one. By handling your media properly and adopting good operating procedures for things like software backup, you can cut operating costs substantially.

THE UNIVERSAL RULES

There are basic rules for handling all media, whether tape, diskette, or hard disk. You've probably seen these mentioned in magazine articles, books, manuals, and even on diskette dust jackets. Nevertheless, they need to be repeated again and again until they sink in and become an automatic and unconscious part of your operating procedures.

The rules aren't just things to think about each time you use a tape or disk. Instead, they must become habits broken only with great effort. Too many users forget there are reasons behind the rules—all designed to maximize the life of the media and thereby ensure continued long-term use with minimum difficulty. But these rules aren't always convenient, and users soon start to ignore them, thinking, "It hasn't hurt yet, so it's okay." Nothing could be farther from the truth. Just because damaged media haven't cost you anything doesn't mean they won't sooner or later. Often, a single lapse may not show up immediately, but the effects are cumulative, and continued failure to obey the rules will add up.

I'll begin by summarizing the rules, and then I'll discuss the rationale for each in individual sections. The essentials are as follows:

1. Always protect the media from dust and dirt, storing them in dustproof containers when not in use. Be especially alert to surface oxidation and corrosive contaminants.

2. Never touch magnetic surfaces with fingers or other foreign objects that could leave deposits or scratch oxide coatings.

3. Never expose media to heat or stray magnetic fields.

4. Take care not to cause static discharges to or across the media.

5. Use only media stabilized at the specified operating temperature, and avoid storing or using media near direct heat sources.

6. Handle all media carefully, whether inserting into a drive, removing from a drive, storing, or transporting.

Media Contamination

The most important rule of media care is to protect tapes or disks from contamination by airborne substances. As pointed out in Chapter 7, abrasive dust caught between a magnetic surface and a read/write head can wreak havoc on both. Therefore, it's crucial that tapes, diskettes, and hard disks be protected from such contaminants.

Naturally, it helps to keep the drive mechanisms clean. The more dust and dirt there is within a drive, the more can be captured by the media. That is not enough. The media must also be protected when not in use, necessitating dustproof storage.

A magnetic tape, diskette, or hard disk belongs in one of two places—never anywhere else! It should be in a drive or in protective storage. Reel-to-reel tapes should be stored in closed boxes. Tape cassettes and cartridges should be stored in individual containers, closed to prevent contamination. Diskettes should be stored in their protective dust jackets and then in a dustproof box because the jackets alone are not sufficient. Hard-disk cartridges should be stored in their shipping containers with protective covers installed and access-doors closed. All media then should be placed in dustproof cabinets.

Never leave media lying out in the open, not even for a few minutes. When you are juggling various items like multiple cassettes or floppy diskettes, there's always a temptation to set one down just for a moment or two until it's needed again. Bad news! Within seconds, airborne particles start settling on the media. Furthermore, the media have a slight magnetic field which can attract minute particles of ferrous compounds, and there's often a slight static charge on the surface that attracts common dust and dirt, grabbing it right off the surface on which the item is placed.

Incidentally, it's a good idea to close storage containers between the steps of removing and returning media. All the care in the world does little good if cassette boxes, diskette dust jackets, storage cabinets, and the like are contaminated internally because they were left open and exposed while the contents were in use. I've seen many users pull a diskette and its dust jacket from a file box, close the box, insert the diskette into a drive, and then leave the jacket propped against some system component. Contaminants settle out of the air into the pocket of the jacket. When the diskette is returned, it's plunged straight into a dirty environment. It's far better to return the empty jackets to the closed storage container until you are finished with the diskettes.

This whole thing becomes even more important when exposure to corrosive compounds is possible. Around major metropolitan areas and industrial centers, corrosive chemicals are often among the normal airborne pollutants. Compounds such as ozone and hydrogen sulphide have adverse effects on oxide coatings, and it's important to minimize the contact with the compounds by minimizing exposure to the atmosphere. Being inside a building isn't much help. A few years ago, I saw some environmental reports that determined indoor pollution was often as bad as or worse than outdoor pollution, due to concentrations developed by slow air circulation combined with indoor contaminants such as cigarette smoke and cooking grease.

You also need to guard against surface oxidation. It's not altogether correct to say that magnetic media rust, but it's a close approximation. Many materials, not just iron, oxidize on exposure to the air, and the compounds used in magnetic coatings are no exception. There are "binders," adhesives, and even lubricants used on tape and disks, many of which either oxidize or dry out when exposed. Recently, I found a tape cassette I'd stashed away in a drawer a few months earlier without a protective container. Looking at the exposed tape, I found the area was white instead of brown and was roughened by uneven splotches and dimpled oxide. The surface had corroded, and the tape was ruined.

Users in high-humidity regions face another problem—airborne moisture. In coastal or southern states, high humidity encourages growth of mildew, mold, and algae in the most inconvenient places. I've seen growths invade camera lenses, boxes of photographic negatives, stamp collections, and virtually every dark, closed area imaginable. Air-conditioning systems help, but such environments may require special treatment to guard against damage to both equipment and magnetic media. One preventive step is to use packs of "dessicant" gels in the media containers. The gels absorb atmospheric moisture, making a comparatively dry environment for the media. However, check with suppliers before purchasing gels so you don't get one that emits harmful vapors or contaminants. Also, you have to remember to renew the dessicants every week or so (usually by heating in an oven) so that they remain effective.

Fingers and Foreign Objects

Keep your fingers off the media surfaces! That's an ironclad rule! Fingerprints are destructive for two reasons. First, skin oils can attract and hold dust and dirt particles, concentrating the contaminants in ridges. Furthermore, the oils and the contaminants they carry can be transmitted to heads or spread out in smudges across the media. Such oils also may cause a gradual breakdown in the chemical structure of oxide coatings, possibly loosening the adhesives that hold coatings to the base materials and eventually causing oxide to peel, chip, or flake.

Second, salts and other compounds in perspiration are corrosive. For optical devices like camera lenses, special cautions are issued about removing fingerprints from all glass surfaces. If not removed, the fingerprints etch the glass, permanently damaging the elements. The same is true of magnetic coatings—fingerprints can etch into the coatings, causing uneven surfaces that don't contact a head properly and thereby lose data during read or write operations. The difference is that magnetic coatings, unlike optical lenses, usually aren't cleanable. Therefore, touching a surface means a permanent fingerprint and possibly the destruction of the entire tape or disk.

Always handle a reel-to-reel tape by the metal or plastic reel, keeping fingers away from the tape. The only safe place to touch is the clear leader that precedes or follows the recording area, and it is necessary to touch that area to thread the tape onto the drive. A cassette or cartridge should be handled only by the side edges, well away from the opening through which the read/write head contacts the tape. A floppy diskette should be handled only from the back edge nearest the label, and special pains must be taken not to touch the surface through the head-access holes cut in the plastic jacket. A hard-disk cartridge should be grabbed only by the built-in handle.

It's a tough rule to obey, particularly if you're as fumble-fingered as I get at times. Sooner or later, a finger comes in contact with a magnetic surface. I used to ignore the occasional contact, but I've had so many problems with drives and diskettes over the years that I'll no longer take any chances. If my finger touches down on a magnetic surface, I toss the media in the trash, cut a new working copy on fresh media from a backup, and proceed from there. It seems a pity to throw away a $5 to $10 diskette, but I prefer that to risking more serious losses later.

Foreign objects are a danger. Keep pens, pencils, screwdrivers, paper clips, staples, and similar "tools" away from tapes or disks. Never poke around the media with any hard object. The principal risk is physical damage to the oxide. Since foreign objects are harder than the oxide, it's easy to scratch, chip, or mar the surface, eventually causing a media failure. If, for some reason, something like a fragment of paper gets lodged in a cassette or disk housing, the odds are it's already done its damage before you try to get it out. Besides, attempts to remove the item can only cause additional damage, so it's advisable, once again, to toss the media and start fresh with a new copy.

Magnetic Fields and X-Rays

All magnetic media rely on changes of magnetic "flux" to store information. Flux changes are created by magnetic fields in the read/write heads, and they can be altered by magnetic fields from any source. Therefore, tapes and disks must be protected from all devices that contain magnets or may become magnetized. That includes most common tools such as screwdrivers, pliers, tweezers, and the like. It also includes the bell coils in telephones, magnets and coils in speakers, transformers, and many others. Virtually any electrically powered device contains at least one transformer, including display terminals, video monitors, printer buffers, ac-powered modems, and many more.

Each such device has the potential of damaging recorded information by altering the magnetic flux. It takes only one exposure to trash all or part of a tape or disk. One telephone ringing too close. One audio speaker activating nearby. One slip-up in placing a tape or disk on top of a printer or CRT. One pass near a magnetized screwdriver or a flashlight with a magnetic handle. These and more can easily cost a user stored data and programs.

As usual, the best remedy is prevention. Keep idle media in approved storage containers, and keep those storage containers several feet from all possible magnetic fields. That means several feet from all metallic objects and electrical or electronic devices. Never set disks or tapes on top of drives, printers, CRTs, monitors, or other system components. Don't even carry them past active printers, particularly printers that have "magnetic induction" drives.

A related problem involves demagnetizing media. Sudden physical shock can alter magnetic fields of objects or the magnetic flux of recording media. There's a trick with metal tools that serves as an illustration. Sometimes, a tool like a screwdriver becomes magnetized, which can be a nuisance to some users. A common remedy is to rap the tool sharply with a heavy hammer. Usually, that physical shock partly demagnetizes the tool, at least enough so that you can use it without grabbing hold of nearby objects. Well, the same thing can happen to magnetic recording media. Dropping a cassette or diskette, particularly so that it hits on its edge, can disturb the magnetic flux and alter the data patterns. Even slamming a box of tapes or disks onto a tabletop can be enough shock to alter data. Therefore, treat media with respect and handle them carefully. If you do drop a cassette or diskette, examine the files stored thereon for possible alteration or damage before using the media again.

Exposure to X-rays also can demagnetize or alter recording media. This is a problem for people who travel and have baggage inspected by

X-ray, people who ship disks through the mails or other common carriers that may use X-rays, and people using systems in medical or dental offices and wandering too near the X-ray room with a diskette in their hands. Any magnetic media being carried onto airlines or shipped by common carrier should be labeled in large letters, "Delicate Magnetic Recordings, DO NOT X-RAY." But even that isn't sufficient, and it's advantageous to package tapes and disks in lead foil for transport. Good products are available from professional photography stores. They sell lead-lined bags for transporting film, and those same bags are useful for magnetic media. The protection may not be absolute, but it does help.

Static Electricity

Electrostatic charges are a common nuisance. Much has been said about the subject in previous chapters, but it must be brought up again. If it discharges across or onto a magnetic surface, an electrostatic charge can severely damage recorded information—possibly even the media itself.

Again, the best remedy is prevention. First, avoid handling media in high-static environments. That means not carrying a disk or tape across a carpeted area. If you must, at least discharge to metal objects as you proceed, but be sure to discharge with something other than the media in your hand. Second, take the appropriate measures to reduce or eliminate static problems as outlined in a previous chapter. Anti-static mats under and around the installation are the most valuable preventive measures of all. Third, don't just walk up to a box of disks or a drive and grab the media—discharge any accumulated static to something else first.

Always be sure the disk or tape drives are properly grounded. First, the grounding is a barrier between you and the media. Second, the ground bleeds off any charge building up in the drive or on the disk during use, preventing spontaneous internal discharges.

Temperature Control

Each type of magnetic media has a specified operating temperature. For example, floppy diskettes should be used only at temperatures between 50°F and 125°F (10°C and 52°C).

One common error is to store or transport media under conditions that allow excess heat. The tapes and disks are on a plastic-like base material that can melt, warp, or distort if overheated, thereby making it impossible to use them in the drives. Keep all tapes and disks out of direct sunlight and away from uncovered windows. If light from a window reaches a storage box, the internal temperature can rise well above media tolerance. Similarly, keep away from radiators, stoves, and other heat sources. If you transport disks in your automobile, don't leave them in a closed car during warm, sunny weather. Glove compartments, trunks, rear decks of station wagons, and other locations all are unsafe because they build high temperatures. It's far better to carry the media with you rather than leave them in a vehicle.

Extreme cold is just as much a danger, but is encountered less often. Most homes and offices aren't likely to get colder than the operating temperature of the media, and few owners are going to be dumb enough to store disks or tapes in a refrigerator or freezer. There is, however, a danger if you are transporting disks or receiving shipments, especially during the winter months. Never use a tape or disk until it has stabilized at room temperature. If you bring one in from outdoors, allow at least four to six hours for stabilization.

The first problem associated with cold is brittleness. The plastic base material gets stiff when cold, and attempting to run the media through a drive can overstress it, thereby causing cracks, or even shattering tapes and disks.

A more serious problem is condensation. We all know what happens to eyeglasses or sunglasses when you enter a warm building during the winter. They fog up, just as a pitcher of lemonade or a glass of iced tea frosts on a hot, summer day. Well, the same can happen to a disk or tape carried from cold to warm environments. Moisture condenses on the surface, possibly damaging heads and media on attempting to use it in a drive. Therefore, always allow at least four to six hours for temperature stabilization before using such media. Don't even open the box, since the container is a protective barrier against moisture penetration during the warming period.

MAGNETIC TAPE

In addition to the general rules, magnetic tapes have other requirements. Things like packing, tape grades, and storage positions usually aren't addressed in the instruction manuals that accompany the popular drive units.

Tape Packing

The way in which magnetic tape is packed onto the supply reel or spool can affect the performance. It's essential for a tape to feed with uniform tension and speed for reliable recording and playback. That leads to the matter of repacking tapes—something necessary for all new tapes and after any shipment of tapes whether they are reel-to-reel, cassette, or cartridge types.

When a tape is bounced around during transport, the coils slip and loosen on the reel or spool, but they don't loosen uniformly. As a result, one section may be wrapped loosely, another tightly. As tape feeds through a drive, differences in tension can affect the speed and, thus, the data being recorded or read back. To minimize the effect, a newly acquired tape or any tape that has been transported from one place to another (other than between drive and storage box) should be cycled through its entire length before use.

The easiest way to repack a tape is to install it onto the drive and perform a fast-forward from beginning to end, followed by a fast-reverse from the end back to the beginning. It takes a few minutes, but the tape ends up on the supply with near-uniform tension. The operation is an easy way of dramatically improving media reliability. I perform this operation on any tape stored longer than 30 days without having been used. It ensures that the tape feeds without binding or stalling. Some people recommend always storing the tape in the fully wound position, making it necessary to rewind before the next use.

Tape Positioning

The storage position also affects reliability. For cassettes and cartridges, the tape should be fully wound or rewound before removal from the drive; never remove one while it is positioned midway through the recording area. By having the tape at one extreme or another, the spool is packed, and the cutouts in the casing for contact with heads and rollers expose only clear leader. The packing helps produce subsequent uniformity of speed, while positioning on clear leader moves the sensitive recording surface into the protective casing where it's less likely to be damaged by dust, dirt, fingerprints, oxidation, and other hazards.

Once packed and inside dust-proof containers, tapes should be stored standing vertically on edge. Even reel-to-reel tapes should be stored on edge, not flat or horizontally. This helps keep reels and casings from warping, and it maintains packing and tape tension by preventing coils from slipping during storage. For cassettes and cartridges, there is some argument about which edge should be the base. However, most recommendations are to position it so that the full spool is on the bottom. This is supposed to reduce strain on the tape and help reduce stretching and distortion.

Write Protection

Cassettes and cartridges may be protected against writing data. This is a safety feature to prevent accidental erasure of valuable information. On cassettes, the protection is implemented by prying off a tab on the rear edge, preventing the write/head of the drive from being engaged. On a cartridge, there usually is a movable tab that can be positioned to either protect or unprotect the medium.

There is a potential problem with cassettes. Often, it's necessary to unprotect a cassette, perhaps to add or change data. With the tab broken off, the usual advice is to place a piece of tape over the notch, thereby simulating an unprotected tape. What the instructions don't tell you is to remove the tape when you're finished. The object isn't to reprotect against recording, but to prevent dangerous adhesive deterioration.

If adhesive tape is left over the cassette protection notch while in storage, that tape can "leak" or grow brittle. You've probably seen what happens to mending tape left on paper for months or years. The tape discolors and chips, while a gummy residue appears around the edges. The same happens if you leave such tape on a cassette. As it ages, the adhesive leaks, attracting dirt and dust, which threaten drive contamination. The tape itself gets brittle and could fragment, leaving pieces that could damage the works or the recording medium.

If you must unprotect a cassette, either buy some commercial plugs made just for that purpose, or remember to remove the adhesive tape before storing the cassette.

Initial Tape Tension

When you first remove a cassette or cartridge from storage, there is usually slack between the supply and take-up spools. That slack should be eliminated before use. Doing a fast-forward/fast-reverse cycle from end to end is one way. The alternative is to rotate one spool by hand. On cassettes, the notched drive hub is accessible to a fingertip or pencil, and it may be rotated until the tape is taut. This isn't a highly recommended procedure, but it does work and shouldn't cause problems if you're gentle. Just don't use so much pressure on the spool notches that you break or chip them.

Tape Grades

There are different grades of tape you can use. Among cassettes, you have the choice of audio-quality or computer-grade tape. And there are differences between them. Since audio tape is less expensive, recreational users tend to rely on it. For the less sophisticated recorders and tape drives, such quality may be adequate. However, the more expensive computer tape is certified to specific standards, meaning that the tapes have been tested for uniformity of coating, few dead spots or dropouts, and so on. Furthermore, many low-cost audio tapes have splices, but computer tape is supposed to be splice-free.

As a rule, you should enjoy better performance from computer-grade tape than from audio-quality tape within almost any system. If you have purchased expensive and delicate recorders, then you almost have to adopt the more expensive type to get the best results from your investment.

Tape Splicing

Eventually, a tape will break, and you'll be faced with the task of replacing or repairing it. Most audiophiles have splicing equipment and supplies to repair and even edit recordings. But for computer use, the best advice about splicing is to avoid it like a plague.

There's no such thing as a perfect splice, and there is always some loss. If you accidentally record data over a splice, you're likely to lose something. Occasionally, people with fancy tape drives having read-after-write verification of recorded data can get by because the machine automatically detects a bad block of data and erases and records the block again and again in different locations until it gets it right. Low-

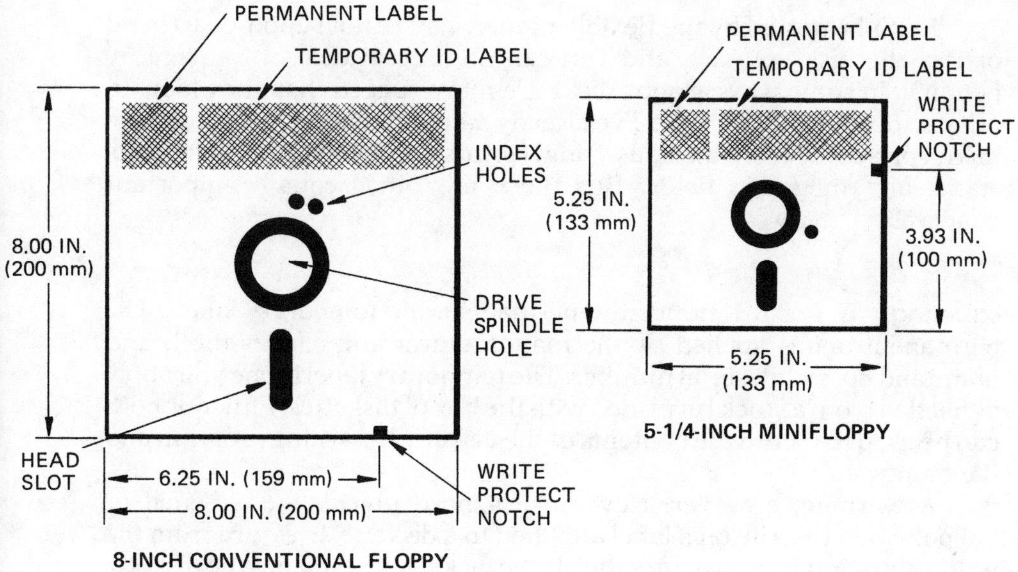

FIG 8-1 Typical floppy-disk features.

quality recorders don't have that capability, however, and a splice could cost you a valuable program or irreplaceable data.

Yet there's a greater danger. The adhesive splicing tape may leak and ooze as it ages, or it may grow brittle. It's unavoidable that the adhesive eventually contacts the heads, rollers, or capstan, where it leaves a deposit that can ruin subsequent tapes. If the splicing material chips or shatters, jagged pieces can lodge in the works and plow through other media, severely damaging recordings.

Don't splice! Don't even attempt to pull tape out of a cartridge or cassette for inspection. There's no safe way to do it!

FLOPPY DISKETTES

Like tapes, floppy disks require care over and above the universal rules for handling magnetic media. Some concerns, such as write protection and storage positioning, are similar, but others—surface certification and using the flip sides—differ.

Special Handling Problems

Floppy diskettes are characterized by physical flexibility. A thin, magnetically coated disk of plastic is housed within a flexible plastic jacket that has openings for the center mounting hub or drive spindle, the timing or index holes that the drive reads with photodetectors, and a small section of disk surface for contact with the read/write heads and, where present, the pressure pad. Inside the plastic jacket, a felt-like liner cleans the diskette as it spins. Figure 8-1 illustrates the typical diskette configurations and parts for both 8-inch and 5-1/4-inch types.

Don't be misled by the flexible nature. You're not supposed to bend or flex the disk yourself, and you can do a great deal of damage by bending. In some ways, floppy disks are more rugged than they look. In others, they are more fragile. I've already mentioned the need to keep the media protected from dirt, dust, fingerprints, foreign objects, heat, cold, static, and magnetic fields. But there are other equally important concerns.

Labeling. In Fig. 8-1, notice the permanent and temporary labels. The permanent one is applied by the manufacturer and carries the brand name and possibly a serial number. The temporary label is one you apply as needed from a stock furnished with the box of diskettes. Either or both can be used to record the contents of the diskette by writing program and file names.

A warning, however! Never use a hard object like a pencil or ballpoint pen to write on a label attached to a diskette. Pressure from the writing instrument penetrates the plastic jacket and damages the diskette surface. Instead, use only soft, felt-tip pens, with the emphasis on soft. The hard, plastic-tipped or reinforced markers should not be used. Neither should the ultra-fine line types. Even with a soft tip, keep the pressure light. I've been known to soften up felt-tip pens by dropping them point-first onto the floor a few times, squashing the tips and flattening them out so they don't press into diskettes. Of course, the writing is hard to read, but it's adequate for my purposes.

I shouldn't have to say it, but I've seen someone actually try this. Don't attempt to put a labeled diskette through a typewriter or printer. They're just not built for that. Even if the diskette somehow survived being wrapped around the roller, it won't survive the impact of the typewriter keys.

Of course, there's bound to be a problem removing a "temporary" label if you rerecord or reassign the diskette. I've seen labels ranging from ones that can't be made to stick at all, to ones that seem welded to the plastic jacket. The first type causes problems because edges and corners rip off as it is being inserted into or removed from a drive, thereby losing a sticky piece of paper inside the drive where it can attach to the head or the magnetic surface of a later diskette. If I see a label working loose, I remove it (this is usually not too difficult), and destroy any spare labels that came in the same box.

At the opposite extreme, the tightly bonded labels are next to impossible to remove without risking damage to the diskette. Unless the label is literally falling off the diskette, I usually just apply a new label over the old, and I've been known to go six or seven layers deep. Notably, a second label is usually easier to remove than the first.

If you insist on stripping old labels, you assume the risk of damaging the media no matter how careful you are. Yet you can do it, and I'll outline the procedure I've used successfully.

1. With the diskette in its dust jacket, lay it flat on a clean, static-free surface with the label at the right edge (I'm right-handed).

2. Hold the diskette to the surface with the left hand, keeping fingers spread and the label between thumb and forefinger.

3. Take a sharp hobby knife (an X-Acto® No. 11 blade works nicely), and hold the blade flat against the diskette jacket. Then gently lift one or more corners of the label. Be careful not to press down on the diskette jacket, and don't dig into the jacket.

4. While still holding the diskette firmly down with the left hand, gently pull the raised label edges, slowly peeling it from the jacket. Occasionally, stubborn labels can be removed by turning an edge under and rolling it up like a rug.

If you're gentle and all goes well, there should be no damage to the diskette.

Drive Insertion and Removal. People who have worked with floppy drives take the disk insertion process for granted. People having their first contact with such drives are often baffled. There are some rules and recommendations, and none of us can fail to benefit from reviewing them.

Obviously, the first step is to open the drive door. Easy, right? Well, not always that easy! There are all kinds of doors. On some you move the door; on others you operate a release mechanism. Some are pressed inward. Some are pressed downward. Some are raised. Some slide from side to side. And there's at least one I've seen that requires twisting a lever. Novice users acquiring their first drives and experienced users acquiring new drives would do well to have the dealer demonstrate how the door works.

Once the door is open, the fun really starts, and a user has to determine how to insert the diskette. There are some rules. The first is that the edge along the labels (the top edge of Fig. 8-1) is the trailing edge; that is, it's the edge held parallel to the door slot and the last edge to pass through the slot. Second, the side with the permanent label is the "top" surface. If the drive opening is horizontal, the label is always up, facing the ceiling and not the floor.

What if the drive openings are vertical? The label edge is still the trailing edge; that never changes. But the conventional approach is that the labeled side faces the system operator. For example, if the drives normally are to the left of the operator, the diskettes are inserted with the labels to the right nearest the operator. If the drives are to the right, the diskettes go in with the labels on the left, again facing the operator. This works on most standard systems, although a few users with detached drives sometimes place them on the opposite sides and have to reverse the positions.

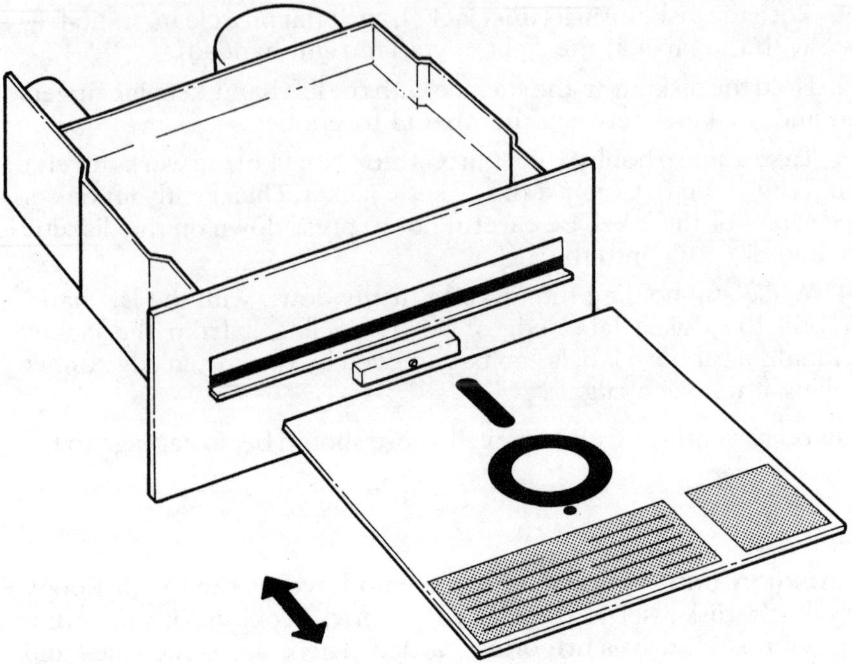

FIG 8-2 Floppy diskette insertion.

There is a rule of thumb—literally. If you use the hand closest to the drives, the diskette should be held with the thumb on the label as shown in Fig. 8-2. The correct diskette position then causes no discomfort and requires no unusual arm twisting.

The diskette must be pressed completely home in the drive to prevent damage when the door is closed. Most drives have a catch or latch that can be felt (or heard as a click) when the diskette is fully inserted.

Now there's the matter of closing the drive door. Here's where even experienced users make mistakes. As the door closes, the center hub or drive spindle engages the large hole in the center of the disk, clamping it firmly in place. The spindle is spring-loaded and moves to center itself in the hole. If the door is closed too quickly or while the diskette isn't in proper position, the hub and clamp can pinch the diskette, possibly damaging the center hole. The best procedure is to work the door slowly and in steps. I call it "jiggling" the door down. By using a slight back-and-forth motion combined with an overall flow toward complete closure, the center hub engages slowly, allowing the disk and hub to be centered. In turn, that cuts down on problems experienced later because of misalignment between the diskette tracks and read/write head.

Removing a diskette is simple. Open the door and grab, right? Well, not quite . . . Some drives have ejection mechanisms and some require lifting an edge or corner with a fingertip to disengage them. If opening the door doesn't shoot the diskette out where it can be grabbed, then lift gently on the center or on either corner of the diskette and it should pop free.

Another warning! Most disk drives have an "in use" indicator. When it is illuminated, a read or write is in progress, and the diskette must not be removed. Attempting to remove (or insert) a diskette while the "in use" indicator is glowing may cause irreparable damage. There are exceptions, however. Some drives, such as those built into the KayPro computer, have an indicator that doesn't mean "in use" but merely indicates which drive was accessed last. Be sure to check the manuals for the exact meaning of lights and indicators.

Yet another warning! There is a difference between 8-inch and 5-1/4-inch drives. The latter spend most of their time idle, spinning only when disk accesses are in progress. They are designed to have the diskettes inserted and removed when they are not spinning. Always insert or remove such diskettes while the drives are quiet to prevent accidental damage to stored files.

Conversely, 8-inch drives spin continuously. These are designed for diskette insertion and removal only while powered and spinning. Never attempt to insert a diskette before powering up or to remove one after powering down. If you suffer a power failure, it's usually better to leave the diskette in the drive until power returns, but be alert to any damage that might be caused by power transients as the system comes back on line. If I take a power failure with the 8-inch drives, I set the drive and computer power switches off, leave the diskettes in place, and wait for the electricity to return to normal. I'll sometimes wait a half-hour or longer to get past surges and fluctuations that typically follow an outage. Then I just switch the system back on, reboot, and proceed normally.

Diskette Storage

There are numerous devices now being marketed for diskette storage, some good but others a bit questionable. The emphasis is and should be on protecting the diskettes from airborne contaminants by limiting the air flow around them. Nearly every commercial storage container does that, but a few may create other problems.

For example, consider plastic notebook sheets with pockets for diskette storage. They're popular because they permit paging through a book of diskettes quickly. They also protect diskettes from airborne dust. However, I dislike them for several reasons. First, there's the possibility of a static discharge while sliding a diskette in or out of the pocket. Some of the newer plastic pocket pages are made of low-static materials, but there's always a chance of creating a charge by rubbing a disk against a pocket, especially in a dry climate.

Second, they sometimes stick to the diskette, especially when the humidity is high. Moisture can work between the layers of plastic, causing an adhesion that's difficult to break. I've had some stuck so tightly it was almost impossible to remove the diskette without bending it or overstressing it. Furthermore, I've seen the plastic lift the printing off labels, thereby contaminating the pocket itself with ink or photocopier residue.

Third, the diskettes can be difficult to remove even under optimum conditions. Some of these pocket pages are so tightly fitted to the diskette size that it takes considerable force and manipulation to work the media out. Of course, that exposes diskettes to potential physical damage.

Fourth, I've had some of the pages fold under as I've closed a binder. That lets diskettes slip toward the binder rings. When the book is closed, the rings dig into and dent the diskettes or jackets. The damage then is similar to but more severe than writing on a label with a ballpoint pen.

I much prefer storage boxes that hold diskettes vertically. My favorites are the flip-top, smoked-plastic boxes sold under various brand names. Available for standard floppies or minifloppies, each box holds up to 50 diskettes, with indexing dividers for subject categories. The lids offer adequate dust protection, and they simply rise upward and tilt back behind the box to access the diskettes. The diskettes remain in their original dust jackets, but the full set of 50 is immediately accessible by flipping through the file. The principle is the same as a box of index cards and just as effective.

Such storage boxes can become expensive, however. I have hundreds of diskettes among three computers, and it would cost a small fortune to put them all in flip files. Instead, I keep the 50 most-used diskettes for each machine in such a box. Backup copies, archival masters, and seldom-used diskettes are kept in the manufacturer's original shipping boxes. That way, I have quick access to the diskettes I need frequently, while the others are out of my way, yet protected.

One point is extremely important. No matter what type of storage container you choose, diskettes should be stored vertically—standing on edge. Storing them flat or horizontally encourages warping or distortion. Vertical storage also prevents the weight of the media from piling up on the lowest diskettes in a stack, possibly pressing contaminants trapped by the felt liners into the magnetic surfaces.

For my most important diskettes, I've replaced paper dust jackets with vinyl DiscSavers™ from RockRoy, Inc. One advantage is color coding to identify software categories quickly. More important, they provide improved protection against spilled liquids, abrasions, and so on. As I used diskettes for several years, original paper sleeves became worn and unsightly, while shedding paper fibers that attached to diskettes. With vinyl sleeves on the most-used diskettes, I eliminate the wear and paper fibers, removing another possible source of contamination. Notably, these single sleeves don't suffer the problems of plastic notebook pages. They don't seem to stick, and I've had no static problems.

Write Protection and Flip Sides

In Fig. 8-1, notice the write-protect notches. By exposing or covering these notches, you can either allow or prevent recording onto the entire diskette. The rationale is that some programs and data should be protected against accidental erasure or overwriting. Therefore, the notches indicate to a drive whether a diskette may be written; if it is protected, power to the write electronics is interrupted.

There are several points to remember. The foremost is that the notches on minifloppies function in the opposite way to that of 8-inch floppies. This is a difference that catches even experienced users off guard when changing systems or diskette sizes. In the 8-inch formats which usually employ optical sensing, the diskette is protected when the notch is open and is "write-enabled" when the notch is covered. Conversely, 5-1/4-inch drives which use mechanical switches consider the diskette unprotected when the notch is open and protected when covered. If you work several machines and formats as I do, it's important to remember the reversal and consciously think about it when changing machines.

The time you'll probably get caught is when you open a new box of diskettes and prepare them for use. Since manufacturers provide 8-inch diskettes in the protected (notch open) state, it's necessary to apply a tab before the diskette can be formatted or recorded. If you try to use an 8-inch diskette and get error messages, be sure to check that you've installed a tab over the notch. Minifloppies are the opposite, coming out of the box unprotected (notch open), so a conscious effort is required to protect them.

Not all diskettes are equipped with write-protect notches. Often, a manufacturer provides diskettes with and without notches. I recommend buying notched diskettes whether you're in the habit of write-protecting or not. Sooner or later you may need to secure a diskette, and you'll need the notch. Of course, you can cut your own, but it's not always the best procedure. You must place a cutout of the appropriate size in the exact position shown in Fig. 8-1. The cutout extends 1/8 or 1/4 inch (3.2 to 6.4 mm) in from the edge of the diskette. An easy way to place one is to lay a notched disk on an unnotched one, mark the outline, and cut through the jacket with a sharp knife (again, an X-acto No. 11 blade is ideal). A 1/4-inch paper punch also works; again, mark the position and then punch a semicircle through the jacket (the edge of the diskette is usually centered in the punch hole).

Not all drives recognize write protection. Some drives lack the optical detectors or mechanical switches, so there is no way to protect a diskette other than through software control such as locking individual files. It's also possible for a detector to fail when an optical sensor burns out or a mechanical switch breaks down or shifts position. For some commercial software, this can cause problems. On an Apple II, for example, certain software requires write protection or it won't boot. If the switch is inoperative, the diskette won't work and the software is inaccessible. I've even heard of some companies using a copy protection scheme whereby an unprotected diskette automatically erases itself on booting—that story from a user who erased nearly a dozen disks (original and replacements) of a commercial package. The write-protect switches were out of position, failed to register the protection, and triggered the software into an automatic erase and self-destruct cycle.

To complicate the situation further, many software houses aren't supplying their products on protected diskettes. This is happening often on 8-inch media, and many suppliers now use unnotched and unprotected distribution masters. It's then possible to make a mistake during the preparation of working copies, say designating the wrong drive as the receiver, and thereby erasing the master. I don't recommend cutting notches in distribution diskettes, so you have to be extremely careful when making those first copies.

About the only way I can see to stop the practice is to return the unprotected diskettes without using them, accompanied by a demand for refund or a protected diskette. On 8-inch diskettes, lack of a write-protect notch serves no useful purpose other than to reduce the suppliers' costs a few pennies per copy. But at the retail price of commercial software, users shouldn't have to accept a cost-reduction maneuver at the risk of damaging the package.

A caution! When covering a write-protect notch either to unprotect an 8-inch diskette or to protect a 5-1/4-inch diskette, use only the tabs that come with the diskettes. They are coated with a nonleaking adhesive that won't gum up your machine. At all costs, avoid conventional mending tape, electrician's tape, "friction" tape, and similar products. Use of those invariably causes contamination and other problems. For optical sensors in 8-inch drives, write-protect tabs must be opaque, so foil tabs are usually provided. I once got some that weren't opaque and erased a diskette I thought was protected. The light beam penetrated the tab and was detected at a high enough level to register as an unprotected diskette.

The ability to cut write-protect notches opens some interesting possibilities, especially for minifloppies where the notch must be open to allow recording. On some machines, it's possible to cut a new notch, flip the diskette over, and use the reverse side, thereby doubling the storage surface without paying for double-sided diskettes. Apple II users discover this quickly, since the drives don't recognize or use the index holes. Therefore, Apple drives don't care if the diskette is flipped, provided the write-protect notch is on the left side.

Some companies even sell "nibbling tools" to cut new notches that allow conversion of single-sided diskettes to double-sided operation, but remember to paper punch or hobby knife does the job just as well. It sounds like a good deal—two disks for the price of one. Not quite! This is a high-risk operation, placing software, diskettes, and drives in extreme jeopardy. I admit I do it myself, but on a limited basis for archival copies I don't consider crucial for the system. Those are things I can afford to lose, and the diskettes are used for tasks that are not "disk-intensive." I know and recognize the risks and have deliberately chosen to accept them for certain things. I do not recommend using flip sides as a day-to-day operating practice.

All that's necessary to flip over an Apple diskette is to place one diskette upside down on top of another, mark the position of the write-protect notch on the uncut side edge, and cut a new notch. However, the second side of a single-sided diskette is not certified and there are no guarantees. Cutting the second notch voids any existing warranty, so if the primary side fails on a diskette that otherwise might be returnable, you're out of luck because the manufacturer won't honor a warranty on items with which you've tampered.

Not only are flip sides not certified, they may have failed certification tests. Most suppliers make all diskettes double-sided. When the blanks fail to pass certification on one side but do pass on the other, they are packaged as single-sided. Therefore, the flip side could be defective, and you run a good chance of losing what you attempt to record.

You can purchase commercial surface-certification software that will detect flaws. Some even "lock out" bad sectors to prevent their use, thus allowing continued use of the good part. Such programs aren't always reliable, however, and they never do intensive testing necessary to certify media fully. Typically, they make one pass across the diskette, writing data, reading data back, and then logging the diskette sector or block as good or bad, according to whether what was read matched what was written. Yet that's not foolproof. A sector can go bad yet be undetected as a result of the test itself, or at any time thereafter. It may also read correctly one time out of a hundred, with that one time being when the certification test passed across.

Even with certified surfaces, flipping diskettes is risky. Remember that single-sided drives have a fiber pressure pad holding the diskette against the head. That pad accumulates dirt and contamination, and it cannot be cleaned by conventional techniques. Therefore, it can scratch or abrade the surface it contacts. With single-sided diskettes used as intended, damage is limited to the unused side where it does no harm. Flipping the disk subjects the good side to the same dangers, however, since it now presses against the pad it was never intended to touch. The result—both sides of the diskette can be damaged.

As I've said, I do some flipping, but I'm fully aware I could lose everything. Therefore, nothing of real value is stored on such diskettes. I also change the pressure pads every month or so, just to play it safe.

Hub Reinforcements

Diskettes are available with or without "hub rings." The rings are reinforcements to the drive spindle holes (Fig. 8-1) that prevent the clamping action of the spindle from damaging diskettes. For many brands, there is a small premium for reinforced diskettes, but it's well worth paying to increase the usable life of the media.

Without a hub ring, the drive spindle clamps directly onto the diskette, causing two potential problems. One is oxide wear, contributing to increased contamination within the drive. As the spindle clamps around the opening, friction wears oxide from that area, freeing oxide particles, which then can be transported onto diskette and drive surfaces.

More serious, however, is the physical damage the spindle does to the diskette. No matter how well everything is aligned as the drive doors are closed, there is always a certain amount of spindle self-centering during mounting. That applies pressure to the edges and area around the hole, stressing the diskette and eventually bending, creasing, or tearing the media. After a while, the center hole becomes ragged, uneven, and possibly "eccentric." When that happens, the diskette no longer mounts correctly, and misalignments severe enough to interfere with data storage and retrieval are possible.

A hub ring protects a diskette from wear by keeping the spindle out of direct contact with the oxide on at least one side. Furthermore, there is far less distortion of the center hole during normal use, and there is also less likelihood of damage resulting from closing the doors too quickly before the spindle has been allowed to center itself.

I recommend using only reinforced diskettes. I've tried buying diskettes without rings, but they've had useful lives less than a quarter of the lives of reinforced diskettes.

If you have nonreinforced diskettes, I recommend you add rings as quickly as possible. There are kits available to do just that, providing a centering and mounting tool with a package of self-adhesive vinyl rings. Again, this is an area where it's not a good idea to cut costs. Buying the cheapest rings may lead to later difficulties as adhesive deteriorates and leaks from between the ring and diskette. That kind of contamination can destroy not only the treated diskette but any other it contacts as well, plus contaminating the drives.

I've had good luck with Inmac's product called The Fortifier, shown in Fig. 8-3. It includes a two-stage tool and rings for both 8- and 5-1/4-inch diskettes. The tool is easy to use, providing good centering of the reinforcement if directions are followed. The adhesive seems substantial, showing no deterioration or leakage a year after application to some test diskettes. Naturally, rings are most effective when used before the diskettes are first inserted into drives, but I've used The Fortifier successfully to rejuvenate old and already damaged media.

Diskette Quality

Here's something I can't emphasize strongly enough. Never try to cut costs in purchasing blank diskettes. When users discover the ongoing costs of keeping a system supplied, there's a tendency to try to reduce expenses by purchasing cheaper brands. Many computer stores now

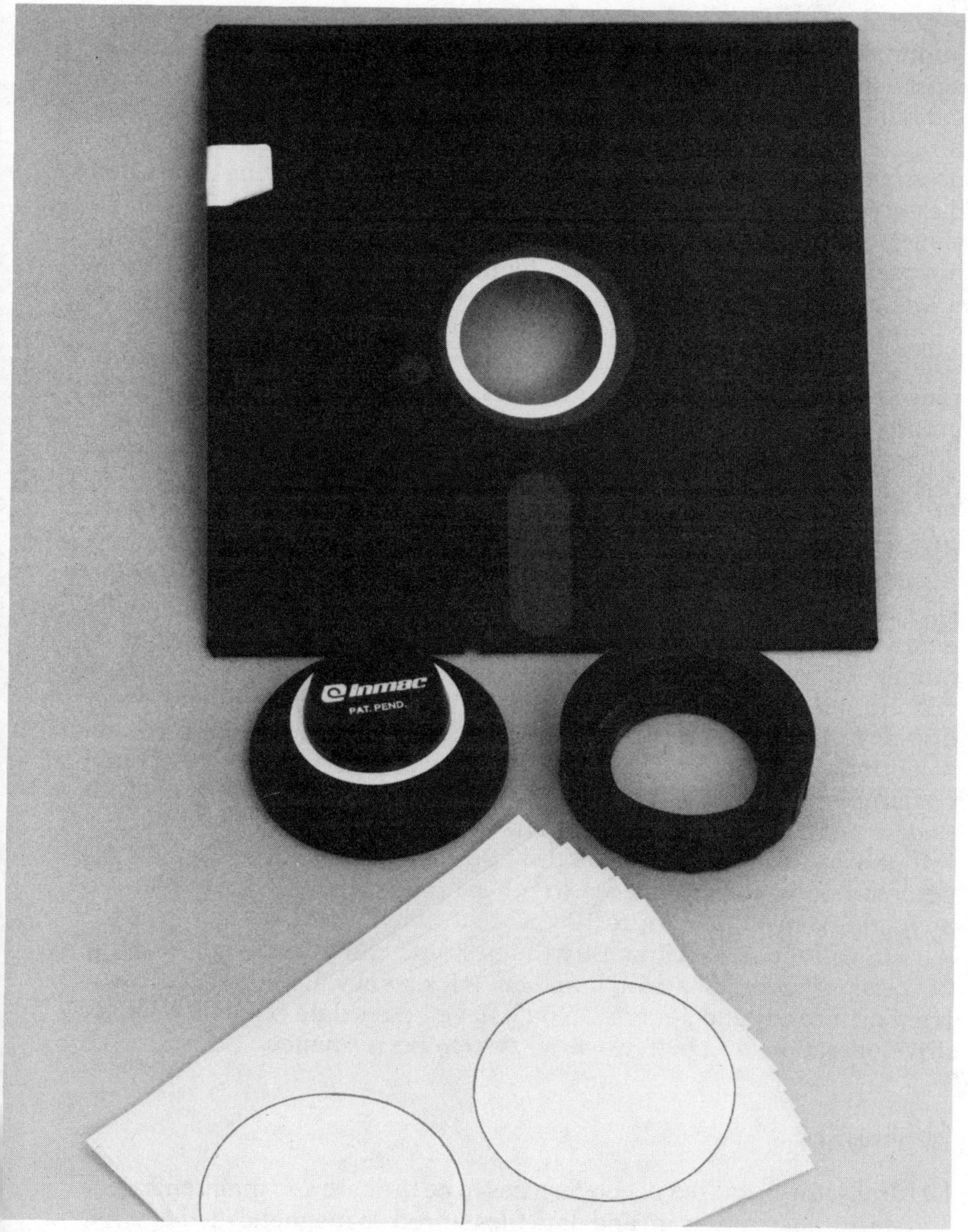

FIG 8-3 Typical diskette reinforcing tool. *(Photo by author)*

offer "generic" diskettes with no brand labels but with prices as low as half to a quarter of that of brand names.

This is false economy! You might save some money on the purchase price, but a subsequent media failure can wipe out hours, days, weeks, or months of work and cost far more. I'm speaking from personal experience, having used many diskette brands and having lost many hundreds of working hours to diskette failures. I won't repeat the stories cited earlier in this book, but I've gone through as many as 180 disks of a national, though inexpensive, brand without finding a single good diskette. I've had bad diskettes cause severe drive contamination that destroyed other diskettes. I've had head crashes resulting from bad diskettes, damaging the drives and incurring high costs for repair. In short, I've learned my lesson the hard way, and now won't use anything but premium-grade diskettes—the highest priced I can find, because this is one area where I believe you get exactly what you pay for.

In particular, I don't like generic diskettes. Sure, the dealer says you can return them if they go bad. Yet what good is that when the diskette failed just as you were storing off hours of work? The data are gone! Just getting a refund or a replacement diskette doesn't pay you for your lost time. And remember, you could lose the time twice—first when your original work is destroyed, and again when you have to redo it.

I've gotten fussy, just as you should. My 8-inch diskettes cost more than $90 for a box of 10. I won't identify the brand name because that would necessitate talking about unsatisfactory brands. And that could lead to legal problems. However, I've chosen a brand unconditionally guaranteed against media failure indefinitely, not for a limited number of months or years (so far, the manufacturer has honored the guarantee without question). The diskettes are 100 percent certified—that's every diskette, not just a few out of the lot. Each diskette is pre-polished to a smooth finish, thereby removing excess oxide that could wear off and contaminate drives. These and other features are built into the price, but they've proved their value over years of use. With this particular brand, I've only lost two of nearly 500 diskettes to media failures. That's a 0.4 percent failure rate compared to other brands where I've experienced anything from 10 percent to 100 percent failure rates.

In short, don't scrimp. Buy the best you can afford—consider the best even if you can't afford it and cut back somewhere else. Stay away from off-brands and generics. You'll have better data reliability, longer drive operation, and better overall system performance.

SOFTWARE

Naturally, the next area of concern has to be the care and maintenance of software, that is, program and data files stored on magnetic media. While proper drive and media care greatly reduce software losses, they are not sufficient by themselves. With the best care, things still go wrong. Tapes break, disks wear out, files are erased accidentally, power disturbances disrupt storage processes, and so on.

The remainder of this chapter is devoted to things you can do to enhance software reliability. Since floppy diskettes are the most popular medium, I'll deal with that software only. Tape and hard-disk users will have to do some digging to locate parallel information for their devices.

Backup Copies

Another ironclad rule! Nothing should exist on magnetic media without at least one backup copy—preferably several copies! That includes purchased software, programs written by the user, output data from a program run, word-processing text files, and anything else that might normally be stored on disk, whether for a few hours or for many years.

Media can fail suddenly and without warning. A diskette that's perfectly good at 9:00 in the morning may go bad by 10:00 and prevent storing a program or file modified during the intervening hour. A diskette that reads perfectly at the end of one day's work may fail to read the next morning. Without backups, unbelievable amounts of work can be lost with a single failure. With backups, other copies exist, so it's simple to recopy as necessary and get back into operation.

There's no excuse not to back up software. Nearly all disk operating systems have some type of copying utility. Under CP/M, the Peripheral Interchange Program PIP.COM can copy one file, several files, or an entire diskette (except the operating system itself). On an Apple II, the master system diskette includes the programs COPY (Integer BASIC) and COPYA (Applesoft) to backup entire diskettes, plus a binary program FID to copy and verify individual files. Making a backup of an entire diskette or a single working file takes only a few minutes, so it's not overly inconvenient and is far better than losing materials. The cost of the extra diskette isn't a valid excuse either; after all, what are a few dollars when the loss of time and output can be prevented?

As a rule, make backup copies frequently. The more often you make copies and the more copies you make, the safer your software will be. When you're programming, it's a good idea to store off your work after every major section of the program has been coded. For applications like word processing, data should be stored to disk and backed up every half-hour or so, in anticipation of uncontrollable occurrences such as power failures. Commercial software should be backed up before it's ever used.

There are a few general rules to follow for making backups of program and data diskettes. The steps I outline are for purchased software, but you can adapt the procedure for programs and data you create yourself.

1. Never record anything on a purchased prerecorded diskette—the so-called "distribution master." A diskette is in jeopardy whenever something is being recorded, and there's too much chance of damaging the master.

2. Before copying, write-protect the distribution master (remove the tab from 8-inch diskettes or apply a tab to 5-1/4-inch diskettes). If the drives recognize write protection, this prevents accidentally erasing or damaging the master by giving the wrong copy parameters.

3. Follow instructions for the copy utility carefully. When it is allowed, put the blank diskette to receive the copy in the drive that later

will use it. With a dual-drive system, I always put programs on the boot drive (low number or letter drive) and data on the high drive. Therefore, I have fewer alignment and timing conflicts by making the working copies on the same drives (low for programs and high for data).

4. Make at least two working copies from the distribution master. These are the "working master" and "working backup" and they must be on separate diskettes. It does no good to have two copies of a file on one diskette if that diskette fails, nor does it help much to have copies on both sides of the same diskette when flip sides are used.

5. Store the distribution master in a safe place. If anything happens to your working copies, it will be needed to reinstate them. The distribution master should be in an area separated from the computer system to avoid accidentally using it and to protect it from mishaps such as spilled drinks around the computer. I prefer a safety deposit box in a bank vault.

6. Perform system-specific installation procedures for the software on both the working master and the working backup. I prefer to "install" the software separately on the two diskettes, just in case I make an error or damage one copy.

7. Test the installed software to be certain it works as it should. Then make additional working copies as needed from that installed software.

It's important that copies be verified whenever possible, to avoid lost or garbled data caused by the copy operation itself. Again, most utilities have some kind of verification procedure. With PIP.COM under CP/M, it's the "[V]" option to the copying instruction, causing the copy to be read back and checked against the data read from the original. If they are the same, the copy is verified; otherwise the operation halts with an error message. I never use PIP.COM to copy anything without verification. With the Apple II, there is a file-verification option in the FID program that performs a checksum calculation and comparison on recorded files. If a number generated from the original data and stored in the file doesn't match a number recalculated during verification, the file is assumed to contain errors and a nonverification message is displayed.

Commercial Copying Utilities. It's sometimes an advantage to obtain and use a commercial copy program. Depending on the machine and system software, such separate programs may contain features not otherwise provided.

To illustrate, my original Altair system could initialize and copy diskettes through its own Peripheral Interchange Program. However, the facilities were so slow that I wouldn't use them as often as I should have. It took a half-hour or more to format a diskette and then copy another entire diskette to it. However, a company called The Software Store marketed a package called DISK FIX which contained a high-speed DISKCOPY program. That program initialized a new disk and recorded all information from another disk in a single operation taking about 90 seconds. The advantage was substantial time reduction, making it easier to back up my software. I could make backups more often and reduce the chances of being caught without a current copy if a diskette failed.

Under CP/M systems, I've not found anything equal to or better than the PIP.COM utility. It's fast and flexible, and it allows verification of the copy, so there's been no reason to look for anything else. Occasionally, I bump into a specialized copy routine included with some other software, but I always come back to PIP.COM as the principal copier.

However, the Apple II can use special copiers to good advantage. Even if we disregard problems of "protected" software, the standard copy programs are slow and, therefore, unlikely to be used as often as they should be. Alternatives include The Filer from Central Point Software, Inc., Super Disk Copy III from Sensible Software, and PenultiCopy from ALF Products.

The Filer provides several specialized facilities, including routines to copy individual files, to copy only the tracks with the disk operating system, and to change the booting process. It features a fast-copy routine that makes high-reliability copies of Apple-compatible diskettes (DOS, CP/M, and Pascal) in as little as 40 seconds while using read- and write-error checking; it also works with 35-, 40-, and 70-track diskettes. As bonuses, The Filer includes a speed-certification program for the disk drives (refer to Chapter 7) and a set of disk diagnostics that check the mechanical operation of drives and the integrity of diskettes' physical surfaces (certification) and data reliability (bad sector scan). Overall, it's an effective utility package.

Super Disk Copy III is a capable copying utility that includes provisions for single files, the disk operating system, and entire disks. It also performs a brute-force copy of Apple Pascal and Fortran disks, and has a number of specialized routines for recovering deleted files, optimizing sector reading order ("skewing"), alphabetizing catalog entries, rearranging files to occupy contiguous sectors and use minimum disk space, and others. It even allows copying back and forth between 13- and 16-sector Apple Diskettes. While it doesn't copy quite so quickly as the The Filer or Penulticopy, those extra features are attractive.

PenultiCopy is intended for high-speed, high-reliability copying of Apple 13- and 16-sector diskettes. It contains drive-speed adjustment instructions and a timing routine, several copying options, and some information on drive maintenance. ALF Products is in the business of commercial diskette duplication for mass distribution. The self-formatting, self-verifying copy routine can use up to ten drives (a master and nine slaves), allowing commercial users to produce numerous copies quickly. But it works well on a two-drive system for personal copies.

I can't say that the choice among The Filer, Super Disk Copy III, and PenultiCopy is easy, or that one is better than another for all applications and users; I say only that they are different. For straightforward, two-drive copying of standard Apple diskettes, they get the same result, and I've experienced no difficulty with any of the three. Users with a single-drive system, however, should be aware that The Filer will work with just one drive while PenultiCopy will not. Super Disk Copy III definitely works better with two drives, although some of the functions can be made to work with just one drive.

Copy-Protected Software. I can hear Apple owners screaming, "What about protected software?" For those who don't own Apple computers, you should be aware that their disk operating system is unusual in that it allows many approaches to keeping a disk from being copied. Most software houses play little games, inventing "locks" for diskettes, hoping to make it impossible, or at least difficult, for users to duplicate programs.

Piracy is a problem in all communications industries including radio, television, motion pictures, home video, and computing. But the oddities of the Apple give software suppliers an edge on almost everyone else. Instead of having to rely on copyright and patent law to protect their interests, they can "doctor" a disk. I can't really blame them for using the capability because piracy is the major factor in lost revenues. After all, those who have put months or years into designing a program are entitled to be paid for their efforts. When unauthorized copies are made and sold or given away, the programmer and distributor are being robbed of their earned and well-deserved income.

On the other hand, the buyer or licensee of software has a reasonable right to run programs without having to contend with losses due to media failure, drive malfunction, or operator error. Since all media fail sooner or later, disk drives can malfunction at any time, or a simple keying mistake can erase a whole diskette, a user needs a backup copy or copies. Otherwise, a user is deprived of the merchandise and denied his or her rights. If a business hinges on a software package, its loss, even temporarily, deprives the business of income. As a result, nearly all software distributors outside the games industry have a provision for obtaining backups, but some are outright "ripoffs." There are three general approaches, summarized as follows:

1. Backup is provided with the purchased software. Two diskettes are furnished. It's not a bad approach because when one diskette fails, it can be returned with a nominal payment for replacement, while the second is used in the interim. But it's not a great solution either. Suppose the second diskette fails before the replacement arrives. If it's business software such as a word-processor or accounting package on which an entire commercial operation depends, the user is effectively out of business and suffers financial loss.

2. Often a single diskette is provided, and a second diskette is made available on returning a registration card, sending an additional payment, or a combination of both. This method suffers the same disadvantage since only two diskettes are available at any time. Besides, what happens if the original fails within hours of its first use? (It's happened.) Furthermore, some suppliers are using the backup as a source of

additional revenue, charging anything from $5 to $80 for the second disk. If I purchase a $200 word processor, I'm not about to spend more money for a second diskette.

3. The least-used method provides a limited copying facility within the software. Southwestern Data Systems is typical. The user receives one diskette, but it has a copying routine. The routine copies the diskette, but does not move the copy facility itself to the new diskette. A copy cannot be used to make another copy. After three copies of the original have been made, the copy routine self-destructs. That allows the user a total of four diskettes—enough for normal use but not for distribution to others.

The user is between the proverbial rock and a hard place. On one hand, backups are needed to minimize downtime due to failed software or media. On the other, suppliers have the right to protect their own interests. Short of boycotting companies who make unreasonable demands for backup copies, I doubt that much can be done to alleviate the problem.

I consider the existence of copy protection self-defeating. Any "lock" that someone designs can be broken by someone else, given enough time, patience, and ingenuity. Meanwhile, forbidden things tend to be temptations, and some people treat breaking into copy-protection schemes as a game. I've even talked with schoolteachers who have admitted they've watched or helped students break protection schemes on disks brought into the classroom. They also claim that students don't even need help—fourth graders often can break into a protected disk within minutes, distributing bootleg copies within an hour while the schools look the other way. It's a sad commentary on the state of ethics, but it happens.

So who's being punished? It's the honest user who just wants a couple of copies to protect an investment. That user doesn't have the time or inclination to break locking schemes and gets stuck with whatever price and inconvenience the supplier wants to impose.

There is some relief, however. So-called "nibble copiers" are available to copy protected diskettes, although they aren't always the easiest things to use. The immediate question is, "Is it legal?" There's some argument, with one side saying no in any circumstance and the other saying yes if within certain guidelines. There doesn't seem to be a definitive answer, but the limited rights are being accepted by many. I quote the following from the packaging of a game sold by Edu-Ware, Inc. It would be to their advantage to claim that copying is illegal, but they make some specific statements that are gaining support among many suppliers.

> Subject to the copyright act of 1980, as specified in Public Law 94-553, dated December, 1980 (94 STAT.3028-29) and amended as Public Law 96-517, the duplication of computer programs without prior consent of

> the publisher, for the purpose of barter, trade, sale, or exchange is a criminal offense for which the offender may be subject to fine, imprisonment, and/or civil suit. Under the provisions of Section 117 of Public Law 96-517, it is not an infringement for the owner of a computer program to make or to authorize the making of another copy or adaptation of that computer program, provided that such new copy or adaptation is created *for archival purposes only* and that all archival copies are destroyed in the event that continued possession of the computer program should cease to be rightful.

According to that, users can take steps to create backup copies if they don't distribute them in any way. Giving or lending a copy to a friend, with or without charge, violates the law. Furthermore, users cannot legally obtain a copy, make a backup, and then return the original while keeping the copy. This is the principle under which companies market their nibble copiers—they feel users are entitled to a reasonable backup procedure within these guidelines. As I've said, there's still much argument about the subject, and I can't say which side is right or wrong. After all, I'm not a copyright lawyer, and the lawyers are at odds among themselves.

Nevertheless, nibble copiers exist. They are sold over the counter in most computer stores. And they are useful for breaking copy protection. The most notable of the Apple II nibble copiers are Omega Microware's Locksmith, Computer:applications' Nibbles Away II, Sensible Software's Back It Up II, and Central Point Software's Copy II Plus. Each is capable of copying protected disks, although the procedure isn't so simple as it sounds. I don't think any package has a clear-cut advantage over the others, but there are differences in auxiliary functions provided. One package may be better at copying a particular diskette than another, while some other copier may be better on a different diskette from the first. Sometimes a protected diskette that's difficult to copy with something like Locksmith may be easy for Back It Up II.

Each package incorporates its own set of functions plus the nibble copying. Locksmith includes a drive-speed test, a routine to erase or degauss all or parts of diskettes, a quick scan of diskette contents, and a "nibble editor" to modify individual bytes of a file when necessary. Nibbles Away II also has a speed test, degaussing function, diskette verification, and an editor. Back It Up II lacks any speed tests or diagnostics, but they are available in other software. Copy II Plus is actually called a "bit copier" instead of a nibble copier, and it includes routines for straight copying of unprotected diskettes, speed checks, file and disk verification, restoration of a deleted file, and other utilities. The choice is one of personal preference, though it's often handy to have more than one of these programs.

A caution is necessary, however. Using a nibble copier is tricky. You have to know the disk formats and storage techniques to use them with newer software. The programs are packed with parameters that can be changed to accommodate different protection schemes, but you have to determine how to manipulate those parameters. Lists of parameters are provided by the suppliers, but they're soon out of date, and getting new lists can be difficult. The most current lists are maintained in files on national communication networks like The Source™ and the CompuServe Information Service™, but access requires a telephone modem. It's also expensive, since you pay by the minute for time logged onto a network.

Before acquiring or attempting to use a nibble copier, Apple users should read two books, namely *Beneath Apple DOS* and *Bag of Tricks.* Both are by Don Worth and Pieter Lechner and are published by Quality Software. They contain invaluable information on Apple disk-storage techniques and the operating system.

Surface Certification

In discussing diskette quality, I mentioned surface certification. Now I'll elaborate. Understand that reputable diskette manufacturers certify media they produce. That's a quality-control procedure supposedly assuring that media you receive do not have defects that would destroy programs or data. Few manufacturers test every diskette they turn out, however, preferring to spot-check manufacturing lots or batches. Therefore, it's possible to open a new box of diskettes and get certified, defective diskettes. Furthermore, the first time you use a diskette, it's no longer certified. It's like using an adhesive bandage, where sterility is guaranteed only to the instant you open the package.

Certifying your own diskettes is an important step in caring for software, and commercial programs are available to help. The principle of certification is that data are recorded to a diskette, then read back and compared to what was output originally. If data coming back match data sent out, the surface is good. If they don't match after a predetermined number of tries, the surface is assumed bad.

I insist on certifying every disk surface before I use it the first time, and I turn up a few bad sectors occasionally. Those diskettes are returned for refund or replacement before they can do any damage. Every time I erase or re-format a diskette, I also re-certify the surface before recording new material. Finally, I run a certification test whenever I see two disk or I/O errors on the same diskette in a single day.

There are many certification programs available for popular machines. Some computers, like the Morrow Designs' Decision 1, even build one into the disk-formatting procedure. For example, when running the CP/M formatting program that came with the Decision 1, I find that it first formats the diskette by recording track and sector marks and some test data. Then it goes back through and verifies each track. As a preliminary step, it's helpful but not totally reliable. In six months, it's detected one bad diskette, but let two others slip through.

Under CP/M I've tried several commercial packages. One was Advanced Micro Techniques' DPATCH™, which is a general-purpose utility providing surface analysis as just one of several functions. Of the capabilities it offers, surface certification was the only function I couldn't get operational. It refused to recognize the double-sided, double-density diskette format used by the Decision 1. People have told me they've had good results with it on single-sided, 8-inch diskettes, but I've been unable to verify it without single-sided drives.

One I have used successfully is BADLIM™ from Blat Research & Development Corp. This program has received some less-than-favorable reviews in computer magazines, but I've been happy with it. The biggest criticism seems to be overpricing, but it's saved me twice from using defective diskettes for major projects. By preventing possible loss of those projects, it was worth far more than the purchase price. One good thing about BADLIM and something to look for in any certification program is that it identifies bad sectors and locks them out so they can't be accessed by other programs. Therefore, an identified bad sector can't hurt files recorded later. Incidentally, BADLIM is the program that caught the two bad diskettes that slipped by the Decision 1 formatting verification.

Similar programs exist for other machines. Some available for the Apple II include the following:

1. Disk Prep™ by Sympathetic Software. This has been advertised as a sector-checking program for certifying the flip sides of diskettes. I've already recommended against that procedure, but Disk Prep is equally effective for checking sectors and certifying the front side. It locks out the flawed sectors by assigning them to a file in the disk directory (catalog).

2. Disk Doctor™ from Creative Computing Software is a general-purpose utility for examining and changing disk sectors. It does, however, contain routines to verify a diskette's contents by checksum or to format and verify a blank diskette. It does not lock out bad sectors.

3. The Filer, by Central Point Software, Inc., along with other useful routines, checks surface integrity by writing and then reading data or checks the integrity of data already recorded by reading and verifying files. Both are useful functions, though bad sectors are not locked out.

4. Disk Recovery™ by Sensible Software, Inc., is designed for certifying surfaces, locking out bad sectors so they can't be used, and recovering from some types of disk "crashes." It enables subsequent use of a diskette after an I/O Error, but it's also an effective initial certification before a diskette is used.

5. Three nibble copiers cited earlier contain some surface checking or certification. The are Locksmith, Nibbles Away II, and Copy II Plus. However, none locks out bad sectors. The assumption is that since a defective disk would be unable to receive a track-by-track or sector-by-sector copy anyway, it should be discarded. Generally, I consider these surface checks most suitable for whole-disk copying operations, and I believe it's an advantage to have another program for stand-alone certification and sector lockout.

Regardless of the technique, some certification software is a "must" item for any serious user. Using diskettes without your own testing is asking for trouble, no matter how reliable the manufacturer or how thoroughly the media are guaranteed. If you decide to cut corners and buy inexpensive media, though you've been warned against it, you'll find frequent certification an absolute necessity.

Software Recovery

The ability to recover damaged or lost software is as important as the need to prevent losses in the first place. As careful as you might be, there's bound to be a time when a sector goes bad within a stored file, a power failure during recording scrambles data, you accidentally erase the wrong file, and so on.

Again, there are many utility packages for recovering damaged or lost files. However, most require an understanding of the disk-storage parameters and operating systems. As usual, it's necessary to do some research into software and approaches for particular installations, but the following paragraphs give some starting points for CP/M and Apple systems, defining types of programs available.

For CP/M systems, there are numerous choices. A few are identified as follows:

1. FILEFIX™ by Alan Miller (available through Digital Marketing) contains an effective program for recovering erased files if new files haven't been stored. While that's also accomplished by other programs, FILEFIX contains some clever utilities to manipulate programs among CP/M user areas, examine directory-block allocations, create multiple accesses to a file from different user areas, display file dumps under keyboard control, delete groups of files selectively, verify whether two files are identical, and so on. This is an attractive collection of routines and programs having practical applications in CP/M systems.

2. DPATCH, by Advanced Micro Techniques, was mentioned under surface certification. It also has facilities to view and alter files and directories, recover undamaged data from a diskette with an I/O error, and restore erased files. While the surface certification routine wasn't functional with my double-sided, double-density diskettes, all other routines operate as the supplier claims. Recovery from an erasure is easy. Given sufficient knowledge of disk storage methods and operating systems, recovery from an I/O error or even complete restructuring of files is possible.

3. DISK DOCTOR™ from SuperSoft, Inc., is intended for recovering from erasures, disk crashes, and other common operating hazards. It's divided into major procedures that the supplier calls "wards," and the user chooses a ward or progresses from one to another according to the failure encountered. The documentation indicates some attractive possibilities, but I've been unable to use them. The program excludes double-sided drives, so I'm unable to perform the system installation. I've also tried it under Apple CP/M (MicroSoft SoftCard) and on single-sided

disk systems owned by acquaintances, but without any luck in getting it operational. It's possible I received a bad distribution master, but that's not what the symptoms indicate. Therefore, I must advise caution with this package.

4. Disk Fix™ from The Software Store, Ltd., is a general-purpose disk editor and file-recovery utility. It displays, edits, and copies any sector of a CP/M floppy diskette or hard disk. It allows file recovery when the directory is damaged, file reconstruction when there are bad sectors, file restoration after erasure, and overall disk editing. This program may be slightly more difficult to use than others, but it is somewhat more versatile. Where others rely on menu selections, Disk Fix allows more manual control that may be essential after some media failures or during some editing chores.

A similar selection of editing and recovery utilities is available for most other systems as well. Many exist for the Apple II, and the functions are included in the nibble copiers such as Locksmith, Nibbles Away II, and Copy II Plus. (Note that Back It Up II does not include a disk editor.) Some of the other utility programs for the Apple include the following:

1. The Inspector™ and Watson™ from Omega Microwave, Inc. Used in combination, these two comprise one of the most complete utility systems for the Apple. When a nibble copier such as Locksmith is added, the power is even greater. The Inspector is the primary package with facilities for mapping and searching disks, searching memory, editing sectors, and fixing file erasures and I/O errors. Watson enhances The Inspector by adding reconstruction and disassembly facilities, the ability to follow disk files, and other useful capabilities. Users should be aware that The Inspector can be used without Watson, but Watson requires The Inspector.

2. Disk Recovery™ from Sensible Software, Inc., complements Back It Up II (the nibble copier) by providing bad-sector scanning, track and sector mapping, and a facility to recover from certain types of I/O errors. It does not contain a disk editor, however, or some individual utility routines available in other software.

3. MasterDisk™ from Masterworks Software, Inc., is an adequate utility for most users. It has a sector editor and facilities to reconstruct the disk directory or undelete an erased file, and that's about all. This program is suitable for casual users who don't need all the capabilities and lack the expertise needed by programs of The Inspector and Watson types. The capabilities cover the most common disk problems and are usable if one's needs aren't too exotic.

4. Disk Doctor from Creative Computing Software is a limited utility, containing routines to view and modify disk sectors (an editor) and verify diskettes. It does not have automatic undeletion of erased files or other facilities for recovery from I/O errors. All changes and all attempts at fixing problems or recovering from failures require manipulations with the editor instead of menu selections.

5. DiskEdit™ from SoftKey Publishing fits somewhere between the extremes of the extensive Inspector/Watson package and the limited packages. It has a disk editor for inspecting and modifying files. It's also able to move sectors on the same disk or between disks to recover from errors, undelete erased files, conceal file names, alter file names to remove illegal characters, and so on.

6. *Bag of Tricks* from Quality Software is a combined book and software package complementing the book, *Beneath Apple DOS.* The two books provide complete documentation of diskette storage and the operating system for Apple II computers, while the diskette provides useful utility programs. It contains a complete sector editor, fully automated directory repair to reinstate lost files (erased or lost to other hazards), initialization of individual tracks to recover from I/O errors while retaining undamaged sectors, and a facility to change the order in which sectors are read by the drives ("reskewing") to achieve disk-access speed improvements.

There are many approaches to disk utilities for each computer system. But they share a common thread: the need for the user to know and understand the disk formats and operating system. Without that knowledge, application of such software is limited, consisting mainly of a few menu selections, when available, to recover an erased file or rebuild a disk directory. Although the editing and recovery functions are probably needed most by business and professional users to protect the software and data, it's the hobbyists who spend the time tinkering with the media and wind up with the best understanding.

Yet users who don't have the time or inclination to play around with media storage still are advised to own a disk editor. If one important data file or program can be saved after a disk crash, accidental erasure, or other failure, the cost is more than justified.

On the subject of software recovery, there's something else to consider. What happens if a program in memory is killed by accidentally miskeying an instruction or keying one at the wrong time? The keyboard error is my nemesis, particularly on the Apple II, where I get in a hurry and change programming languages, jump to the monitor, or instruct the system to start a new program when that's really not what I intended. I have a tendency to do those things while writing programs and before getting a developed section properly stored to disk.

For some computers, there are ways to restore a killed program to memory if no new program has been loaded. In an Apple II, the old program is still in memory until overlaid by something else, and the killing action simply resets memory "pointers" so that the computer doesn't know where the program is stored. If pointers can be restored, the program can be revived. With an Apple, one easy way involves installing a Utility ROM (UTL) from Soft Control Systems. The ROM itself is inexpensive, but it must be housed on a "ROM board," which can impose significant but worthwhile costs. I've used both an Andromeda

ROMBoard™ (two ROM sockets) and a Mountain Computer ROMPlus™ (six ROM sockets) successfully.

With the UTL ROM installed and active, a single command from the keyboard restores a lost program in memory if nothing else has been loaded and the system has not been reset or powered down between the loss and the recovery attempt. The same ROM also has facilities that aid a programmer in automatically numbering lines, alphabetically sorting disk catalogs, controlling on-screen listing speeds, and removing DOS from a diskette to gain storage space. But I consider program recovery the most valuable function because it's saved many hours of effort that otherwise would have resulted from a single careless keystroke.

Under CP/M, recovery is sometimes possible by simply executing a zero-length program. It's characteristic of such an operation that the computer "jumps" to the start of the last program executed. Assume a program, say one being edited under BASIC, has been exited prematurely. The recovery would involve the following:

1. Without executing any other program, save a zero-length command file on disk, if one is not already in place. Use any name desired, such as SAVE 0 RESTART.COM.

2. Type the zero-length file name as a command line; in this case, enter RESTART at the CP/M prompt.

3. The display should show that you are back to the program you exited.

General Disk Utilities

General utilities are available for different systems to accomplish different tasks. Whether these are important depends on the applications involved, the need for extra memory space, the need for increased speed, and so on. I don't want to get too deeply involved in this subject, other than to mention that these exist for nearly any computer system. As the user, you are the only one who can determine your needs and whether the products would be cost effective.

To illustrate the types of software to which I'm referring, I'll again use the Apple II as the sample system, citing three utilities as follows:

1. MASTERDOS™ from Masterworks Software, Inc., allows a user to change the names of commands used by the disk-operating system and change the standard name of the greeting program that must reside on a diskette. Personally, I don't see a big advantage since it could lead to rampant confusion. The package also contains a facility to strip the disk-operating system from the initial tracks of a diskette, thus freeing up storage space for other uses. That's a practical function but is available in other software products as well.

2. Diversi-DOS™ from Diversified Software Research, Inc., is a three-way utility. It provides a high-speed disk-operating system that allows disk accesses to proceed much faster than the normal operating

system. However, it's not compatible with many commercial software products. It also has a keyboard buffer that allows high-speed typing without losing characters and a printing buffer that makes use of any memory card as a holding buffer for the printer so the computer can proceed to other tasks more quickly.

3. The Manager™ from Omega Microware, Inc., can be used to move the Apple disk-operating system from motherboard memory to a plug-in memory board, effectively freeing an additional 10.5K of memory for programming and other uses. It is also capable of setting up a 16K memory-expansion card as a small but fast disk emulator for high-speed data transfers to and from temporary storage.

4. Macrodisk™ from Macrotech Computer Products, Ltd., also serves to convert Apple memory boards to disk emulators for high-speed data transfers. This one allows the size of the memory-disk emulation area to be selected by the user.

5. Companies such as Legend Industries, Ltd., can provide specialized software for their hardware products. For example, Legend can provide various utilities to use their 128KDE Soft Disk card as a 128K disk emulator, a general-purpose memory expansion, or an enhancement to a spreadsheet system.

If these are capabilities you feel you need, spend some time researching the field. Check the literature. Visit dealers and see the products in operation. In short, be sure a utility has the features and capabilities you need before you buy.

Conclusion

Throughout this chapter, I've tried to show how complex but important proper care and maintenance can be for both magnetic media and software. I've given you an idea of the areas of greatest concern and the types of products available to accomplish the tasks.

The key is that software is invaluable. The programs you've bought or designed and the data you've developed are indispensable. After a year or two of operating a system, you're likely to find that the software is worth more than the hardware, so don't be fooled by people who say software is expendable. It's not. The hardware may be expendable, but never the software.

With a little time and care, use of effective backup techniques, and willingness to purchase the supporting products, you should be able to develop a high degree of confidence in your media and software. Proper care for these things is not cheap, but the alternative is far more expensive in the long run.

NINE

POWER CONDITIONING

This chapter is devoted to the computing topic least talked about and most ignored by system sellers and users alike, namely the need for power conditioning. The subject was introduced in Chapter 3, with brief descriptions of types of power disturbances, effects on systems and warranties, and basic preventive steps. In this chapter, I'll provide more information, although a book of this scope cannot and should not be an exhaustive study of power problems and remedies. Instead, I'll provide a fundamental introduction intended to get you to recognize the problem and examine some possible ways to avoid serious damage.

Throughout, remember it's your responsibility to provide acceptable power. If you don't, neither equipment manufacturers nor retailers are responsible. Also remember that power disturbances can do anything from causing "computer amnesia" (the loss of memory) to destroying electronic components, media, and software. Finally, remember that warranties and service contracts assume acceptable power and can be voided if there is evidence of power-caused malfunctions.

TYPES OF POWER DISTURBANCES

The three principal types of power disturbances are noise, voltage fluctuations, and outages. It's been claimed that noise accounts for about 88.5 percent of the computer-disrupting disturbances, with fluctuations accounting for about 11 percent and outages for about 0.5 percent.[1] This would indicate that noise, the type of interference that affects a TV picture, should receive the most attention.

That's not necessarily the case, however, since one has to weigh effects as well as number of incidents. Line noise, which includes voltage

1 Ruxton Tucker, "The Glitch Stops Here," *Computer Design*, February 1982.

spikes, can be caused by such actions as utility switching, lightning, appliances switching on and off, and even the operation of computer components. Printers and disk drives, especially, can create power-line noise. The effects range from mildly annoying to severely damaging, depending on the type of noise, when it occurs, and how the computer components are designed. Most systems are sensitive to some degree, if only because manufacturers don't want to incur the cost of protective circuitry and components. Therefore, noise can contribute to or cause errors in program operations at runtime, errors in data entered from a keyboard or mass storage, garbled data stored to disks and tapes, and a host of other problems. Severe noise, especially high-voltage spikes, can cause physical and electronic damage ranging from blown chips and circuit boards to disk head crashes.

Are your lights dimming periodically? Have you noticed your video screen pulsate, with the image shrinking, expanding, or distorting? Are you blowing fuses or circuit breakers in your building, appliances, or computer without obvious cause? Do light bulbs seem to last only a fraction of the expected life, requiring frequent replacement? If you answer yes to any of these, you've seen effects of voltage fluctuations. Within a computer system, these fluctuations contribute to data losses, processing errors, memory disruptions, disk-drive speed changes (and data losses), electronic failures, and others.

While it may be true that voltage fluctuations, including power cutbacks (brownouts) and overvoltage or undervoltage conditions, comprise only 11 percent of the actual disturbances, it has been claimed that they cause nearly half of all power-originated computer failures. Personally, I feel they're responsible for an even higher number of failures, and they've historically been the most disruptive of all power problems in my three systems. Some days I've had to shut down entirely because disk drives were changing speed every few minutes—I could hear the differences in sound as the ac drives would either speed up or slow down.

Outages or blackouts are total interruptions lasting from a fraction of a second to many hours. These are hard to miss, since the system typically shuts down. Most systems tolerate extremely brief outages lasting less than a few cycles (a cycle is 0.017 second on 60-Hz ac power), but some will not. Volatile memories are erased, programs are stopped, data transfers are interrupted (possibly causing permanent I/O errors on the media), drive heads crash, and so on. To complicate the situation, power often restores erratically, with wild fluctuations that cause circuits and components to oscillate or "ratchet" unpredictably, risking further damage to components and media.

The three types of failures all are serious, too serious to ignore. Whether you use a computer for recreational or business purposes, the wires connecting the system to a wall outlet are an ever-present threat to your operation and investment. There's little you can do to control when a power disturbance will hit, or how severe it will be. Most originate outside your building on the utility lines, and the only control you have is to be careful about when and how you turn appliances and machinery on or off. That at least can minimize some local or internal interferences.

You have to be alert to power problems and shut your system off if you see them and haven't taken steps to protect the equipment. I've already mentioned that I shut down if I hear ac-driven disk drives change speed (change of pitch is audible). Dimming lights and pulsating screens are other indications of imminent problems, and they too justify a shutdown. I've also learned to use other electrical devices as warning systems. For example, I have a programmable video cassette recorder that is extremely sensitive to power interruptions. Even outages too quick to affect the computer cause the recorder clock to reset, loudly "popping" any set switches to the neutral position, whether the unit is turned on or not. I keep the play switch pressed down even while not using the machine, and when I hear it release while I'm working at a computer, I know it's time to shut down, because power has just become too unpredictable.

If you notice an unusually high incidence of burned-out light bulbs, you may be seeing the effects of a long-term overvoltage condition, not just fluctuations. Whenever I've had a group of bulbs go bad almost simultaneously or too soon after being installed, I've had the utility company monitor the lines for a week. Half the time, it turns out that I'm receiving a voltage higher than the "normal" level, and steps have to be taken to rectify the situation. Continued operation of electrical or electronic devices at constant overvoltage conditions can only shorten the operating life.

POWER-PROBLEM SOLUTIONS

There are several approaches to alleviating power problems, and every system user must decide which approach is the most suitable. Much of this depends on the degree of accuracy and reliability required. Since increased levels of protection necessitate higher and higher levels of spending, a user must weigh costs of lost data, disrupted programs, wasted time, and damaged equipment or media against the costs for the protective devices. The more critical the application, the more protection is needed and the more it costs. Recreational users who can tolerate occasional losses and have low-cost computers may not find it cost effective to pay for more than minimum noise or surge protection. Business or professional users whose profits depend on the computer most likely need all the protection available, regardless of price.

There are five basic categories of protective devices. Progressing upward in price and protective capability, they are filters and suppressors, isolation transformers, voltage regulators, line conditioners, and standby or uninterruptible power supplies (UPS units). Table 9-1 categorizes types of power disturbances for which protective devices are used.

Table 9-1. **Power Disturbances and Protective Devices.**[2]

Power line problems	Recommended Solutions* Ultra-isolators	Power conditioners	AC Line regulators	Uninterruptible power systems
Power line noise				
Lightning strikes causing up to 3000-volt transients	x	x		x
Spikes caused by utility network switching	x	x		x
Transients produced by machine tools, air conditioners, copiers, lighting systems, and other equipment	x	x		x
Ringing disturbances caused by switching carried out by utility	x	x		x
Voltage problems				
Brownouts		x	x	x
Undervoltages or overvoltages		x	x	x
Voltage fluctuations		x	x	x
Chronic low line voltage		x	x	x
Power outages				
Temporary outage				x
Momentary interruptions from faults or overloads on power line				x
Blackouts				x
Other problems				
Ground not dedicated or isolated	x	x		x
Shock hazard to systems, operators, or users	x	x		
Frequency variations				x

*Filters are not included.

Filters and Surge Suppressors

The least expensive devices are filters and surge suppressors sold in computer retail stores, but they give the lowest level of protection. Often, dealers tout the devices as cure-alls, and users purchase them expecting to solve all power problems. Typically, filters electrically block certain frequencies while allowing others to pass, thus removing noise from the lines. However, inexpensive filters are most effective for noise frequencies at 50 kHz and higher, offering little or no protection against common transients and noise occurring between 400 Hz and 50 kHz. For example, Fig. 9-1 illustrates the manufacturer's claimed performance for the

2 Adapted from: Ruxton Tucker, "It's Your Job to Get Adequate Power to Run Your Computer," *Industrial Research & Development*, November 1980.

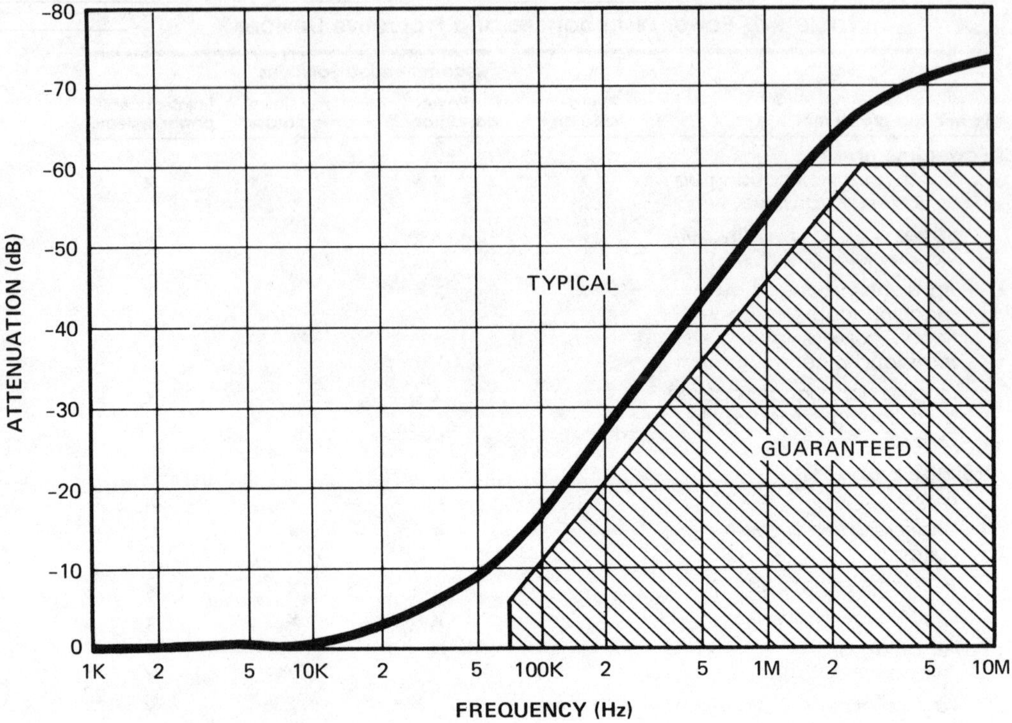

FIG 9-1 Typical noise filter performance. *(Courtesy of Panamax)*

Panamax surge suppressor and noise filter. Notice the solid line designated "typical." It indicates attenuation of frequencies from 10 kHz to 10 MHz. Then notice the shaded area designated "guaranteed," which extends only from 50 kHz up.

Suppressors are designed to stop voltage spikes, clamping or shunting high voltages to the ground wire where they can't harm equipment. Note that suppressor effectiveness assumes the ground is properly connected. Since no computer should be operated without proper grounding anyway, that shouldn't be a problem.

There are too many of these types to attempt to cover the field. Dozens of manufacturers make scores of models in every imaginable size, shape, and configuration.

Two Panamax units were shown in Fig. 3-8, combining both noise-filtration and surge-suppression functions. The SS-120/2 model plugs directly into a wall receptacle and provides two protected outlets. The SS-120/4 provides four outlets at the end of an extension cord, and it has an on/off switch controlling all four outlets simultaneously. Both units are protected with external fuses and have indicator lights that go dark when the fuses blow. This is an important feature for surge protectors. If they are not fused, it is possible for a surge to burn out the suppressor but leave it capable of powering the connected equipment. Therefore, a user could unknowingly have a suppressor that is nonfunctional, providing no protection.

A slightly different approach is taken by RKS Industries, marketing surge suppressors—with no claim of any noise suppression—under the name Surge Sentry®. I've used two of their models successfully. The SS-120H is similar in physical appearance to the Panamax SS-120/2 shown in Fig. 3-8, while the SS-120D resembles the Panamax SS-120/4. I point out the similarity only in approximate size and appearance, not in function, since the Surge Sentry is not a noise filter.

The Surge Sentry model SS-120H provides two outlets and an indicator light. At first, I thought it lacked a fuse, since none shows from the outside. While there was an internal fuse, replacing it is not considered a user function. This unit is supposed to be returned to RKS Industries for repair or replacement, ensuring that a unit with inadequate or damaged suppresion is not used.

The Surge Sentry model SS-120D is a four-outlet box on an extension cord. This one took some getting used to. It has two indicator lights and a reset switch. Normally, both lights are illuminated. If the "S" light is dark, the unit is unplugged, a power failure is in progress, or the unit has failed. If power fails and comes back on, the "S" indicator illuminates. However, the "D" indicator goes dark and stays dark when there is any power interruption or "dropout." That power dropout doesn't just affect the "D" indicator; it also cuts off power to the four outlets until the reset switch is operated. The only way to restore operation, power the outlets, and illuminate the "D" light, is with the reset switch—the unit is not self-restoring on being powered up. That may or may not be an advantage, since it seems sensitive even to short dropouts that the computer might be able to accept, cutting power immediately. It does, however, prevent erratic power fluctuations from reaching the connected equipment as power returns.

Figure 9-2 illustrates four of many devices available from Electronic Specialists, Inc. These are isolators and "super isolators" that provide noise filtration and high-voltage spike suppression, while preventing interaction among devices plugged into the outlets. The latter function is of special interest. The filter-isolation techniques isolate individual sockets or banks of sockets from the others on the same box. That keeps electrical noise generated by one component, like a printer, from interfering with components such as computer mainframe or disk drives. Filtering noise that comes from outside the installation is important, but it's just as important to eliminate disruptive noise created within, or transmitted between devices through electrical lines.

As mentioned earlier, these are just a few representative products. There are many other suppliers as well, including private-label distribution outlets. For example, Inmac carries four models. The least expensive is a two-stage spike suppressor that plugs into a wall outlet and assertedly protects the entire electrical circuit in the room, although it provides no

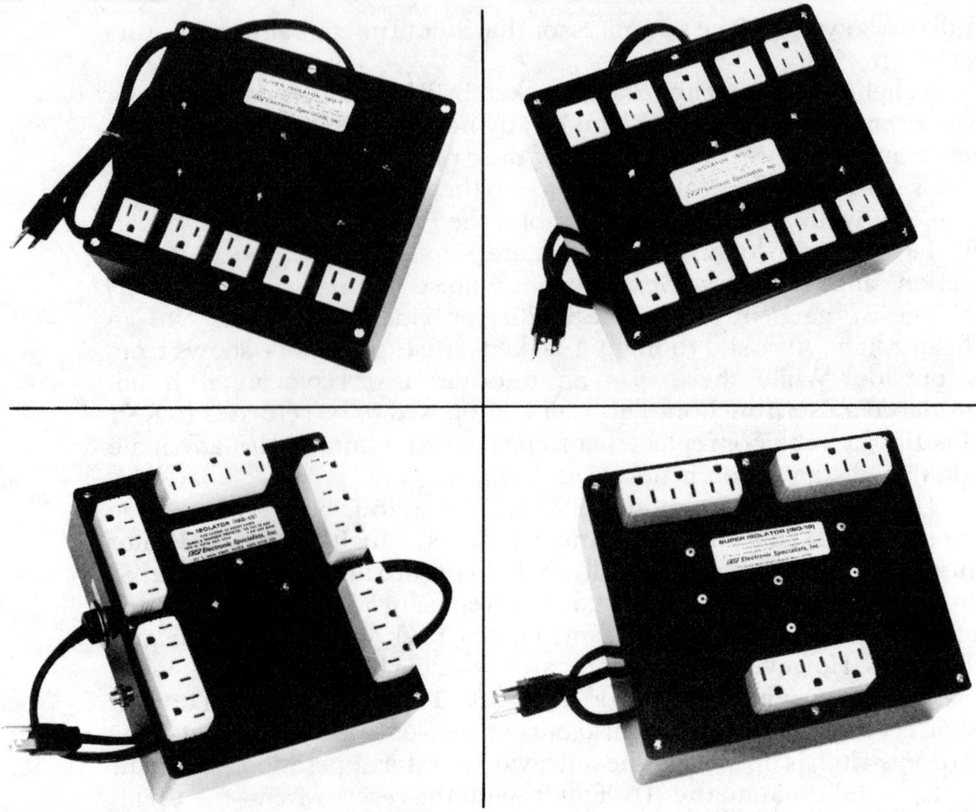

FIG 9-2 Power-line noise control devices. *(Courtesy of Electronic Specialists, Inc.)*

noise filtration. At the top of their line is an eight-outlet filter and surge suppressor with individually switched outlets.

Although these devices can cost anything from under $50 to several hundred dollars, the cost is negligible when compared to the potential hardware and software losses that could result from power disturbances.

Isolation Transformers

When power lines are particularly noisy or system components are especially sensitive, it's necessary to consider the next higher level of protection. These are isolation transformers, not to be confused with the filter isolators mentioned in the previous section. Such devices generally use ferro-resonant transformers to achieve a high degree of noise isolation, with many designed to eliminate noise in the 400 Hz to 50 kHz range not covered well by simple noise filters. Typically, isolation transformers attenuate noise in both directions—noise entering the installation from the utility lines and noise leaving the installation.

Transformers also are effective for eliminating voltage spikes and conditions known as "common-mode noise" and "transverse-mode

FIG 9-3 Isolation transformer. *(Courtesy of Electronic Specialists, Inc.)*

noise." By definition, common-mode noise is an interference that occurs between the ground wire and both current-carrying wires of a power line. Transverse-mode noise occurs between the two current-carrying wires. Both types are difficult to control by filtration techniques, but are eliminated easily with a transformer.

Such transformers are more expensive than simple filters and suppressors, carrying prices upward of several hundred dollars and reaching into the thousands for "ultra-isolation" transformers.

One device of this general type is the Electronic Specialists' Kleen Line™ KLR-500 regulator, filter, and suppressor shown in Fig. 9-3. This particular model is rated for a 500-watt load, but other models are available up to 2-kilowatt (2 KW) loads. The supplier claims that the KLR units provide voltage regulation, noise elimination, spike and surge suppression, and, as an option, electrical isolation of the individual outlets.

Incidentally, some devices are rated by watts and kilowatts (KW), while others are rated by volt-amperes (VA) and kilovolt-amperes (KVA). According to the dictionary, a volt-ampere is a dc-power measurement equivalent to a watt, so I convert all ratings in this chapter to watts and kilowatts where 200 watts would correspond to a specified 200 volt-amperes.

Similar isolation transformers are available from other sources. The Electronic Power Conversion Division of Gould, Inc., offers Super Isolation Transformers capable of handling loads from 500 watts to

5 KW. SOLA Electric offers CVS- and CVN-series constant-voltage transformers or power protectors that provide isolation from line noise and voltage fluctuations for loads from 30 watts to 7.5 KW.

These types of units can reach substantial sizes and weights. For example, the 30-watt SOLA CVS transformer weighs about 8 pounds (3.6 kg) and measures about 6 × 5 × 3 inches (152 × 127 × 76 mm). But the 7.5-KW model weighs about 330 pounds (150 kg) and measures about 20 × 9 × 38 inches (508 × 229 × 965 mm). However, most microcomputer users probably impose loads of 500 watts or less, requiring a unit weighing less than about 46 pounds (21 kg) and measuring 13 × 7 × 8 inches (330 × 178 × 203 mm) or smaller.

A caution! Transformers have magnetic fields. Therefore, isolation transformers must be well separated from other equipment and magnetic media. Be especially careful not to place transformers next to media storage cabinets, tape drives, disk drives, and other sensitive devices.

Voltage Regulators and Line Conditioners

Line voltage regulators are effective for constant or intermittent high- or low-voltage operating conditions. They are effective also when an installation is subject to utility brownouts. Generally, these units use transformers to regulate the voltage level on the power line, providing a steady level to the connected equipment. They are capable of correcting for either high or low voltage on the lines, whether that voltage is short-term such as during a brownout or long-term where the normal power condition is "out of spec."

There is an element of confusion between voltage regulators and line conditioners, but a line conditioner normally combines a voltage regulator with noise filtration, isolation, surge suppression, and so on. Regulators are effective for out-of-voltage conditions if noise and surges aren't a problem. Though more expensive, combination line conditioners are more effective where noise and surges are a problem because they protect against virtually all power problems other than outages.

As usual, there are many choices available for both regulators and conditioners. Topaz, Inc., provides several models and sizes of a unit called the Line 2® Power Conditioner. The large, cabinet-style version, handling loads as great as 10 KW, was shown in Fig. 3-11. The smaller floor-or-desk-mount unit is shown in Fig. 9-4 and is available for loads from 400 watts to 2 KW. As line conditioners, these units control power transients, voltage spikes and surges, undervoltages and overvoltages, and similar disturbances.

SOLA Electric manufactures minicomputer regulators with outputs from 70 watts to 2 KW in portable versions and 120 watts to 7.5 KW in non-portable, hard-wired versions. They also provide Solatron/Acuvolt™ line voltage regulators, typically for commercial applications and extremely sensitive equipment.

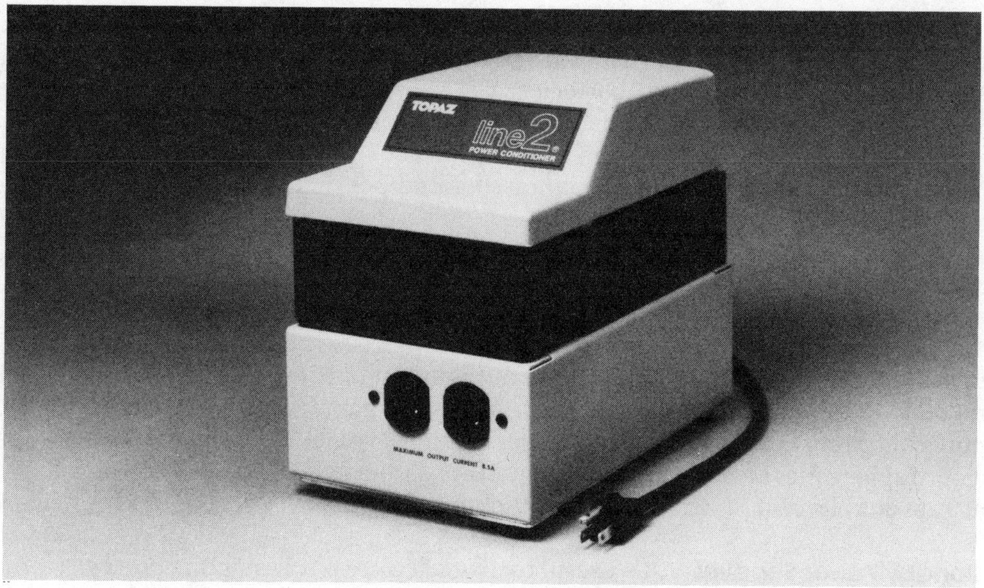

FIG 9-4 Line 2 Power Conditioner. *(Courtesy of Topaz, Inc.)*

Gould, Inc., offers the GPC-series of power conditioners rated from 500 watts to 5 KW. They also have a DLC-series for critical applications with loads ranging from 1 to 60 KW.

These units are nearly at the top of the line, at least for equipment protection. The only things they don't guard against are blackouts, which are in the realm of the standby and uninterruptible power supplies. Note, however, that since regulators and line conditioners contain transformers, the usual care is necessary to keep them away from media, drives, and other sensitive electronics.

Backup Power Supplies

King among the power treatment devices is the uninterruptible power supply or "UPS." The idea is to protect connected equipment from all disturbances, including voltage problems, spikes, surges, noise, and outages—especially outages. These units provide continuous power to a computer system during periods when utility lines have failed. While utility lines are active, the units charge and maintain storage batteries. When power fails, battery output takes over and is converted to a form usable by connected devices. All such units can deliver limited power for specified intervals during a blackout.

It is necessary to differentiate between two types of power supplies, both sometimes called UPS units. Switching standby supplies aren't really UPS devices. It's more appropriate to call them SPS units. They switch to battery backup when power fails, usually within a short enough time that operations aren't interrupted.

True UPS supplies power the equipment from the batteries and charger or inverter circuitry whether power lines are active or not. While incoming power is present, batteries are recharged as they are being used, so they remain at full capacity if power should go off. When power fails, the batteries are already on-line and merely continue to power the installation without switching or an associated possibility of interfering with equipment operations.

True UPS units seem more desirable than switching SPS units because there's less chance of data loss. However, they are more expensive, both to acquire and to operate.

In installing backup power units, the object is to keep equipment operating not through unusually long outages but only through the short, nuisance-type cutoffs that erase memories and garble disk contents. If power is going out for more than several hours, you're not going to find affordable units for backup throughout those intervals. What you can do at reasonable cost is ride over the quick interruptions.

Standby Power Supplies. It's useful to take a look at a few standby power supplies. Most are general-purpose units designed to be interposed in the power lines between the wall plug and the computer system. At least one, however, is machine-specific and connects inside a computer. Again, many manufacturers and brands are available. I'll be describing units I have used on one or another of my systems. I present these descriptions only as indications of what is available and what you might seek, not as a definitive study of the subject or as comprehensive equipment reviews. The units in question are:

1. The RBS-DC Reserve Power System, which replaces the APS-5 Reserve Power Supply, both from Control Technology, Inc. The units tested were designed for Apple II/Apple II Plus systems, but versions are available for Apple III and IBM Personal Computers.

2. The Guardian Angel™ from R.H. Electronics, Inc. It installs in the power line between the computer system and the wall receptacle. It supports all systems and components with a total load of 150 watts or less.

3. The SPS-0200 Standby Power System provided by SAFT-America, Portable Battery Division. It installs on the power line and can be used with any system having a total load up to 200 watts.

4. The Mayday™ 60+6S supply from Sun Research, Inc. It outputs up to 600 watts, installs in the power line, and is independent of the system.

Control Technology's RBS-DC supply and its predecessor, the APS-5, represent the system-specific approach. Shown in Fig. 9-5, this unit interposes between the computer's internal power supply and the remaining computer circuitry. The computer's normal power supply converts ac line input to dc currents for the electronics. The RBS-DC draws a "trickle" of dc power from those lines for battery charging,

FIG 9-5 RBS-DC Reserve Power Supply for an Apple II. *(Courtesy of Control Technology, Inc.)*

detects interruptions only on the dc lines, and supplies dc power directly to those lines during an interruption.

The RBS-DC supply keeps the computer running during the interruption, including the motherboard, memory, plug-in cards, and disk drives powered from a plug-in controller. It does not support external peripherals such as video displays or printers, although Control Technology is expected to introduce an "inverter" unit to provide backup ac power for those.

An obvious disadvantage is that the display is lost, leaving a user "blind" during the power outage. That means leaving the computer alone until the power returns, attempting to exit a program and shut down without seeing what is happening, or connecting a battery-powered TV set to monitor operations. However, the RBS-DC has the longest "hold-up" time of any unit tested. It should keep an Apple II operating for about 115 minutes (1 hour, 55 minutes) if there are no lengthy or frequent disk accesses. Each disk use causes a significant battery drain and reduces the hold-up time, but that's true of any backup supply.

Installation can be a problem. The RBS-DC connects inside the computer and could void a warranty or service contract. In an Apple II, the power leads from the internal supply must be unplugged from the motherboard and connected to a special cable adapter. That adapter then connects to the original plug on the motherboard. A cable to the external battery/supply box is the problem. It's short (27 inches) and rather difficult to handle and position so that it doesn't interfere with circuit boards.

When power fails, the RBS-DC takes over, powering the electronics. A front panel indicator flashes, and a "beeper" sounds. When power comes back on, the unit returns to standby status and all operations continue normally.

The RBS-DC does require changing operating procedures. Since it's between the Apple power supply and the motherboard, switching off the Apple appears as a power failure. To shut off the computer, it's necessary either to hold the RBS-DC reset button while throwing the computer switch or to throw the computer switch and then hit the RBS-DC reset. The first method is preferable because it eliminates a momentary but unnecessary battery drain. If a user likes to boot the computer with the power switch, the RBS-DC reset must be used at the proper time; otherwise, the computer doesn't power down.

R.H. Electronics' Guardian Angel® is a line-type reserve power supply adaptable to any equipment within its power specifications. That means any computer, peripheral, or combination drawing 150 watts or less. It should work with loads up to 200 watts, but hold-up time would decrease.

Installation requires nothing more than plugging Guardian Angel into a grounded wall socket, plugging the computer power cord into a receptacle on the supply, and turning on the supply's power switch. Being external, it responds to interruptions in the main ac power. Furthermore, it can power several devices, including a monitor, if the total load is within tolerances.

Switching time between power interruption and battery takeover is specified as less than 10 milliseconds and is fast enough that the connected system components suffer no adverse effects. The manufacturer claims the unit will take over during undervoltage conditions (below 100 volts ac) and overvoltage conditions (above 140 volts ac).

Guardian Angel has a comparatively short hold-up time. At full load, it provides backup for only two to six minutes. At a half load of 75 watts, the backup interval increases to 15 minutes. Since most small systems impose less than a full load, actual backup times generally are longer. Nevertheless, users should commence an orderly shutdown when the alarm sounds. Guardian Angel doesn't offer the luxury of sitting back to wait out a power loss.

SAFT-America's SPS-0200, shown in Fig. 9-6, formerly was marketed under the Gould brand name. There's also an SPS-0400 model that offers twice the output but just under half the hold-up time. Both models install in the ac power line between the wall socket and the supported equipment.

Like other line units, the SPS-0200 responds to interruptions in the main power line, can be used to power several devices, and is not specific to any one computer brand. This particular unit has a rated output of 200 volt-amperes or 200 watts, with the hold-up time rated at 20 minutes for a

FIG 9-6 SPS-0200 Standby Power Supply. *(Courtesy of SAFT-America)*

full 200-watt load. The companion model SPS-0400 is supposed to give a 400-watt output, but it's rated for only eight minutes at full load.

Switching time between power interruption and battery takeover is specified at less than 10 milliseconds and is fast enough that the connected system components suffer no adverse effects. It takes over nicely during undervoltage conditions and responds well to brownouts. There is a line filter or suppression network to keep transient voltage spikes from reaching connected equipment.

It's interesting that the SPS-0200 has a 12-month warranty, which is longer than most other units. And the warranty includes the battery most others exclude. It has four receptacles for connecting equipment, generally enough for most 200- or 400-watt loads. It has external, user-accessible fusing that isn't provided by some others. It even has a low-battery cutoff to prevent extended outages from completely draining the battery. The RBS-DC literature doesn't mention excessive battery drain, but Guardian Angel literature cautions against a complete drain because it could and often does weaken or destroy the battery.

The Mayday 60+6S from Sun Research, Inc., shown in Fig. 9-7, is a more powerful unit than those previously cited. This is the top-of-the-line

FIG 9-7 Mayday 60+6S backup power supply. *(Courtesy of Sun-Research, Inc.)*

model for the supplier and provides 600 watts with a hold-up time exceeding 30 minutes. The unit also includes a surge suppressor and voltage regulator, and it features a sine-wave output instead of the square-wave or modified square-wave outputs of the Guardian Angel and SAFT SPS-series.

That sine-wave output is important because not all units output the same type of power. Specifically, some output a "sine wave" just like normal ac line power. Others output a rectangular wave that approximates normal power. For many computers and peripherals, this is no problem, but motorized equipment such as ac-driven disk drives, hard disks, and the like don't always tolerate a rectangular waveform. A power-type mismatch is recognizable by the sound of the motors slowing when reserve power takes effect. Similarly, there are some internal computer supplies that may not tolerate rectangular waveforms, and they can start ratcheting, sometimes destructively. Therefore, users must be careful about matching power supplies and equipment. Manufacturers such as Sun Research sometimes offer units with both square- and sine-wave outputs, although the sine-wave versions typically are more expensive.

The Mayday 60+6S did take some getting used to. It's not quiet like the smaller units. It continuously buzzes whenever it's plugged in, indicating that the trickle charger is always active and always draws some power, even when all switches are set off. I reduced the noise by replacing some vibrating storage capacitors but couldn't eliminate the sound entirely. Switchover time has been fast enough to prevent losses of computer operations, memory, and disk operations, but not fast enough to hold up my CRT without glitching the screen (the CRT is particularly sensitive and quick to respond to a power failure anyway).

The unit runs somewhat hot, unlike others that remain cool to the touch. I've been assured it's normal, however, and that thermal cutoffs inside will interrupt power if it begins to overheat. Another notable difference is that other types I've used all had internal gelled lead-acid batteries, but the Mayday unit uses external batteries and normally is provided with wet-cell storage types. Those are contained in an external marine-quality, acid-proof case.

So far, I've not found any reserve power supplies attempting to use nickel-cadmium batteries. First, they don't have the capabilities of gelled lead-acid or wet-cell types. Second nickel-cadmium batteries are subject to charge-memory problems. They must be cycled from full charge to low charge periodically to keep them from taking a "set" that would prevent full cycling when it's really needed for equipment backup.

Most suppliers say their gelled batteries are "maintenance-free" because they don't require adding water or electrolyte. Like all storage batteries, however, they do break down in time and eventually have to be replaced. Depending on whom you ask, you'll hear of life expectancies ranging from two to five years, but most seem to be rated for about three years.

Batteries should not be enclosed in cabinets, drawers, or other confined or airtight areas. There are two reasons. One is that the batteries may overheat during charging or discharging if there is insufficient air circulation. The other is that some batteries, if mistreated or overstressed, can vent gases, principally hydrogen. Such gases must be diluted with fresh air to prevent fire and explosion hazards. Wet cells naturally demand a great deal of respect. It's easy to spill electrolyte if they're mishandled, and the sulfuric acid can burn badly.

Uninterruptible Power Supplies. The true uninterruptible power supplies—the kind that do not require switchovers to backup batteries—are the elite in the world of power conditioning. They also are the most expensive though most effective form of power backup available. Because of the costs involved, most people who choose these units have ultra-sensitive installations and equipment running ultra-critical applications.

Although I've not tried any of these units with my own systems, I'm aware of their existence. They do not have a high visibility in the microcomputing field, but they are well known by users of minicomputers and large-scale mainframes.

One major supplier is SOLA Electric. The company provides UPS units in various sizes and capacities to meet almost any need. The Mini-UPS models are shown in Fig. 9-8. The standard models provide 400 to 600 watts for 10 to 24 minutes. They weigh between 85 and 135 pounds (39 and 61 kg). These are well suited to microcomputer installations, providing sine-wave outputs with voltage regulation and other line-protection features. The ac line never powers the connected equipment directly, since all power is drawn through the inverter. The units also may be equipped with auxiliary battery packs to increase the hold-up times normally available.

FIG 9-8 Mini-UPS uninterruptible power supplies. *(Courtesy of SOLA Electric)*

For comparison, SOLA Electric also makes larger UPS installations such as those shown in Fig.9-9. A 1.5 KW unit is shown in the foreground. Their catalog lists UPS installations up to 325 KW, though such units weigh over 14,000 pounds (6,350 kg)—that's 7 tons.

Gould, Inc., also offers true UPS units. The GSU-series is suitable for low-power installations with loads up to 500 watts. Normally, they provide up to 10 minutes of power, although external battery banks can be added to extend the time. The DSU-series, one of which is shown in Fig. 9-10, provides outputs from 500 watts to 1.8 KW and hold-up times of 5 or more minutes. With three external battery packs, the hold-up times can be extended to about 300 minutes for the 500-watt model or to 78 minutes for the 1.8 KW model. There are other models as well. The 5000A series extends the power loads to 20 KW, while the 6000A series reaches 45 KW.

POWER MONITORING

Power monitoring isn't directly a part of controlling power problems. Instead, it's a means of determining whether a problem exists and what the best course of remedial action would be.

If you suspect power problems such as overvoltage or undervoltage, often the first step is to contact the utility company and ask them to monitor the lines in your building. With enough persistence, you should be able to persuade them to attach a small recording monitor to one of your outlets for a week or so. They then can tell if you are consistently over or under the nominal voltage or if periodic rises and dips may be a problem. Sometimes, they can correct the situation at the source. Most such monitoring does not include spikes, surges, noise, and other interferences. Those you have to check out for yourself.

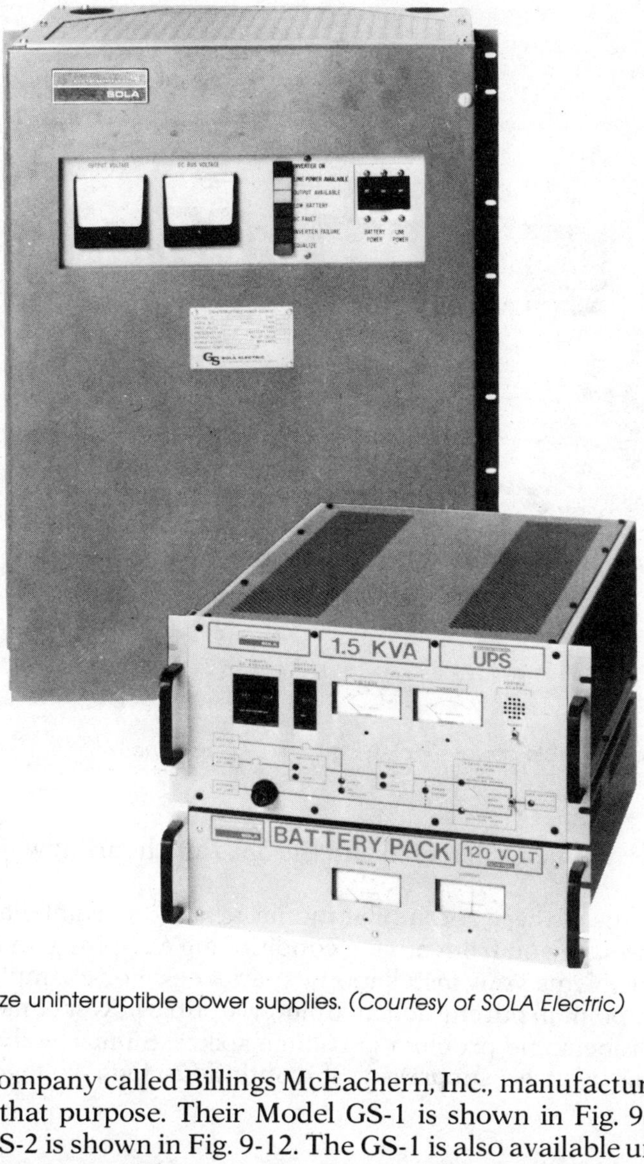

FIG 9-9 Medium-size uninterruptible power supplies. *(Courtesy of SOLA Electric)*

A company called Billings McEachern, Inc., manufactures monitors for just that purpose. Their Model GS-1 is shown in Fig. 9-11, and the Model GS-2 is shown in Fig. 9-12. The GS-1 is also available under private label from Inmac. These monitors are rather expensive, but they can provide important information if you suspect line problems.

The less expensive GS-1 uses indicator lights to show whether one or more power failures, low voltages, high voltages, voltage spikes, voltage drops, or incidents of high frequency noise have occurred since the unit was last reset. The thresholds are adjustable. By resetting the unit at regular intervals, say daily or even hourly, a pattern of power problems can be isolated to indicate the type of conditioning equipment needed.

The GS-2 is more sophisticated and more expensive. It has the same tests as the GS-1, plus tests of high- and low-line frequency (drifts from the designated ac current frequency). It also includes clock and timing circuitry and a printer with which to output a continuous record of the

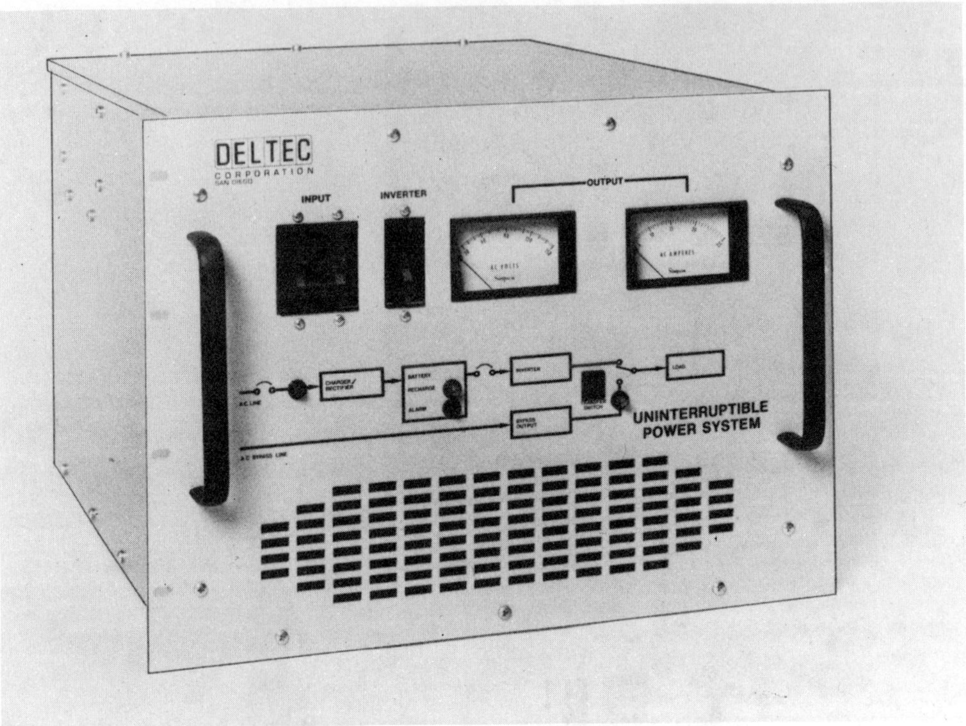

FIG 9-10 Medium-size uninterruptible power supply. *(Courtesy of Gould, Inc.)*

types of power problems detected and the days and hours at which they occurred.

The outputs of these and similar monitors are important diagnostic tools. They can save you from buying conditioning equipment overqualified for the problems your installation experiences. For example, there might be little point in purchasing an uninterruptible power supply if the only regular repeatable problem is voltage spikes. Similarly, there's no point in using a surge suppressor if continuous high voltage is the problem.

CONCLUSION

Power problems are serious matters. They can disrupt operations, destroy programs and data, and damage equipment. While disturbances and sources often cannot be controlled directly, equipment can be protected from the adverse effects.

That protection is available, but at a price. Power conditioning is not an inexpensive proposition, and a user must be willing to pay the price for the level of protection needed. For all but recreational users, the simplistic surge protectors and noise filters available at the normal retail level are far from sufficient. Serious users have to be more protective of

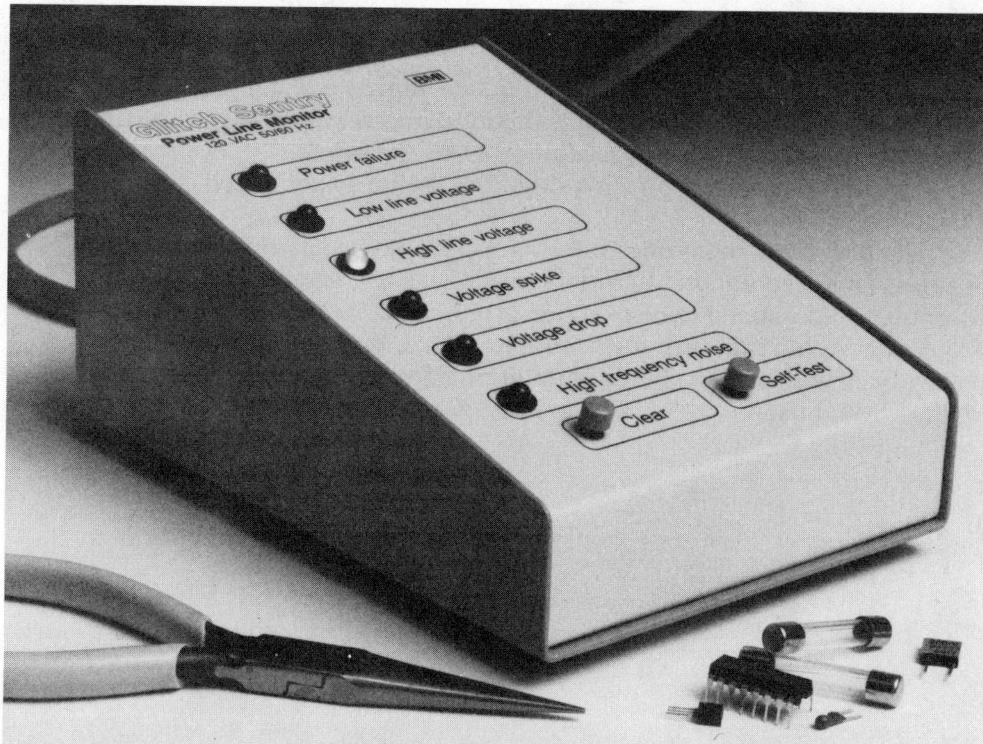

FIG 9-11 GS-1 Power Line Monitor. *(Courtesy of Billings McEachern, Inc.)*

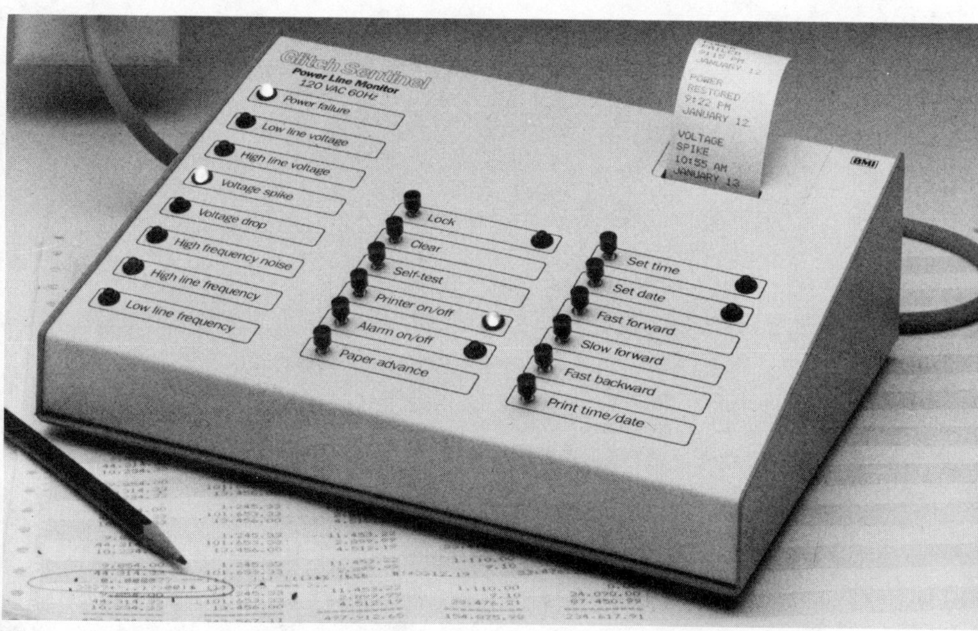

FIG 9-12 GS-2 Power Line Monitor. *(Courtesy of Billings McEachern, Inc.)*

their investments and have to look to more sophisticated means of blocking out power disruptions.

Because of the complexities involved and the sheer number of products available, this chapter is limited to an overview. As part of the responsibility to provide adequate power to the computer, every user must examine both the power conditions being experienced and the available solutions.

Having used microcomputers for several years now, for both business and recreation, I find it necessary to recommend that no computer of any size or configuration ever be operated without some line protection. At a minimum, surge suppression and noise filtration should always be provided. The choice of additional features then must be left to the individual user.

TEN

INTERFACING

Interfacing peripherals to microcomputers may seem a little misplaced as the topic of the final chapter of this book. In fact, it may not even seem to be a care or maintenance item. Interfacing is a critical requirement for operation, however. Normally, users will probably have all components initially interfaced by a dealer, so there's little concern when first hooking up a new system. But somewhere down the line, there's bound to be a need to connect some new piece of equipment.

I can't hope to present all the information you might need, but I can call your attention to some pertinent facts, the particular areas of difficulty, and a few products available to help you solve communication problems between devices.

Keep this in mind, however. Interfacing equipment is a difficult job. There are so many variations and so many approaches to constructing an interface that the process of connecting two devices often boils down to trial and error. Even suppliers and dealers are often baffled trying to get a new printer to work, connecting a new modem, or hooking up a printer buffer. Even the so-called "experts" sometimes have to spend hours or days getting one device to talk to another. Then, when the hardware is wired correctly, it's still necessary to have appropriate software. Some of the intricacies were described in Chapters 5 and 6 on switch settings for terminals and printers.

Since they are the most common connections, I'll be concerned only with parallel Centronics-compatible interfaces and serial RS-232C connections. These are the ones with which most microcomputer owners connect printers, terminals, modems, buffers, and similar devices to the mainframe computer.

Remember that this is not a tutorial on interfacing, but merely a means of pointing out some areas that may prove troublesome.

PARALLEL INTERFACES

Parallel interfaces are custom-designed for virtually every computer-to-peripheral hookup. There are no standards, not even among devices using the 36-pin Centronics-style connector. About the only reliable statements that can be made are that parallel interfaces have eight data lines (one per bit) and assorted other signal lines for printer or computer control.

The principle of parallel interfacing is that all eight bits of a data character are transmitted simultaneously on eight signal lines—actually eight pairs of lines, since each has a ground-wire signal return. Other signal lines then inform the devices when data are valid for "strobing" into the electronics. Strobing means that the receiving device gets a signal from the sending device and accepts valid data at that time. In addition, there may be one or more other signals transmitted back and forth between the connected units, informing each of the other's status. For example, if a printer is busy and can't accept data, it informs the computer via a signal line. If the printer has data to send and is awaiting some place to send them, it might inform the printer that data are available.

The problem with parallel interfaces is that different devices use different signals. Furthermore, two devices with the same signals may not have them on the same connector pins, so a busy signal on pin 11 of one device might be a ground line on pin 11 of some other unit.

It's an advantage to have parallel interfaces completed by a dealer or supplier. Few individuals can cope with the complexity of figuring out the signal requirements at each end of the line and then work up a suitable cable. Normally, prewired cables can be ordered for most equipment. For example, when ordering a Compulink SooperSpooler (printer buffer) for an Epson MX-80 printer, a user should buy a cable from Compulink specifically configured for the Epson. Similarly, when installing a printer interface card such as an Interactive Structures' PKASO board or an SSM Microcomputer Products' APIO board for the Apple II, a user must specify the exact printer brand, model, and optional equipment being connected.

Parallel interfaces usually are not interchangeable. To illustrate, the PKASO board for an Apple II and an Epson MX-80 is not fully compatible with an Okidata Microline 84 printer. It's not the cabling but the preprogrammed instructions in the interface board for controlling the graphics capabilities that cause problems. With something like the SSM APIO board having no inherent graphics capabilities, the same board and cable can be used to drive an Epson or an Okidata printer, but a different cable is required if a Compulink SooperSpooler is interposed in the line to buffer outputs.

Obviously nonstandard approaches make it difficult to alter an installation, once set up. If it becomes necessary to change printers, say to achieve faster operation or more features, it may also be necessary to buy a new cable, which isn't too expensive, and perhaps a whole new interface board, which is expensive.

Often, parallel interfaces are used by system assemblers—original equipment manufacturers or OEMs—specifically to keep users from breaking up a preconfigured system into individual components. The interfaces are unique, so a printer furnished with a system cannot be removed and used elsewhere. Similarly, the host computer cannot drive a printer brand not sold by the original supplier. Often, this is a deliberate means of keeping users locked into specific brands and product lines, and such systems should be avoided. Before buying any system or peripheral with a parallel interface, check that the units in question can be used with other peripherals and host computers, with or without new cables or interface boards.

I'm not fond of parallel interfaces. Although they often allow faster communication than serial interfaces, I shuffle systems and peripherals too frequently. I do use some parallel units, but normally I'll go out of my way to avoid parallel interfaces that keep me from moving printer A to system C one day, to system B the next, and back to system A the third. It's much easier to do that kind of shuffling with a serial interface where leads can be "jumpered" or "shorted" as necessary. Many devices sold with parallel interfaces, notably the Epson and Okidata printers, also have serial-interface options that permit such versatility.

I'll repeat my admonition. Unless you're an electronic whiz, you should have your parallel interfaces constructed by a supplier or dealer.

SERIAL INTERFACES

In contrast, serial interfaces are flexible, particularly the ones compatible with RS-232C specifications. They can be adapted, modified, jumpered, and otherwise altered to accommodate different computer-to-peripheral hookups, thereby allowing a system to use various printers at different times and permitting a single printer to be moved from one system to another.

This doesn't mean connecting a serial interface is easy. On the contrary, it can be extremely difficult. The biggest problem is that manufacturers rarely interpret the RS-232C specification the same way, sometimes altering the function of one or more signal lines or adding lines unique to their own product and intended application. With that, it's often necessary to jumper or short lines to achieve the necessary signals at the other end. For example, a printer might require a signal known as Data Set Ready (DSR) to indicate the computer is ready to transmit data, but the computer might not be equipped for that signal. It's then necessary to jumper the DSR line to some other line to provide a constant signal, thereby making the printer think the computer is ready all the time.

There's also the matter of whether a device is defined as Data Communications Equipment (DCE) or Data Terminal Equipment (DTE), affecting how signals function and whether a given line is an input to or an output from the unit. Sometimes, DCE/DTE terminology isn't used, the owner relying instead on definitions of a Data Set or Data Terminal device but having the same problem of signal compatibility. Normally, a computer is considered Data Communications Equipment or a Data Set, while a printer or other peripheral is considered a Data Terminal. But this is not always the case, especially when modems are involved. There's also a problem in connecting one computer to another because both might be using interfaces defined as Data Terminals.

To better understand what happens, take a look at some common signal lines of an RS-232C interface. Remember that the connector usually has 25 pins, but only a few of those pins are used for most devices.

1. Pin 1 is a Protective Ground (PG) line. Typically, it ties the chassis or frame grounds of the two devices together. Thus far, I've never seen any variation on this pin—it's always been a ground and it always has to be connected from pin 1 of one device to pin 1 of the other. Failure to provide a good connection on pin 1 can, however, cause damage to the attached devices by leaving them unprotected against voltage transients, static, and other adverse conditions.

2. Pin 2 is Transmitted Data (TD). That seems straightforward, but it isn't, because some manufacturers use TD for data transmitted from their device to the connected device, while others use it for data transmitted from the connected device to the one in question. This may be affected by the device definition as a Data Terminal or Data Set. It's necessary to determine whether the TD line is incoming or outgoing for the devices at either end, and pin 2 on one end may have to connect to pin 2 or pin 3 on the other.

3. Pin 3 is Received Data (RD) and is the complement of the TD line on pin 2. In some units, it may be defined as incoming data received from the connected device, but other devices have been known to define it as outgoing data to be received at the other end. Depending on the device, it may connect to pin 2 or 3 at the other end.

4. Pin 4 usually is the Request to Send (RTS) line, activated by a unit to initiate a data transfer. Typically, a device activates this line as an indication that it has data to send and is awaiting some response from the other end to indicate a readiness to receive. Some devices use this line, others do not. Some route it straight through from pin 4 of one device to pin 4 of another, while others route it to another pin.

5. Pin 5 is usually the Clear to Send (CTS) line, activated to indicate that a unit is ready to accept data from another. Most often, this signal is a response to the device that sent an RTS signal, indicating the communication lines aren't busy and data transfers may proceed. Like the RTS line, the CTS signal is used by some devices, ignored by others, and cross-connected to different lines in still others.

6. Pin 6 is used for a Data Set Ready (DSR) line, normally activated any time the Data Set device or Data Communication Equipment end is switched on. Usually, it indicates only that the unit is on, not that it's ready to receive or send data. In modem communications, for example, this signal may be used to inform the modem whether the computer is turned on or off and, therefore, whether to accept or reject connection with and transmission from the telephone line. Again, the line may be used, ignored, or cross-connected, depending on devices in question.

7. Pin 7 almost always carries a signal ground, which is different from the protective ground on pin 1. The signal ground is necessary to complete the electrical paths of other lines, although it may be strapped to the protective ground within the device at either end. In almost all interfaces, pin 7 on one end connects to pin 7 on the other.

8. Pin 8 normally is the Carrier Detect (CD) line, used most often to indicate the detected presence of a carrier signal when connected to a modem. However, various manufacturers use this line for all kinds of things, including control of tape-writing operations, indication of power-on status of a device, indication of cable connection, and so on. Of all lines, this is usually the most difficult to connect and frequently ends up being strapped to pin 5, 6, or 20 to provide a constant signal.

9. Pin 20 is the Data Terminal Ready (DTR) line that complements the DSR signal on pin 6. It often serves no purpose other than to indicate that the Data Terminal device has been switched on. Usually, pin 20 can be used as a jumper connection to provide a constant signal to other lines whenever the terminal device is on.

Those are the basic signals. However, some manufacturers add other lines for special purposes. For example, an Okidata Microline 84 printer may or may not use an "SSD" signal on pin 11 for connection to a BUSY signal in another device. Others I've seen have required lines on other pins going by names such as Data Set Testing, Secondary Received Date, Secondary Transmitted Data, Clear to Write, Secondary Request to Send, Ring Indicator, and so on.

Names alone don't mean much when one is trying to connect two devices. In fact, trying to get an interface to work properly can be an exercise in frustration because just one wrong wire can either prevent any communication or garble data because there's no handshaking between devices to start and stop transmissions.

The first time I ran into a problem was while temporarily replacing a Qume Sprint 5 printer with a Diablo 630 when the regular unit was shipped out of town for repairs. I could not get the new printer to run at all. No data made it through. Eventually, I found that the Diablo required a DSR signal on pin 6, while the computer had that signal "cut dead" in its interface circuitry—the signal wasn't even present at the connector. The solution was to solder a wire between pins 6 and 20 at the connector so

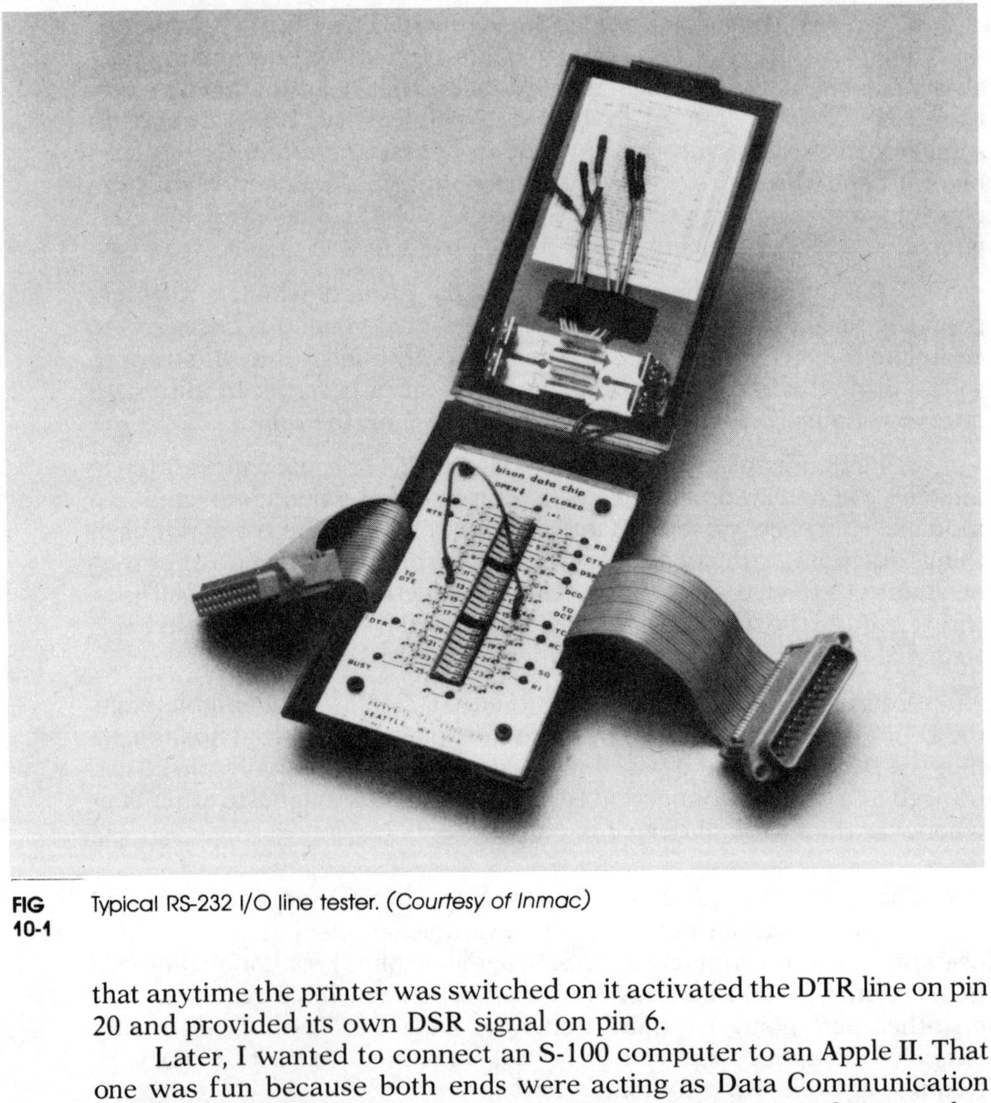

FIG 10-1 Typical RS-232 I/O line tester. *(Courtesy of Inmac)*

that anytime the printer was switched on it activated the DTR line on pin 20 and provided its own DSR signal on pin 6.

Later, I wanted to connect an S-100 computer to an Apple II. That one was fun because both ends were acting as Data Communication Equipment! I had to build a special connector with pins 2 and 3 crossed so that the transmitted data at one end became the received data at the other end. Then, I had to jumper or short together pins 4, 5, 6, and 20. Switching one unit on activated DTR on pin 20 and fooled the unit into believing that RTS, CTS, and DSR also were present and active. Of course, that overrode any hardware handshaking, and communications had to be slowed to a speed where there was no danger of overrunning a buffer but also no need for starting and stopping transmissions.

Most of the time, there doesn't seem to be much logic to interface connections. I've watched both service technicians and dealers spend hours or days trying to get one printer to work with one computer. I've encountered a couple of interface setups that work, and I haven't the vaguest idea why; I stumbled on the right combination of signals and

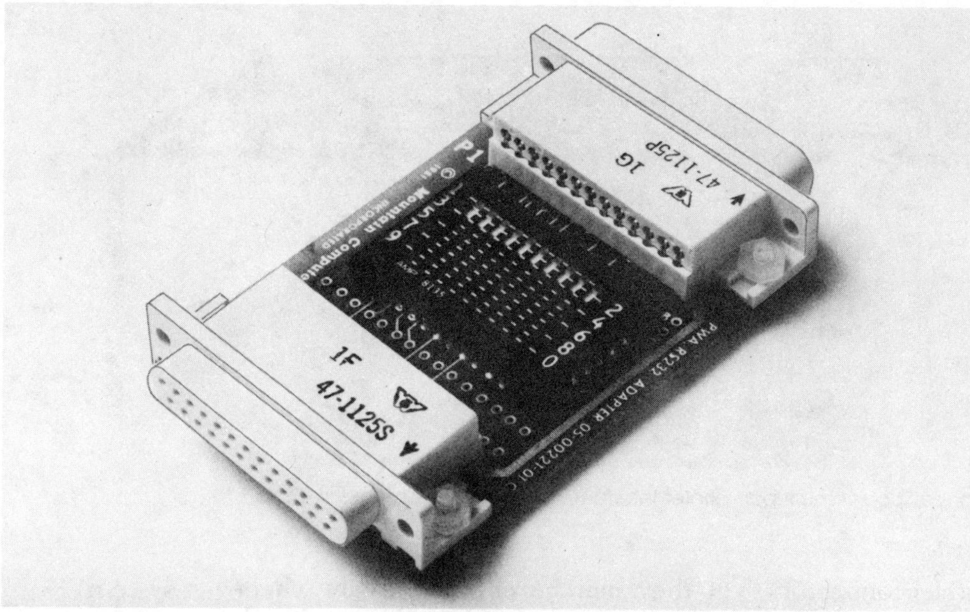

FIG 10-2 RS-232C reconfiguration adapter. *(Courtesy of Mountain Computer, Inc.)*

jumpers purely by chance. There's no easy way out of the situation either, unless it's to reduce transmission speed and eliminate the need for handshaking or go to strictly software-protocol systems where starting and stopping is controlled by codes included in the data stream. Even then, some lines still must be connected correctly.

RS-232C INTERFACING AIDS

There are some interfacing aids. Perhaps the most important for anyone who reconnects or changes equipment frequently is something known as a "breakout box." Actually, it's an RS-232 I/O Line Tester, like the Inmac model shown in Fig. 10-1. There are many models and variations on these devices, but they all cut the interfacing time by allowing users to identify signal discrepancies. The status of individual signal lines is shown by the illuminating or darkening of LEDs (light-emitting diodes), and signals are easily jumpered with short patch cords requiring no soldering. Once a working interface is set up, a permanent connector can be assembled to match the patch cords, and the box can be removed from the circuit. The devices are handy in testing for malfunctions as well, since they can indicate whether a failure is in the interface cable, within the computer, or within the connected device.

Another useful device is a "crossover connector." The one shown in Fig. 10-2 is an RS-232C Reconfiguration Adapter from Mountain Computer, Inc. It allows semipermanent patches to be made with slide switches. The connections require no soldering and no disassembly of

FIG 10-3 SooperSpooler multi-port printer interface. *(Courtesy of Compulink Corp.)*

cable connectors, yet they can be changed easily whenever system parameters or components are changed. Without a breakout box, an adapter like this can be used to set up an interface by trial and error, although it doesn't provide the LEDs to indicate which lines are active or inactive.

SPECIAL DEVICES

While on the subject of interfacing, there are two devices of special interest because of their applications. The first represents a category of equipment popularly known as printer spoolers. The other provides a means of communicating between components without an interface cable.

Printer Spooler

Figure 10-3 illustrates a 62K SooperSpooler Intelligent Printer Interface from Compulink Corp. This unit represents a whole category of similar devices used to buffer computer outputs before they reach the printer. The obvious application is that printouts can be dumped quickly from the host computer to the buffer, allowing the buffer to control actual printing operations while the computer returns to available status for other processing chores. Effectively, this allows two computing tasks to be performed at the same time.

SooperSpooler is microprocessor-controlled, with selectable functions for postprocessing data. Switch settings or software commands from the host computer allow it to format printouts, providing pagination, single-sheet or continuous-form printing, page headings, numbered and formatted pages, formatted lines, and so on. It has several capabilities designed to improve the efficiency of the entire installation.

FIG 10-4 LCM-100 Line Carrier Modems. *(Courtesy of Communications Research Corp.)*

The reason I mention this unit under interfacing is that it can be equipped with two input and two output ports. With the option installed, serial and parallel inputs are available, as are serial and parallel outputs. Therefore, two computers may be connected—one to the serial port and the other to the parallel port. Similarly, two printers may be connected, with one receiving serial data and the other receiving parallel data. The attractive part is that the output port is switch-selectable (a rear-panel DIP switch), so a computer providing parallel data can be switched to drive a serial printer, and vice versa.

I have both an S-100 computer and an Apple II connected through this device to serial Qume Sprint 5 and parallel Epson MX-80 printers. Either computer can drive either printer without having to disconnect cables, replace interface cards, or otherwise tamper with the equipment. Of course, I can't have both printers or both computers working at the same time, but that's not my principal concern. I'm far more interested in being able to switch printers so I can use the high-speed, dot-matrix one for rough drafts and the slower letter-quality one for final outputs without having to disassemble and reassemble things.

Wireless Communication

Figure 10-4 shows a pair of LCM-100 Line Carrier Modems from Communications Research Corp. These are among the most intriguing devices I've come across because they allow a computer to connect with another serial device through existing electrical wiring in a building. By eliminating the interface cable between devices like a CRT and a computer, they provide what might be considered wireless communication. It may sound impossible, but it's not. The LCM-100s superimpose a "frequency shift keying" signal on the electrical lines, putting the signal on the lines with one modem and decoding it anywhere else in the building with the other modem.

This means that users are free to move a CRT from room to room without dragging a cable behind or tearing walls apart to route special cables. It's possible to have the computer in the basement and the CRT in the attic. It's possible to have the computer on one side of a solid fire wall and the CRT on the other side. In fact, any desired locations are possible if the rooms are served by the same main power feeds coming into the building, even if they are on separate circuits within the building.

The modems require serial RS-232C interfaces to the computer and peripheral, using the basic signal lines previously described. However, they transmit only the data signal across electrical lines, not the handshaking signals. Therefore, hardware handshaking to drive a remote terminal or printer isn't practical, but the communications line can be controlled by software protocol transmitted with the data stream.

As might be expected, the data transmissions aren't perfect. Electrical lines are subject to noise and interference, and the same disturbances affect the modems. The ones I tested were difficult to get operational, but that was due to some special problems with the power in my building. The manufacturer was able to provide a "phase coupler" for the circuit breaker box to eliminate almost all the interference. There are still occasional glitches showing up as a random character, but they're infrequent enough that they don't cause major problems. When mobility is a concern, the tradeoff between convenience and "pure" data transmission may be justified.

The point is that these devices do work, and they work well. Furthermore, they provide a whole new option in equipment interfacing—an option that may prove valuable to users requiring mobility or having special installation problems.

CONCLUSION

Equipment interfacing is extraordinarily complex, and thorough coverage is beyond the scope of this book. This chapter has touched lightly on parallel and serial RS-232C interfaces, but it hasn't even attempted to cover others such as current loops and IEEE (Institute of Electrical and Electronic Engineers) interfaces commonly found on many computers. Yet the subject is important because equipment cannot work if not interfaced correctly. Furthermore, interface failures can and often do affect installations at every level of application.

In spite of the aids and devices available to help users with interface problems, most people will remain totally baffled by the many wires and possibilities. As a result, users should leave interfacing to professionals like dealers and technicians whenever possible. Before buying any peripheral or add-on, be sure to ask the manufacturer for the interface configuration applicable to your host system. It's annoying to acquire something like an expensive printer only to find that nobody knows how to wire it into your particular system.

APPENDIX

PRODUCT GUIDE

This appendix provides information on sources for products cited in this book, companies that provided information used in the development of the book, and companies providing information considered useful or potentially useful in the care and maintenance of microcomputer systems. The presentation is alphabetical by company name, with no attempt to categorize products by system or application.

This is not a comprehensive list, nor is it intended to be one. There are many companies and products not represented here. Reasons for omission are numerous: some products are specific to systems other than those the author could test; manufacturers sometimes failed to respond to repeated inquiries for information; and some products were introduced after completion of this edition (among other reasons). Readers should consider this list a general guide to be used as a starting place in the search for suitable products. Furthermore, this list is provided for information only; it does not necessarily indicate endorsement of the product or products by the author or publisher.

An "(N/A)" following the name and address information indicates a company that is known to provide applicable products but which failed to respond to the author's inquiries for information. Their products are not described elsewhere in this work, and information in this list is for reference only. Telephone numbers and prices are not included because they are subject to frequent change.

ALF Products, Inc., 1448 Estes, Denver, CO 80215.
PenultiCopy: high-speed, high-reliability copy program for Apple II diskettes that are not copy protected.

Accupower, 2216 Lundy Ave., San Jose, CA 95131. (N/A)
A100 Power Supply: replacement 100-watt internal power supply for the Apple II computer.

Advanced Logic Systems, 1195 E. Arques Ave., Sunnyvale, CA 94086.
Synergizer kit contains a *Z-Card* Z-80 CPU, a 16K RAM expansion card, and a *Smarterm* 80-column display card for the Apple II.

Advanced Micro Techniques, 1291 E. Hillsdale Blvd. #209, Foster City, CA 94404.
DPatch: disk-recovery software for CP/M-based systems.

Andromeda, Inc., P.O. Box 19144, Greensboro, NC 27410.
Expansion ROM and other plug-in boards for the Apple II.

Answer Corporation, 502A N. Second Ave., Sandpoint, ID 83864. (N/A)
Lost Program Recovery: disk-recovery software for Apple II.

Applied Engineering, P.O. Box 47031, Dallas, TX 75247.
Time II: real-time clock card for the Apple II.

ATS Cases, 25 Washington Ave., Natick, MA 01760. (N/A)
Light-duty carrying cases for Apple and other computers.

ATV Research, 13 N. Broadway, Dakota City, NE 68731.
RF modulators for Apple-to-television hookups.

B&B Electronics, Box 475, Mendota, IL 61342. (N/A)
Various interfacing aids including RS-232 testers, "gender reversers," tee-connectors, and so on.

BK Technologies, CAT Div., 3204 Monroe St., Rockville, MD 20852. (N/A)
Gameport extenders for the Apple II.

Basis, Inc., 5435 Scotts Valley Dr., Scotts Valley, CA 95066.
Basis-108: personal and small-business computer system.

Billings McEachern, Inc., 402 Lincoln Centre Dr., Foster City, CA 94404.
GS-1 and *GS-2 Power Line Monitors:* nonrecording and recording monitors for identifying and analyzing power-line disturbances.

Blat Research & Development Corp., 8016 188th St. S.W., Edmonds, WA 98020.
Badlim: disk-surface certification software for CP/M-based systems.

California Computer Systems, Inc., 250 Caribbean Dr., Sunnyvale, CA 94086.
Assorted parallel and serial interface cards for the Apple II.

Central Point Software, Inc., P.O. Box 19730-#203, Portland, OR 97219.
The Filer: Apple II disk utility software for fast copying, drive testing, and other functions.
Copy II Plus: Apple II disk utility software for copying, drive testing, bit-copying protected disks, and so on.

Communications Research Corp., 1720 130th Ave. N.E. Bellevue, WA 98005.
LCM-100 Line Carrier Modems: communicate between a computer and peripheral device using existing electrical wiring instead of serial interface cable.

Compdent, 542 Lake St., Hancock, MI 49930.
Reset Guard: shield to prevent accidental use of Reset key (Apple II).

Compulink Corp., 1840 Industrial Circle, Longmont, CO 80501.
SooperSpooler: a 16K to 62K intelligent printer spooler and postprocessor for systems using serial or parallel interfacing.

Computer:applications, Inc., 13300 S.W. 108 St. Circle, Miami, FL 33186.
Nibbles Away II: nibble copier for the Apple II. Package distributed by Micro-Ware Distributors, Inc., P.O. Box 113, Pompton Plains, NJ 07444.

Computer Case Co., 5650 Indian Mound Court, Columbus, OH 43213.
Various carrying cases for Apple II and other small computers.

Computer Station, Inc., 11610 Page Service Dr., St. Louis, MO 64141.
Station Master: Apple II interface cards with graphics-dump capabilities for parallel printers.

Control Technology, Inc., 8200 N. Classen Blvd. No. 101, Oklahoma City, OK 73114.
RBS-DC Reserve Power Supply: system-specific backup power for Apple II, IBM PC, and other computer systems.

Corvus Systems, Inc., 2029 O'Toole Ave., San Jose, CA 95131.
Corvus Concept: small-business and professional computer system.

Creative Computing Software, 39 E. Hanover Ave., Morris Plains, NJ 07950.
Disk Doctor: disk-recovery software for the Apple II.

Creative Software Development, 4657 Thayn Dr., West Valley City, UT 84120.
Time Machine II: real-time clock for the Apple II.

Davong Systems, Inc., 1061 Terra Bella Ave., Mountain View, CA 94043.
DSI-series Winchester hard-disk subsystems.

Digital Marketing, 2670 Cherry Lane, Walnut Creek, CA 94596.
Distributing numerous software items for CP/M and other computers; markets *File Fix,* a disk-recovery and general-purpose CP/M disk utility package, among others.

Diversified Software Research, Inc., 5848 Crampton Court, Rockford, IL 61111.
Diversi-DOS: a high-speed, enhanced, Apple II disk operating system.

Dymarc Industries, Inc., 7133 Rutherford Rd., Baltimore, MD 20207. (N/A)
Clipstrip and *Clipper* power-line conditioners (suppressors and filters).

Electronics Specialists, Inc., 171 S. Main St., Natick, MA 01760.
Extensive line of power-conditioning equipment including filters, suppressors, isolators, and so on.

Epson-America, Inc., 3415 Kashiwa St., Torrance, CA 90505.
MX-series dot-matrix printers, *HX-20* microcomputer, and other microcomputing products.

Evasco Computer Systems, Inc., 845 Third Ave., New York, NY 10022. (N/A)
Programmer's First Aid: Apple II disk utility package.

Fiberbilt/Ikelheimer-Ernst, Inc., 601 W. 26th St., New York, NY 10001.
Extensive line of carrying cases for Apple II and other computers or peripherals.

Franklin Computer Corp., 7030 Colonial Highway, Pennsauken, NJ 08109.
Ace-1000: personal and small-business computer system.

Gould, Inc., (Deltec), 2727 Kurtz St., San Diego, CA 92110.
Extensive line of power-conditioning equipment, including regulators and uninterruptible power supplies.

Happ Electronics, Inc., 4640 Island View, Oshkosh, WI 54901.
GS-1 and *GS-2:* gameport extenders for the Apple II.

Hutton Industries, Inc., P.O. Box 1413, Tacoma, WA 98401.
QWK Cover: fitted rigid cover for Apple II keyboards.

IBM, P.O. Box 1328, Boca Raton, FL 33432.
IBM Personal Computer: personal, small-business, and professional computer system.

IMS International, 2800 Lockheed Way, Carson City, NV 89701.
5000SX and *8000SX:* small-business and professional computers.

Inmac, 2465 Augustine Dr., Santa Clara, CA 95051.
Varied product line includes cleaning, care, and maintenance products of many types. Catalog should be requested.

Innovative Computer Products, 18360 Oxnard St., Tarzana, CA 91356.
PerfectData cleaning kits; extensive line of diskette and hard-disk cleaning products.

Intertec Data Systems, 2300 Broad River Rd., Columbia, SC 29210.
SuperBrain II: small-business and professional computer system.

Ithaca Intersystems, Inc., P.O. Box 91, 1650 Hanshaw Rd., Ithaca, NY 14850.
Ithaca-series small-business and professional microcomputers.

Kay Computers, Div. Non-Linear Systems, 533 Steven Ave., Solana Beach, CA 92075.
KayPro computer for personal, small-business, and professional use.

Kensington Microware, Ltd., 300 E. 54th St., New York, NY 10022.
System Saver: Apple II cooling fan with power surge suppression.

Ladco Development Co., P.O. Box 464, Olean, NY 14760.
Ramlok: reserve power supply for small microcomputer systems.

Langley-St. Clair, Instrumentation Systems, 132 W. 24th St., New York, NY 10011.
I-Protect: lead-impregnated, acrylic-screen overlays to guard against X-ray and ultraviolet radiation emitted by cathode ray tubes.

Last Electronics, P.O. Box 1300, San Andreas, CA 95249.
Plexa-Lok: clear acrylic, slip-on keyboard shields for personal and small-business computers.

Legend Industries, Ltd., 2220 Scott Lake Rd., Pontiac, MI 48054.
Memory products for the Apple II, including the *128 KDE Soft Disk.*

Lobo Drives International, 358 S. Fairview Ave., Goleta, CA 93117.
Assorted disk drives for microcomputer systems.

Lynx Design & Technology, Inc., 3880 Chesswood Dr., Downsview, Ontario M3J 2W6, Canada
Lynx-300: disk-drive adjustment tool.

Macrotech Computer Products, Ltd., 1370 Marine Dr., North Vancouver, BC V7P 1T4, Canada.
Macrodisk: software to make Apple II memory boards emulate RAM-disks. The company also provides *Macromem*-series memory boards and other products.

Mark Four Imports, P.O. Box A, San Gabriel, CA 91776.
Cool-Mark II: internally mounted cooling fans for Apple II computers.

Masterworks Software, Inc., 1823 W. Lomita Blvd., Lomita, CA 90717.
Masterdisk and *Masterdos* utility software packages for Apple II computers.

Micro-Sci, Inc., 17942 Irvine Blvd. No. 205, Tustin, CA 92680.
A40 and *A70* disk drives for Apple II computers.

Microstand, P.O. Box 96, Tolvana Park, OR 97145.
Microstand MS-II: support stand for Apple II computer, disk drives, and monitor.

Mountain Computer, Inc., 300 El Pueblo Rd., Scotts Valley, CA 95066.
Extensive line of Apple II and other add-ons, including the *ROMPLUS+* card and *RS-232C DB25 Pin Reconfiguration Adapter,* among others.

National Field Sales, 2660 W. Chester Pike, Broomall, PA 19008.
Line of *Stedi-Watt* power conditioners (suppressors and filters).

Nikrom Technical Products, 25 Prospect St., Leominster, MA 01453.
Master Diagnostics + plus: Apple II disk cleaning kit with diagnostic software.

Novation, Inc., 18664 Oxnard St., Tarzana, CA 91356.
Extensive line of telephone modems and data communications devices.

Ohm/Electronics, 746 Vermont Ave., Palatine, IL 60067.
Powermaster line of power conditioners (suppressors and filters).

Okidata Corp., 111 Gaither Dr., Mt. Laurel, NJ 08054.
Microline series of dot-matrix printers, including the 200 cps *Microline-84*.

Omega Microware, Inc., 222 S. Riverside Plaza, Chicago, IL, 60606.
Locksmith: a nibble copier for the Apple II.
Inspector: a general-purpose disk utility for the Apple II.
Watson: an extension and enhancement to *Inspector*.

Omni Communication, R.D. 3, Box 200, Jackson, NJ 08527.
Blitz Bug: lighting and surge suppressor for electrical lines.

Osborne Computer Corp., 26500 Corporate Ave., Hayward, CA 94545.
Osborne-1: portable microcomputer for personal, small-business, and professional applications.

Otrona Corp., 4755 Walnut St., Boulder, CO 80301.
Otrona Attache: portable professional and small-business computer.

Panamax, 150 Mitchell Blvd., San Rafael, CA 94903.
Multiple-product line of power-conditioning devices (filters and suppressors).

Personal Computer Products, 16776 Bernardo Center Dr., San Diego, CA 92128.
Appli-Card: Z-80 microprocessor plug-in for the Apple II, plus numerous applications packages and associated products.

Practical Peripherals, 31245 La Baya Dr., Westlake Village, CA 91362.
Microbuffer II: plug-in 16K to 32K printer buffer for the Apple II, plus free-standing printer buffers for numerous other systems.

Quadram Corp., 4357 Park Dr., Norcross, GA 30093.
Extensive line of memory products, printer buffers, and associated equipment for various microcomputer systems.

Quality Software, 6660 Reseda Blvd. No. 105, Reseda, CA 91335.
Beneath Apple DOS: book explaining the Apple disk operating system.
Bag of Tricks: book and software to supplement *Beneath-Apple DOS*.

R.H. Electronics, 566 Irelan, P.O. Bin CC, Buellton, CA 93427.
Super Fan II: Apple II external cooling fan with or without ac line protection.
Guardian Angel: reserve power supply for small microcomputer systems.
Super RAM II: 16K plug-in memory expansion for the Apple II.

RKS Industries, 4865 Scotts Valley Dr., Scotts Valley, CA 95066.
Surge Sentry line of power-conditioning equipment, including suppressors, filters, and interruptors.

Rock Roy, Inc., 7721 E. Gray Rd., Scottsdale, AZ 85260.
DiscSavers: protective vinyl diskette sleeves.

SAFT-America, Inc., Portable Battery Div., 931 N. Vandalia St., St. Paul, MN 55114.
SPS-0200 and *SPS-0400 Standby Power Supplies:* in-line reserve power for systems drawing up to 200 or 400 watts respectively.

Santa Clara Systems, Inc., 560 Division St., Campbell, CA 95008.
MiniMega: a 5-1/4-inch Winchester hard-disk subsystem.

Sanyo Business Systems, Computer Div., 51 Joseph St., Moonachie, NJ 07074.
MBC-series of personal, professional, and small-business microcomputers.

Sensible Software, 6619 Perham Dr., West Bloomfield, MI 48033.
Back It Up II: nibble copier for Apple II software.
Super Disk Copy: high-speed copier for standard Apple II software.
Disk Recovery: disk-recovery utility software for Apple II.

Shugart Associates, 435 Oakmead Parkway, Sunnyvale, CA 94086.
Extensive line of floppy, minifloppy, and Winchester hard-disk drives.

Soft CTRL Systems, Box 599, West Milford, NJ 07480.
Useful preprogrammed ROMs for the Apple II, including the *UTILITY ROM* for recovering programs in memory after killing them.

Softkey Publishing, 14404 East D St., Tacoma, WA 98445.
DiskEdit II: general-purpose disk utility software for Apple II.

Software Store, 706 Chippewa Square, Marquette, MI 49855.
Disk Fix: a general-purpose CP/M disk editor and file recovery utility.

SOLA Electric, Unit of General Signal, 1717 Busse Rd., Elk Grove, IL 60007.
Extensive line of power-conditioning equipment, including regulators and uninterruptible power supplies.

Sorrento Valley Associates, 11722 Sorrento Valley Rd., San Diego, CA 92121.
AMS 5000 Megabyter: Winchester hard-disk subsystem for Apple II.

Square 1, 1134 Crane St. F-3, Menlo Park, CA 94025.
Floppy Armour: rigid protective containers for shipping floppy diskettes.

SSM Microcomputer Products, 2190 Paragon Dr., San Jose, CA 95131.
Extensive line of Apple II interface cards, including the *ASIO* serial, *APIO* parallel, and *AIO-II* combination serial/parallel boards.

Sun Research, Inc., Box 210, New Durham, NH 03855.
Mayday line of standby power systems for small computers.

SuperSoft, Inc., P.O. Box 1628, Champaign, IL 61820.
Diagnostics II: system diagnostics for CP/M-based microcomputers.
Disk Edit: general-purpose disk utility for CP/M-based systems.
Disk Doctor: file recovery utility for CP/M diskettes.

Sympathetic Software, 9531 Telhan Dr., Huntington Beach, CA 92646.
Disk Prep: Apple II diskette formatter and surface certifier.

Texwipe Co., 51 Prospect Place, Hillsdale, NJ 07642.
Extensive line of cleaning and care products for computer installations. Catalog should be requested.

3M Company, 3M Center, St. Paul, MN 55144.
Anti-static mats and anti-static service kits.

Topaz Electronics Div., 3855 Ruffin Rd., San Diego, CA 92123.
Several models of *Line 2* power conditioners for computer installations.

Tovatech, 1903 Fordham Way, Mountain View, CA 94040.
VENTOP: slotted ventilation cover for cooling an Apple II.

Videx, Inc., 897 N.W. Grant Ave., Corvallis, OR 97330.
Apple II enhancement hardware including the *Videoterm* 80-column card and *Enhancer II* keyboard modification.

XPS, Inc., 323 York Rd., Carlisle, PA 17013.
Apple-Cillin II: complete system diagnostic software for Apple II.

INDEX